D0225905

DATE DUE

Library Store #47-0108 Peel Off Pressure Sensitive

Spanish Women in the Golden Age

Recent Titles in
Contributions in Women's Studies

The Several Worlds of Pearl S. Buck: Essays Presented at a Centennial Symposium, Randolph-Macon Woman's College, March 26–28, 1992
Elizabeth J. Lipscomb, Frances E. Webb, and Peter Conn, editors

Hear Me Patiently: The Reform Speeches of Amelia Jenks Bloomer
Anne C. Coon, editor

Nineteenth-Century American Women Theatre Managers
Jane Kathleen Curry

Textual Escap(e)ades: Mobility, Maternity, and Textuality in Contemporary Fiction by Women
Lindsey Tucker

The Repair of the World: The Novels of Marge Piercy
Kerstin W. Shands

Clara Barton: In the Service of Humanity
David H. Burton

International Women's Writing: New Landscapes of Identity
Anne E. Brown and Marjanne Goozé, editors

"Some Appointed Work To Do": Women and Vocation in the Fiction of Elizabeth Gaskell
Robin B. Colby

Women, Politics, and the United Nations
Anne Winslow, editor

Envisioning the New Adam: Empathic Portraits of Men by American Women Writers
Patricia Ellen Martin Daly, editor

Before Equal Suffrage: Women in Partisan Politics from Colonial Times to 1920
Robert J. Dinkin

"Nobody Wants to Hear Our Truth": Homeless Women and Theories of the Welfare State
Meredith L. Ralston

Spanish Women in the Golden Age

Images and Realities

Edited by
Magdalena S. Sánchez and Alain Saint-Saëns

Contributions in Women's Studies, Number 155

GREENWOOD PRESS
Westport, Connecticut • London

UNIVERSITY OF TULSA MCFARLIN LIBRARY
WOMEN'S LITERATURE

Library of Congress Cataloging-in-Publication Data

Spanish women in the golden age : images and realities / edited by
   Magdalena S. Sánchez and Alain Saint-Saëns.
      p.   cm.—(Contributions in women's studies, ISSN 0147–104X   ;
   no. 155)
      Includes bibliographical references and index.
      ISBN 0–313–29481–X (alk. paper)
      1. Women—Spain—History.   2. Sex role—Spain—History.   3. Spain—
   Social conditions—To 1800.   I. Sánchez, Magdalena S.   II. Saint-
   Saëns, Alain.   III. Series.
   HQ1692.S66   1996
   305.4′0946—dc20   96–36432

British Library Cataloguing in Publication Data is available.

Copyright © 1996 by Magdalena S. Sánchez and Alain Saint-Saëns

All rights reserved. No portion of this book may be
reproduced, by any process or technique, without the
express written consent of the publisher.

Library of Congress Catalog Card Number: 96–36432
ISBN: 0–313–29481–X
ISSN: 0147–104X

First published in 1996

Greenwood Press, 88 Post Road West, Westport, CT 06881
An imprint of Greenwood Publishing Group, Inc.

Printed in the United States of America

The paper used in this book complies with the
Permanent Paper Standard issued by the National
Information Standards Organization (Z39.48–1984).

10 9 8 7 6 5 4 3 2 1

Woman?
HQ1692
.S66
1996

Copyright Acknowledgments

The editors and publisher gratefully acknowledge permission to quote from the following:

Earlier versions of Chapter 2, "Charisma and Controversy: The Case of María de Santo Domingo" by Jodi Bilinkoff, were presented at the annual meeting of the Society for Spanish and Portuguese Historical Studies, Vanderbilt University, 8–10 April 1988, and published in *Archivo Dominicano* (Salamanca) 10 (1989), 55–66. It appears in this volume with the kind permission of the editors.

Every reasonable effort has been made to trace the owners of copyright materials in this book, but in some instances this has proven impossible. The editors and publisher will be glad to receive information leading to more complete acknowledgments in subsequent printings of the book, and in the meantime extend their apologies for any omissions.

Contents

Preface   ix
Alain Saint-Saëns

Acknowledgments   xi

PART I: RELIGION AND SOCIETY   1

1. Spaces of Women's Religiosity in the Military Order of
   Santiago in Late Medieval Castile (Twelfth to Sixteenth
   Centuries)   3
   María Echániz

2. Charisma and Controversy: The Case of María de Santo
   Domingo   23
   Jodi Bilinkoff

3. Behind the Veil: Moriscas and the Politics of Resistance
   and Survival   37
   Mary Elizabeth Perry

4. A Case of Gendered Rejection: The Hermitess in Golden
   Age Spain   55
   Alain Saint-Saëns

PART II: POLITICAL REALMS   **67**

5. The Female Figure as Political Propaganda in the "Pedro el Cruel" Romancero   69
Anne J. Cruz

6. Pious and Political Images of a Habsburg Woman at the Court of Philip III (1598–1621)   91
Magdalena S. Sánchez

7. Women and Factionalism in the Court of Charles II of Spain   109
JoEllen M. Campbell

PART III: FEMALE IDENTITY   **125**

8. Images and Realities of Work: Women and Guilds in Early Modern Barcelona   127
Marta V. Vicente

9. Conversions of the Woman Monarch in the Drama of Calderón de la Barca   141
Mary Lorene Thomas

10. Rhetorical Canons and Female Portraits in Pastoral Romances   157
Sylvia Trelles

11. The Gendered Context of Melancholy for Spanish Golden Age Women Writers   171
Teresa S. Soufas

Bibliography   185

Index   209

Contributors   227

Preface

⎧his volume seeks to attain two methodological goals. First, to offer new
⎩ results of current research on the history of women in Early Modern Spain.
Second, to provide an interdisciplinary view, through articles about literature
and psychoanalysis, social, political, religious, and artistic history, by respected
specialists from different countries, including the United States, France, and
Spain, and from different historical and literary schools. This book clearly
enlightens the debate around this newly developing field and demonstrates,
through refined and accurate analysis, that women's history and gender history
are two inseparable parts of a same, until now, too neglected ensemble.

❧

In Early Modern Spain, church and state, helped by the powerful Inquisition,
rapidly extended their ascendancy from the control of basic expression of faith
to the domain of daily life, of personal privacy and inside this sphere, sexual
behaviors. Women were not spared in this general domestication of minds and
bodies. In a patriarchal society, on the contrary, all eyes were focused on their
writings, talk, body and its image, sexuality, and faith, even their dreams and
visions. What the authors of this book, *Spanish Women in the Golden Age:
Images and Realities*, point out very well, however, is that women successfully
struggled to be listened to, and to save, conquer, or increase, when it was
possible, a space of liberty in which they could promote their own agenda in
Early Modern Spain.

In this collection, Spanish women are first put in perspective within a
socio-religious context. Caught between scorn, fear, misogyny, shame, guilt,

and solicitation, women of Spain had indeed more than one reason to protest against unfair treatment from God and his representatives on earth.

Turning to the political realm, the authors study women who were in close relation to power—that is, directly in contact with the king—and completely reconsider the generally accepted stereotypes of these women. They were, in many aspects, in a key position to influence their royal spouse, brother, or son.

The volume also considers working women who, dealing with men inside or outside guilds, tried to gain recognition for their work. These women, who were manipulated by the different powers of the city in which they lived, also defended their own interests before them. Imagination was on the side of these courageous female workers, who found ways to overcome a repressive and rigidly sexist legislation.

Spanish literature and theater at that time, far from ignoring the debate about the role and place of women in the society, reflected it, with all the ambiguity and the complexity of a codified message. As shown in the final chapters of the book, Spanish women had to try to define their own space of liberty through literary discourse and most often against the diminishing vision of themselves that it projected. But the frustrations that they all experienced generated a sense of "sisterhood" that was able to transcend boundaries of class.

In Early Modern Spain a narrow but real path enabled all of these different women to contour the rigid model imposed on them. In a Spanish society, too much and too well defined by a principle of exclusion, women were active and visible participants.

❦

This book, *Spanish Women in the Golden Age: Images and Realities*, complements my earlier edited works, *Religion, Body and Gender in Early Modern Spain* and *Historia silenciada de las mujeres españolas* (siglos XV–XIX). Finally, it will help in the wait for the forthcoming monographs on which several of the chapter authors are currently working.

I would like to thank my friend, Dr. Magdalena Sánchez, from the Department of History at Gettysburg College, who accepted to join me as co-editor of this book. With patience, firmness, and wisdom, she helped to transform my initial project into a more accomplished and publishable manuscript and enriched it by building a strong, stimulating, and precise bibliographical essay that should be able to satisfy any reader eager to know more about specific aspects of the subject.

Alain Saint-Saëns

Acknowledgments

The editors gratefully acknowledge the Spanish Ministry of Culture, the Program for Cultural Cooperation between the Spanish Ministry of Culture and North American Universities, and Gettysburg College for their generous support of this publication. The editors also thank Terri Jennings for her work in preparing the manuscript for publication.

Magdalena Sánchez also thanks the contributors for their work and patience. She is particularly grateful to Jodi Bilinkoff, Anne Cruz, and Betsy Perry for their editorial suggestions in the preparation of this manuscript. Finally, she wishes to thank William Bowman for his untiring support and assistance throughout the completion of this volume and Adam Fernandez for his help with the final editing of the manuscript.

Spanish Women in the Golden Age

Part I

RELIGION AND SOCIETY

1

Spaces of Women's Religiosity in the Military Order of Santiago in Late Medieval Castile (Twelfth to Sixteenth Centuries)

María Echániz

In 1492, the community of Sancti Spiritus of Salamanca wrote to the Master of the Order of Santiago, Alonso de Cárdenas, telling him that they were "religious women, with whom no man had to be with, nor to have power over, nor to rule, nor to govern, especially because the people of this house were so honest, wise and prudent to rule the government of the monastery."[1] This vigorous defense of the power to govern themselves and of the concept of a women's community constituted the reply to the master's attempt to impose his niece as commander of the monastery, despite the fact that the community had enjoyed the right to choose their own commander since its foundation in 1268. At a time when few women could express their desire to defend spaces of their own, these *freilas*—as the female members of a military order are called—did so because previous generations of women had ruled themselves and created a space of their own within the order.

This chapter studies the spaces that women created for themselves within the military religious Order of Santiago in medieval Castile. My purpose is to analyze spaces of women's actions that have been misunderstood or even totally forgotten by Spanish (and non-Spanish) medieval historians.[2] Women's participation in the Order of Santiago raises many questions. Why, for example, would a group of medieval women want to take part in a formal and symbolic male space ruled by the values of war and crusade against the Muslims, at a time when the sex/gender roles of medieval culture forbade them from participating totally in those activities? In order to answer this question, it is necessary to study the foundation of the Order of Santiago, its meanings in the context of the religious history of the Middle Ages, the opportunities that it offered to women, and the ways in which women created their own spaces in the order. Subsequently, I will analyze the evolution of these spaces up to the beginning of the sixteenth century.

THE FOUNDATION OF THE ORDER OF SANTIAGO (1170–1175)·

As is well known, the military orders were established during the twelfth century in the Holy Land as a result of the military necessities of conquest and defense of territory, but also as a consequence of the religious reform of the eleventh century and the "vita apostolica" movement of the twelfth century. In 1128, Bernard of Clairvaux addressed a treatise to the Order of the Temple called *De laude novae militiae*, in which for the first time in the history of the Christian Church holy wars were justified. Thereafter, religious life could merge with military life for the purpose of defending the Faith. The military orders also benefited from emerging values of the "active apostolic life" that ended the monopoly of contemplative life as a unique monastic pattern.[3]

The Orders of the Temple and St. John of the Hospital spread from the Holy Land to the Iberian peninsula, which shared an active frontier with Islam. Their influence was essential for the foundation of the Hispanic military orders during the second half of the twelfth century. Also important was the existence in Spain of religious and military fraternities. Between 1170 and 1175, the quick evolution of one of these, the Fraternity of Cáceres, gave rise to the Order of Santiago.

On the first of August, 1170, a new military and religious fraternity apparently formed by a group of knights with a master, Pedro Fernández, received the newly reconquered town of Cáceres from Fernando II, King of León. Six months after this first documentary mention, the *fratrum of Canceris* (as the fraternity was then called) and Pedro, Archbishop of Santiago de Compostela, reached an accord by which the fraternity adopted a fundamental symbol, that of the Apostle Santiago, who had been defined in the Iberian "reconquest" as the bastion of Spanish Crusade ideology. Between February and September of 1170, the brothers of Caceres were referred to more and more as the militia of Santiago or *militie Sancti Iacobi*.[4] The primitive rule of the militia, a group of spiritual principles addressed to both single and married laymen and laywomen, can be dated between 1170 and 1173, and demonstrates that women were members from this early period.[5] In 1175, the militia—now known as the Order of Santiago—and its rule received papal approval. By the time of the 1175 bull of Alexander III, the order already had a defined structure, a more complex rule, three specific vows (obedience, poverty, and conjugal chastity), and a new kind of member—the canon. These canons joined the order between 1173 and 1175 and were certainly Augustinian regular canons.[6]

From its very foundation, the Order of Santiago had some distinctive features. It was the only Hispanic military order founded by and for lay persons, men and women, and the only one from Castile-León that was not linked to another religious order. It also engaged in a wide variety of activities in addition to those central to the military purpose of the Order. Moreover, it was the first religious order to allow its members to marry by transforming the traditional vow of *complete* chastity to the vow of *conjugal* chastity.[7]

According to the bull of 1175, men and women, laity and clergy, single and married, could belong to the order, and all would be considered "religious," although each would have different functions. These included the *freiles caballeros*, or knights of Santiago, married and single, who lived with their families or in common, and whose main function was making war against the Muslims; the *freiles clérigos*, Augustinian canons, who lived in their convents or along the frontier with the knights, giving spiritual assistance to them and their families and educating their children; and finally the freilas, married and single, who lived with their families or together, and whose main function was to help the military effort spiritually by performing the divine office.[8] Those freilas who lived in community had, like the freiles clérigos, a didactic function: they educated the daughters of members of the order. Both freilas and knights were under the authority of the Master of Santiago, who was always a knight, while canons were under the authority of priors.

These distinctive features of the Order of Santiago explain, in my opinion, why some medieval women were interested in the spiritual and material projects of the order. In the context of the religious movements of the twelfth and thirteenth centuries, the foundation of the order met not only military needs, but also desires for lay participation in religious life, desires emerging throughout Europe in this century and particularly difficult for women to fulfill.[9] For them, the Church had already defined a primary religious space—the convent—and even though women participated as well as men in the search for new ways of religious life, there were few substantial changes in the institutional options that the Church gave them to pursue their religious experiences.[10] Only outside the cloister could medieval women find alternatives to the monastic pattern as beguines, anchoresses, or as participants in heretical movements.[11]

Santiago accepted lay participation in the sense that women (or men) could become members without necessarily adopting a monastic life. The laity kept its preponderance within the order during all of its history. Moreover, even though women could not fulfill completely the spiritual ideal of the order because they could not participate in war, this ideal gave them an orthodox and very prestigious—in the context of a frontier society—type of religious life. Furthermore, Santiago gave some women possibilities of access to economic, political, and social power through Santiago's property tenure—holding and ruling both whole commanderies as well as just some possessions of the order—and it permitted women to create their own space, especially within female monasteries. While a high proportion of Spanish female monasteries were under the direct control of local bishops, these of Santiago were exempted from Episcopal jurisdiction—as was the whole order—and depended directly on the master of the order and the pope. These communities were ruled by women who received the name of *comendadoras* (commanders)—in Castile—or prioress—in Aragón. Also, the monastic option of the order had, at least until the beginning of the sixteenth century, some original features. These included the complete absence of normative enclosure, the personal administration of property of each freila, a relaxed common life, the profession of the vow of conjugal chastity—by which they kept the possibility of getting married without losing the habit but by just leaving the communities—and the maintenance of strong familial relationships outside and inside monasteries through the educational and charitable roles of the communities as defined by the Rule of Santiago. The women's communities had to be "open"—not cloistered—because they had to accept as temporal members married freilas and their daughters. Finally, even though women could not look for social promotion within the order through military activities, their association with Santiago through different types of spiritual and economic relations did provide opportunities for promotion.

Nevertheless, women never had a central position in the Military Order of Santiago nor "symmetric" roles as knights and canons. Neither participation in war—the main role of knights—nor priesthood—one of the main roles of canons—was open to freilas. In Santiago's hierarchy, women could be only sub-commanders and commanders. They could not be Masters of the Order, members of the Council of the Thirteen—a council of leading commanders who gave advise to the master—mayor commanders—chief of one regional grouping of commanderies—nor visitors. They usually did not participate in General Chapters where *establecimientos*—temporal and spiritual laws of the order—were dictated and offices were elected. This lack of participation in governing institutions of the order left women in a weak position, without the capacity to take part in decisions that affected their life in the order. Thus, if the Order of Santiago was innovative in the extent of the participation it allowed women within the order and in the ways it permitted them to express their spirituality, it nevertheless never transgressed role divisions inherent in the medieval gender system. Moreover, a diacronical analysis of women's participation in the order from its foundations until the sixteenth century shows that their position within the order changed in ways that reflected a transformation of female spaces.

THE RULE OF SANTIAGO

The Rule of Santiago is the principal source for the study of the order's organization and women's position within it, especially in the first century of its existence. The semi-definitive text of the Rule of Santiago may be dated to the middle of the thirteenth century. With one exception, later texts of the rule introduced few and insubstantial variations.

Until recently, four different versions of the Rule of Santiago were known: the primitive rule in Latin, which can be dated between 1170 and 1173;[12] the brief version in Latin, which is included in the bull *Benedictus Deus* of Alexander III, in 1175;[13] the full version in Castilian from the middle of the thirteenth century;[14] and a fifteenth-century full version in Latin.[15] We have to add to these four versions a new one that I have found, which is dated 1480 and written in Castilian, and which is an adaptation of the Rule to the female community of the Sancti Spiritus of Salamanca made by the General Chapter of the order celebrated in Ocaña in that year.[16]

A comparative study of the rule's first three versions reveals significant changes in the position of women within the order from 1170 to 1260. According to the primitive rule, women were members of the order from the inception of the fraternity. They could live the ideal of spiritual life in two ways: within their families or in a community. Moreover, the primitive rule made explicit that freilas could decide whether or not to marry.

> Unmarried women are to be asked if they wish to marry. Those who wish to do so may marry. Those who do not wish it shall be placed in appropriate places and monasteries of the order, where necessities shall be administered to them.[17]

This reference to "appropiate places and monasteries" suggests that there existed different types of communal life. The first known female monastery of the order, Santa Eufemia de Cozuelos, was founded after 1186, so it is possible that before that time women lived in "appropriate places," probably just houses or perhaps the two hospitals that the order had at that time.

From the version of 1175 on, the rule consistently displayed concern for the integration of women who were relatives of freiles in an attempt to establish control—protection structures that could include all members of Santiago's spiritual family. The *Benedictus Dei* bull of 1175 basically was concerned with justifying the order's more innovative features, such as participation of married members and the change of vows from absolute chastity to conjugal chastity. According to the bull, Santiago's ideal of spiritual life could be reached through marriage or celibacy, but it is clear that the second option seemed more valuable to the papacy. More important for us, the text suggested that women could only reach this ideal through marriage to freiles—or by remaining unmarried within monasteries, as other parts of the bull let us assume—but not through marriage to men unaffiliated with the order, as the primitive rule had apparently allowed.[18] The marriage had to be chaste, meaning, according to the bull, that husband and wife had to be faithful to each other and to refrain from intercourse on specified days.[19]

The previously quoted reference to single women from the primitive rule disappeared in the bull and was replaced by a reference to widows. The text referred exclusively to widows of freiles who had received the order (*qui Ordinem susceperunt*), that is, the ones who were freilas and who desired to marry again.[20] Widows could get married again with whomever they wanted, but they needed the master's or commander's consent, which the primitive rule had not required.

In the mid-thirteenth–century rule, the tendency to include within the order women who were relatives of freiles—their widows, wives, and daughters—while carefully controlling their ways of life became more noticeable. This rule never referred to these wives, widows, and daughters of knights as freilas, but its dispositions considered them objects of regulation and control since they were members of the order. Women who were wives of knights had to respect the periods in which sexual intercourse was forbidden, and these periods were considerably extended.[21] During the two Lenten periods, couples had to separate in order to live communally with members of the order of their own sex.[22] Wives had to join "women who do not have husbands," that is, the freilas who lived communally. They could also live in these communities while their husbands were away at war or on other business.[23] Dispositions concerning widows of knights are the most detailed, perhaps because of the order's emphasis on the paternalistic control of women. A widow had three options: stay in the monastery, marry again with the permission of the master or the commander, or live outside the monastery if she led a "good life" and the master thought it appropriate. Thus, while the Rule of Santiago considered that a widow was released from "men's law," she was not released from the order's control because she was now considered subject to its dispositions whether or not she had, in the words of the earlier bull, "received the order" (*Ordinem suscepe-runt*).[24] Finally, the daughters of widows of freiles were also objects of protection and control until they were fifteen years old, when they had to decide for themselves whether or not to assume the habit of the order. The order was to protect their virginity and to raise and educate them until that moment.[25]

Analysis of the first three versions of the rule, which reflected the history of the order between 1170 and 1260, reveals three main processes with respect to the position of women within the order. First, according to the primitive rule, the freilas—single or married—were not necessarily relatives of male members, and possessed their own identity within the order. In the mid-thirteenth–century rule, even though the order never referred to women linked by kinship with male freiles as freilas, it considered them subject to the principles of the rule, which attempted to define their material and spiritual life. Second, in the primitive rule, common life could take place not only in monasteries but also in other places, while in the thirteenth-century rule only monasteries were considered appropriate. Third, women were allowed more power to make their own decisions in the primitive rule, whereas in the following versions control over women was increased.

At least three factors help explain these changes in the position of women within the order. First, in its process of formation, the order was very quickly transformed from a lay fraternity to a religious order of lay people and canons who were more influenced by the ecclesiastical guidelines. Second, in its first century of life, the economic success of the order had created increasing concern over Santiago's property and, as a consequence, led to tighter control over the families of freiles since they occupied properties belonging to the order.[26] Finally, as the Order of Santiago consistently defined its structure and institutions, it lost interest in independent attachments of women to the order, attachments that once were considered to be part of the original features of the ideal of Santiago and and probably were regarded in the middle of the thirteenth century as troublesome.[27] As a consequence, the order tried, first to restrict increasingly women's participation in forms of conventual life, which were easier to control, and second, to control strictly the lives of female relatives of freiles. The fact that freilas were excluded from the governing institutions of the order made their position weak, ambiguous, and vulnerable to these kinds of restrictions. Nevertheless, women's spaces in Santiago endured and kept many of their original characteristics until the end of the fifteenth century, when they confronted another process of change, this time defined by the male governors of the order and by the monarchy of the Catholic Kings.

The adaptation for women of the Rule of Santiago made by the General Chapter of Ocaña in 1480 constitutes one of the first signs of this new process. Master Alonso de Cárdenas justified this adaptation because, he said, the order was founded more for men—knights and canons—than for women, and the rule was addressed more to men than to women, so that when the freilas read the rule they encountered many difficulties.[28] The master recognized in this way the marginal position of women in Santiago. But, in fact, the adaptation formed part of an arrangement between the order and the female community of Sancti Spiritus of Salamanca, to whom the text was addressed. The community wanted the order to guarantee their right to choose their own commander, and in exchange they accepted this new text, which introduced, among other things, an important change: the vow of conjugal chastity was changed to one of perpetual chastity.[29]

Among other reasons, this Rule of Santiago adapted to women is interesting because the attempt to make a text addressed mainly to men more relevant to women—or vice versa—demonstrates, from the point of view of the adapter, what the contents of the feminine and masculine were in a given context. Thus, for example, the new text eliminated all of the chapters of the rule that were dedicated to the exaltation of the military ideal and of war for the faith. This was a basic change: the originality of the order consisted of the union of military and religious ideals. To prevent women from participating in the Holy

War—even if only in symbolic terms—radically limited women's possibilities of fulfilling Santiago's ideal. The text also eliminated all references to the central institutions of the order, that is, the general chapters, the council of the Thirteen, the master and his election, the visitors and their powers. The freilas had almost never participated in the governing institutions of the order, but this suppression represented their definitive and complete exclusion. Another important change, as I have said, was the change of the vow of conjugal chastity to one of perpetual chastity. Other changes were not so substantial. The rest of the text can be defined as a "translation to the feminine" of the Rule of Santiago.

The contents of the Rule of 1480 were restrictive to the freilas of Sancti Spiritus, to whom the text was addressed. We do not know what the first reaction of the community was to this text, but from the beginning of the sixteenth century the freilas rejected these innovations and refused to profess the Rule of 1480. For them, after the Council of Trent, to accept this new rule meant to accept that they were traditional nuns (because of the vow of perpetual chastity) and, as a consequence of that, they were subjected to enclosure. But, as we will see, the importance of this text is that it is the first documentary proof of a new process of change in the position of women within the order.

SECULAR AND CONVENTUAL FREILAS

The normative model designed by the different versions of the Rule of Santiago reveals how the position of women changed within the order in two differents periods during the Middle Ages. However, these versions of the rule reflect exclusively the interests and points of view of the men who ruled the order from its central institutions. It is necessary to verify the normative model with the other source of information that we have: the documentary source.

From the very foundation of the order, the Rule of Santiago and several documents refer to women who were full members of the Order of Santiago in two different ways. I will call the ones who lived with their families "secular" freilas and the ones who lived in common, "conventual" freilas. Both of them took the same vows—poverty, obedience and conjugal chastity—and both were under the Rule of Santiago and the master, but their way of life was in practice different. In addition to these two types of "full" membership, others types of female association to the order also are documented, especially in the period 1170–1260. Examples of such associations reveal the determined support lent by women to the religious ideal of the new order.

During the first twenty-five years of the order, this support was reflected by a substantial amount of female or mixed female-male donations of property to the order. Twenty-one percent of the documented private donations to the order were made by women and 37 percent by married couples.[30] If we consider documentation from a particular commandery, as, for example, private donations to Vilar de Donas, a male monastery of the order in Galicia, during the period 1194–1300, women made 33.3 percent of the donations and married couples 13.3 percent; men accounted for 40 percent of the donations.[31] In the commandery of Montalbán in Teruel, for the period 1210–1327, women made 43 percent of donations, compared with 37 percent made by men; married couples made only 12 percent of the donations.[32] Finally, in the commandery of Uclés (Cuenca) for the period 1174–1310, male donations represented 44 percent of private donations to the house, married couples 41 percent, and female donations only 8.8 percent.[33] These numbers indicate that women, whether by themselves or with their husbands, brothers, or sons, decided to support the new order by giving it property. Women gave property to Santiago for a variety of purposes: to procure the salvation of their soul or the souls of their relatives, to found or endow a hospital of the order, to assist economically in the redemption of christian captives, or just to help the order fulfill its general goals.[34] The variety of activities in which the order engaged—military, hospitable, redemption of captives, educational, parochial—and its prestige in the Spanish Christian kingdoms, where the "reconquest" and the characteristics of a frontier society occupied a central position, help to explain why women wanted to support the order. Some of the female donors went further and affiliated themselves with Santiago as familiars.

Familiaritas was an institution through which people from different social backgrounds gave "their bodies and souls" to a religious order or to a particular house. The familiar usually promised to enter into the order if she or he decided to take vows, gave some goods to the institution (though the donor normally administered them until his or her death), and chose to be buried in a house of Santiago. In exchange, the order promised that the familiar would receive spiritual and material benefits, and sometimes established special economic agreements.[35] Three examples of women who became familiars of the order are the following. In 1189, Mayor Isidoro confirmed the sale of some properties made by her son to the prior of San Marcos de León and donated additional properties with the proviso that the order give her spiritual and material assistance.[36] In 1190, Vitalia, the widow of Vidal de Palombar, affiliated to the order and gave one-half of her property, on the condition that Santiago should nourish her and bury her with her husband.[37] Lucía, the widow of Martín de la Chica, gave her "body and soul" to the order in 1244, donating 200 Alfonsin maravedís. Santiago accepted Lucía and her dead husband as familiars, sharing its spiritual and material goods with them.[38]

Until the middle of the thirteenth century, we document women who became secular freilas both with their husbands or in an independent way. One example of a married couple who became freiles is María and Pascual of Alberit in 1185. The couple promised to donate to the order all of their property if they died without issue, or one-half of it if they had children. If María became a widow, she would keep possession of their goods until her death, living in her house, as the master would order. If Pascual became a widower, he would live on the frontier, if the master so decided.[39] Some examples of independent women who were or became members of Santiago are the following. In 1216, Sancha Luz, *fratrisa* of the order, together with her sons Lope and Juan Sánchez, signed an agreement with the master and the prior of Vilar de Donas about the presentation of priests for the church of Santiago de Dorra.[40] In 1229, Aurembiaix, countess of Urgel, who one year before had promised that if she took vows she would do it in the order, became a freila of Santiago.[41] Some years later, in 1242, Sancha Pérez de Azagra, *soror Ordinis de Ucles*, and her daughter Milia gave to the order several possessions in Teruel, goods that they would keep in usufruct until their death. Even though close relations between Sancha Pérez and the order were documented since 1221, it was only in 1242 that she called herself a *soror* of Santiago.[42]

From the middle of the thirteenth century, there is less and less information about secular freilas who were not relatives of Santiago knights. One of the reasons for this decrease of information is the limited amount of documentation for these types of private donations. The disappearance of this kind of documentation complicates the study of the participation of women as secular freilas, and also as familiars and donors. But this decrease of information is also closely related to a process analyzed earlier: from the middle of the thirteenth century, the order was no longer interested in instituting relations with women who were not relatives of freiles or else conventual freilas. Thus, documentation about secular freilas during these centuries is very scarce, and it makes almost exclusive reference to aristocratic female relatives of freiles. For example, at least two commanders of the female monastery of Sancti Spiritus de Salamanca were secular freilas before moving to the convent, and both of them were also relatives of knights. Inés Alfonso was the widow of the commander Martín Alfonso de Valdevieso. She ruled the command from 1379 until 1394. María Ramírez de Guzmán was the widow of the master García Fernández, lord of Villagarcía, and she was commander between 1411 and 1427.[43] In 1480, the General Chapter of Ocaña mentioned Clara Albernáez, chambermaid of Queen Isabel and wife of commander Gonzalo Chacón, saying that she was a secular freila and held properties from the order.[44] New references to secular freilas date from 1494. The secular freila Isabel de Nurueña arranged to be buried in the monastery of Sancti Spiritus, "house of my order, where I have always wanted to end my life," donating to the community diverse properties on the condition that the freilas pray for her and celebrate a Requiem mass once a week. Isabel de Nurueña probably had lived in this monastery, perhaps before her marriage. When she made her will, she was a widow working in the service of the noble María de Luna, wife of Enrique Enríquez, *mayordomo mayor* of the Catholic Kings.[45]

The decreased mention of secular freilas is inversely proportionate to the information about conventual freilas and female monasteries. The tenure of master Pelay Pérez (1242–1275) coincides both with the elaboration of the extent rule and with the period in which many female monasteries were founded or experienced a decisive moment in their organization. It is easy to observe the order's interest in supporting this kind of female participation during this period.

From 1195 to 1268, the order had seven female monasteries. The first known was Santa Eufemia de Cozuelos, in Palencia, a male monastery founded in the middle of the tenth century that King Alfonso VIII gave to the Order of Santiago in 1186. After the donation, the monastery continued to be male and, in 1195, had a double community of women and men, with a female commander and a prior. From the end of the twelfth century, the monastery was exclusively for women.[46] The community grew during the period of the tenure of Pelay Pérez under the patronage of the Infanta Sancha Alfonso, who donated considerable property to the house, lived in the community, and was buried there.[47]

In 1194, King Sancho I of Portugal gave to Master Sancho Fernández some properties and houses in Santos, Lisbon, to build a male monastery of Santiago. A female monastery was built instead, and was called Santos-o-Velho. In 1271, Pelay Pérez donated to the community all the properties of the order in Lisbon.[48] In 1212, a group of noblewomen led by Maria de Terrassa founded the monastery of Sant Vicens de Jonqueres, in Sabadell, near Barcelona. Some years after, in 1234, Countess Garsenda de Bearn linked the community with the Order of Faith and Peace, affiliated to the Order of Santiago. From 1269, the monastery was under the direct control of Santiago.[49] The first news concerning the double community (female-male) of the Hospital of San Mateo de Avila dates to 1256. At that time, the community was ruled by a female commander, Dominga Xemeno, and there was at least one conventual freila called Doña María. The double community still existed in 1286, although afterward the women seem to have disappeared.[50]

In 1260, Master Pelay Pérez gave to Constanza, *fratrissa* and widow of the noble Guillem d'Anglesola, a group of properties in Lérida in order to found a new female monastery in that city. Constanza promised the master that she would donate as much as she could to the foundation and was nominated patroness of the house. This monastery encountered serious economic difficulties from its inception because of the continuous intervention of members of the order and of the local nobility who wished to control its property. Its existence was brief, and it was incorporated in Jonqueres in 1342.[51]

There is little documentation concerning the female monastery situated in Destriana, León. In 1266, the order limited the number of freilas to thirteen and we know that the community still existed in 1290.[52] Finally, in 1268, Infant Martín Alfonso—brother of Sancha Alfonso- and his wife María Méndez started to endow, with the master Pelay Pérez, the female monastery of Sancti Spiritus de Salamanca. The monastery was founded in what had been an urban domain of the Order of Santiago since 1223—the *puebla* of Sancti Spiritus.[53] The founder María Méndez played an active role after her husband's death in establishing the position of the community within the order, and succeeded in obtaining for the freilas the power to govern themselves through the choice of their own commander.

All of these female communities shared some of the same characteristics. They observed the rule and the *establecimientos* of Santiago, were subject to visits from and regulation by the order, and used the rituals of profession and novitiate of Santiago. The initial endowment of these communities was formed by donations from founders or principal donors and from the order. In those communities where enough documentation survives to support any conclusion, the patrimony seems to have grown throughout the thirteenth century, both because of private and royal donations, and because of royal privileges and exemptions. After this period, new property principally was brought to the communities by new members joining the monasteries. Nevertheless, the monasteries enjoyed various degrees of economic success, depending on such factors as women's possibilities of access to property (which changed in Castile and Aragon during the later Middle Ages), community location,[54] possibilities for self-management (the interference of male commanders or priors could be very negative to communities),[55] external intervention in a community's property (often related to the feudal violence of the fourteenth and fifteenth centuries), and the geographic distribution of the patrimony.

One common characteristic shared by the female communities of Santiago was that the freilas belonged to the nobility, at least from the middle of the thirteenth century when the order underwent a quick process of "aristocratization."[56] In Sancti Spiritus of Salamanca, for example, the freilas were members of the urban patriciate (middle and low nobility), whose male members were knights and *hidalgos* with great social, economic, and political power within the city and its hinterlands, while some of the commanders of the community belonged to the high nobility of the Castilian Kingdom.

Another common characteristic of these communities was that the freilas were related through bonds of kinship. In Sancti Spiritus, the freilas were usually members of lineages who had lived in the monastery through generations, especially ones from the families Flores, Paz, Nieto, Maldonado, and Monroy.

One of the main vehicles for the creation of these female genealogies was the rearing of female children related to the freilas. An example is Leonor Pérez and her daughter Catalina González, who entered the community in 1379. Catalina was raised and educated in Sancti Spiritus. In 1427, she was still a freila. In 1498, nine of the twenty-three freilas of Sancti Spiritus had spent periods of their childhood in the monastery, periods that oscillated between three and fifteen years.[57]

At the end of the fifteenth century, the female monasteries of Santiago passed through a very difficult period. When the order lost its original ideals, it also lost the character of an institution that originally had combined the spheres of the religious and the military. From the thirteenth century, breaks between the two spheres appeared within the order, but it was as the "reconquest" drew to a close in the Spanish Kingdoms that Santiago began to find the two spheres incompatible. During the fourteenth and fifteenth centuries, the order, controlled by the Castilian high nobility, actively participated in the feudal violence and in the continous political struggles. The knights consistently changed their ways of life, refusing to observe the Rule of Santiago. From the General Chapter of Ecija in 1485 onward, to be a knight of Santiago no longer meant having different religious duties from other laymen. The canons, instead, were reincorporated into the ecclesiastical structure and had to observe strictly the Rule of Santiago and the Rule of St. Augustine.[58] But the conventual freilas did not easily find a space in which to reincorporate because of the original characteristics of their position. The Order of Santiago attempted to resolve the question by trying to assimilate their position with that of the canons—without giving them their power, of course—and changing their way of life, which is only understandable when one takes into account the original ideals of the order as a whole. One of the main changes that Santiago wanted to impose on them was the enclosure.

At the same time, Castilian society was undergoing another process characterized by the strengthening of the central state. One consequence of this process was that in 1493 the Catholic Kings incorporated the Order of Santiago to the crown. From that time, the monasteries of Santiago were placed under the direct control of the kings and were subject to their religious reforms. These reforms were an important part of the monarchs' program of consolidation of state power. Significantly, the first papal brief that Isabel and Fernando received from Alexander VI concerning the reforms was *Exposuerunt Nobis* (27 March 1493), where the pope authorized them to name clergy to reform the female monasteries of their kingdoms. The program of reform reflected the state's view that female monasteries were homogenous. A uniform model was applied to all monasteries with complete enclosure—the main point of the reform—perpetual chastity, common property, and life in common as its goals.[59] The new wave of foundations of female monasteries of Santiago that began at the end of the fifteenth century was partially influenced by this reform.

This second wave began around 1479 with the foundation of Santa Olalla de Mérida by the master Alonso de Cárdenas.[60] In 1501, Queen Isabel moved the community of Santa Eufemia de Cozuelos to Toledo.[61] In the same year, the Catholic Kings founded and endowed the monastery of Santiago de la Madre de Dios in Granada. Queen Isabel's interest in this foundation was reflected in a letter of 1500 addressed to the bachelor of Sepúlveda. She had known that his daughter, "la latina"—who knew Latin—wanted to take vows in the monastery of Sancti Spiritus. The queen ordered that she profess in Granada in order to teach Latin to the freilas of the monastery that the queen was founding there.[62]

Santa Cruz de Valladolid was similarly tied to the queen because one of the founders, María de Fonseca, was one of the queen's maids. Isabel collaborated in the foundation by giving protection and privileges to the community. The papal approval dated from 1506. In his bull, Julius II gave permission to María de Zúñiga, the other founder, to write the constitution of the community. In this exceptional text—one of the few surviving documents of this type written by a woman in Castilian—Zúñiga ordered her community to take a vow of perpetual chastity and to lead an enclosed life.[63] The last female monastery of the order was Santiago el Mayor de Madrid, which was founded by the freile Iñigo de Cárdenas and his wife Isabel de Avellaneda in 1584.[64]

The monasteries of Santa Cruz and Santiago de la Madre de Dios were especially influenced by the Catholic Kings' program of reform for female monasticism. The freilas of these communities were pressured to take the vow of perpetual chastity and lead enclosed lives, two important changes in the traditional life of the conventual freilas.

Obviously, the Catholic Kings' reform also affected the older monasteries of the order since it tried to introduce new elements into the traditional monastic life of the freilas. The communities defended their traditional way of life in different ways: initially by formally accepting the imposed changes but ignoring them in practice, and later, when this proved insufficient, by trying to defend their rights at law. The conflict became sharper after the Council of Trent and lasted until the eighteenth century.[65]

The systematic reform of female monasticism and the imposition of enclosure on women's communities carried out by the Catholic Kings (without equivalents in male monasticism, which were reformed less systematically and without the imposition of enclosure) suggests that women and their communities were defined by the state as particularly important objects of control as the state grew stronger. Why? I would suggest that this was because the state once again assumed a role as the primary institution of control over the individual, a role previously played mainly by the patriarchal family. Henceforth, the family would occupy a secondary, though still very important, position.

CONCLUSION

From its inception as a lay fraternity, the Military Order of Santiago permitted some women—especially women from the ruling class—to create spaces of their own, spaces with some original features, at a time when the institutional parameters of women's spirituality were severely constrained. Women were members and active supporters of an order that offered them some access to religious, economic, and social powers. The order gave women a prestigious type of spiritual life in the context of a frontier society which integrated aspects of the secular life in an original way. However, the order also used these spaces as a way to control women. The maintenance of the freilas' privileges and of the original features of the space they inhabited demanded the constant exercise of self-defense and resistance. Through this resistance some of the original features of their way of life were preserved throughout the Middle Ages. Their presence within the order was even strong enough to produce an expansion of their communities despite the order's shift away from its primitive ideals.

An analysis of the historical experience of the freilas from the end of the twelfth to the beginning of the sixteenth century demonstrates that Castilian women of the ruling class suffered an important reduction in their capacities for social, economic, and political action, a reduction that men of the same class did not experience. The change in their position was closely related to the strengthening of the state and of the Order of Santiago as an institution. Thus, the freilas' experience supports the hypothesis of Joan Kelly, who argued that European women did not have a renaissance or, at least, did not have one during the Renaissance.[66]

NOTES

I have published a first and partial version of this article: "Espiritualidad femenina en la Orden Militar de Santiago (siglos XII–XV)" in Angela Muñoz; María del Mar Graña, eds., *Religiosidad femenina: expectativas y realidades (ss. VIII–XVIII)* (Madrid: Asociación Cultural AL-MUDAYNA, 1991). I am deeply grateful to Dr. David Nirenberg who helped me to translate this article. The following abbreviations have been used in these notes: AHN: Archivo Histórico Nacional (Madrid); OOMM: Sección Ordenes Militares; AHDE: Anuario de Historia del Derecho Español; AEM: Anuario de Estudios Medievales.

❦

1. "syendo nosotras mujeres religiosas con quien non an de estar varones algunos, nin menos de nos aver de tener en su poder, nin regir, nin governar, quanto más syendo las personas de la dicha casa de tanta onestidad e juyzio e discreçión para lo governar el regimiento de la dicha casa." María Echániz, "Las mujeres de la Orden Militar de Santiago. El monasterio de Sancti Spiritus de Salamanca (1268–1500)," Ph.D. diss. (Barcelona, 1990), doc. 260.

2. I know of only three works that touch specifically on the subject: Alan Forey, "Women and the Military Orders in the Twelfth and Thirteenth Centuries," *Studia Monastica* 29, 1 (1987) 63–92; María Soledad Ferrer Vidal, "La mujer en la Orden Militar de Santiago," *Las mujeres medievales y su ámbito jurídico* (Madrid: Servico de Publicaciones de la Universidad Autónoma de Madrid, 1983), 201–215; and *idem*, "Los monasterios femeninos de la Orden de Santiago en la edad media," *Las ordenes militares en el Mediterráneo occidental* (Madrid: Casa de Velázquez: Instituto de Estudios Manchegos, 1989), 41–50. For a bibliography about particular monasteries, see the notes in that section.

3. Derek W. Lomax, *La Orden de Santiago (1170–1275)* (Madrid: Consejo Superior de Investigaciones Clientíficas, Escuela de Estudios Medievales, 1965) 1–2. See also, Alan Forey, *The Military Orders from the Twelfth to the Early Fourteenth Centuries* (Toronto: University of Toronto Press, 1992) 1–5, and Antonio Linage Conde, "Tipología de la vida monástica en las órdenes militares," *Yermo* 12 (1974), 73–115.

4. In 1173, Pope Alexander III placed the Militia of Santiago and its goods under his protection. José Luis Martín Rodríguez, *Orígenes de la Orden Militar de Santiago (1170–1195)* (Barcelona: Consejo Superior de Investigaciones Científicas, 1974), 17–18, and doc. 59, 234.

5. This rule was edited by Jean Leclercq, "La vie et la prière des chevaliers de Santiago d'après leur règle primitive," *Liturgica* 2 (1958), 347–357.

6. A fifteenth-century tradition of the order stated that they were members of the monastery of Santa María de Loyo (Galicia), but this has been questioned by Derek Lomax, "The Order

of Santiago and the Kings of León," *Hispania* 18 (1958), 5–6. There exist other possibilities to explain the incorporation of the canons, such as the influence of the Augustinian canonical communities along the pilgrimage route to Santiago de Compostela. See, Eutimio Sastre Santos, "El martirologio de Uclés y los orígenes de la Orden de Santiago," *Hispania Sacra* 34 (1982), 217–252.

7. The Orders of Calatrava and Alcántara—linked to the Cistercian Order—did not accept women as members in the beginning. Thereafter, they only accepted nuns. The Alcántara Order founded its first female community in the sixteenth century. The Calatrava Order had two during the Middle Ages: San Felices de los Barrios (Burgos), founded around 1219–1220, and San Salvador de Pinilla (Sigüenza), accepted as a member in 1461. See Joseph O'Callaghan, "The Affiliation of the Order of Calatrava with the Order of Cîteaux," *Analecta sacri ordinis cisterciensis* 16 (1960), 43–44, and Alan Forey, "Women and the Military Orders in the Twelfth and Thirteenth Centuries," 73.

8. That is, performing their own liturgy of the Order of Santiago, especially the canonical hours, the processions, the prayers for the dead, helping to celebrate the mass, and performing other paraliturgical exercises. Liturgy occupied a central possition in the order, and it was especially important for the members of Santiago who lived in community. See, Derek Lomax, *La Orden de Santiago*, 96.

9. As Eutimio Sastre points out, the Order of Santiago can only be understood within the context of the "vita apostolica" movements of the twelfth century. The order was formed by different kinds of people and also had a plurality of goals—military, charitable, and educational. This plurality of goals was a typical feature of many communities originating in the apostolic movement. By merely taking this context into account we can understand, in Sastre's opinion, three original features of the order: the incorporation of married members, the new religious vow of conjugal chastity, and lay superiority within the order's hierarchy. See Eutimio Sastres Santos, "La Orden de Santiago y su Regla," Ph.D. diss. (Madrid: Universidad Complutense, 1981).

10. The "vita apostolica" movement that aspired to imitate the apostolic life defined by complete poverty, itinerant preaching, and active life failed in the long run to fulfill women's expectations of a new monastic model that was different from the contemplative and cloistered one. We can observe in the beginnings of new religious orders a wide diversity of female nonmonastic links, but as orders organized their structures and institutions they terminated these links and, at best, accepted only nuns. See, Carol Neel, "The Origins of the Beguines," *Signs* 14, 2 (1989), 329–330, and John Freed, "Urban Development and 'cura monialium' in Thirteenth Century Germany," *Viator* 3 (1972), 311–327.

11. See, especially, Carol Neel, "The Origins of the Beguines"; Patricia Rosof, "The Anchoress in the Twelfth and Thirteenth Centuries," in Lilian Shank and John Nichols, eds., *Medieval Religious Women, II. Peaceweavers* (Kalamazoo: Cistercian Publications, 1987), 123–144; and Brenda Bolton, "Mulieres Sanctae," in Susan Stuard, ed., *Women in Medieval Society* (Philadelphia: University of Pennsylvania, 1976), 141–158. For an analysis of a heresy that was clearly a woman's option, see Luisa Muraro, *Guglielma e Maifreda. Storia di un'eresia femminista* (Milano: La Tartaruga, 1985).

12. Jean Leclerq, ed., "La vie et la prière."

13. Eutimio Sastre Santos, ed., "La Orden de Santiago y su Regla," 324–329.

14. Discovered in a codex from the canons' monastery of Santa María de Benevívere and edited by Derek W. Lomax, *La Orden de Santiago*, 51–53, doc. 1, 221–231. Lomax dates the text around 1260, taking into account some paleographic features of the manuscript and the use of some linguistic forms.

15. Enrique Gallego Blanco, ed., *The Rule of the Spanish Military Order of St. James (1170–1493)* (Leiden: E. J. Brill, 1971). He edited the version of the codex AHN, Cód. 45b.

16. Edited and studied by María Echániz, "Las Mujeres de la Orden de Santiago. El Monasterio de Sancti Spiritus de Salamanca, 1268–1500," doc. 224. A monographic study of this rule will be published in the near future.

17. "Ab illis mulieribus que viros non habuerint queratur si maritos velint accipere. Volentibus liceat nubere. Nolentes locabuntur locis aptis et monasteriis que sunt de domo, ubi necessaria eis administrabuntur." Jean Leclercq, ed., "La vie et la prière," 354.

18. "habeantur in ipso Ordine qui celibem, si voluerint, ducant vitam et consilium beati Pauli apostoli sequantur qui dicit: 'De virginibus autem preceptum Domini non habeo, consilium autem do'; sint etiam qui iuxta institutionem dominicam ad procurandam sobolem et incontinentie principium evitandum coniugibus suis utantur et una cum eis incolatum superne patrie de con valle lacrimarum et terrena transire peregrinatione intrantur et lacrimis diluant et operibus pietatis." Eutimio Sastre Santos, ed., "La Orden de Santiago y su Regla," 325; S. Paul, I Cor. 7:25.

19. "Qui continere nequiverit, coniugium sortiatur et servem inviolatam fidem uxori et uxor viro nec thori coniugalis continentia violetur." Eutimio Sastre Santos, ed., "La Orden de Santiago y su Regla," 328.

20. "Si autem viri premortui fuerint et relicte ipsorum, qui Ordinem susceperunt, nubere voluerint, denuntietur hoc magistro sive commendatori, ut cum illius conscientia, cui mulier ipsa vult nubat, secundum verbum apostoli Pauli dicentis: 'Mortuo viro soluta est mulier a lage viri, cui vult nubat tantum in Domino.' " Eutimio Sastre Santos, ed., "La Orden de Santiago y su Regla," 328; S. Paul, I Cor. 7:1ff.

21. "Quando ayunaren non convengan con sus mugeres ni en las fiestas de Sancta María ni de Sant Iuan Babtista nin los apóstolos, ni de las mayores fiestas ni en las vigilias." Derek Lomax, ed., *La Orden de Santiago*, doc. 1, 224.

22. "En las dos quaresmas los freyres que ovieren mugeres conviento tengan e las mugeres con aquellas que non an maridos." Derek Lomax, ed., *La Orden de Santiago*, doc. 1, 224.

23. "Mas si los freyres fueren sobre moros o en otros negocios de la casa e sus mugeres quisieran seer en la claustra con las freyras, sean recibidas e ténganlas ondradamientre tro que a sos maridos vengan e aquesto sea en providentia del maestro," Derek Lomax, ed., *La Orden de Santiago*, doc. 1, 224.

24. "Aquelas mugeres a quí transieren sos maridos, estén en los monesterios, e si alguna bona vida fiziere e fueras del monesterio quisiere remaneçer si el maestro por bien lo viere remanezca, e si alguna quisier casar dígalo a so maestro e a so comendador que con so mandado se case e segund que dixo el apostóligo: 'Muerto el varón, suelta es la mugier de la ley del varón, con quiquier case tanto en el nuestro sennor,' " Derek Lomax, ed., *La Orden de Santiago*, doc. 1, 224.

25. "Aquella (viuda) que non quisiere casar more en el monesterio e si fiias oviere sean nodridas consigo en la Orden en virginidad e sean guardadas fasta XV annos e aprendan letras. E si remanecer quisieren en la Orden sean en providentia del maestro, si non, depártanse con aquello que les pertenece." Derek Lomax, ed., *La Orden de Santiago*, doc. 1, 224.

26. Freiles' wives had to be members of the order because this was the only way to guarantee that the order could control them and their property. Widows needed permission to marry again because the order probably discouraged husbands who were not freiles in order to keep control of the widows' properties, part of which might belong to the order.

27. Similar processes happened in the Premontré, where attachments of independent women affiliated to the order performed hospitable and charitable roles, which finished some years after the death of the founder Norbert of Xanten (1134). See, Carol Neel, "The Origins of the Beguines," 332–338. This also happened in the Order of St. John of the Hospital. See, Alan J. Forey, "Women and the Military Orders in the Twelfth and Thirteenth Centuries," 67–68.

28. "nuestra Horden más principalmente ovo respeto a los varones, por rasón de la cavallería, e a los priores e freyles de misa que a las dichas comendadoras e freylas religiosas d'ella, (y) la Regla de la dicha nuestra Horden está más dirigida e enderesçada a los varones que a ellas, e quando la han de leer e usar de los mandamientos e cosas d'ella conviéneles mudar muchos vocablos e cosas d'ella que a las dichas comendaderas e freylas no conviene, en lo qual resçiben fatiga e ofuscaçión e enojo," María Echániz, "Las mujeres de la Orden Militar de Santiago," doc. 224.

29. Two days later, the general chapter dictated an *Establecimiento*, which guaranteed the right of the freilas of Salamanca to choose their own commander. María Echániz, "Las mujeres de la Orden Militar de Santiago," doc. 227. Nevertheless, the same master who signed this *establecimiento*, Alonso de Cárdenas, did not respect it in 1492 when he tried to impose his niece as commander of the monastery (see note 1).

30. I use the documentation edited by José Luis Martín, *Orígenes*. He edited 316 documents, 61 of which were private donations. Married couples made 23 donations (37% of the total); women 13 (21%); men 21 (34%); and mother-son groups, 2 (3.2%).

31. I use the documentation edited by José Luis Novo Cazón, *El priorato santiaguista de Vilar de Donas en la edad media (1194–1500)* (La Coruña: Fundacíon "Pedro de la Maza," 1986). I consider only the 66 documents dated before 1300. There were 15 private donations. Donations made by men were 6 (40%), by women 5 (33.3%), by marriages 2 (13.3%), and by groups 2 (13.3%).

32. I use the documentation edited by Regina Sainz de la Maza, *La Orden de Santiago en la Corona de Aragón. La encomienda de Montalbán (1210–1327)* (Zaragoza: Institucíon "Fernando el Católico," 1980), who edited 236 documents, 16 of which were private donations. Donations made by women are 7 (43%), by men 6 (37%), by marriages 2 (12%), and by brother-sister groups 1 (6.2%).

33. I use the documentation edited by Milagros Rivera, *La encomienda, el priorato y la villa de Uclés en la edad media (1174–1310)* (Madrid: Consejo Superior de Investigaciones Científicas, 1985). She edited 248 documents, 34 of which were private donations. Donations made by men were 15 (44%), by marriages 14 (41%), by women 3 (8.8%), by sister-brother groups 1 (2.9%), and by other groups 1 (2.9%).

34. See, José Luis Martín, *Orígenes*, docs. 48, 68, 71, 72, 182, 200, 208, 220, 271, 309; Regina Sainz de la Maza, *La Orden de Santiago en la Corona de Aragón*, docs. 1, 2, 35; and Milagros Rivera, *La encomienda*, docs. 45, 61, 82, 149.

35. For the subject of *familiaritas*, see José Orlandis, "Sobre la elección de sepultura en la España medieval," *AHDE* 20 (1950), 5–49, and *idem*, "Traditio corporis et animae en las iglesias y monasterios de la Alta Edad Media," *AHDE* 24 (1954), 95–279.

36. "mihi tam in spiritualibus quam in temporalibus secundum facultatem domus provideant, tam in victu quam in vestitu, in victo quotidiano, in pelle mantu et pallio uno de duobus annis in duobus," José Luis Martín, ed., *Orígenes*, doc. 260, 432–433.

37. José Luis Martín, ed., *Orígenes*, doc. 261, 433–434.

38. Regina Sainz de la Maza, ed., *La Orden de Santiago en la Corona de Aragón*, doc. 26, 259–260.

39. José Luis Martín, ed., *Orígenes*, doc. 178, 359.

40. Jose Luis Novo Cazón, ed., *El priorato santiaguista de Vilar de Donas*, 62, doc. 8, 206–207.

41. "offerimus corpus nostrum et anima domino Deo et Sancto Ordini Sancti Iacobi de Uclés, et promittimus obedienciam in manu vestra fratri Lupe Petri, Ordini Sancti Iacobi vobis et domino Petro Gonçalbo, Dei gratia magistro Ordinis, et totius conventui succesive, solempnizantes iuxta regulam Ordinis Sancti Iacobi et statuta et sororem eiusdem Ordinis nos de cetero

confitemur." Regina Sainz de la Maza, ed., *La Orden de Santiago en la Corona de Aragón*, docs. 12, 15, 224, 246–247.

42. They were the widow and the daughter of Lope de Varea. Regina Sainz de la Maza, ed., *La Orden de Santiago en la Corona de Aragón*, docs. 9, 23, 24; 242, 256–258.

43. See, María Echániz, "Las mujeres de la Orden Militar de Santiago, II," 502–503, 505–507.

44. Through her husband, Clara Albernáez apologized to the master for not being in the Chapter (AHN, OOMM, Santiago, Libro 1241C, fol. 72v.)

45. See, María Echániz, "Las mujeres de la Orden Militar de Santiago, II," 546–548.

46. See, María Soledad Ferrer Vidal ànd Díaz del Reguero, "Santa Eufemia de Cozuelos: un monasterio femenino de la Orden Militar de Santiago," *En la España medieval. Estudios en memoria del profesor Salvador de Moxó, I* (Madrid: Universidad Complutense, 1982), 337–348. The document of 1195, Biblioteca Nacional de Madrid, Mss, 13.063, f. 75r–76r.

47. In 1608, Sancha Alfonso's body was found to be incorrupt. This fact and a preexisting tradition of holiness encouraged the community of Santa Fe de Toledo, heir to Santa Eufemia, and the Order of Santiago to start her beatification. Several pseudohistorical works were written about her, the first of which was, Antonio Quintanadueñas, *Serenísima infanta gloriosa virgen doña Sancha Alfonso* (Madrid: P. de Val, 1651).

48. I have found no work about Santos. For references to it, see Francis Gutton, *L'Ordre de Santiago* (Paris: P. Lethielleux, 1972), 213–215; and Derek Lomax, *La Orden de Santiago*, 78, 83.

49. See, María Mercè Costa, "Les dames nobles de Jonqueres," *II Colloqui d'Història del monaquisme català* (Abadía de Poblet, 1974), 253–309; "Les eleccions priorals en el monasterio de Santa Maria de Jonqueres," *AEM* 11 (1981), 419–433; and "Un conflicte monàstic: Valldonzella i Jonqueres," *Estudis Cistercencs* IX (1973), 5–24.

50. AHN, OOMM, Uclés, carp. 56, docs. 2 and 5.

51. See Regina Sainz de la Maza, "El monasterio santiaguista de San Pedro de la Piedra en Lérida," *AEM* 11 (1981), 383–418; *La Orden de Santiago en la Corona de Aragón (1210–1327)* (see note 2), 135–145; and *La Orden de Santiago en la Corona de Aragón, II. La encomienda de Montalbán bajo Vidal de Vilanova (1327-1357)* (Zaragoza: Institucíon "Fernando el Católico," 1988) 99–102.

52. See Derek Lomax, *La Orden de Santiago*, 83.

53. See María Echániz, "El monasterio de Sancti Spiritus de Salamanca. Un espacio monástico de mujeres de la Orden Militar de Santiago (siglos XIII–XV)," *Studia Historica* 9 (1991), and *Las mujeres de la Orden Militar de Santiago*.

54. Urban communities such as Jonqueres or Sancti Spiritus had a more active economic life because they had the continuous socioeconomic support of women members of urban nobility—*caballería villana*. On the other hand, Santa Eufemia de Cozuelos, a countryside community, received no sizable donations during the late Middle Ages.

55. San Pere de la Pedra and Santa Eufemia experienced difficulties because they had, at least during some periods, priors or male commanders. The first community disappeared and the second was eventually moved to Toledo. But even in the communities that did not have a prior or male commander, the order tried several times to control management, sometimes illegally encroaching upon their goods and privileges. See María Echániz, "Formas de agresión al patrimonio," in "Las mujeres de la Orden Militar de Santiago II," 424–446.

56. Since 1249, nobility was a prerequisite for becoming a member of the order. See, *Establecimiento* of chapter of Mérida in 1249 (The Hispanic Society of America, New York), HC Mss, 380/834, f. 2v–3r.

57. Two of them belonged to the lineage of Flores. Inés de Ribas, daughter of Juan Flores and Inés de Ribas, entered the monastery in 1468. At that time, two women from her family

were already religious—María Flores and Aldonza Flores. We can suppose that they took care of her during the ten years in which she learned to read, write, and sing. In 1478, Inés de Ribas took the habit. Catalina Flores joined the community in 1488. She had been raised there for six years and took the habit in 1494. If the disposition of the rule which said that girls living in the monastery had to decide to leave or take the habit when they were fifteen years old was observed, Inés had entered in the monastery when she was five and Catalina Flores when she was nine years old. See María Echániz, "Las mujeres de la Orden Militar de Santiago II," 529–531.

58. The habit of the order was for them more related with the honor, the nobility and the right to hold a commandery than with a model of religious life. In early modern times, because of these changes, historians doubted that knights were really religious persons. See Daniel Rodríguez Blanco, "La reforma de la Orden de Santiago," *En la España medieval* V, 2 (1986), 935–937, and L. P. Wright, "The Military Orders in Sixteenth and Seventeenth Century Spanish Society. The Institutional Embodiment of a Historical Tradition," *Past and Present* 43 (1969), 43.

59. The main goal of the reform was *el encerramiento* of the religious women. See, Tarsicio de Azcona, "Reforma de religiosas benedictinas y cistercienses en Cataluña en tiempo de los Reyes Católicos," *Studia Monastica* 9 (1967), 86–87; and "Reforma de las clarisas de Cataluña en tiempos de los Reyes Católicos," *Collectanea franciscana* 27 (1957), 5–51.

60. Angel Alvárez de Araujo is the only historian who dates the foundation to 1479, although without adducing any evidence. Other historians believe in a later foundation. See, Angel Alvárez de Araujo, *Las órdenes militares de Santiago, Calatrava, Alcántara y Montesa*, (Madrid: Fernando Cao y Domingo de Val, 1891) 47–48, and Francis Gutton, *L'Ordre de Santiago*, 228–229.

61. In 1485, the general chapter of the order decided to move three monasteries—Sancti Spiritus de Salamanca, Santa Eufemia de Cozuelos, and San Marcos de León (a male monastery)—to Llerena, Ocaña, and Guadalcanal, respectively. The pope authorized the moves in 1486, but strong opposition from the communities and the considerable expense of the project caused it to be postponed. In the end, only Santa Eufemia was moved, although not to Ocaña but to Toledo, but then only because of the personal interest of the queen, who paid the expenses and gave the convent of Santa Fe and the *Casa de la Moneda* to the community as a new location. María Echániz, "Las mujeres de la Orden Militar de Santiago," doc. 242. Ecija, 13 March 1485. See also AHN, OOMM, Uclés, carp. 95, n. 5 and 6.

62. María Echániz, "Las mujeres de la Orden Militar de Santiago," doc. 328. See, Rafael G. Peinado Santaella, "La Orden de Santiago en Granada (1494-1508)," *Cuadernos de estudios medievales* VI–VII (1978–1979), 179–228.

63. See María Echániz, ed., "María de Zúñiga. La definición de un modelo de vida espiritual dirigido a una comunidad de mujeres," Cristina Segura, ed., *La voz del silencio, I (siglos VIII–XVIII)* (Madrid: Asociación Cultural AL-MUDAYNA, 1992), 207–218.

64. See Francis Gutton, *L'Ordre de Santiago*, 234–236 and Angel Alvarez de Araujo, *Las órdenes militares*, 55–61.

65. See María Echániz, "Las mujeres de la Orden Militar de Santiago, II," 629–636, 639–656, 698–703.

66. Joan Kelly, "Did Women Have a Renaissance?" Renata Bridenthal and Claudia Koonz, eds., *Becoming Visible* (Boston: Houghton Mifflin, 1977), 175–201.

2

Charisma and Controversy: The Case of María de Santo Domingo

Jodi Bilinkoff

*I*n the last months of 1509 and the first of 1510 a panel of ecclesiastical judges listened to hours of testimony in a case that deeply divided the friars of the Dominican Province of Spain. They were deciding the fate of María de Santo Domingo, also known as the Beata de Piedrahita, a young tertiary from the west of the bishopric of Avila. To her supporters, the Beata was a holy woman who was endowed with the divine gifts of ecstasy, prophecy, and infused wisdom. Her detractors dismissed her as a vain, publicity-seeking fraud.

This case was to determine more than the personal destiny of María de Santo Domingo, however. By 1509 many Dominicans, both male and female, had already joined the Beata in seeking a life of more intense personal prayer and more austere penitential practices in religious houses located in her home districts of Piedrahita and Aldeanueva. Was this, as these enthusiasts claimed, a movement of "genuine" reform within the Order of the Preachers? Or, was it, as the Beata's opponents insisted, a misguided deviation from the "true" Dominican tradition as interpreted by an official hierarchy based in Rome? Not surprisingly, most modern Dominican scholars share the latter opinion.[1]

Here I examine the trial of María de Santo Domingo and the conflicting images of the female and the holy constructed by her supporters and opponents. Her case reveals at their rawest the tensions raised by the issues of authority, charisma, and gender roles in late medieval and early modern Castile, tensions that permeate the entire history of Western Christianity.

We know little about the life or even the identity of the woman who took the name in religion María de Santo Domingo. She was born around 1485 in Aldeanueva, a village in the bishopric of Avila under the jurisdiction of the

Dukes of Alba. A contemporary chronicler suggested that she was raised by devout parents.[2] However, Juan de Setiembre, one of the Beata's supporters testified during her trial that he had heard that her mother had severely punished her as a child for sneaking off to church to pray and neglecting her household chores.[3] This conflict between family duties and religious aspirations occurs frequently in women's autobiographical and hagiographical literature of the period.[4] María de Santo Domingo was either completely illiterate or very nearly so, and apparently dictated the two devotional treatises and pair of letters that make up the body of her original work.[5]

As a teenager, she began what would become a lifelong association with the friars of the Dominican monastery of Santo Domingo in the nearby market town of Piedrahita. She became a tertiary, a person who is affiliated with a religious order but does not take formal vows of profession. María joined the Dominican Third Order around 1502 and lived briefly in the residence for lay sisters, or *beaterio*, in Piedrahita, and then moved to the beaterio of Santa Catalina in Avila.[6]

By 1507, the Beata's strong and controversial personality had begun to assert itself. That year, she left Santa Catalina and, in an unusual move, took up residence at the recently founded male Dominican house of Santo Tomás in Avila, probably in a residence attached to the monastery. During her trial, Juan Hurtado de Mendoza reported that she had quarrelled with the sisters of Santa Catalina, and other detractors intimated that she had disobeyed orders.[7] Her supporter, Diego de San Pedro, acknowledged the Beata's bad relations with the Santa Catalina community, but claimed that the resentments arose only when María criticized the sisters for failing to observe strictly their rule. The Beata's confessor and procurator, Antonio de la Peña, offered a more mystical explanation for her transfer to Santo Tomás, claiming that "the Lord neither wanted nor desired that she remain in an obscure corner of a humble house, and thus carried her into public view," but added that she had secured her superiors' permission to make the move.[8]

María de Santo Domingo stayed a few months at Santo Tomás before, accompanied by a coterie of friars and beatas, she traveled to Toledo, where the notoriety she had already achieved in Avila grew and intensified. There stories circulated about a young woman who prophesied the future and received mystical gifts from God, but who also caused scandal because of her condemnation of the city's conversos and her excessive praise for the Inquisition. According to one witness, her provocative words caused civil unrest on one occasion, and an unnamed bishop publicly scolded the Beata and her followers.[9]

Soon news of María de Santo Domingo's exploits reached the court of Ferdinand of Aragon and members of the Rome-based Dominican hierarchy, including the order's new master general, Thomas Cajetan. Ferdinand responded by inviting her to what was to be the first of several visits to his court at Burgos during the winter of 1507–1508, where she greatly impressed the king, the influential Cardinal Cisneros, and many courtiers.[10]

Cajetan, however, was deeply concerned that the scandalous behavior and public pronouncements of this questionable young woman would bring embarrasment to the Dominican Order. Even more serious, in his eyes, was the possibility of schism within the order, as more and more friars, particularly from the Piedrahita monastery, followed the Beata in her calls for a life of extreme austerity. He took action, attempting to curtail her activities and her access to friars through legislation at several Dominican chaper meetings beginning in March of 1508.[11] Eventually, the master general petitioned and received from Pope Julius II permission to launch a full-fledged investigation into the life and teachings of María de Santo Domingo. Four trials were held between 1508 and 1510, but records remain for only the last, and definitive, one that took place between October, 1509, and March, 1510. At the end of this trial the carefully chosen (some would say, stacked) panel of judges, which included Ferdinand's own confessor, Juan de Enguera, exonerated the Beata of all charges and, in fact, declared that her "exemplary life and doctrine" was "very useful and to be highly recommended."[12]

María de Santo Domingo, her name cleared, was thus free to take up the position of prioress of a convent founded especially for her by the Duke of Alba in her native village of Aldeanueva. In an extraordinary instance of social mobility in premodern Castile, an illiterate peasant woman came to preside over a religious institution with over 100 nuns, all named María in honor of the house's patron, Mary Magdalene. Apparently the Beata remained here until her death, which probably occurred around 1524.[13]

Was María de Santo Domingo a holy mystic and prophetess or an elaborate fake and seductress? During many months of testimony, the Beata's supporters and opponents presented conflicting images of this complex and elusive figure. Except for a fairly brief stint at the witness stand by María herself and two female witnesses, the rest of the testimonies came from male observers, the vast majority of them Dominican friars. Their comments reflect male attitudes toward the proper roles of men and women in religious life as well as competing views of what constituted the "true" Dominican tradition, views heavily gendered in their thrust and content.

Perhaps the most serious charge levelled at the Beata de Piedrahita, and one made by nearly all of her detractors at the trial, was that her fits and raptures were feigned—even staged on request. The friars Juan de Azcona, Agustín de Funes, Juan Hurtado de Mendoza and Damián de Avila all regarded her raptures as faked (*fingidos*). Agustín de Funes insisted further that María staged her false ecstasies in collusion with her confessor, Diego de Vitoria.[14] The relationship between María and Vitoria would come under close scrutiny during the trial, as we shall see.

Many doubted the accuracy of her prophecies as well. Juan Hurtado de Mendoza recounted a complicated series of prophecies uttered by the Beata and recorded by Vitoria concerning a future pope, emperor, and master of the order. Hurtado regarded all this as "a lie that she made up thinking to please those who listened."[15] Lope de Gaibol, a former confessor to the Beata, grew highly suspicious of her claims to be able to distinguish consecrated from unconsecrated Hosts because she could see God in a consecrated Host. Fray Lope decided to put her to the test. On one occasion he told María that he was giving her an unconsecrated Host, and she remained calm, when he had in fact given her a consecrated wafer. Another time he administered a Host he knew to be unconsecrated and watched as she went into one of her raptures. Gaibol thus concluded that the tertiary's ecstasies and her powers of divinition were utterly bogus.[16]

Many learned friars doubted that an ignorant peasant woman could speak convincingly on theological matters. Several found her incoherent and opaque. Juan de Azcona, a generally sympathetic observer, expressed a widely held sense of confusion when he reported that, "in many matters the said Sor María was very sensible and obedient and that in other matters she deviated from the monastic rule." At least one cleric expressed the opinion that the Beata was actually mad.[17] In the 1920s and 1930s, the Dominican historian Vicente Beltrán de Heredia proposed mental illness, hysteria, heart disease, and even epilepsy as explanations for María's bizarre words and behavior. Like his sixteenth-century predecessors, he was perplexed by what seemed to him an unbalanced, even pathetic woman who had nevertheless exerted undeniable influence over mature, experienced, and highly educated friars.[18]

In addition to the charges of duplicity, ignorance, and inconsistency, the Beata faced accusations that touched directly on her position as a woman. For example, many of her detractors commented on her vanity and concern with matters of appearance. Agustín de Funes testified that while he had only seen María wearing the habit of her order, he had heard that she sometimes wore "scarlet petticoats" and "coral necklaces." Juan de Azcona and Juan Hurtado de Mendoza also reported her use of brightly colored fabrics, gold and coral jewelry, and, as they noted disapprovingly, French bonnets.[19] The Beata herself admitted that she wore her hair in long tresses, regarded as a sign of women's beauty and seductive power in the Christian tradition since Paul composed his letters.[20] María de Santo Domingo's claims to holiness were greatly complicated, perhaps even vitiated, in the eyes of these male clerics by the fact that she was a young and possibly attractive woman. Is a pretty beata a contradiction in terms?

These friars were also troubled by a feature of María's spirituality that her supporters found charming—her dancing, especially in public. Evidently, in moments of religious ecstasy the Beata would spontaneously begin to dance, sometimes with other people. Agustín de Funes reported that many had seen her go into trances and dance in churches to the music of the organ, but alleged that at least once, without being in rapture, she had danced with some friars at an inn (*hospedaje*) in Piedrahita. Juan Hurtado de Mendoza admitted that the Beata moved "very gracefully" when she danced, as she claimed, "with Christ and the angels," but complained that she engaged in these performances too frequently and, again, sometimes when not in ecstasy. He worried that even if her actions stemmed from true religious emotions, the sight of a young, attractive woman exhibiting her body and perhaps even her long, flowing hair, in public would seem a "matter of lasciviousness" (*cosa de liviandad*).[21]

The Beata's opponents had further reasons to suspect her sexual purity. Even her supporters admitted that María frequently kept the company of friars, without female escort. She maintained a particularly close, some felt, unhealthy, relationship with her confessor, Diego de Vitoria. María and Vitoria developed a kind of mutual dependency, as has often happened in the history of spiritual direction and friendship. In his testimony Vitoria recalled his first meeting with the Beata, over three years previously. After speaking with her, he claimed, "he felt a degree of fervor and repentence that he had never felt before."[22] For her part, María told the judges that she seldom remembered things that happened to her during her raptures and that "Fray Diego de Vitoria, who was always with her and was the one who heard and understood the truth, could and would tell it."[23]

Many witnesses commented on the "excessive familiarities" between María de Santo Domingo and Diego de Vitoria, and other friars. Clergymen reportedly spent entire nights in her cell, sitting on or even leaning over her bed. On occasion she embraced and even kissed them. Juan Hurtado de Mendoza, who had first ordered Vitoria to confess the Beata, was particularly upset by the appearance of impropriety. He became highly suspicious when, after several "fraternal corrections," Vitoria refused to disassociate himself from his penitent. Hurtado concluded that the fault lay with María for having tempted her confessor and forced him into a compromising situation.[24] No one suggested that Vitoria, by all accounts the main interpreter of the Beata's mystical experiences, might have manipulated her in any way.

Besides using her feminine wiles to deceive and seduce her followers, detractors accused María de Santo Domingo of something absolutely forbidden to women: appropriating the role of the priest. The Beata delivered sermons and heard confessions, at least informally, and signed her letters "Your unworthy chaplain(ess)" (*la indigna capellana de Vuestra Reverencia*). Even Diego de Vitoria, while reluctant to label her addresses as "sermons," admitted that she gave public "exhortations," through which "many people have received great spiritual benefits."[25] Here the Beata was crossing a dangerous line, moving from the traditional role accorded to holy women as private counselors and consolers to a position of leadership in genuinely public apostolate. This was a risky move.[26]

In general, the opponents of María de Santo Domingo objected to the unrestrained, indecorous, and highly public nature of her behavior. Her dramatic, some would say, theatrical raptures and strange prophecies created controversy and dissention. Many saw this young woman who let her hair grow long, wore jewelry, and danced in churches as an exhibitionist. Her nights alone with her confessor and her public sermons seemed to challenge the accepted role of religious women as humble, discrete, and obedient. Recently the Dominican historian Ramón Hernández asserted that "prudence" was at the heart of the "authentic" Dominican tradition.[27] María de Santo Domingo was anything but prudent.

The Beata's supporters, who outnumbered her detractors by about two to one at the trial, strove to counter these negative charges and to portray her as a genuine holy woman. Almost all testified that they had seen her ecstasies and heard her prophecies and believed them to be true. Many reported that María's raptures occurred at the moment of receiving the Eucharist, a common experience in the history of female spirituality. Don Fernando de Toledo, the brother of the Duke of Alba, recalled, for example, that "he had seen her fall into ecstasy many times, at the time of receiving communion, saying in rapture things so marvelous and devout that all who listened were moved to tears."[28]

Moreover, as Diego de Vitoria and others insisted, María's frequent fits, trances, cries, spells of copious weeping, and bodily contortions in imitation of Christ's Passion were gifts sent by God, not actions over which she had any control. Vitoria claimed that he had tested his penitent on this account, explaining that "he had begged her several times that she fall into ecstasy so that certain persons might see it, but that some times she had gone into a rapture and other times no."[29]

The Beata's supporters acknowledged her lack of formal education but asserted that she could understand difficult points of theology through "infused wisdom" received directly from God, another commonplace of mystical literature, especially among female mystics. According to Juan de Ceballos, on several occasions, while in ecstasy, "Sor María was asked by great men of letters (*grandes letrados*) about complicated matters of holy scripture and theological issues, responding to them in such a way that the greatest theologians were amazed."[30]

In sharp contrast to the testimony of María's opponents, who cast her as a vain and frivolous woman, her followers depicted her as an extreme ascetic who urged all Dominicans to adopt a more austere way of life. They told many anecdotes about her simple manner of dress, heroic fasts, and horrific disciplines and mortifications of the flesh, which, according to one witness, began when she was a child.[31] Juan de Setiembre went so far as to claim that certain monks and nuns attacked the Beata only because they were incapable of meeting her high ascetic standards.[32]

María de Santo Domingo's advocates insisted upon her piety, humility, obedience, and chastity. They had to reconcile these claims with the many allegations of dancing, elegant dress, and licentious behavior made by her detractors.

For example, her supporters described the Beata's dancing as an integral part of her experience of rapture and prophecy, a way God moved her body as He moved her spirit. María del Cordero recalled that, "she had seen several times the said Sor María sing and dance with much grace and that with the dance and the hymns she would go into ecstasy and would say such marvelous and devout things that she made all the persons who listened cry piteously." Antonio de Benavente hastened to add that María danced "in a respectable way" (*honestamente*).[33]

As to her wearing fancy clothing and jewelry, both Diego de Vitoria and Diego de San Pedro asserted that the Beata only donned these items to please the female devotees who had given them to her, and she always returned them. Vitoria specified that these women asked María to wear their clothing and jewels while she was in rapture. Perhaps they believed that these exterior items would be consecrated by touching the body of the holy woman while she was being touched by God. In one of the most extraordinary images evoked during the trial María del Cordero testified that the Beata "wore none of the jewels or fine clothing out of vanity or lasciviousness, nor for any bad purpose, nor for looking good, but she wore them as an image might wear them."[34] In this formulation her role became a totally passive one, that of a living statue or icon, dressed by members of the faithful hoping for some contact with the divine.

María's supporters also had to explain her constant association with friars, especially alone in her cell at night. Almost all discussed her continual illnesses and torments at the hands of devils, another classic theme in the lives of saintly women. Her defenders, especially her confessors Diego de Vitoria and Antonio de la Peña, maintained that they had to stay with the Beata during the night to help her through the frequent demonic attacks that tortured her both physically and spiritually. De la Peña used a traditional view of women to justify his actions. He claimed that in times of diabolical violence, "the company of women is not sufficient because women are weak and tremble at the demons that torment them and are not capable of understanding some of the mysteries that take place." Both confessors concluded that it was indeed their duty, and a "service to God," to protect and comfort their besieged penitent, even if it gave the appearance of impropriety.[35]

In fact it was this public, observed aspect of the Beata's spirituality that scandalized her opponents but attracted her followers. For them, María de Santo Domingo's divine gifts distinguished her as an exemplar, a model for others, a morality play. Many, including the generally disapproving Juan Hurtado de Mendoza, commented that this young woman, by her words, her actions, and her graceful dancing, had moved them to tears. Her annual Eastertime experience of Christ's wound in the side and other bodily signs served the Christian community, in the words of Antonio de la Peña, as "a commemoration of the Passion" (*un memorial de la Pasión*).[36] Witnesses recited cases of people they had known who had led dissolute lives or had not confessed for years, who, after encountering the Beata, were moved to repentence or even entered the religious life.[37] To her many followers María de Santo Domingo's gifts of ecstasy, prophecy, extreme asceticism, infused wisdom, and bodily imitation of Christ's Passion set her off from ordinary women. Somehow an illiterate peasant woman had received the power to exhort, edify and amaze, and they hurried to join her ranks.

Did the Beata de Piedrahita adhere to or deviate from an "authentic" tradition of Dominican spirituality? I would like to suggest that by the early sixteenth century there existed not one but two different and at times conflicting concepts of the Dominican life. The case of María de Santo Domingo clearly demonstrates this fundamental tension within the rder and, by extension, within the Western Christian tradition in general.

The mainstrean or dominant view, held by the Beata's opponents, stressed order, hierarchy, and the authority of formal theological education. It took as its model Thomas Aquinas, the great thirteenth-century theologian and teacher. Vicente Beltrán de Heredia claimed that the essence of Dominican spirituality lay in the integration of four elements: regular observance, prayer, study, and apostolate. However, he placed much greater emphasis on the last two, study and apostolate, in chronicling the order's theologians, teachers, missionaries, and administrators.[38] This "Thomistic" tradition was heavily gendered as male, as women were barred from the intellectual and apostolic activities so highly valued here. For holders of this vision, in both the sixteenth and the twentieth centuries, María de Santo Domingo was an utter anomaly. They regarded her reform movement as, at best, a mere curiosity of Dominican history and, at worst, a dangerous detour in the struggle to fulfill the educational and apostolic mission expressed in the very name "The Order of Preachers."

Supporters of the Beata had to turn, therefore, to an alternate vision that stressed charismatic spirituality, ultra-asceticism, and the authority of direct, mystical experience. This tradition had a powerful model as well, Catherine of Siena, the great fourteenth century mystic, ascetic, and reformer. The "Catherinist" tradition of Dominican spirituality emphasized the first two of the elements listed by Beltrán de Heredia, prayer and regular observance, which were open to women. In fact women, especially ones like Catherine of Siena, who were illiterate but spiritually experienced, formed the very core of this tradition.[39] Catherine, who was canonized in 1461, exerted an enormous influence among Dominicans in late medieval and early modern Europe. María de Santo Domingo and her followers were among them.[40]

Thomas Cajetan, the Order's Master General in 1509, understood perfectly that the "Catherinist" movement represented by the Beata de Piedrahita posed a potential threat to the dominant "Thomistic" tradition he worked so hard to maintain. Aside from undermining the hierarchical chain of command and the authority of monastic superiors, the charismatic Piedrahita movement, with its anti-intellectual bent and emphasis on prayer and penitence was viewed as perhaps excessively "feminine" and thus inappropriate for friars.[41] Thus, despite the Beata's favorable sentence at the trial, over the next few years Dominican officials effectively squelched the movement she headed. By 1512, María and her female followers were enclosed in their convent in Aldeanueva and dissident friars such as Diego de Vitoria either transferred to other houses or reduced to obedience.[42]

In the decades following the trial of María de Santo Domingo, Spanish Dominican friars distinguished themselves mainly by their intense efforts to evangelize the peoples of the New World and to revive scholastic theology in the universities, two of the most "masculine" features of the dominant "Thomistic" tradition. It was this vision of Dominican spirituality that decided the eventual fate of María de Santo Domingo, and guaranteed that she would be written out of the order's official histories.

But this episode hardly put an end to the phenonomon of holy women and their male followers, which persisted well into the seventeenth century. Despite efforts of clerical authorities to curtail the activities of beatas and to limit their influence, pious Catholics in early modern Spain, like their counterparts in other times and places in Christian history, anxiously placed their faith in individuals who could offer the promise of direct mediation with the divine. As long as believers looked beyond ordained clergymen and theologians for assurances of personal salvation, charisma would continue to arouse controversy.

NOTES

Earlier versions of this chapter were presented at the annual meeting of the Society for Spanish and Portuguese Historical Studies, Vanderbilt University, 8–10 April 1988, and published in *Archivo Dominicano* (Salamanca) 10 (1989), 55–66. It appears here with kind permission of the editors. I would like to thank the many friends and colleagues who offered help and suggestions, especially William Christian, Jr., John Coakley, Fr. Ramón Hernández, Sr. Suzanne Noffke, Karen Scott, Ronald Surtz, and Richard Trexler.

🐝

1. See particularly the works of Vicente Beltrán de Heredia, especially *Historia de la reforma de la provincia de España (1450–1550)* (Rome: Istituto Storico Domenicano, 1939). The sixth chapter of this work is entitled "La pseudoreforma intentada por la Beata de Piedrahita y los Procesos de esta religiosa." More recently, see Ramón Hernández, "Actas de los Capítulos Provinciales de la Provincia de España del Siglo XVI (II)," Archivo Dominicano VII (1986), 5–28. A more sympathetic view is offered by Alvaro Huerga, "Los pre-alumbrados y la Beata de Piedrahita," *Historia de la Iglesia* vol. XVII, (Valencia: EDICEP, 1974), 529–533.

2. Pedro Martír de Angleria, *Epistolario* vol. II, tr. José López de Toro (Madrid: Góngora, 1953–1957), 300; "criada desde su mas tierna infancia, por voluntad de su padre." [Letter of 6 October 1509].

3. Jesús G. Lunas Almeida, *La Historia del Señorío de Valdecorneja, en la parte referente a Piedrahita* (Avila: Tip. Senén Martín, 1930), 186–187.

4. For two other cases of peasant women from the bishopric of Avila, Mari Díaz and Ana de San Bartolomé, see Jodi Bilinkoff, "The Holy Woman and the Urban Community in Sixteenth Century Avila," Barbara J. Harris and JoAnn K. McNamara, eds., *Women and the Structure of Society*, (Durham, NC: Duke University Press, 1984), 76; Ana de San Bartolomé, *Autobiografía* (Madrid: Editorial de Espiritualidad, 1969), 121–130. For cases in medieval Europe, including that of Catherine of Siena, see Caroline W. Bynum, *Holy Feast and Holy Fast: The Religious Significance of Food to Medieval Women* (Berkeley: University of California Press, 1987), 220–227.

5. José Manuel Blecua, ed., *Libro de la Oración de Sor María de Santo Domingo (Madrid: Hauser and Menet, 1948)*. Mary E. Giles, *The Book of Prayer of Sor María of Santo Domingo: A Study and Translation* (Albany: State University of New York Press, 1990). Ronald E. Surtz, *Writing Women in Late Medieval and Early Modern Spain: The Mothers of Saint Téresa of Ávila* (Philadelphia: University of Pennsylvania Press, 1995), 85–103. Ronald E. Surtz, "The 'Sweet Melody' of Christ's Blood: Musical Images in the 'Libro de la Oración' of Sister María de Santo Domingo," *Mystics Quarterly* 17 (1991), 94–101. "Extractos de las revelaciones de Sor María de Santo Domingo," Biblioteca Capitular y Colombina, Seville, Códice 83-3-16, no.82-2, fol.246r-258r. The Beata's letters can be found in Archivo Histórico Nacional, Madrid, Sección Universidades, Cód.1224 F, fol. 47, and Real Academia de Historia, Madrid, Colección Salazar L-8, fol.120. They also have been published by Beltrán, 255–256, 264; Manuel Serrano y Sanz, *Apuntes para una biblioteca de escritoras españolas*, vol. II, pt. 2, (Madrid: Ediciones Atlas, 1975), 669–670; and Blecua, in his critical essay following the *Libro de la oración* (n.p.).

6. For the sequence of events, see Beltrán, 78ff. For Dominican houses in Piedrahita, see Carmelo Luis López, *La comunidad de villa y tierra de Piedrahita en el tránsito de la edad media a la moderna* (Avila: Institución "Gran Duque de Alba," 1987), 114–118. For Dominican houses in Avila, see Jodi Bilinkoff, *The Avila of Saint Teresa: Religious Reform in a Sixteenth-Century City* (Ithaca: Cornell University Press, 1989), 39–41.

7. Beltrán, 109 (Juan Hurtado de Mendoza); Lunas, 183 (Agustín de Funes).

8. Lunas, 178 (Diego de San Pedro), 204–206 (Antonio de la Peña, "porque el Senor no quiso ni quiere que permanezca en el rincon oscuro de una humilde mansion y si llevarla al publico").

9. Lunas, 206 (Antonio de la Peña), 184–185 (Damián de Avila); 188, 191 (Juan de Setiembre, where she refers to the devil as "el mala casta"); Beltrán, 117-119 (Juan de Setiembre, "por haber dicho . . . muchas veces en sus raptos e amonestaciones cosas favorables a la Inquisicion e castigo de los conversos") According to some accounts, María also visited Dominican houses in Segovia and Madrid on this trip, although in Segovia the religious refused to allow her to enter; Lunas, 171.

10. Pedro Mártir de Angleria, 301, "El Rey . . . cree sinceramente que tiene lugar todo esto en la forma mas correcta, y con sus visitas a la Beata da pábulo al asunto como si se tratara de algo santo. Nuestro fraile purpurado alaba a la Beata." Beltrán, 110 (Juan Hurtado de Mendoza, "En Burgos oyo decir al Cardenal que nunca había visto doctrina viva sino desta Soror María, y el y otros . . . tenían grandísima certidumbre que esta Soror María era grandísima sierva de nuestro Senor." See Marcel Bataillon, *Erasmo y España* (Mexico: Fondo de Cultura Económica, 1950), 61–71 for Cisneros' general interest in mystics and beatas. For María's relationship with Ferdinand, Cisneros, and the Duke of Alba, see Jodi Bilinkoff, "A Spanish Prophetess and Her Patrons: The Case of María de Santo Domingo," *Sixteenth Century Journal* 23-1 (1992), 21–34.

11. Hernández, 5–28. Sebastián de Olmeda, *Nova Chronica Ordinis Praedicatorum* (Rome: n.p., 1936), 188–195. Albertus de Meyer, ed., *Registrum Litterarum Fr. Thomae de Vio Caietani*

O.P. Magistri Ordinis, 1508–1513, (Rome: Institutum Historicum Praedicatorum Historica, 1935).

12. Bernardino Llorca, *La Inquisición española y los alumbrados (1509–1667)* (Salamanca: Universidad Pontificia, 1980), 45–52. See Lunas, 212–215, for sentence. See Beltrán, 83ff, and Lunas, 130–139, for the long and fractious process of choosing judges.

13. This is the last approximate date she is mentioned in a chronicle of the Convent of Santa Cruz de la Magdalena, Aldeanueva, compiled by the nuns in the eighteenth century. AHN Clero libro 445.

14. Lunas, 185 (Damián de Avila, "el testigo sabia que dicha Sor María se arrebataba . . . para que la vieran muchas señoras que alli estaban"), 170 (Juan de Azcona); Beltrán, 113 (Juan Hurtado de Mendoza). The allegation of feigned sanctity was a common and serious one, especially for women in Catholic Europe in the early modern period. For cases in Spain, see Richard L. Kagan, *Lucrecia's Dreams: Politics and Prophecy in Sixteenth-Century Spain* (Berkeley and Los Angeles: University of California Press, 1990). Jesús de Imirizaldu, *Monjas y beatas embaucadoras* (Madrid: Nacional, 1977). The phenomenon has been particularly well studied for Italy; see, for example: Judith C. Brown, *Immodest Acts: The Life of a Lesbian Nun in Renaissance Italy* (Oxford: Oxford University Press, 1986), especially ch. 5. Luisa Ciammitti, "One Saint Less: The Story of Angela Mellini, Bolognese Seamstress (1667–17[?])," in Edward Muir and Guido Ruggiero, eds., *Sex and Gender in Historical Perspective* (Baltimore: Johns Hopkins University Press, 1990). Fulvio Tomizza, *Heavenly Supper: The Story of Maria Janis*, tr. Anne Jacobson Schutte (Chicago: University of Chicago Press, 1991). Cecilia Ferrazzi, in Anne Jacobson Schutte, ed., *Autobiografia di una santa mancata 1609–1664* (Bergamo: Pierluigi Lubrina, 1990).

15. Beltrán, 111, "Y que a este testigo parecio esto una patrana que componia pensando que habian dado placer los que la oian."

16. Lunas, 203–204. The Beata's supporter Antonio de la Peña attacked Gaibol's methods, 210–211.

17. Lunas, 169. Tomás de Matienzo, one of María's supporters, opposed the appointment of Alfonso de Fonseca as a judge for her trial, charging that "el Reverendo Patriarca ha dicho muchas veces que la dicha beata es una gran locura." 134. Fonseca was later removed from the case.

18. Beltrán, 103, 127, 137, and comments scattered throughout his works.

19. Lunas, 183 (Agustín de Funes), 167 (Juan Hurtado de Mendoza), 170 (Juan de Azcona, "Que el declarante siempre habia visto que las vestiduras de dicha Sor María eran blancas y negras, conforme a su orden, pero que debajo de la gobella llevaba paño colorado a manera de forradura . . . y que tambien llevaba un sombrero frances y, algunas veces, corales."

20. Lunas, 159–160. María del Cordero angrily denied that the Beata bleached her hair blond, pp. 189–190. For St. Paul on women's hair see Bernadette J. Brooten, "Paul's Views on the Nature of Women and Female Homoeroticism," Clarissa W. Atkinson, Constance H. Buchanan and Margaret R. Miles, eds. *Immaculate and Powerful: The Female in Sacred Image and Social Reality* (Boston: Beacon Press, 1985), 75–77.

21. Lunas, 168 (Juan Hurtado de Mendoza), 183–184 (Agustín de Funes), 170 (Juan de Azcona).

22. Lunas, 175, "Siendo entonces cuando conocio a dicha beata . . . y que antes de marchar para Toledo . . . la rogase que se dignara por caridad, encomendarle a Dios para le diese contricion de sus pecados y que, durante el camino, sintio tal fervor y arrepentimiento como nunca lo habia sentido."

23. Lunas, 158–160, "Que nada sabia de esas cosas puesto que las decia en rapto, y que despues del rapto muchas veces no se acordaba de nada, por cuyo motivo, fray Diego de Vitoria, que siempre estaba con ella y era el que oia y sabia la verdad, podria decirla y la diria." See also

pp. 206, 185. For the relationship between María de Santo Domingo and her confessors, as well as other cases from the diocese of Avila, see Jodi Bilinkoff, "Confessors, Penitents, and the Construction of Identities in Early Modern Avila," Barbara B. Diefendorf and Carla Hesse, eds., *Culture and Identity in Early Modern Europe: Essays in Honor of Natalie Zemon Davis* (Ann Arbor: University of Michigan Press, 1993), 83–100.

24. Lunas, 166–167 (Juan Hurtado de Mendoza, "era dicha Sor María la mayor culpable porque le forzaba a ello"), 188–189 (Juan de Setiembre—usually a supporter); Beltrán, 109, 117–119.

25. Lunas, 177 (Diego de Vitoria), 1669 (Juan Hurtado de Mendoza); Beltrán, 114. Pedro Martír de Angleria, 300, "En algunas ocasiones emulando al sacerdote que celebra el Santo Sacrificio . . . profiere frases de amor hacia Cristo, que hacen pedazos los corazones del auditorio." I have attempted to analyze the Beata's modes of discourse and the meanings they may have held for contemporary readers and listeners; see Jodi Bilinkoff, "Establishing Authority: A Peasant Visionary and Her Audience in Early Sixteenth-Century Spain." Paper presented at Western Michigan University, March 1994.

26. Jodi Bilinkoff, "Woman with a Mission: Teresa of Avila and the Apostolic Model," Guilia Barone, Marina Caffiero, and Francesco Scorza Barcellona, eds., *Modelli di santità e modelli di comportamento: Contrasti, intersezioni, complementarità* (Turin: Rosenberg and Sellier, 1994), 295–305.

27. Hernández, 7. See also Juan López, *Quinta parte de la historia de Santo Domingo y de Su Orden de Predicadores* bk. I, (Valladolid: Juan de Rueda, 1621), 60–62 for the disapproving tone of an official Dominican chronicler.

28. Lunas, 193, also, 190–191 (María del Cordero), 194 (Doña Aldonza de Pimentel), 171–173 (Juan de Ceballos, "Que estando un dia diciendo misa fray Diego de Vitoria . . . al tiempo de dar la comunion a la sierva de Dios . . . vieron todos maravillados que la hostia no estaba en los corporales, habiendo comulgado dicha religiosa por manos de Dios o de algun angel.") Caroline W. Bynum, "Women Mystics and Eucharistic Devotion in the Thirteenth Century," *Women's Studies* 11(1984), 179–214.

29. Lunas, 176.

30. Lunas, 172–173, also, 194 (Don Fernando de Toledo); Beltrán, 107 (Francisco de Porres).

31. Lunas, 178 (Diego de San Pedro), 182 (Antonio de Benavente), 189 (María del Cordero), 187 (Juan de Setiembre, on childhood ascetic practices), 210 (Antonio de la Peña, "tanta perfeccion que se hace visible en la austeridad de sus vestidos, en la parvedad de su alimentacion, en su devotisima oracion, en la abundancia de lagrimas, en el rigor de sus disciplinas.")

32. Lunas, 188, "conocio que muchos religiosos las contradecian [her contemplations and conversations] porque les repugnaba hacer las austeridades de la religion que ella amonestaba." Beltrán, 119–120.

33. Lunas, 192 (María del Cordero), 181 (Antonio de Benavente), 171 (Juan de Ceballos).

34. Lunas, 176 (Diego de Vitoria, 179 (Diego de San Pedro), 192 (María del Cordero, "Que ninguna de las joyas ni ropas finas que se ponia lo hacia por vanidad, no por liviandad, nor por ningun mal fin, no por parecer bien, sino que las llevaba como podria llevarlas una imagen.")

35. Lunas, 201–203 (Antonio de la Peña), 175 (Diego de Vitoria), 191–1921 (María del Cordero), 181 (Antonio de Benavente, who also indicated that friars stayed with her to witness late night raptures, "Si alguna vez se habian quedado en la celda de dicha María determinados religiosos era para ayudarlas en sus tormentos y para presenciar los raptos que solia tener a media noche.")

36. Lunas, 168 (Juan Hurtado de Mendoza, "Que aquella noche estando en mitad del placer del baile, comenzo la dicha María a decir cosas tan santisimas que hizo llorar al testigo y a los demas que la escuchaban"), 177 (Diego de Vitoria), 202 (Antonio de la Peña), 173 (Juan de Ceballos). William A. Christian Jr., "Provoked Religious Weeping in Early Modern Spain," J.

Davis, ed., *Religious Organization and Religious Experience* (London: Academic Press, 1982), 97–114.

37. Lunas, 181–182 (Antonio de Benavente), 195 (Cristóbal Brochero), 189 (María del Cordero), 173–174 (Juan de Ceballos), 201–202 (Antonio de la Peña).

38. Vicente Beltrán de Heredia, "Directrices de la espiritualidad dominicana durante las primeras decadas del siglo XVI," *Miscelánea Beltrán de Heredia*, vol. III (Salamanca: Universidad de Salamanca, 1972), 407.

39. John Coakley, "Friars as Confidants of Holy Women in Medieval Dominican Hagiography," Renate Blumenfeld–Kosinski and Timea Szell, eds., *Images of Sainthood in Medieval Europe* (Ithaca: Cornell University Press, 1991), 222–246. See the many lives of "siervas de Dios" related in the chronicle of Juan López cited in note 27 above.

40. John W. Coakley, "The Representation of Sanctity in Late Medieval Hagiography: Evidence from *Lives* of Saints of the Dominican Order," Th.D. Diss., (Cambridge: Harvard Divinity School, 1980). In a discussion of the *Lives* of the tertiaries Columba of Rieti (d.1501) and Osanna of Mantua (d.1505), Coakley comments, "what is especially remarkable about both *Lives* is the extremely strong influence which they show Catherine of Siena to have exerted on both of these saints. Catherine's role in these works shows her continuing importance for Dominican women," pp. 44–45. See Alvaro Huerga, *Santa Catalina de Siena en la historia de la espiritualidad hispana*, (Rome: n.p., 1969) and "Santa Catalina de Siena, precursora de Santa Teresa," *Cuadernos de Investigación Histórica* 10 (1986), 197–214 for treatment of María de Santo Domingo and the Piedrahita movement in this context.

41. Beltrán, *Reforma*, 123–125.

42. Beltrán, *Reforma*, 125–126, 143ff. *Registrum litterarum Fr. Thomae de Vio Caietani.*

3

Behind the Veil: Moriscas and the Politics of Resistance and Survival

Mary Elizabeth Perry

Moriscas, those women who had converted to Catholicism from Islam either voluntarily or under duress, appeared to many Christians of Golden Age Spain as sensual and lewd, wearing exotic clothing as they danced and sang; but in historical records moriscas emerge only dimly, as quiet and indistinct figures. Despite laws forbidding women to cover the face, which could permit them to hide their licentiousness behind anonymity, moriscas appear as obscurely in history as though they were veiled.[1] Doubly silenced, first by their own culture that emphasized the seclusion of women, and again by Christians who saw them as members of an increasingly distasteful minority group, moriscas nevertheless played a crucial role in resisting Christian attempts to obliterate their culture.

A portrait of these women, who so often were ignored or discounted as mere victims of the violence and oppression in Muslim-Christian conflicts, emerges from a combination of many different sources. Royal documents, ecclesiastical reports and letters, chronicles, and city regulations provide Christian views of moriscas. Inquisition records augment these views, but hidden among them are testimonies that suggest a morisca voice. Even closer to an authentic morisca voice is the literature written in *aljamía*, a combination of Arabic script and Castilian Spanish.[2]

The limitations of these sources should be noted, however. Since literacy was rare among moriscas, *aljamiado* literature must be considered as writings by men who generally used the voice of conventional religious beliefs to refer only indirectly to actual morisca experiences. Moreover, testimonies of moriscas in Inquisition cases must be analyzed for their subtext, that is, the power context for the testimony: who asked the questions, under what circumstances, who recorded responses, and what was not said and why?[3]

These varied sources can be woven together within a historical context using analysis based on feminist criticism and theories of social boundaries, cultural persistence, and hegemony. Antonio Gramsci's hegemonic theory, for example, points out the significance of culture in struggles of political domination and the active roles of popular culture in particular.[4] Seeking to level out differences, hegemony works through the smallest details of everyday life, those tasks so often left to women.[5] Behind their silent submission, moriscas actually subverted Christian policies by preserving in their homes the language, rites, and customs of their people.[6] Hidden in the subtext of most historical documents, their subversion becomes apparent when the focus centers on their experiences and their subcultures, not merely for ascribed status and internalized gender definitions, but also for their work, interactions, and consciousness.[7]

Any portrait of these women must show them in their historical context, and regional variations in this context should be recognized. Although Muslims had lived in the Iberian peninsula since even before the invasion of 711 from North Africa, their regional differences intensified during the centuries-long struggle of the Reconquest. Those Muslim women who remained in the north as the Christians pushed southward lived within dispersed families, usually in smaller communities where they appeared to assimilate more readily into Christian culture, some intermarrying and eventually forgetting their own Arabic dialects.[8] Required to pay special tributes for which their *aljama*, or religious community, was responsible, Muslims nonetheless enjoyed religious freedom for some time under Christian rule. In this system of *convivencia* they did not have to live in *morerías*, or prescribed areas, until later in the medieval period.

Muslim women in the east, in the kingdoms of Aragon and Valencia, clustered together in higher density rural communities where they retained their Arabic dialects and customs. When Christian forces defeated Muslim rulers, they accepted Muslim residents as highly prized agricultural workers who were especially noted for their skills in irrigation. Christian landlords favored convivencia as a way to protect the Muslim farmers and families who were so important in defending their lands against plunderers and in cultivating profitable crops such as rice, sugar cane, and silk worms.[9]

In the south, Muslim women lived in especially high concentrations in urban centers, such as Córdoba, Seville, and Granada. They also worked to produce flax, cotton, wheat, and olives in the surrounding countrysides. From the eighth-century marriage of Sara la Goda, granddaughter of the Visigoth ruler Witiza, and 'Isa ben Muzahim, intermarriage between Christians and Muslims had blurred the boundaries between the two groups.[10] When Seville fell to the Christians in 1248, thousands of Muslims fled to North Africa, but others recognized their deep Spanish roots; they stayed as *mudéjares*, or "those allowed to remain," and continued their lives as doctors, agrarian workers, and artisans, such as bricklayers, tilemakers, and iron workers.[11] By the fourteenth century, females predominated in the population of Seville and participated actively in the economy not only as spinners and silkmakers, but also in selling food and working as laborers for masons and tilemakers.[12]

Muslim women found that the status of mudéjares soon changed as the forces of Ferdinand and Isabella defeated the last Muslim stronghold at Granada in 1492. In the terms of capitulation, the Catholic monarchs promised their new Muslim subjects that they would be free to practice their own religion and implied that they intended to continue the policy of convivencia. As first Archbishop of Granada, they named Hernando de Talavera, a man who wanted to convert the Muslims of this kingdom, but favored persuasion over coercion.[13] Realizing that conversion sermons would have to be in Arabic because so few Muslims of Granada understood Castilian, Talavera tried to attract clerics who knew Arabic and even sponsored the publication of an Arabic vocabulary and grammar book written by Pedro de Alcalá.[14] His efforts focused on wooing individuals and small groups of Muslims away from their community at large, and in teaching Christian doctrine especially to Muslim children who then would carry it into their families.[15] Not surprisingly, then, the most significant arena for the conflict that grew between Muslims and Christians was not a battlefield nor royal chambers, nor even the secret prisons of the Inquisition; rather, it was the *morisco* home, a bastion of cultural resistance in which women played leading roles in preserving Muslim traditions and resisting Christian hegemony.[16]

As the resistance of these women slowed the pace of conversions in Granada, Isabella sent Francisco Jiménez de Cisneros to bring more fervor into the efforts. Preaching so fervently that, according to some sources, he baptized 3,000 or 4,000 Muslims at a time, Cisneros substituted for the traditional individual ablution a sprinkling of holy water among the multitude.[17] His harsh methods to hasten conversion, such as burning all Arabic books pertaining to religion, provoked a military rebellion that began in the Albaicín, a hilly Muslim quarter across the river from the Alhambra in Granada.

Muslim women lost religious freedom as well as husbands, brothers, sons, and fathers who died or were enslaved as Christian forces put down the rebellion. Royal pragmatics of 1502 decreed that any Muslim remaining in Castile must be baptized or leave the kingdom. Baptisms made Muslims into nominal Christians, but few of the new converts actually understood or embraced their new religion. The problem of actually "Christianizing" so many new converts intensified after the *Germanía* rebellion of 1520–1522 in Valencia, when Christian farmers attacked Christian nobles through their Muslim vassals and forcibly baptized thousands of the Muslims whose lords could not protect them. Increasingly, converted Muslims, now called *moriscos*, or "little Moors," became suspect as false Christians who continued their own religion in secret and had neither the desire to conform to the Church nor loyalty to the Spanish kingdoms.[18]

Despite their regional differences in assimilation in the past, Muslim women throughout Spain became moriscas subject to the same restrictions. With active support from the Church, the Spanish Crown moved to extinguish any remnants of Muslim presence. After winning papal permission for relief from his solemn vow to tolerate Muslims in Aragon, Charles V announced in 1525 that no Muslim could remain in his kingdoms except as a slave.[19] Receiving assurance from ecclesiastical officials that moriscos' baptisms were valid even if they had been carried out forcibly, Charles V invited the Inquisition to send representatives to visit moriscos throughout his kingdoms and instruct them in the Christian faith. In 1526 he reached an agreement with the moriscos where, in exchange for a payment of 40,000 ducats, the Inquisition would not prosecute them and they would have ten years in which they could use their own cemeteries, language, and dress, and would have recognition of consanguine marriages already consummated.[20]

In that same year of 1526, however, a junta meeting in Granada agreed to forbid all morisco "particularism," expanding the list of prohibited behavior from Islamic rites to almost all Muslim cultural practices.[21] The Inquisitor General, concerned with the large morisco population in Valencia, directed his subdelegates there to establish schools to educate the morisco children. Meant to teach "good customs" as well as Christian doctrine, the schools were compulsory for morisco children, and the Church sent rectors and lay sheriffs to enforce attendance at the schools and at Mass.[22] Some clerics considered morisco women their greatest rivals for the souls of morisco children, and they believed that moriscas were particularly "obstinant" in holding on to their Muslim practices and preventing their children from going to Christian schools.[23]

Royal, ecclesiastical, and local regulations increased pressure on moriscos to seek assimilation. The Edict of Grace issued by the Inquisition in Seville in 1548, for example, confirmed the exemption of moriscos from prosecution for past errors and from confiscation of their goods, but it went on to repeat the royal prohibition on more than one conjugal morisco family living together in a single household. The edict also asserted that moriscos must live among Old Christians, have Old Christian servants, marry their sons and daughters to Old Christians, and provide dowries for their daughters. They must bury their dead in parishes and monasteries in the Christian manner, and they must live faithfully as Catholics. Finally, moriscos were to be instructed in their new faith and send their children for instruction. Those who violated any of these regulations should confess to the Inquisition or be subject to denunciation by others.[24]

Marriage provided a particular problem in Christianization, for Islamic law permitted marriage between first cousins. Once they had been baptized, some morisco couples found that they were violating the canon law of Christians that prohibited marriages within certain degrees of consanguinity. Moreover, promoting intermarriage between Old Christians and moriscos seemed to prohibit Old Christians from marrying one another, which violated natural law, as one cleric noted, and required "pure" people to marry the "impure."[25] Some Old Christians did marry moriscos, but much intermarriage must have been discouraged by the "purity of blood" statutes that restricted certain offices, privileges, and university positions to people whose parents and ancestors did not include Muslims, Jews, or those who had converted to Christianity. In trying to protect the purity of Christian society, these laws actually undercut any Christian efforts to facilitate morisco assimilation.[26]

Women actively participated in resisting pressures on the morisco community to assimilate. Forbidden to meet in mosques, to observe Islamic rituals, to possess books printed in Arabic, or to use the Arabic language, moriscos withdrew into their private homes or small kinship groups where they might more safely continue their language and religious traditions. Moriscas played a major role in preserving these traditions, for the sexual division of labor directed to them the tasks of child-rearing, cleanliness, and food preparation. Dietary prohibitions against wine and bacon, for example, could be observed discreetly within a household, and so could Islamic days of fasting. Even the great festival of Ramadan, held after thirty days of fasting, could be continued within a family group, as it included a special meal and called for the children to kiss the hands of their parents and ask their pardon and blessing.[27]

Christians required all morisco infants to be baptized, but this did not preclude traditional Muslim ceremonies to welcome a new baby, so long as they took place quietly and privately. On the seventh day following the birth, morisco men would gather in a home for ritual ablution and reading of the Koran as the father presented the child, gave it a name, and declared it a Muslim.[28] Women held their own ceremony on this same day, placing the infant in a packet in which grains of wheat and barley and small items of gold and silver had been placed.[29] After praying, they dressed the newborn in clean clothing and placed a silk cloth on it. Together they named the child and held it up, ululating "li, li, li." They then placed an Arabic book on the mouth, nose and eyes of the child as they said, "Allah make you a good believer."

Moriscos could also preserve their own death rituals if a priest did not come too soon to administer the Last Rites or supervise the burial. Safe among family members, the dying morisco could call aloud for Muhammed and ask to be turned to face the direction of Mecca. After death, no one was to touch the body until the phrase, "Lord God, forgive me" was said three times. The women then washed the body, repeating, "God is very great," wrapping the body in a clean cloth as men of the family helped them move it.[30] After Christian prohibitions against Muslim burials became more stringently enforced, the prayer for the dead moved from the grave to a home where the name of the dead person could be pronounced within the family "so the angels would write it down."

Christian authorities who learned of the persistence of Muslim rites hardened their resolve to obliterate them. They called for expelling all *alfaquíes*, or Muslim holy leaders, but they also identified another dangerous group: the women of the morisco community. Criticizing the perfidy of these women, Christian officials prohibited moriscas from acting as midwives who could facilitate Muslim circumcision and hide the infant to avoid baptism. Some authorities called for the strict surveillance of morisco housewives in Valencia, believing that they were the ones who circumcised newborn infants. When a child was found to be circumcised, the wife of the household usually confessed to the deed, perhaps because she had actually acted as circumciser, or because she believed that the Inquisition would be more lenient with women.[31]

Moriscas found their homes increasingly invaded as Christian officials recognized their families as the focus of cultural resistance. Attempting to enforce Christianization attempts, commissioners entered morisco homes to compel parents to send their children to Christian schools. These visitors were also to seize baths, musical instruments, and any Arabic books that they found. Moreover, Old Christian sheriffs were directed to enter morisco homes unexpectedly at meal time when they could find evidence of Muslim diet and fasting, as well as the Muslim practice of eating while seated on the floor.[32] Such invasions of the home transformed it from a safe space to one of danger and ambiguity, where boundaries separating moriscos and Christians could shift and even disappear.

As restrictions on them increased, many moriscas appeared to adopt *taqiyya*, the Muslim tradition of "precaution."[33] Developed as a protection for Muslims who wanted to preserve their true beliefs in situations of severe persecution, this tradition counseled external conformity to a dominant culture while maintaining internal resistance that could save true Islam from extinction. As a Muslim leader in North Africa advised moriscos in 1563, "Maintain prayer and give alms, even though you do it symbolically, for God is not concerned with your exterior attitude, but with the intention of your hearts. . . . And if they tell you to denounce Muhammed, denounce him by word and love him at the same time in your heart."[34]

Such quiet and serene subversion became far less possible, however, as atrocities escalated in the morisco rebellion of 1568–1570 that began in the Alpujarras, a mountainous region near Granada.[35] Armed only with stones or roasting spits, morisco women joined the rebels in the battles. Their ululations became battle cries to frighten the Christians and unify the men with whom they fought and died.[36] For the defeated moriscos, rebellion ended with death, enslavement, and dispersion. Morisco boys younger than ten and one-half years and girls younger than nine and one-half years were not to be enslaved, but distributed among Old Christians to be raised as Christians, although a royal *pragmática* of 1572 noted that, "from ignorance or malice," some Christians had sold children even younger after branding them on the face as a slave.[37] Many morisco families simply disintegrated, but those that escaped death or slavery were rounded up to be dispersed as intact units throughout the Spanish kingdoms so that Old Christians could more effectively isolate and surround them.

Moriscas must have sensed that a new and even more tragic chapter had begun in their lives as they complied with orders to relocate themselves and their families. Some 50,000 moriscos expelled from Granada were sent in groups of 1,500, each escorted by 200 soldiers, to march northward and westward.[38] As they laboriously covered about twenty kilometers a day, at least one-fourth of the moriscos died, many from typhus.

The effect of this dispersion may be seen by looking at a single city, Seville, that was ordered to receive 4,000 moriscos from Granada following the rebellion.[39] Here new inhabitants found themselves the object of close ecclesiastical scrutiny ordered by the archbishop.[40] Now not only required to attend instruction by a cleric on Sundays and feast days, moriscos were also to pay each time for the instruction and to pay a fine if they missed it. Priests of parishes in which moriscos had settled were made responsible "to know how they live, and not to consent to their speaking Arabic, nor that they teach it to their children; and they must see that they do not live too many together, nor that they meet together, because in this way they hide their language and customs."[41]

Surrounded by Old Christian neighbors, moriscas could no longer join together in the neighborhood or family rituals that they had preserved in secret. Their private households could not safely conceal the foods and baths, the festivals and musical instruments with which they had maintained their Muslim identity; nor could they depend upon a royal exemption to protect them from prosecution by the Inquisition. Some cases before the Holy Office indicate lack of Christian instruction, as that of Alonso Martín, who was convicted in 1592 for having told a group of farm laborers that he was not keeping the feast day of Saint Anne, the mother of the Holy Virgin, because the Virgin had not been born, but descended through the air to the earth.[42] Other cases indicate the persistence of Muslim rites and customs, such as the ritual bathing that Magdalena Morisca was denounced for by two neighbors who had seen her outside her house washing "in the Muslim manner" in the very early morning hours.[43]

For moriscas, inquisitional prosecution spelled the end of any protection they might have enjoyed within their homes and families. Morisco cases from the tribunal in Seville frequently involved family members testifying against one another, for it was usually in a private home and among family members that moriscos continued to observe Muslim rites and customs. María Xérez, for example, was only fifteen years old and denounced by her own parents who had been imprisoned and interrogated by the Inquisition.[44] Under questioning, she confessed that with them she had kept the fast of Ramadan and said Islamic prayers, wearing customary Muslim clothing. In 1609, five moriscos who were found guilty of having engaged in Muslim rites in the home of Juan Valencia, a morisco, also testified against their "accomplices" after torture and confession.[45] Those convicted of meeting in this home included the son, daughter, and son-in-law of Juan Valencia.

It is difficult to know how many of the moriscos consciously engaged in the forbidden activities as a means to preserve their own religious beliefs. Changing into clean clothing on Fridays and eating meat cooked in oil rather than lard might merely represent customary cultural practices more than religious subversion. Whether consciously religious or not, moriscos carried out these activities among family members who became targets for interrogation by the Inquisition. Diego Martín, for example, defended himself from the accusation that he changed into clean clothing on Friday by saying that he had done so only at the persuasion of his wife, Leonor de Morales. Accused of other Muslim practices, this woman steadfastly refused to testify against "accomplices," although interrogators subjected her to six turns of the cord during torture.[46]

One of the most common charges made against moriscas, that they "communicated with others," troubled inquisitors who repeatedly heard in confessions that moriscos had learned the rites and beliefs of Islam from women. Leonor Hernández was denounced by her eldest son in 1592 for having taught him and his younger brother "the sect of Muhammed."[47] Under torture, Lucia de la Cruz, mother of the teen-aged María Xérez noted above, confessed to all of the charges against her and added that she also washed five times a day and taught the Muslim religion to others.[48] Lucia de León and María de León, two women penanced as moriscas by the Inquisition in 1609, confessed that they had learned to "keep the sect of Muhammed" from their mother and mother-in-law, respectively.[49] In that same year, Hieronymo Rodríguez de Guiomar told inquisitors that he had learned the religion and law of Islam from María Hernández, who had already died.

It is not clear that moriscas actually played a major role in teaching Islam to others, for the subtext of their testimony before the Inquisition cannot be ignored. They were, after all, answering questions under duress and were often trying to give the answers that they assumed the inquisitors wanted to hear. They may have taken responsibility for teaching Islam to protect their men, believing that the Inquisition would punish women less severely than men. In addition, inquisitors may have wanted to discredit Islam further by showing that it was merely the product of talkative women who presumed to instruct others. However, since the expulsion of all *alfaquíes*, who were male Islamic religious leaders, it is likely that women stepped in to fill the void, especially in instructing their own children. Not all moriscas were illiterate and uneducated, and some of them may have known of the many women religious leaders who had been revered in Islamic tradition.[50]

Gender beliefs combined with religious and racial prejudices in the persecution of moriscos. Christians, who identified moriscos as a separate race still clinging to an abhorrent religion, often attacked moriscos as a group through criticism of their women and sexual practices. Local ordinances, for example, prohibited women of Muslim descent from traditional female occupations, such as selling baked goods, healing, and midwifery.

Complaining that "many women, especially *moriscas* and even *moras*," were selling baked goods that they made, pastry makers appealed to the prejudices of city officials in Seville and got from them a prohibition that forbade guild nonmembers to bake and sell pastries and bread.[51] A cleric, in writing a justification for expelling all moriscos, criticized the women for going about freely, dancing and singing and wearing "little clothing, almost only a chemise."[52] Others decried the great fertility of moriscas, blaming it on sensuality and licentiousness, and said that moriscas married at the age of eleven. One friar accused moriscos of engaging in sodomy with both men and women.[53]

Recent historical studies have refuted contemporary Christian accusations of morisco immorality. It is true that morisco culture valued marriage far more than celibacy for both women and men, although Sufi mystics had long taught the importance of celibacy for those who wanted to attain union with God.[54] There is no evidence that moriscos engaged in more promiscuous sex than Christians, nor, with few exceptions, did moriscos practice child-marriage. Ages at first marriage were the same for Christian and morisco men, and moriscas married only twelve to fourteen months earlier than Christian women.[55] Moreover, a manuscript written in aljamía entitled *Caxtigo para lax gentex* indicates the genuine concern that moriscos had with marriage and the family. Separate chapters detail husbands' and wives' rights within a marriage, and other chapters describe the obedience that children owe to both parents.[56]

Rarely do moriscas appear in historical records except as wives or daughters. "La Mora de Ubeda" is a major exception, for she is reported in a sixteenth-century *aljamiado* mauscript as a very old single woman, illiterate, but with such a great knowledge of Koranic law that she governed Granada.[57] Most morisco daughters, however, married by the age of eighteen, and widows often remarried.[58] The persistence of polygamy may explain why most moriscas appeared to be married, but even though the Koran allowed a man to have up to four wives, he had to be able to support them. After the defeat of the Alpujarras rebellion in 1570, some moriscos of Valencia purchased moriscas from Granada as wives. Whether or not they had already married another woman in the Christian manner, they now married these women "a la morisca," simply signing before an *alfaquí* a statement of giving a dowry for the new wife.[59] Moriscos regarded them as married women, although Christian clerics and officials were more likely to see them as concubines.

Polygamy, which had been disappearing before the rebellion of 1568, undoubtedly reappeared as a strategy for taking care of a population that became predominantly female. Males in the morisco population were killed or taken as galley slaves, and some of those who survived disappeared into the mountains where they joined outlaw groups.[60] A clerical census of the moriscos in Seville during the 1580s shows males outnumbered females only for the age group of children younger than fifteen years.[61] Women, who had few ways of earning a living, sometimes worked in brothels where moriscas and *moras de allende* (foreign Muslims) were especially valued for their knowledge of spells.[62] They may also have known about popular contraceptive remedies in Muslim culture.[63]

Moriscas who practiced healing arts came under special attack. As medicine in Christian Europe became increasingly formalized as a profession during the sixteenth century, the reputation of Arabic medicine declined. Women such as María de Luna became important agents for preserving this traditional medical knowledge after most of its books had been burned, for she taught it to her sons and neighbors who acted as doctors in villages that lacked a licensed physician.[64] Ynés Yzquierda, another woman prosecuted by the Inquisition, testified that a Moor had given her a book of remedies that she used for healing. Accused of healing two mortally ill women by using sheets, shirts, head coverings, and warm water, she replied that she had only asked for these items to prepare their bodies for burial. She had not even attempted to cure them, she said, much less to use sorcery or instructions from the Muslim book.[65]

Much of the healing done by moriscas resembled magic and sorcery. They used water baths for curing and sometimes burned an article of clothing of the patient. Fumigations that they used seemed closely connected to demoniacal beliefs about illnesses. Frequently they projected curative power into an object such as an amulet or into certain secretions such as the healer's saliva.[66] Old Christian women as well as moriscas practiced such magic and also faced prosecution by the Inquisition.[67]

Magical healing by moriscas was closely associated with love magic and superstitions that the Church considered blasphemous. "Libro de dichox marabilloxox," a sixteenth-century manuscript written in *aljamía* that was hidden beneath a false floor in a house near Zaragoza, compiled many popular morisco beliefs.[68] One recipe called for tying a live frog to a beast that could not urinate, another explained how to make a depilatory, to cure hemorrhoids, to get rid of warts, and to make a man love a particular woman. Cabalistic signs were prescribed for preventing miscarriages, for weaning a baby, for love within a marriage, and for a love affair. Fourteen amulets that had been hidden with the manuscripts were written in both Arabic and aljamía to protect the wearer from illnesses and misfortune. Although both men and women could engage in these practices, most Inquisition cases of sorcery were against women, perhaps because healing was so often carried out in the home where domestic medicine was one of women's tasks.[69]

Christians complained that moriscas held on to the Arabic language more tenaciously than the men, and they declared that these women showed little remorse when they were punished by the Inquisition.[70] One woman who was sentenced to wear a *sanbenito*, the penitential garment marked with the person's offenses and meant for public humiliation, requested another one for her child to help protect it from the cold.[71] Decrying the ineffectiveness of inquisitional punishments, Fray Nicolás del Río declared that the sanbenito had become a decoration of honor to them.[72]

Yet moriscas could not always maintain such bravado in the face of persecution. By the beginning of the seventeenth century, these women faced the agonizing realization that their children had become a major issue in the debate on whether to expel moriscos. Ignacio de las Casas, a morisco Jesuit who had been trained in one of the schools that the Christians had established for morisco boys, continued to insist that Christians could more effectively bring moriscos into the church through improving the methods of teaching them.[73] Whether they had been well instructed in Christian doctrine or not, children of moriscos had been baptized, and many Christians argued that they should not be expelled, particularly if they would be leaving with their parents for Muslim areas such as North Africa.

Many Christians also agreed, however, that older children were less likely to become good Christians because they had already learned the Muslim faith of their parents and a strong aversion to Christianity.[74] Allowing the children to remain with their parents would facilitate the expulsion, avoiding the problem of what to do with such a large number of parentless children, and also the problem of distraught parents refusing to leave without their children. One letter advising the king on this issue declared that morisco parents could be consoled by pointing out the effort it would take to keep their children with them and the pain they would feel if their children died while they were traveling into exile.[75] Another order that called for keeping morisco children of ten years and younger noted that authorities had the right to kill parents who protested, and that the childen who protested should be kept in a prison or in some other "secure place" until the expulsion had been completed.[76]

Clerics and nobles sent more advice to the king on how to take care of morisco children once their parents had gone into exile. A group of Jesuits and the bishop of Morocco wrote that children of seven years and less should be kept in seminaries where they would be trained in occupations that would be useful, but not in arms production because this would damage Christian interests.[77] Children for whom no seminaries were available should be sold as slaves to Old Christians, who would protect them from the sin of apostasy. In addition, enslavement would "secure the great benefit of finishing off this evil race, because slaves seldom marry." One priest proposed a less punitive policy that would keep morisco infants only if wetnurses could be found for them, although the royal council had also suggested assigning two of these infants to each wetnurse and finding alternative animal sources for milk.[78]

As Philip III issued orders in 1609 for the expulsion of moriscos in the several parts of his kingdom, he carefully noted that he had consulted with theologians and learned people in deciding that moriscos going to Christian lands should be able to take their children with them, but those going to Muslim lands must leave their children of seven years or younger with clerics or other devout persons.[79] He exempted from the expulsion those who were clerics, nuns, or slaves, and—significantly—families of mixed marriages with Old Christian husbands and morisca wives. In the latter case, the royal order upheld a gender view that identified families through the father. It also ignored the lack of Christianization that inquisitors had found even among Old Christian males, and it discounted the active role that women had played in the preservation of Muslim rites and customs.

When the expulsion order was published, moriscos responded with great lamentations, "particularly the women," as one cleric wrote.[80] Some Christians criticized moriscas for leaving the country with jewels and gold and silver sewn into their clothing, which the royal order had prohibited.[81] Another cleric reported that moriscas wept as they left with their husbands and older children in a "disordered procession," full of "dust, sweat, and gasping.[82] Exile promised great hardship for these women. The 30,000 moriscos who went to France found such an unfriendly reception that fewer than 1,000 remained in that country.[83] Most moriscos went to "Berbery," or North Africa, where they received such bad treatment that one report estimated that "three parts of those who went have died."[84]

Moriscas who remained in Spain as slaves, nuns, or wives of Old Christians appear sporadically in historical records. A seventeenth-century report on Muslims, both slaves and free, in Seville described their "very great number" and said that they engaged in retail, were accused of stealing children and teaching Muslim doctrine.[85] In the years following the expulsion, the Inquisition penanced several women who were accused of Muslim practices that they were evidently still attempting to keep alive as the external symbols of their culture.

If tragedy and pathos mark the portrait of moriscas in Golden Age Spain, so also do resistance and survival. Relegated as much as possible to domestic seclusion by Islamic tradition, and discredited by Christians as sensual and obstinant, these women assumed a major role in keeping alive a culture under attack. Patriarchal systems of both Christians and Muslims oppressed them, and yet, ironically, the very gender system that decreed their inferiority—relegating them to domestic seclusion—ensured their primary place in the cultural struggle between Christians and Muslims.

In this portrait of moriscas, the real veil is not that of Islamic tradition nor of Christian contempt; rather, it is the veil of phallocentric assumptions that has obscured the roles of many women who have been far more active in history than most historians have acknowledged. By challenging these assumptions and bringing women's experiences into central focus, we have brought a new perspective to reading historical documents. A picture emerges of women who developed their own power, not as public officials nor military leaders, but as wives and mothers. Their power included domination of others, but it meant, even more often, a degree of autonomy to determine their own identity and a capacity to nurture, educate, and influence others to accept and preserve the values of their own traditions.

NOTES

1. For example, in 1639 the city council of Seville approved for the fourth time the prohibition against women covering their faces; see Archivo Municipal de Sevilla (hereafter AMS), Sección 4, siglo XVII, Escribanías de Cabildo, tomo 29, número 18. Note that moriscas may have chosen obscurity in order to survive.

2. For further information on aljamiado literature, see Ramón Alba, ed., *Leyendas moriscas* (Madrid: Miraguena, 1984); Alvaro Galmés de Fuentes, "La literatura aljamiado-morisca, literatura tradicional," in *Les morisques et leur temps: Table Ronde Internationale 4–7 juillet 1981, Montpellier* (Paris: Centre National de la Recherche Scientifique, 1983); F. Guillén Robles, *Leyendas de José Hij de Jacob y de Alejandro Magno sacadas de dos manuscritos moriscos de la Biblioteca Nacional de Madrid* (Zaragoza: Hospicio Provincial, 1888); Julián Ribera y Mariano Sánchez, *Colección de textos aljamiados publicada por Pablo Gil* (Zaragoza: Comas Hermanos, 1888); and Antonio Vespertino Rodríguez, ed., *Leyendas aljamiadas y moriscas sobre personajes bíblios* (Madrid: Editorial Gredos, 1983).

3. Annette Kuhn, "Passionate Detachment," *Women's Pictures: Feminism and Cinema* (Boston: Routledge and Kegan Paul, 1982), 15; see also Mary Elizabeth Perry, *Gender and Disorder in Early Modern Seville* (Princeton: Princeton University Press, 1990), 10.

4. Antonio Gramsci, *Letters from Prison* (New York: Harper and Row, 1973), esp. 204; Antonio Gramsci, *Selections from the Prison Notebooks of Antonio Gramsci* (New York: Interntional Publishers, 1972), 169–70; 238, 258, 260. For an anthropological view, see Manning Nash, *The Cauldron of Ethnicity in the Modern World* (Chicago and London: University of Chicago Press, 1989), 1–2.

5. Trinh T. Minh-ha, "Not you / Like you: Post-Colonial Women and the Interlocking Questions of Identity and Difference," *Inscriptions*, 3–4 (1988), 72.

6. Ricardo García Cárcel, *Herejía y sociedad en el siglo XVI: La inquisición en Valencia 1530–1609* (Barcelona: Ediciones Penínsulas, 1980), 229. For examples of feminist literary critics who have found women's subversion beneath appearances of conformity, see Sandra M. Gilbert, "What do Feminist Critics Want? A Postcard from the Volcano," Elaine Showalter, ed., *The New Feminist Criticism: Essays on Women, Literature and Theory* (New York: Pantheon, 1985), esp. 35; and Mary Beth Rose, "Gender, Genre, and History: Seventeenth-Century English Women and the Art of Autobiography," in Mary Beth Rose, ed., *Women in the Middle Ages and the Renaissance: Literary and Historical Perspectives* (Syracuse: Syracuse Universiy Press, 1986), esp. 267.

7. See the discussion of gynocriticism by Elaine Showalter, "Towards a Feminist Poetics," in Showalter, ed., *The New Feminist Criticism*, 131.

8. For example, see Robert I. Burns, S.J., *Muslims, Christians, and Jews in the Crusader Kingdom of Valencia: Societies in Symbiosis* (Cambridge: Cambridge University Press, 1984).

9. Antonio Domínguez Ortiz and Bernard Vincent, *Historia de los moriscos: Vida y tragedia de una minoría* (Madrid: Revista de Occidente, 1978), 112–113.

10. Jacinto Bosch Vilá, *La Sevilla islámica, 712–1248* (Seville: Universidad de Sevilla 1984), 61–62; H. Montgomery Watt, *A History of Islamic Spain* (Edinburgh: Edinburgh Universiy Press, 1965), 54.

11. Ramón Carande, *Sevilla, fortaleza y mercado: Las tierras, las gentes y la administración de la ciudad en el siglo XIV* (Seville: Diputación Provincial de Sevilla, 1982), 38–40, 53–55, esp. Alonso Morgado, *Historia de Sevilla* (Seville: Andrea Pescioni y Juan de León, 1587), estimates that 100,000 Muslims left Seville, but that 300,000 wanted to remain in Iberia, 102.

12. Carande, 50–51; Antonio Collante de Terán Sánchez, *Sevilla en la baja edad media: La ciudad y sus hombres* (Seville: Ayuntamiento, 1977), 335–336, 362–375.

13. This was in agreement with a long-standing tradition formally established in *Las siete partidas*, the thirteenth-century legal code, Partida VII, Título XXV, Ley II.

14. Domínguez Ortiz and Vincent, 95.

15. Henry Charles Lea, *The Moriscos of Spain: Their Conversion and Expulsion* (New York: Burt Franklin, 1968), 25–27.

16. García Cárcel, 229.

17. Pascual Boronat y Barrachina, *Los moriscos españoles y su expulsión: Estudio histórico-crítico*, vol. I (Valencia: Francisco Vives y Mora, 1901), 108.

18. Domínguez Ortiz and Vincent, 17–20. For a more complete examination of the Muslims of Valencia, see Mark Meyerson, *The Muslims of Valencia in the Age of Fernando and Isabel: Between Coexistence and Crusade* (Berkeley: University of California Press, 1991).

19. Lea, 82–85.

20. Domínguez Ortiz and Vincent, 24.

21. Domínguez Ortiz and Vincent, 22. See also Fredrik Barth's Introduction in Fredrik Barth, ed., *Ethnic Groups and Boundaries* (Boston: Little, Brown and Company, 1969), for a discussion of the boundaries of pariah groups that break basic taboos, 31, esp.

22. Lea, 142–148; see also Francisco de Borja de Medina, "La Compañía de Jesús y la minoría morisca (1545–1614)," in *Archivum Historicum Societatis Iesu* 57 (1988), 69–73, for reports on schools established by Jesuits especially in Granada.

23. Mercedes García Arenal, *Los moriscos* (Madrid: Editora Nacional, 1975), 122.

24. Archivo Histórico Nacional (hereafter AHN), Inquisición, libro 1254.

25. Damián Fonseca, *Justa expulsion de los moriscos de España: con la instrvccion, apostasia, y traycion dellos: y respvesta á las dudas que se ofrecieron acerca desta materia* (Rome: Iacomo Mascardo, 1612), Biblioteca Nacional (hereafter BN) R11918.

26. Purity of blood statutes are discussed in Henry Kamen, *Inquisition and Society in Spain* (Bloomington: Indiana University Press, 1985), 115–133; and in Albert A. Sicroff, *Los estatutos de limpieza de sangre: Controversias entre los siglos XV y XVII* (Madrid: Taurus, 1985). For a theory of social boundaries believed necessary to separate purity and profanity, see Mary Douglas, *Purity and Danger: An Analysis of Concepts of Pollution and Taboo* (New York and Washington: Frederick A. Praeger, 1966). See Barth for pariah groups that are prevented from assimilating by boundaries of exclusion, 31, esp.

27. García Arenal, 93.

28. Pedro Longás, *Vida religiosa de los moriscos* (Madid: Ibér ica, 1915), 256–260.

29. García Arenal, 96.

30. Longás, 285–290.

31. See the interesting essay by Bernard Vincent, "The Moriscos and Circumcision," in Anne J. Cruz and Mary Elizabeth Perry, eds., *Culture and Control in Counter-Reformation Spain* (Minneapolis: University of Minnesota Press, 1992), 80–81, 87–89, esp. For a regulation against morisca midwives in Granada, see Luis García Ballester, *Los moriscos y la medicina: Un capítulo de la medicina y la ciencia marginada en la España del siglo XVI* (Barcelona: Editorial Labor, 1984), 116.

32. See the "Instrucción" and "Informe" reprinted in García Arenal, 106–125.

33. See H.A.R. Gibb and J. H. Kramers, eds., *Shorter Encyclopaedia of Islam* (Ithaca: Cornell University Press, 1961), 561–562; and H. Lammens, *Islam. Beliefs and Institutions*, Sir E. Denison Ross, tr. (London: Methuen & Co., 1968), 168.

34. "Respuesta que hizo el mufti de Oran a ciertas preguntas que le hicieron desde la Andalucía," dated May 3, 1563, reprinted in Mercedes García Arenal, *Los moriscos* (Madrid: Editora Nacional, 1975), 44–45.

35. Advice to the moriscos to practice *taqiyya*, or outer conformity while maintaining Islam internally, is in "Respuesta que hizo el mufti de Oran a ciertas preguntas que le hicieron desde la Andalucía," in García Arenal, 44–45. For an example of the atrocities reported, see Jaime Bleda, *Coronica de los moros de España* (Valencia: Felipe May, 1618), 695; and *Relación muy verdadera sacada de vna carta que al Illustre Cabildo y regimiento desta ciudad* (Seville: Alonso de la Bar, 1569), n.p.

36. *Relación muy verdadera sacada de vna carta*, n.p.

37. *Pragmática y declaración sobre los moriscos del Reyno de Granada* (Madrid: Alonso Gómez, 1572), n.p.

38. Domínguez Ortiz and Vincent, 50–52.

39. Antonio Domínguez Ortiz, *Orto y ocaso de Sevilla. Estudio sobre la prosperidad y decadencia de la ciudad durante los siglos XVI y XVII* (Seville: Diputación Provincial de Sevilla, 1946), 57. For an account of the arrival in Seville of 4,300 moriscos from Granada, see the 15 December 1590 letter of the Conde de Priego in Archivo General de Simancas (hereafter AGS), Camara de Castilla, leg. 2157.

40. *Constituciones del Arcobispado de Sevilla* (Seville: Alonso Rodríguez Gamarra, 1609), 19–20.

41. *Constituciones*, 19–20. In 1589, Philip II directed each bishop and archbishop to conduct a census of resettled moriscos under their jurisdiction and report on how they were living and carrying out the Christian faith.

42. AHN, Inquisición, legajo 2075, número 8. Ricardo García Cárcel, *Herejía y sociedad en el siglo XVI: La inquisición en Valencia 1530–1609* (Barcelona: Ediciones Península, 1980), 234, found that moriscos prosecuted by the Inquisition in Valencia were completely ignorant of Christian doctrine.

43. AHN, Inquisición, legajo 2075, número 19.

44. AHN, Inquisición, legajo 2075, número 11.

45. AHN, Inquisición, legajo 2075, número 19.

46. AHN, Inquisición, legajo 2075, número 11.

47. AHN, Inquisición, legajo 2075, número 8.

48. AHN, Inquisición, legajo 2075, número 11.

49. AHN, Inquisición, legajo 2075, número 19.

50. See, for example, Margaret Smith, *Rabi'a the Mystic and Her Fellow-Saints in Islam: Being the Life and Teachings of Rabi'a al-Adawiyya Al-Qaysiyya of Basra together with Some Account of the Place of the Women Saints in Islam* (Cambridge: Cambridge University Press, 1984); Miguel Asín Palacios, *Vidas de santones andaluces: La "epístola de la santidad" de Ibn 'Arabi de Murcia* (Madrid: Estanislao Maestre, 1933); and also Mary Elizabeth Perry, "Delusions, Assimilation, and Survival: A Christianized-Muslim Holy Woman in Seventeenth-Century Spain," unpublished paper presented to the American Historical Association, December, 1992.

51. AMS, Sección Especial, Papeles del Señor Conde de Aguila, Libros en folio, tomo 27, número 3.

52. Padre Aznar Cardona, *Expulsión justificada de los moriscos españoles y suma de las excelencias christianas de nuestro Rey D. Felipe Tercero deste nombre* (Huesca, 1612), quoted in García Arenal, 230, esp.

53. Ricaldo de Montecrucio, *Reprobación del Alcoran*, BN, 4.037.

54. Bernard Vincent, *Minorías y marginados en la España del siglo XVI* (Granada: Diputación Provincia de Granada, 1987), 48; Smith, 167; but cf. Lammens, 135.

55. Vincent, 48–51.

56. Hidden under a false floor in the village of Almonacid de la Sierra, this was one among several manuscripts found in 1884 that have been catalogued, transcribed, and described in Julián Ribera and Miguel Asín, *Manuscritos árabes y aljamiados de la biblioteca de la junta* (Madrid: Junta para Amplicación de Estudios é Investigaciones Científicas, 1912), 48–49.

57. See manuscript LXII, *Tafcira*, by Mancebo de Arévalo, in Ribera and Asín, 223–224.

58. Vincent, 49.

59. Vincent, 55–57.

60. Vincent, 173–176.

61. Tomás González, ed., *Censo de población de las provincias y partidos de la corona de Castilla en el siglo XVI, con varios apéndices para completar la del resto de la peninsula en el mismo siglo, y formar juicio comparativo con la del anterior y siguiente, segun resulta de los libros y registros que se custodian en el Real Archivo de Simancas* (Madrid: Imprenta Real, 1829), 365; see also Vincent, 138–140.

62. Vincent, 65.

63. As an example of these remedies, see Norman E. Himes, *Medical History of Contraception* (New York: Schocken Books, 1970), 136–149.

64. See the case of Roman Ramírez before the Inquisition in Cuenca, discussed in García Ballester, 82.

65. AHN, Inquisición, legajo 2075, número 15.

66. García Ballester, 121–122. Widespread beliefs in practices such as these are described in María Helena Sánchez Ortega, *La Inquisición y las gitanas* (Madrid: Taurus, 1988), 97–101, esp.

67. Sánchez Ortega, 102–133.

68. In Ribera and Asín, 98–106.

69. Perry, *Gender and Disorder*, 20–26. Sánchez Ortega points out that Old Christian women, as well as moriscas, practiced such magic and faced prosecution by the Inquisition, pp. 102–133.

70. *Para que lo cotenido en la nueva Pragmática de los Moriscos se pueda mejor en execución, y se preuenga y disponga a este effecto lo necessario, han de guardar las justicias y personas a cuyo cargo esto ha de ser, la orden siguiete* BN, ms. V.E. 26–39, n.p.

71. Fonseca, 126–127.

72. See his letter of 13 June 1606, to Philip III, in García Arenal, 127.

73. Borja de Medina, 3–134.

74. Boronat y Barrachina, II, 528.

75. Consulta from Segovia, 1 September 1609, quoted in Boronat y Barrachina, II, 524–526.

76. Quoted in Boronat y Barrachina, II, 528.

77. Consulta quoted in Boronat y Barrachina, II, 542–544. Presumably, the lack of seminaries for morisco girls meant that most of them would be enslaved.

78. Padre Sobrino's letter is in Boronat y Barrachina, II, 537–542; the royal council report is in the same volume, 548–551.

79. *Declaración del Bando que se a publicado de la expulsión de los moriscos* (Sevilla: Alonso Rodríguez Gamarra, 1610), n.p.

80. Fonseca, 255.

81. Luis Cabrera de Córdoba, *Relaciones de las cosas sucedidas en la corte de España, desde 1599 hasta 1614* (Madrid: J. Martín Alegria, 1957), 396. See also Fonseca, 273.

82. Padre Aznar Cardona, quoted in García Arenal, 235.

83. Domínguez Ortiz and Vincent, 226–228.

84. Cabrera de Córdoba, 396; Domínguez Ortiz and Vincent, 230–231.

85. BN, ms. 81.735, "Informe sobre los moros esclavos y libres de Seville," quoted in Domínguez Ortiz and Vincent, 266.

4

A Case of Gendered Rejection: The Hermitess in Golden Age Spain

Alain Saint-Saëns

*E*remitical life experienced a true Golden Age during the Roman Empire with Paul, the First Hermit, and Anthony the Abbot. Following in their footsteps, some women fled the world and went to the deserts of Egypt and Thebaid to battle the devil on his own turf, struggle without giving quarter, and gain eternal salvation. Thanks to their ascetic exploits, these women attained a fame that was able to stand the test of time. In the Middle Ages hermitesses were clearly vivid examples of sanctity, as the case of a Joan of Signa in fourteenth-century Toscany, studied by French historian Jacques Dalarun, demonstrates perfectly.[1] The eremitical ideal, created not only by the Desert Fathers, but also by their female counterparts, was still very much flourishing in Habsburg Spain.[2] Spanish women, however, had to face a suspicious, even hostile environment if they followed in the footsteps of their revered forerunners. As Teresa of Avila confessed with regrets in the Libro *de la vida*: "These days are not the old days."[3] Whereas their idealized models continued to receive recognition within their religious society, the anchorite penances that Golden Age hermitesses some-times tried to practice and the isolated lives they led close to hermitages failed in inspiring either admiration or even benevolent indifference; on the contrary, from the moment they dared lay claim to their gendered eremitical inheritance, women faced scathing comments and unequivocal rejection.[4]

❦

The feminine example of ascetic life led to subsequent anchorite vocations. Angela Teodora Parra y Carvajal (1674–1745) subjected herself from the age of twelve to very hard and extreme penances. Never incorporated into a religious

Order, she lived the greater part of her lonely life in a cave hollowed out in the garden of her house in Auñón. She eventually moved to another grotto carved out of a rock.[5] For Sor Margarita de Espíritu, the cave in which Mary Magdalene had retired near Marseilles still seemed to be a very tangible reality. In 1655 she stated, "then I intended to take refuge into saint Mary Magdalene's cave."[6]

Perhaps the case of Catalina de Cardona, evoked by Teresa of Avila in the *Libro de las fundaciones*, is the most interesting. Guided by a hermit from Alcalá, she went to live in a cave: "There was a small cave," Teresa says, "with scarcely any room; he left her there." She remained inside for eight years.[7] Catalina, even more than Peter of Alcántara, represents the quintessence of the eremitical ideal. In her book, Teresa of Avila first explained at length the desire of this woman to live like an anchoress; then she described the stages of her life, from her retreat to the desert until her death.[8] Cardona, as a modern anchoress, had reached a harmonious synthesis; she had assimilated and integrated in her personal experience some of the achievements of Elias, Magdalene, Jerome, Paula the Roman, and Mary the Egyptian. Teresa of Avila, in her *Libro de las fundaciones*, drew paralells between her eremitical models and Catalina, turning her writing into a true panegyric worthy of inclusion in some *Lives of the Fathers*. The Carmelite must have felt herself closely related to Catalina Cardona, who herself eulogized Mary the Egyptian and clearly expressed her desire to be called by the only name she thought she deserved, "sinner."[9] "Mary the Egyptian," stated Jacobo da Voragine, "performed austere penance."[10] Writing about Catalina, Teresa established an obvious parallel.[11] Voragine talked about Mary the Egyptian's "three breads"; they also appeared under the pen of Theresa: "Three breads that were left by the one who came with her [Cardona]."[12] Catalina's mortifications bring to mind the paintings of José Ribera, such as the *Saint Mary the Egyptian* (1640–1641) of the Prado Museum, which shows a penitent woman worn out by privations, praying inside her cave, and the *Saint Mary the Egyptian* (1651) of the Gaetano Filangieri Civic Museum, which marks a less mystical and more natural reflection on the sanctified model. Lastly, when Teresa of Avila gave a description of the vision she had had of the deceased Catalina, the figure of Mary Magdalene guided her hand: "This holy woman was represented to my mind in an intellectual vision, as a glorified body, surrounded by angels."[13] Due to the great respect that she had for Cardona, Teresa exhorted the Carmelites to follow that anchoress' example: "Let us try, for the love of our Lord, to follow this sister of ours."[14] She considered herself to be lagging far behind Catalina Cardona, her penances, and, implicitly, her life as an anchoress. Thus the *Pecadora* was transformed into a highly praised and cited model; for she was all that Theresa, in the depths of her person and her soul, wanted to be but could not be.[15] Such an extraordinary person could not remain unknown, and according to Efrén de la Madre de Dios, she was very controversial in her day. However, it is evident that this hagiographer of Teresa of Avila does not approve of the fact that the Carmelite, whom he eulogizes, showed such fervor in regard to Cardona. He tries to exonerate Teresa *a posteriori*, explaining, "Mother Teresa was too noble and too humble to disparage Cardona, and perhaps she lost many in dedicating praises to her and in being envious of her penances."[16] What the Carmelite theologian wrote is revealing of the permanency of the discredit upon the hermitesses in a historiographical trend. Forgetting any kind of moderation, Efrén de la Madre de Dios, in another part of his writings, characterizes Cardona as "a grotesque figure of female hermit (*ermitaño femenino*)," thereby denying both her feminity and the very existence of the Spanish word for "hermitess" (*ermitaña*). Only madness, that convenient alibi for gendered misconduct, and a "primitive mentality" can account for this "sprout of the Thebaid."[17] This modern repulsion for the hermitess devalues not only the importance given to the Desert Fathers by Teresa of Avila, but it also calls into question Teresa's absolute conviction that Catalina perfectly complied with the message they had left.

The rejection of the female anchorite model was matched by the rejection of the modern anchoress, in spite of the warm eulogy coming from a person with the spiritual dimensions of Teresa of Avila. Perhaps because she was a woman like Magdalene, Mary the Egyptian, and Catalina, Teresa was better able to understand the nuances and subtleties of female anachoresis; as she said in regard to Cardona in the *Libro de las fundaciones*: "She was a woman like me but more delicate, being who she was."[18]

❦

The Castilians also showed their devotion to Magdalene by giving her name to several hermitages.[19] While few of them were given the name of Mary the Egyptian, they were quite famous, such as the hermitage of La Cabrera, where an illustrious man, Luis Antonio de Umares, "Procurator of the Royal Councils of His Majesty," retired in 1661.[20] Women, however, did not serve uniquely as inspirational models of penitence for contemporary men. Following the example of saint Mary of the Head, saint Isidro's chaste spouse, some women also became attached to hermitages during the Golden Age, although they were less frequently mentionned than men in books of pastoral visits, registers of the archiepiscopal Chancellery, and trial records of the Inquisition. Documents in the sixteenth century as well as in the seventeenth century confirm their existence and suggest a ratio in New Castile of one female hermit for every nine men.[21] As in the case of male hermits, the Tribunal of the *Suprema* called such women either *ermitañas* or *santeras* without differentiating clearly between the two terms. The proceedings from a 1676 case in Pastrana show an inquisitor speaking of "the *ermitaña*" at one point, but mentioning her dwelling as the "house of the *santera*."[22] Nonetheless, the wider use of the word "santera," in particular in documents dealing with their connection to the *ermita*, appears to designate more specifically the practical role of such women as caretakers.[23]

They received a license from the bishop,[24] insured the cleanliness of the hermitage and were responsible for the venerated image.[25] The specified duties of women holding the *officio de santera*[26] apparently did not preclude them from being married and having children. The two successive wives of Fernández Serrano, a hermit in Daymiel, share his life as a *santero*,[27] while the *santera* Ynés de Campo from Albaladejo is married in 1584, and the mother of a daughter.[28] In Fuente in 1601, a son even embraces his mother's profession. He is identified as "Juan García, *santero*, son of Quinteria, *santera*."[29] Isabel Cara, hermitess of the hermitage of San Salvador in Pastrana, lived with her husband Juan Rojo in a small dwelling that adjoined the chapel of the hermitage and had two living units: a kitchen at the entrance, and a bedroom that gave access to the sacristy.[30] Did Isabel lead an angelic life with her husband like Renato and Eusebia, the couple of hermits imagined by Miguel Cervantes in his *Persiles y Sigismunda*? These chaste fictional spouses claimed, "We sleep apart, eat together, speak of Heaven, despise the world, and faithful in the mercy of God, we wait for eternal life."[31] Although records do not give details in the case of Juan and Isabel, however, this was assuredly not always true.

Real or imagined promiscuity on the part of santeras fueled a great deal of mockery leaving traces in Spanish literature. Their supposedly excessive carnal needs inspired Francisco de Quevedo for one. In a poem from *El parnaso español*, he saw in such solitary women the makings of a never tiring sex machine and wrote, "Wrong would be the hermit/who would forget in the midst of all this/the permanent desires of a hermitess from La Mancha."[32] Miguel Cervantes' Don Quixote also spoke extensively of the *gallinas* (hens, but also girls), adding that "Few hermits are without them."[33] Moreto y Cabaña, in his work *Yo por vos y vos por otro*, gave an equally ambiguous definition of *gallinas*, in which double meaning and sexual insinuations insulting for santeras were evident for all.[34] Quevedo's own verses form an apt summary of such jokes: "I could say more but this is enough, for people to know that the flower of the so-called sanctified persons is bawdy, even if it is said to be sterile."[35] While all hermits, men and women, were open to such accusations, the virulence of attacks on ermitañas and santeras reflect well the danger that was perceived in the existence of solitary women.

As severe as Golden Age literature appears, reality often was yet more unkind to santeras, who were effectively marginalized in their villages on two levels: first as theoretically holy but in fact ever suspicious hermits, second, and perhaps above all, as women. In the hamlet of Pareja, in 1562, Fernando de Contreras exclaimed simply, "God is grieved with the *santera*, this whore!"[36] Actual verbal assaults did indeed match literature's bad jokes. Witness the case of three drunkards who profaned the hermitage of San Salvador in Pastrana while the hermit was away. Onlookers maintained that they dared accuse the santera of their own vice, telling her "she is a drunk."[37] Recurring instances of such denigration clearly indicate an overwhelming rejection of the santera by her contemporaries, refusal that flew in the face of their theoretical and collective respect for such women's models in early Christianity.

The general disgrace in which santeras lived, however, could be far more tacit and insidious than violently insulting. Catalina Martínez was santera of the hermitage of Our Lady of the Valley in Molina. During High Mass on Holy Thursday in the year 1561, she knelt before the altar to receive communion. When the priest approached, Catalina became extremely nervous, trembling and weeping. All those attending Mass looked at her in stupified disbelief. Unable to swallow the consecrated Host, she finally stammered between sobs, "Father, I have eaten this morning."[38] The shocked parish priest put a finger between her lips to retrieve each particle of Host, made a little ball, and placed it into the mouth of the next person waiting for communion.[39] Apart from the question of her guilt, the Inquisition trial record shows how strongly isolated the woman was in the rustic society. No one testifying knew her name nor that of her husband, the santero. Nobody could even assert that she herself *was* a santera,[40] although most witnesses did at least consider her as some sort of wise woman, in spite of her incoherent words. As for the priests who listened to the prematurely aged hermitess, they "yelled at the old woman, repeating many times: 'What are you doing?' "[41] This dramatic scene of a terrified santera totally paralyzed by her sense of guilt, illustrates the exacerbated beliefs while the Council of Trent was still taking place, as well as the santera's position on the edge of her community.

Molina's imperfect santera, well aware of her wrongdoing, appeared as even more reprehensible in the light of popularized models whose representations only accentuated her failings. Magdalene's life had ended, according to Jacobo da Voragine's account, with the very sacrament that Catalina had wrongly wished to receive. "She received the body and blood of the Lord from the hands of the bishop with a great abundance of tears. Afterward she prostrated herself at the base of the altar and her most holy soul ascended to the Lord."[42] Pictorial representations of this scene were as common in Spain as they were in Italy, from the beginning of the fourteenth century on, when a disciple of Giotto painted it in fresco for the first time in the chapel of the Podestà in Florence.[43] A painting by Jerónimo Jacinto de Espinosa, for example, *The Last Communion of Magdalene* (1665), of which Fernando Benito Domenech said, "it is the most beautiful expression of the theme in Habsburg Spain," depicts a similar scene.[44] Significantly, however, the priest here is at least as important as the penitent. This painting and others like it may well have played an active part in the discredit of the santera. In the context of the Catholic Reformation, Catalina's difficulties bespoke not only her imperfect relationship to her eremitical model but also her inferior role to duely appointed ministers of the faith. By his presence in the central axis, the priest confirms the major role that the Council Fathers at Trent attributed to him in their decisions concerning the sacrament of order. The juxtaposition of the priest's magnificent chasuble and Magdalene's ragged clothing summarizes the abyss separating the glorious Church from a lonely santera whose ill-defined garments denote no added holiness.[45] Francisco López de Ubeda, in *The Picaresque Justina*, seems to address all such poorly perceived santeras when he states that "Hypocrites and people who do not live communally, who ostentatiously perform exercises and ceremonies, and wear clothes created only to satisfy a whim, these people always were suspect on the way to virtue."[46] The inhabitants of Molina lacked confidence in Catalina Martínez particularly because they thought that beneath her harsh penances— which actually could explain her precocious ageing —one would find some real hypocrisy.[47]

❦

The rejection of the hermitess was indeed an unquestionable reality of the Spanish Golden Age. It was part of the devaluation of the woman as much in her discourse[48] as in her body.[49] In this gendered process the Church played a decisive role, and assertions like those of the priest in charge of visiting the Diocese of Cuenca in 1633 were far from being atypical: "Many sins and indecencies are usually committed in that church," he writes, "women talk and other unedifying things."[50]

Above all, hermitesses were suspect because they were survivers of a dying tradition. Steadfast and rebel souls would be tolerated only if they joined a religious order or put themselves under the strict control of a bishop[51] or a confessor.[52] Henceforth the new model of sanctity was inside convents,[53] while hermitesses/santeras had no other choice than to endure a situation day after day, in which they were forever distrusted, even if a few more open-minded people encouraged them to keep on struggling, like Juan de Avila. "Enough, Madam, that the road your grace has followed has passed through the desert," he notes down in his *Epistolario*, "and it seems that the desert has not ended yet; it is still a long way to go."[54]

NOTES

The following abbreviations are used in this chapter:

A.D.C. = Archivo Diocesano de Cuenca

A.D.T. = Archivo Diocesano de Toledo

A.H.N. = Archivo Histórico Nacional

B.A.C. = Biblioteca de Autores Cristianos

B.A.E. = Biblioteca de Autores Españoles

Exp. = Expediente

Inq. = Inquisición

Leg. = Legajo

M.C.V. = Mélanges de la Casa de Velázquez

R.de C.= Relaciones de Causas

A first version of this text was presented at the SSPHS Annual Meeting in Saint Louis, MI, in April 1989, under the title: "Women and the Eremitical Life during the Spanish Golden age"; and a shorter one, entitled: "The Santera in the Golden Age: A Case of Gendered Rejection," at the XIVth Mediterranean Conference, in Mallorca, Spain, in July 1992. I thank Bartolomé Bennassar, Francisco Bethencourt, Richard L. Kagan, Anne E.McCall, Sally Nalle, and Ricardo Saez, who helped me, with their suggestions, to elaborate this article.

❦

1. See Isabel Morán Suárez, "La influencia de Oriente en el eremitismo cristiano," *Lecturas de historia del arte* (Vitoria-Gasteiz: Ephialte. Instituto de Estudios Iconográficos, 1990), 60–68; and Benedicta Ward, *Harlots of the Desert: A Study of Repentance in Early Monastic Sources* (Kalamazoo, 1987). Also, Jacques Dalarun, "Jeanne de Signa, ermite toscane du XIVème siècle, ou la sainteté ordinaire," *Mélanges de l'Ecole Française de Rome 98* (1986–1), 161–199; and André Vauchez, *La sainteté en Occident aux derniers siècles du moyen age, d'après les procès de canonisation et les documents hagiographiques* (Rome: Bibliothèque de l'Ecole Française de Rome, 1981); *Eremitismo nel francescanesimo medievale. Atti dei convegni della società internazionale di studi francescani in Assisi* (Napoli: Edizioni Scientifiche Italiane, 1990); and Teresa-María Vinyoles y Elisa Varela, "Religiosidad y moral social en la práctica diaria de las mujeres de los últimos siglos medievales," in Angela Muñoz y María del Mar Graña, eds., *Religiosidad femenina: expectativas y realidades* (ss.VIII–XVIII) (Madrid: Asociación Cultural Al-Mudayna, 1991), 41–60. In the same volume, see Cristina Papa, " 'Tra il dire e il fare': Búsqueda de identidad y vida cotidiana," 73–91. See also Ann Kosser Warren, *The Anchorite in Medieval England. 1100–1539* (Cleveland: Case Western Reserve University, 1980).

2. See Alain Saint-Saëns, *La nostalgie du désert. L'idéal érémitique en Castille au Siècle d'Or* (San Francisco: Mellen Research University Press, 1993). See also Margot H. King, *The Desert Mothers: A Survey of the Feminine Anchorite Tradition in Western Europe* (Saskatoon, Sask.: Peregrina, 1985); and Sebastian P. Brock and Susan Ashbrook Harvey (trs. and eds.), *Holy Women of the Syrian Orient* (Berkeley: University of California Press, 1987).

3. Teresa de Jesús, Efrén de la Madre de Dios and Otger Steggink, eds. in *Obras completas* (Madrid: B.A.C. 1986): *Libro de la vida*, 147, chap. 27, 16.

4. See Caroline Walker Bynum, Stevan Harrel, and Paula Richman, eds., *Gender and Religion: On the Complexity of Symbols* (Boston: Beacon Press, 1986). See also Jodi Bilinkoff, "The Holy Woman and the Urban Community in Sixteenth-Century Avila," in Barbara J. Harris, and JoAnn K. McNamara, eds., *Women and the Structure of Society* (Durham, NC: Duke University Press, 1984), 74–80; Margaret L. King, *Women of the Renaissance* (Chicago: University of Chicago Press, 1991); and Arlette Fage and Natalie Zemon Davis, eds., *Histoire des femmes en Occident. De la Renaissance à l'époque moderne* (Paris: Plon, 1991).

5. See *Escritoras españolas*, Manuel Serrano y Sanz, ed. (Madrid: B.A.E. 270, 1975) 123, no. 303.

6. Sor María del Espíritu Santo, in Manuel Serrano y Sanz, ed., *Escritoras españolas* (Madrid: B.A.E. 269, 1975), 400.

7. Teresa de Jesús, *Libro de las fundaciones*, chap. 28, 24, 783; chap. 28, 27, 784. See also Alain Saint-Saëns, "Thérèse d'Avila ou l'érémitisme sublimé," *M.C.V.* 25 (1989), 125–143.

8. Teresa de Jesús, *Libro de las fundaciones*, chap. 28, 21–36, 782–786. For a more precise definition of the concept of anachoresis, see Jean Sainseaulieu, *Etudes sur la vie érémitique en France de la Contre-Réforme à la Restauration* (Lille: Ateliers de Thèses, 1974), 9.

9. Teresa de Jesús, *Libro de las fundaciones*, chap. 28, 21, 783.

10. Jacques de Voragine, *La Légende Dorée* I, 284.

11. Teresa de Jesús, *Libro de las fundaciones*, chap. 28, 26, 783. See also Alison Goddard Elliott, *Roads to Paradise: Reading the Lives of the Early Saints* (Hanover and London: Cambridge University Press, 1987).

12. Compare Jacques de Voragine, *La Légende Dorée*, I, 285, with Teresa de Jesús, *Libro de las fundaciones*, chap. 28, 27, 784.

13. Ibid., chap. 28, 36, 786.

14. Ibid., chap. 28, 36, 786.

15. Ibid., chap. 28, 21, 782; also chap. 28, 25, 783. See also Ignacio Elizalde, "Teresa de Jesús, protagonista de la dramática española del siglo XVII," *Letras de Deusto* XII, 24 (1982), 173–198; and Alison Weber, "The Paradoxes of Humility: Santa Teresa's *Libro de la Vida* as Double Mind," *Journal of Hispanic Philology* 9 (1985), 211–230.

16. Efrén de la Madre de Dios and Otger Steggink, *Tiempo y vida de Santa Teresa* (Madrid: B.A.C., 1968), 410. See also Sara T. Nalle, *God in La Mancha. Religious Reform and the People of Cuenca, 1500–1650* (Baltimore: The Johns Hopkins University Press, 1992), 136.

17. Efrén de la Madre de Dios, "La escisión de Pastrana," *Actas del congreso internacional teresiano I* (Salamanca: Universidad, 1983), 389–407. Pedro Saínz Rodríguez, in *Axerquía*, 8 (September 1983), 337, formulates a very severe judgment on Efrén, much more hagiographer than biographer of Teresa of Avila. See also Teresa Scott Soufas, *Melancholy and the Secular Mind in Spanish Golden Age Literature* (Columbia and London: University of Missouri Press, 1989); and Juliana Schiesari, *The Gendering of Melancholia. Feminism, Psychoanalysis, and the Symbolics of Loss in Renaissance Literature* (Ithaca: Cornell University Press, 1992).

18. Teresa de Jesús, *Libro de las fundaciones*, chap. 28, 35, 786. See also Dominique Deneuville, *Sainte Thérèse d'Avila et la femme* (Lyon: Edition du Chalet, 1964).

19. See, for example, A.H.N., Inq. Toledo (1540–1541), Leg. 497, Exp. 3, Visitas, Ocaña, fol. 31v; A.H.N., Ordenes Militares, Calatrava (1568), Leg. 3, Exp.6, Visitas, fol. 8; A.D.T., Libro de Visitas no. 1201 (1682–1686), fol. 28v; A.D.C., Libro no. 204, Relación de Visita (1583), fol. 29. See also Miguel Angel Zálama Rodríguez, *Ermitas y santuarios de la Provincia de Valladolid* (Valladolid: Diputación de Valladolid, Editora Provincial/ Publicaciones Gráficas Andrés Martín, S.A., 1987); Ismael Gutiérrez Pastor, *Ermitas de la Rioja* (Logroño: Caja de Ahorros de Zaragoza, Aragón y Rioja, 1985); and María Soledad Lázaro Damas, "Ermitas y santuarios de la ciudad de Jaén en el siglo XVI," *La religiosidad popular* III, 282–301.

20. A.D.T., no. IV/1495 (1659–1661), Libro de Visitas de Zorita, Almoguera, Butrago con el valle de Lozoía, fol. 62. About this hermitage, see also A.D.T., no. IV/1240 (1647–1648), Libro de Visitas, fol. 47; no. IV/1498 (1649), Libro Quenta y Raçón, fol. 1v: "Vissitóse la hermita de santa María Jipciaca es hermita de mucha devoción."

21. See some examples in A.D.C., L–351, Inq. Cuenca, R.de C. (1535), fol. 34v, and (1591), fol. 406v; A.H.N., Inq. Logroño, Libro 838, R.de C. (1649), fol. 38v; A.H.N., Inq. Toledo, Leg. 224, Exp. 10 (1676); A.D.T., no. IV/1494 (1692–1693), fol. 3v. See also William A.Christian, Jr., *Local Religion in Sixteenth-Century Spain* (Princeton: Princeton University Press, 1989), chp. 3, 70–125.

22. A.H.N., Inq. Toledo, Leg. 224, Exp. 10 (1676–1678), fols. 37 and 192 v.

23. A.D.T., Libro de las Visitas, no. IV/1355 (1654–1655), fol. 71 v. See also A.D.C., L–351, Inq. Cuenca, R. de C., Sigüenza, fol. 34v; A.D.C., Inq.Cuenca, Leg. 702, Exp. 274, fol. 1.

24. A.D.T., Registro de Cancillería, Cardenal Pasqual de Aragón, no. 818 (1671–1672), fol. 68 v. For another license, see fol. 122.

25. A.D.T., Libro de Visitas, no. IV/1355 (1654–1655), Pastrana, fol. 190. See also Fuente Novilla, fol. 152.

26. A.H.N., Inq. Toledo, Leg. 224, Exp. 10 (1676–1678), fol. 5 v and fol. 88. See also A.D.C., Inq. Cuenca, Leg. 702, Exp. 274 (1561), Molina, fol. 1 v.

27. A.H.N., Inq. Toledo, Leg. 86, Exp. 1 (1662–65), Daymiel, fol. 57 and 57 v.

28. A.D.C., Inq. Cuenca, L–351, R. de C., Sigüenza (1584), fol. 577 v.

29. A.D.C., Inq. Cuenca, R .de C., Leg. 752, Exp. 25 (1601), fol. 1.

30. A.H.N., Inq. Toledo, Leg. 224, Exp. 10 (1676–1678), fol. 5v: "Isabel Cara, mujer. . . . que su exercicio es asistir en compañía de su marido a cuydar de la hermita de san Salvador." See also Alain Saint-Saëns, "Une nouvelle approche de l'ermitage du XVIIème siècle," *M.C.V.* 26 (1990), 56–61.

31. Miguel Cervantes, in B. Carlos Arribau, ed., *Persiles y Sigismunda* (Madrid: B.A.E. 1, 1943), 620.

32. Francisco Quevedo, in Florencio Janer, ed., *El Parnaso español* (Madrid: B.A.E. 69, 1953), 174, no. 479. See also Michela Ambrogetti, "La fortuna dell' *ermitaño* nel teatro del Siglo de Oro," in Francisco Ramos Ortega, ed. *Actas del Coloquio "Teoría y realidad en el teatro español del siglo XVII. La influencia italiana."* (Roma: Instituto Español de Cultura y Literatura de Roma, 1981), 463–470; and Alain Saint-Saëns, "Saint ou coquin. Le personnage de l'ermite dans la littérature espagnole du Siècle d'Or," *Revista Canadiense de Estudios Hispánicos* XVI (1991), 123–135. See also Everett W. Hesse, *La mujer como víctima en la comedia y otros ensayos* (Barcelona: Puvill, 1987).

33. Miguel Cervantes, in B. Carlos Arribau, ed., *Don Quijote de la Mancha* (Madrid: B.A.E. 1, 1943), 455.

34. Agustín Moreto y Cabaña, in L. F. Guerra y Orbe, ed., *Yo por vos, y vos por otro* (Madrid: B.A.E. 39, 1950), 375: "Las gallinas, / Hijo mío, sustentan a quien las cría / Dan huevos, pollos y pollas / Y aseguran un buen día." Moreto, like Cervantes, enjoys playing with the meaning of several words, and here offers some verses that may have an innocent sense or a very sexual and dirty one (*huevos* are eggs, but also a very vulgar word for testicles; *pollas* might mean hens but, more often, *polla* is used to talk vulgarly about an erection). See also Everett W. Hesse, *Theology, Sex, and the "Comedia," and Other Essays* (Potomac, MD: Studia Humanitatis, 1982); Mary S. Gossy, *The Untold Story: Women and Theory in Golden Age Texts* (Ann Arbor: University of Michigan Press, 1989); and Mélanges Henk Oostendorp, *España, teatro y mujeres* (Amsterdam: Rodopi, 1989).

35. Francisco Quevedo, *El parnaso español*, B.A.E. 69, no. 479, 174–175. Quevedo plays here on the double meaning of *verde* and *seca*. See also Diane Debra Andrist, "Love, Honor and the Male-Female Relationship in Representative Authors of the Spanish 'Comedia,' " Ph.D. diss. (Buffalo: State University of New York-Buffalo, 1986).

36. A.D.C., Inq. Cuenca, R. de C., Sigüenza (1562), fol. 178.

37. A.H.N., Inq. Toledo, Leg. 224, Exp. 10 (1676–1678), Pastrana, fol. 7.

38. A.D.C., Inq. Cuenca, Leg. 702, Exp. 274: Martínez (Catalina), Santera, Molina (1561), fol. 1 r. See also Caroline Walker Bynum, *Holy Feast and Holy Fast: The Religious Significance of Food to Medieval Women* (Berkeley: University of California Press, 1987); and by the same, *Fragmentation and Redemption: Essays on Gender and the Human Body in Medieval Religion* (New York: Zone Books; Cambridge, MA: Dist. MIT Press, 1991), 119–150.

39. A.D.C., Inq. Cuenca, Leg. 702, Exp. 274, fol. 1 r. See also fol.1 v: "Llamó este testigo a Fernando Jérez clérigo de la dicha villa. . . . y le dió el sanctíssimo sacramento que avía sacado de la boca de la dicha muger y el dicho Fernando Jérez lo rescibió e consumió y esta es la verdad y lo hize por descargo de su consciencia." See also Sara T. Nalle, "Inquisitors, Priests, and the People during the Catholic Reformation in Spain," *The Sixteenth Century Journal* XVIII, 4 (Winter 1987): 557–587.

40. A.D.C., Inq. Cuenca, Leg. 702, Exp. 274, fol. 1 r; also fols. 2 r and 2 v. See Augustin Redondo, ed. *Les problèmes de l'exclusion en Espagne (XVIe–XVIIe siècles). Idéologies et discours* (Paris: Publications de la Sorbonne, 1983); and Francisco Tomás y Valiente, "Delin-

cuentes y pecadores," *Sexo barroco*, 11–32. Also in the same volume, Bartolomé Clavero, "Delito y pecado. Noción y escala de transgresiones," 57–90.

41. A.D.C., Inq. Cuenca, Leg. 702, Exp. 274, fol. 2 v, concerning the woman's words: "abierta la boca, diciendo ay, ay, ay." For the testimonies, see fols. 2 v and 3 r. For the priests yelling at her, see fol. 2 v.

42. Jacques de Voragine, *La Légende Dorée* I, 464. See also A.M. Allchin, ed., *Solitude and Communion* (Oxford, 1977), 1–84.

43. See Sara Wilk, "The Cult of Mary Magdalen in Fifteenth Century Florence and Its Iconography," *Studi Medievali*, XXVI (1985), 685–698. See also Edmund Leach, "Late Medieval Representations of Saint Mary Magdalene," *The Psychoanalytic Review* 75 (1988), 95–109.

44. Fernando Benito Domenech, *Catálogo Los Ribalta y la pintura valenciana de su tiempo* (Madrid: Museo del Prado, 1987), 281. See also Alain Saint-Saëns, *Art and Faith in Tridentine Spain. 1545–1690* (San Francisco: Peter Lang, 1995), Part I, 29–84: "Non-Apocryphal Holy Images;" and Palma Martínez Burgos García, *Ídolos e imágenes. La controversia del arte religioso en el siglo XVI español* (Valladolid: Universidad de Valladolid y Caja de Ahorros de Salamanca, 1990).

45. See José Orlandis, "La disciplina eclesiástica española sobre la vida eremítica," *Ius Canonicum* IV (1964), 147–163; and Tomás Moral, *Otras aportaciones al eremitismo peninsular* (Pamplona, 1970), 2. See also Alain Saint-Saëns, "Antón de la Fuente, ermite-pélerin de Castille au XVIIème siècle," *Histoire, Economie et Société* (1987–1), 47, note 18. For some interesting examples, see A.H.N., Inq. Toledo, Leg. 204, Exp. 21, fol. 3: "Hombre que anda en ávito de hermitaño o pelegrino;" also, A.H.N., Inq. Logroño, R. de C., Libro no. 835 (September 1600), fol. 20 v: "Juan del Campo hermitaño de Tofalla del reyno de Navarra. . . . sea despojado del ávito de hermitaño. . . . y que perpetuamente no se vista de semejante ábito ni de otro que paresca religioso ni persona recoleta sino que ande en ábito de mero lego."

46. Francisco López de Úbeda, in Eustaquio Fernández Navarrete, ed., *La pícara Justina* (Madrid: B.A.E. 33, 1950) chap. 2, 111.

47. Francisco Quevedo, in Florencio Janer, ed., *Doctrina de Epicteto puesta en español, sin consonantes*, (Madrid: B.A.E. 69, 1953) chap. 52, 404. Despite all that, the same poet recognized the value of attempting severe penances. In a letter to a friend, in Aureliano Fernández Guerra y Orbe, ed., *Epistolario* (Madrid: B.A.E. 48,1951), 589, letter no. 111: *A su amigo Adán de la Parra*, he reflects seriously on the subject. See also Joaquín Rodríguez Mateos, "La disciplina pública como fenómeno penitencial barroco," *La religiosidad popular* II, 528–539.

48. See Claire Guilhem, "L'Inquisition et la dévaluation des discours féminins," in Bartolomé Bennassar, ed., *L'Inquisition espagnole, XVe–XIXe* (Paris: Hachette, 1979), 197–229. See also my Introduction in Alain Saint-Saëns, ed., *Religion, Body, and Gender in Early Modern Spain* (San Francisco: Mellen Research University Press, 1991), 2–16.

49. See Alain Saint-Saëns, "Apología y denigración del cuerpo del ermitaño en el Siglo de Oro," *Hispania Sacra* XLII, 85 (1990), 169–180. See also Mary-Elizabeth Perry, "Subversion and Seduction: Perception of the Body in Writings of Religious Women in Counter-Reformation Spain," *Religion, Body, and Gender in Early Modern Spain*, 67–78; Anne J. Cruz, "The Princess and the Page: Sexual Transgressions and Marriage in the Spanish Ballad *Gerineldos*," *Religion, Body, and Gender in Early Modern Spain*, 110–122. Also, Augustin Redondo, ed., *Le corps dans la société espagnole des XVIème et XVIIème siècles* (Paris: Publications de la Sorbonne-Nouvelle, 1990). See also Linda L. Caroll, "Who's on Top? Gender as Societal Power Configuration in Italian Renaissance Drama," *The Sixteenth Century Journal* XX, 4 (1989): 531–558.

50. A.D.C., *Libro de Visitas*, no. 205 (1633), fol. 132: "conversaciones de mujeres y otras cosas indevidas." See also Nina M. Scott, "Sor Juana Inés de la Cruz: 'Let Your Women Keep Silence in the Churches. . . . ,' " *Women's Studies International Forum* 8 (1985), 511–19; Bonnie S. Anderson and Judith P. Zinsser, *A History of Their Own* (New York: Harper and Row, Publishers, 1989), 214–263; and Richard C. Trexler, *Gender Rhetorics. Posture of Dominance and Submission in History* (Binghamton: MRTS, 1994).

51. See Teresa de Jesús, *Libro de las fundaciones*, chap. 17, 8, 732: "Como vino el santo concilio de Trento, como mandaron reducir a las órdenes los ermitaños;" and André Michel, *Les Décrets du Concile de Trente*, 388, LVIII, canon 6; 390, canon 11; 464, LIX, canon 9; 500, canon 16. See also Sergio Bertelli, *Rebeldes, libertinos y ortodoxos en el barroco* (Barcelona: Ediciones Península, 1984); Mary Elizabeth Perry, *Gender and Disorder in Early Modern Seville* (Princeton: Princeton University Press, 1990), 177–180; and compare with what Maurice Devroede says, in "Erémitisme et instruction dans les Pays-Bas autrichiens et la principauté de Liège au XVIIIe siècle," *Revue d'Histoire Ecclésiastique* LXXXVI, 3–4 (Juillet-Décembre 1991), 295: "C'est au XVIIe siècle, que, dans le cadre de la Contre-Réforme, les évêques sont intervenus pour réglementer la vie d'ermites. Ils ont pris l'habitude de les traiter comme des religieux, quoique la plupart fussent des laïcs. Les mesures épiscopales n'avaient d'autre but que de combattre les abus."

52. See Isabelle Poutrin, "Le voile et la plume. Mystique et sainteté féminines" (Paris-Sorbonne: Thèse de Doctorat, 1993), chap. 3, 32–43, 102–113. See also Merry Wiesner-Hanks, *Women and Gender in Early Modern Europe* (New York: Cambridge University Press, 1993).

53. See José Luis Sánchez Lora, *Mujeres, conventos y formas de la religiosidad barroca* (Madrid: Fundación Universitaria Española, 1988). See also Gabriella Zarri, "Le sante vive: per una tipologia della santità femminile nel primo cinquecento," *Annali dell'Istituto Storico Italo-Germanico in Trento* 6 (1980), 371–445. Also, Isabelle Poutrin, "Souvenirs d'enfance: l'apprentissage de la santeté dans l'Espagne moderne," *M.C.V.* 23 (1987), 331–354; and Electra Arenal, "The Convent as Catalyst for Autonomy. Two Hispanic Nuns of the Seventeenth Century," in Beth Miller, ed., *Women in Hispanic Literature. Icons and Fallen Idols* (Berkeley, 1983). By the same Arenal, with Stacey Schlau, *Untold Sisters: Hispanic Nuns in Their Own Works* (Albuquerque: University of New Mexico Press, 1989).

54. Juan de Avila, in Luis Sala Balust, ed., *Obras completas* (Madrid: B.A.C., 1952), Vol. I, *Epistolario*, 671, letter 97. On the *desierto* as a theme, see Alain Saint-Saëns, *La nostalgie du désert*, Part I, 15–78. See also Fernando Rodríguez de la Flor, "La ciudad de Yahve," *Caracola* 3 (1989), 46–51; and by the same, *De las Batuecas a las Hurdes* (Mérida: Junta de Extremadura, 1989). Also Palma Martínez-Burgos García, "Los tópicos del paisaje en la pintura española del siglo XVI," *Fragmentos* 7 (1986), 66–83.

Part II

POLITICAL REALMS

5

The Female Figure as Political Propaganda in the "Pedro el Cruel" Romancero

Anne J. Cruz

From their first oral beginnings in the mid-fourteenth century to their collection in *romanceros* and their influence on such authors as Cervantes, Lope de Vega, and Góngora in the sixteenth and seventeenth centuries, the Spanish *romances* gained widespread popularity due to their evocative poetics and dramatic engagement. Yet these ballads offer far more than aesthetic pleasure: cutting across social categories in their depiction of women from various social groups as well as in their wide appeal to differing audiences—laborers and nobles, townspeople and countryfolk—they recreate and delimit certain modes of gender behavior. Through their normative narratives, the audience is reminded, even as it is informed and entertained, of the roles deemed socially and morally acceptable for women within patriarchal systems of power.

Thus, although the romances' portrayal of women's roles serves a primarily literary function, their representations nonetheless contribute to gender expectations. The large number of ballads chronicling the dynastic conflicts between Pedro of Castile, the fourteenth-century monarch, and his bastard half-brothers, Fadrique and Enrique of Trastámara, are instructive in that they exemplify the oral texts' codification of gender behavior.[1] The depictions of female figures are themselves embedded in social perceptions: by juxtaposing the monarch's wife to his mistress in a binary structure embodying two warring political factions, the "Pedro el Cruel" ballad cycle not only divides male and female roles into the traditional active/passive binomial, but explicitly compares and condemns female agency over feminine victimization.

Comprised of Spain's oldest *romances noticieros*, the ballad cycle recounts the fratricidal struggles from approximately 1357 that precipitated a civil war and established the Trastámara succession to the Castilian throne after Pedro's death in 1369. The legitimate heir of Alfonso XI of Castile and María of Portugal, Pedro ascended to the throne after displacing his preferred half-brothers borne by the king's mistress, Leonor de Guzmán. The young king inherited his father's political troubles: the nobility's strong dislike of Alfonso's authoritarian rule, and the border disputes between Castile and Catalonia-Aragon. Despite the nobility's lack of support and his half-brothers' constant attempts to dethrone him, Pedro nevertheless succeeded in protecting the interests of the lower nobility within Castile and in maintaining Castilian hegemony outside the kingdom, efforts recognized by his partisans in his epithet of "el Justiciero," against that of "el Cruel" given him by his opponents.

Modern historians acknowledge Pedro's reign as no bloodier than usual for its time and, in contrast to the succeeding Trastámara monarchy that encouraged a seignorial regime, supportive of a centralizing policy curbing domination by the nobility.[2] Since the majority of the extant romances alleged that Pedro was the issue of his mother's adultery with a Jew, and accused him of murdering Fadrique and his abandoned French bride, Blanca de Borbón, they have rightly been considered political propaganda in support of the Trastámara faction. That Pedro is now known by the sobriquet of "el Cruel" is due in great part to the ballads' success in denouncing his so-called atrocities.

Louise Mirrer's sociolinguistic analysis brilliantly clarifies both the ballad narratives' intrinsic "tellability" and their ideological rhetoricity, strategies influencing the audience's political attitudes in their use of evaluative devices.[3] A look at the ballads' positioning of its female figures further uncovers how their distortion of historical facts not only underwrites their structural function, but their moral and political stance as well. By purposely focussing on the female characters' relationships with men rather than on their individuated political worth, the ballads constitute the women through phallocentric symbolization.[4] Thus, the anti-Petrine ballads contrast Pedro's wife, Blanca de Borbón, with his mistress, María de Padilla, in the traditional virgin/whore dichotomy, while the pro-Petrine romances depict her as an adulterous spouse willing to seduce her own brother-in-law. Such a dualistic depiction—the female figures are martyrs or seductresses, in either case dependent upon a patriarchal system of values—perpetuates female stereotypes by divesting them of any psychological complexity or agency.

In usurping the female character's historicity, then, the romances metaphorize them into abstract categories that reflect and serve male interests. To a greater extent than is usually the case in medieval univocal discourses, whose protagonists are employed as abstractions or divided according to heroic virtues, the female figures of the "Pedro el Cruel" cycle occupy a symbolic space where racial, class, and national differences are acted out.[5] However, although the point certainly bears repeating, I am less interested in belaboring the domination of women by patriarchal society than in studying the manner in which these romances selectively combine historical information with fictionalized accounts in their efforts to win popular support for the Trastámara regime. In recontextualizing the ballads historically, my purpose is twofold: to reveal the rhetorical strategies in their political positionings, and to recover their narratives' feminine presence by demonstrating how this presence is categorized, exploited, and diminished through gender codification.

Recent studies show that, in Spain, women's legal and social conditions improved from the eleventh through the thirteenth centuries owing to their participation in the Reconquest, the restriction of family authority to conjugal family, and the weakening of legislation based on the Roman *patria potestas*.[6] The romances' symbolically repressed female figures, however, contrast sharply with the many aristocratic women of the period who wielded considerable power in their own right. Pedro's first conflictive encounters with women, in fact, were with his mother, María, Queen of Portugal, and his father's mistress, Leonor, who, as a Guzmán, belonged to one of Spain's most powerful families.

María de Portugal is generally considered a virago by historians: Antonio Pérez Gómez, for one, notes that she often sided with her son's enemies and behaved with "an imprudent impropriety" that forced Pedro to murder several of her lovers.[7] Leonor de Guzmán's conduct, in comparison, has elicited contradictory reports: contemporary accounts paint her as a forbidding opponent, constantly interfering in royal matters: the Portuguese bishop attested to her constant harassment of the queen. She was also alleged to have hired a Moorish witch to murder María and her only surviving son, Pedro, during childbirth.[8] Later, in the eighteenth century, the historian Henrique Florez praised Leonor's political acumen in rejecting the suggestion from Juan Manuel, the king's foe, that she pressure Alfonso XI into a second marriage, a deed sure to alienate Alfonso IV of Portugal, Alfonso's father-in-law and strong ally.[9] Most recently, María Helena Sánchez Ortega, no doubt taking into account the fact that Leonor bore the king nine children, has disallowed any possible intrigue on her part, and sees her as remaining "almost in the shadow devoted to her function as prolific mother and loyal companion."[10]

Royal liaisons, in any case, could not be so easily separated from politics, since they touched directly upon queens' rights and prerogatives; also, aristocratic mistresses often demanded special privileges. Certainly, María de Portugal was not only personally humiliated, but politically affected by Alfonso's preference for Leonor, especially since he lived openly with her, lavishing honors upon her family, while the queen and her son remained in isolation from court.[11] After Alfonso's death, the queen incarcerated Leonor and, with Pedro's compliance, gave orders for her assassination. Yet, although she avenged her marginalization by Alfonso, she remained under her son's control, her pent-up frustrations vented in their violent relations.

The tensions between mother and son may have originated not nearly so much from her evil temper as from the male fear of motherhood, kept in check through patriarchal authority and masked by male dominance. Maternal sovereignty, seemingly promoted by the cult of Mariology that took hold in the thirteenth century, instead contributed to female disenfranchisement. Encroaching upon the courtly love ideal, Mary assumed a paradigmatic role for Christian women, for as a virgin mother, she was deemed Queen of Heaven and Mother of the Church, but remained doubly subjected to a masculine god who was, besides, her son.[12] While women who entered the convent came under some measure of control, those who remained in society continued to signify potential disruption: Ave, the salutation to the Virgin, easily reverted to Eva, the originary cause of men's ills. María's support of her daughter-in-law, Blanca de Borbón, and her alliance with his half-brothers so angered Pedro that she escaped with her life only by retiring to Portugal.[13] There, she was rumored to lead a "dishonorable" life, for which her father—in a fit of patriarchal temperament—attempted to have her murdered.[14]

Despite their restricted positions, therefore, María de Portugal and Leonor de Guzmán's actions led to the overthrow of a dynasty and the creation of a new aristocracy, the most important political events of the century. Pedro's usurpation in his mother's name of Leonor's properties, which included the estate of Medina Sidonia, and her murder, again in vindication of his mother, were significant factors in the Trastámaras' rebellion against their brother. In rejecting his legitimate wife, Blanca de Borbón, for his mistress, María de Padilla, Pedro followed in his father's footsteps, emulating a patriarchal model that nonetheless depended on the women's strategic competition for monarchical power through their male offspring. The romances' insistence on containing the women's range of action to an idealist opposition of good versus evil lays bare their propagandistic strategies. Those depicting Blanca as the cuckholding wife, her adulterous relationship made all the more treacherous by its incestuous overtones, attempt to win support for Pedro, while the ballads codifying Blanca and María de Padilla within the virgin/whore dichotomy intend to gain credibility for the rival faction.

Pedro's illicit relationship with his mistress was itself due to the queen's minister and cousin, Juan Alfonso de Alburquerque, who introduced the young king to María de Padilla, seeking to manipulate him through a sexual alliance.[15] When María's family instead gained power over Pedro, the minister encouraged the king to marry the French princess Blanca de Borbón both to produce a legitimate heir and to collect the large dowry promised by France in return for Castile's support against England.[16] The wedding ceremonies were abruptly terminated after only three days by Pedro's inexplicable departure and return to his mistress. The ballads in defense of the king exploited the occasion to accuse Fadrique of adultery with his sister-in-law; the ballads against Pedro blamed his defection on his mistress's having bewitched him, as rumors of

María de Padilla's powers over the king gained increasing currency.[17] A century later, Florez tells us, the Jews were accused of having intervened in the sorcery, since Blanca was supposed to have encouraged Pedro to expel all Jews from the kingdom.[18]

A more plausible explanation for the king's abandonment of Blanca and his break with Alburquerque and with his mother, who joined with Blanca's supporters, was his discovery that France did not intend to make good its promise.[19] The coalition against Pedro included the French, his former minister Alburquerque, the Trastámara brothers, the Aragon princes Joan and Ferran, and Pope Innocent VI. The ensuing civil strife, which was to draw Castile into the Hundred Years' War between France and England, scarcely relented in 1369 with Pedro's murder at the hands of Enrique. The greater number of surviving ballads in favor of the Trastámaras testify to their final victory, yet certain contradictions in several variants indicate that the outcome was none too certain during the decades that followed Pedro's death, and that the *juglares* allowed their audience their choice of political factions through the different variants.

One version of *Yo me estaba allá en Coimbra*, an anti-Pedro ballad recounting the death of Fadrique, reflects the uncertainty of the turn of events in its ambivalent narrative, accusing Pedro of Fadrique's death but ending with the king's repentance.[20] Fadrique narrates how Pedro tricks him to come to Seville from Jumilla, where he is assaulted by the king's men:

> "Yo me estaua alla en coymbra
> que yo me la oue ganado
> quando me vinieron cartas
> del rey don Pedro mi hermano
> que fuesse auer los torneos
> que en Seuilla se han armado
>
> . . .
>
> Las puertas me auian cerrado;
> quitaronme la mi espada,
> la que traya a mi lado,
> quitáronme mi compañia
> la que me auia acompañado.
> Los mios desque esto vieron,
> de traycion me an auisado."

Translation:

> "There I remained at Coimbra
> after conquering the town
> When I received letters
> From King Pedro, my brother
> inviting me to the tournaments
> taking place in Seville
>
> . . .
>
> The doors were barred to me;
> My sword was taken from me;

the one I wore by my side,
My company was taken from me
those who had accompanied me.
My men, when they observed this,
soon warned me of the betrayal." (100:1-6; 107:50-56)

Fadrique characterizes himself as entirely innocent of any wrongdoing and loyal to the king, whose faction perfidiously has him murdered.

The circumstances of the murder at first point to Pedro's treachery and lawlessness, but the ballad ends by blaming Fadrique's death on the king's weak will instead. He gives in to the murderous desires of his mistress, María de Padilla, who asks for Fadrique's head in reprisal for the presumed betrayal of his brother:

"Porque es aquesso, buen rey?
Nunca os hize desaguisado
ni os dexe yo enla lid
ni con moros peleando . . . "
aun no lo ouo bien dicho
la cabeça le han cortado;
a doña Maria de Padilla
en vn plato la ha embiado . . .
"aqui pagareys traydor
los de antaño y de ogaño
el mal consejo que diste
al rey don Pedro, tu hermano."

Translation:
"To what do I owe this, good King?
I've never done you any harm
nor left you abandoned in battle
nor left you fighting the Moors . . . "
No sooner has he had his say
when they've cut off his head;
to the lady María de Padilla
they've sent it on a platter . . .
"Here you shall pay, you traitor,
your deeds past and present,
the evil counsel you gave
to King Pedro, your brother." (107–108:73–77; 108:79–82; 87–90)

Falsely accusing Fadrique of treason, María is portrayed as the archetypal castrating woman who comes between the brothers, severing their fraternal bond. The graphic image of Fadrique's bloody head served on a platter recalls as well the Biblical tale of Salome, whose mother exploited Herod's sexual passion for her own purposes. Thus, although historical records show that Pedro murdered Fadrique only after he had pardoned him several times for rebelling with other nobles against him, the ballads downplay Pedro's struggles with his rebellious brother to stress the role a woman plays in bringing about his downfall.[21]

Other anti-Petrine romances emphasize the female figures' binary representation by opposing María de Padilla's power over the king to the French princess's innocence, her virtue winning out over her rival's ill will. In the romance *Doña María de Padilla*, a love-besotted Pedro begs his mistress's pardon for having married Blanca. The following variant foreshadows Blanca's murder in the blood-red pennant that the king cruelly demands sewn for his sullen mistress:

> "Doña Maria de Padilla,
> no os mostredes triste vos,
> que, si me case dos vezes
> hizelo por vuestra pro
> y por hazer menosprecio
> a doña Blanca de Borbon;
> a Medina Sidonia enbio
> a que me labre vn pendon
> sera el color de su sangre,
> de lagrimas la labor;
> tal pendon, doña Maria,
> lo hare hazer por vos."

Translation:
> "Lady María de Padilla,
> do not look so sad and forlorn,
> since, if I married twice,
> I did so for your benefit alone,
> and to express my disdain
> for Lady Blanca de Borbón;
> To Medina Sidonia I shall order
> that she embroider a pennant
> red as the color of her blood,
> a handiwork tearfully sewn;
> such a pennant, Lady Maria,
> for you I'll have fashioned." (155:1–12)

The king's offering to María de Padilla not only implies his usurpation of Blanca's dowry—the estate of Medina Sidonia, previously seized by his mother from her rival, Leonor de Guzmán, and the site where Blanca, the legitimate queen, is imprisoned—but the sure promise of her death. As the virginal Blanca awaits her martyrdom, she not only forgives the king and his henchmen, but her rival as well:

> "Ya se a que venis, amigos,
> que mi alma lo sintio;

no avedes vosotros culpa,
pues el rrey os enbio;
de doña Maria de Padilla
tanpoco me quexo yo
que los daños que ella pudo
sienpre me los estorbo;
¡o Françia mi tierra buena!
¡o mi casa de Borbon!
oy cunplo xviij años
xviij, que mas non;
el rrey no me ha conoçido,
virgen y martir me voy;
yo os perdono la mi muerte;
tanbien al rrey mi señor; pues que matarme le plaze
alegre la çufro yo."

Translation:

"I know why you've come, friends,
I felt it in my soul;
not one of you is to blame,
since the king has sent you;
of Lady Maria de Padilla
I'll not complain to you
as from what harm she could
she has always protected me;
Oh, France, my good country!
Oh, my house of Bourbon!
Today is my eighteenth birthday
Eighteen, not a day more;
The King has not touched me,
I die virgin and martyr;
I forgive you my death;
as I forgive the King my lord;
since my death is his pleasure,
I accept it joyously." (156:33–48)

Although there is no historical evidence of Blanca's murder by Pedro, the ballad intentionally underscores the monarch's decision to sacrifice his saintly bride under his mistress's vindictive spell in order to debase him in front of his audience. Pedro's mistreatment of his legitimate Christian spouse, against the pope's wishes that he reconcile with Blanca, raised further suspicions of the king's reputed Jewish origins. Noted for his support of Jews, Pedro had earlier been criticized for lifting Alfonso XI's ban on usury that had penalized the Jewish community during the first half of the fourteenth century.[22] The Trastámara campaign against Pedro took advantage of the popular unrest spurred by rising costs and interest rates, and engaged the French and the pope in a renewed crusade against this "infidel." Enrique charged his brother with "increasing and enriching Moors and Jews and raising them to noble status."[23]

As the economy suffered the effects of the Black Plague and the civil war, the ballads contributed to the increasing antisemitic sentiment that resulted in attacks against Jews and the looting of Jewish neighborhoods that anticipated the violent pogroms of 1391.[24]

One anti-Petrine romance thus dwells on the apocryphal story circulated by the Trastámara faction of Pedro's Jewish origins, a thinly veiled accusation of his mother's adultery.[25] It was said that María de Portugal had originally given birth to a girl who was then replaced by the male child of a Jew named Pero Gil. Supporters of the Petrine faction were despectively called "emperegilados," a pun combining Pedro's averred father's name with the derogatory term "emperejilado," meaning "fancied up" and intimating an effeminate nature.[26] In the ballad *Cercada tiene a Baeza*, Pedro, as the traitor Pero Gil, fights with the Moors against the Christians:

> Cercada tiene a Baeça,
> esse Arraez Audalla Mir,
> con ochenta mil peones
> Cavalleros cinco mil.
> con el va esse traydor,
> el traydor de Pero Gil.

Translation:
> Baeza is now besieged
> by that Arraez Audalla Mir,
> with eighty thousand laborers,
> [and] five thousand knights.
> Accompanying him is that traitor,
> the traitor known as Pero Gil. (183:1–6)

The disparaging name conflates Pedro's perceived affinities with both Jews and Moors. In a letter to the pope, Enrique accused his brother of betraying the Christian cause: "you well know how the traitor, the heretical tyrant, Pero Gil, had the city of Ubeda destroyed by the Moors, entering, and burning and destroying it all, and killing many of its families and residents."[27]

Pedro's representation as Jew corresponds to María de Padilla's depiction as a witch in the romance *Mañanita de los reyes*. In this ballad, the court ladies' joyous requests to the king for Epiphany gifts for their lovers clash shockingly with María de Padilla's gruesome plea for Fadrique's head:

> Mañanita de los Reyes
> la primera fiesta del año,
> cuando damas y doncellas
> al Rey piden aguinaldo;
> unas le pedian seda,
> otras el fino brocado;
> otras le piden mercedes

para sus enamorados
Doña Maria, entre todas,
viene a pedirle llorando,
la cabeza del Maestre,
el Maestre de Santiago.

Translation:

Joyful Epiphany morn
the first holiday of the year,
when all the ladies and damsels
ask for a present from the King;
some would ask him for silk,
others delicate brocade;
others ask him special favors
for their lovers.
Lady María, alone among them
comes crying to ask from him
the head of the Maestre,
the Maestre of Santiago. (119:1–12)

Mirrer explains that this startling juxtaposition is in itself sufficiently intriguing in its "reportability" to continue to interest audiences, its timelessness confirmed by the *canto aguinaldero*, or offering song, still sung today in Segovia and Zamora during the Christmas holidays.[28] The ballad ending, however, projects a moral and religious judgment onto the historical figure of María de Padilla, as it condemns her spirit to fly forever through the air, rejected by both God and the devil:

Doña Maria de Padilla
por los aires va volando;
por sus buenas fechorias
no la quiere Dios ni el Diablo.

Translation:

Lady María de Padilla
goes flying through the air;
because of her many misdeeds
neither God nor the Devil
loves her. (122:89–92)

The antisemitic pairing of Pedro and María as Jew and witch also reflects on the class struggles that accompanied Castile's civil wars, since Pedro allied himself with the lower nobility and *legistas* along with the Jews, while Enrique represented the interests of the high nobility. The war resulted in a victory for conservative values: historians have remarked upon the largesse (the noted *mercedes enriqueñas*) with which Enrique treated his noble allies.[29] Grants of townships, land, rents, and jurisdictional rights, as well as the creation—for the first time in Castile—of new titles of nobility established wealthy families that consolidated the power of the aristocracy.[30] Enrique's support of the *mesta*, the league of noble sheepowners, and his increased taxation further destabilized the agrarian economy, leading in many cases to peasants' forced emigration and abandonment of their lands. In light of the worsening economic situation in Castile and the escalating tensions among Christians and Jews, the anti-Petrine ballads functioned as a political tool that at once drew attention away from the Trastámaras to Pedro's previous reign of terror and contributed to the further marginalization and mistreatment of Jews.

Indeed, Pedro's choice of a mistress over a wife who could give him a legitimate heir is presented in the ballads as a rejection of true Old Christian, Castilian values. His own father's abandonment of his wife for his mistress, a liaison that produced bastard progeny, ironically serves as an example of the chaotic familial situations brought on by extramarital relations, as the Trastámaras constantly strove to wrest power from the legitimate son. Historically, illicit love most often results in unstable political alliances; Pedro's daughter by María de Padilla married John of Gaunt, Duke of Lancaster, who in 1371 challenged Enrique's right to the Castilian throne to claim it for himself.[31]

The continuing struggles between the Trastámaras and Pedro's heirs are echoed in the romance *Por los campos de Xerez*, which prophesies the outcome of the civil war through a messenger from God in the guise of a shepherd. Composed after Pedro's death, the romance presages the events that led to the conflict between John of Gaunt and Enrique for the Castilian throne, with the former signing a treaty with Portugal against Castile and its ally, France.[32] Mirrer is right in stating that the romance seeks to affirm Trastámaran authority as "a predetermined consequence of [Pedro's] unjust rule."[33] But it also registers its strong opposition to the king's relations with María de Padilla, since their illicit union conceived the very reason for John of Gaunt's claim. The ballad enforces the people's wish for a rightful heir by stipulating that Pedro will be blessed with a son only if he returns to Blanca. If he persists in his sinful life, his daughters (who had in fact been legitimized by the Castilian Cortes and by the Bishop of Toledo) will take part in his downfall:

> "tienes presa a doña Blanca
> enojaste a Dios por ello;
> que si tornas a quererla
> dar te ha Dios vn heredero
> y si no, por cierto sepas
> te vendra desman por ello.
> Seran malas las tus hijas
> por tu culpa y mal gouierno;
> y tu hermano don Henrique
> te haura de heredar el reyno;
> moriras a puñaladas
> tu casa sera un infierno."

Translation:

> "You've imprisoned Lady Blanca
> by this act, you've angered God;
> if your love for her rekindles
> you'll be granted an heir by God;
> but if not, then know for certain
> that you'll suffer greatly for it.
> Your daughters will become evil
> through your fault and evil rule;
> and your brother, don Enrique
> will wrest the kingdom from you.
> You will die stabbed to death
> Your house will be a living hell." (154:43–54)

Even the few extant ballads on Pedro's behalf impute his political problems to women, depicting them either referentially as limited by their own sexuality, or metaphorically as symbols of Castile's financial woes. The *Romance de doña Blanca* attributes her husband's rejection to her amoral behavior: When Blanca is escorted from France by her brother-in-law Fadrique, the two commence an affair that produces an illegitimate child:

> Entre las gentes se suena
> que d'ese buen Maestre
> don Fadrique de Castilla
> la reina estaba preñada;
> otros dicen que parida.
> No se sabe de por cierto,
> pero el vulgo lo decia:
> Ellos piensan que es secreto,
> ya esto no se escondía.

Translation:

> People are gossiping
> that that so-called good Maestre,
> don Fadrique of Castile
> has gotten the Queen pregnant;
> others say she has given birth.
> No one can say for sure,
> but everyone has been talking:
> the two think it a secret,
> but it can no longer be hidden. (85–86:1–5; 7–10)

Analyzing the ballad's evaluative language, Mirrer points out that the argument, which presupposes the audience's knowledge of Blanca and Fadrique's death by the king, is set in the context of John of Gaunt's ongoing claim to the Castilian throne against Enrique's son, and aims to redirect the audience's sympathy from the Trastámaras to Pedro's family.[34] It is not coincidental, therefore, that Fadrique appears as the villain in the piece, dishonoring Blanca and timorously leaving her to face her predicament—and Pedro—alone. When the ballad assumes Blanca's voice, the personal pronoun carries with it both the acknowledgment of queenship and its responsibility, yet its qualifier, *desventurada*, already alludes to the punishment she will suffer at the hands of the king.

In this variant, Blanca is presented as no better than Fadrique; Pedro's abandonment cannot justify her incestuous relationship with her brother-in-law, and she admits she is even more to blame than he for having violated her role as queen:

> "Yo, desventurada Reina
> mas que cuantas son nascidas
> casaronme con el Rey
> por la desventura mia.
> De la noche de la boda
> nunca mas visto lo habia,
> y su hermano el Maestre
> me ha tenido compañia.
> Si esto ha pasado
> toda la culpa era mia.
> Si el rey don Pedro lo sabe,
> de ambos se vengaria;
> mucho mas de mi, la Reina
> por la mala suerte mia."

Translation:
> "I, the most hapless Queen
> of all who have ever been born
> was married to the King
> to my great misfortune.
> Not since our wedding night
> Have I ever seen him again,
> and his brother, the Maestre
> has kept me company.
> For this turn of events,
> I'm the only one to blame.
> if King Pedro finds out,
> he'll take vengeance on us both;
> much more so on me, the Queen,
> to my ill fortune." (87–88:53–66)

Since the ballad supports the Petrine faction, its narrative assumes a highly moralistic tone, punishing Blanca's illicit love for Fadrique first through her maternal grief at having to give up their child, then with her murder. Yet, as the audience was well aware, Pedro abandoned Blanca, not because of any dalliance with Fadrique, but because the French were not forthcoming in their promise of a large dowry.[35] Blanca's depiction as an unfaithful wife serves to remind the audience of France's participation in Pedro's overthrow. The adultery thus becomes a political allegory, as the romance denounces the current alliance of the Trastámara regime with France in favor of the rival Anglo-Portuguese alliance with Lancaster.[36]

The pro-Petrine romance opposing an affiliation with France was soon countered by an pro-Trastámara ballad censoring Pedro's rejection of French support. Again, the romance dehistoricizes the female figure by cleverly metamorphosing her into the various categories implied in her name. Thus, *En triste prision y ausencia* displaces Blanca from her historical position as queen to both the real and metaphorical target (*blanco*) of the king's scorn and, synechdochally, to the rejected French alliance. In that her devalued position allows for yet another play on her name, she also represents the debased currency of the realm, since at half a *maravedí*, the *blanca* was among the lowest fractional coins minted:

> Doña Blanca de Borbon
> mi padre me puso en Francia,
> no entendiendo que mi suerte
> tan en blanco me dejara.
> Bien pensó mi padre El Duque
> que su Blanca acá en España
> que valiera una corona
> y ante el Rey no valgo blanca.
> Como no me selló el Rey
> con el sello de su gracia
> soy moneda forastera
> que en este reino no pasa.
> Soy Blanca, o blanco do el Rey
> contino tira sus jaras
> y como no son de amor
> de ordinario me traspasan."

Translation:
> "Lady Blanca de Borbón
> in France my father named me,
> never thinking that my fortunes
> would disappoint me so bitterly.
> My father, the Duke, had thought
> that his Blanca, here in Spain
> would be worth a crown,
> yet to the King I'm less than nothing.
> Since the King has not stamped me
> with the seal of his approval
> I am but a foreign coin
> uncirculated in this kingdom.
> I am Blanca, or a bull's-eye
> for the King's constant arrows,
> and since they're not love's kind,
> they pierce me every time." (142:17–32)

The romance relies on two opposing conventions: the courtly love tradition of unrequited love and woman as exchange value in the symbolic economy. In the former, the Petrarchan conceit of the unfeeling lover applies to the woman; in the ballad, however, the conceit is reversed, as the pun on Pedro's name points to his—not Blanca's—harshness. The trope incorporates a seemingly blasphemous allusion to a New Testament passage: Pedro's name is taken to mean rock, evoking Christ's words to the apostle Simon Peter when appointing him leader of the new Church (Matthew 16:17–19). What is suggested, however, is not Peter's designation as the first bishop of Rome, but his remorse over having denied Christ during the Passion, unlike Pedro, who remains stonily unmoved by Blanca's suffering:

> "Pedro te dicen, que el nombre
> tiene a piedra semejanza
> y eres mas duro que piedra
> pues con sangre no te ablandas."

Translation:
> "You are called Peter, a name
> likened to rock
> and you are harder than rock,
> as blood does not temper you." (143:37–40)

The Petrarchan simile with its religious reverberations in part counteracts the materialist metaphor of Blanca as a foreign coin whose circulation is proscribed within the realm. Both tropes, however, have the effect of reducing the female figure to a visual sign within the libidinal economy. The pun on Blanca's name as *blanco*, a bull's-eye pierced repeatedly by the flint of a hardened husband, also resonates with mystical and mythological overtones, even while it negates its allusions—the object of desire erotically penetrated by love's arrows—since her victimization is motivated by Pedro's hatred rather than his love. The ballad's metaphoric language intends Blanca's final disappearance, as the ballad's first line, *en triste prisión y ausencia*, defines her *locus* and condition as both prison and absence, a space where she can ultimately neither be seen nor heard.

Similarly, the pun on Blanca as the Spanish coin *blanca* relies on the audience's perception of the loss of French funds for which Pedro was unduly criticized. The romance utilizes yet another pun on her name: Blanca reflects the whiteness of the French fleur-de-lis stamped on the *écu*, the rejected coin left unmarked by the Spanish eagle. The uncirculating French coin's high value is lowered to that of the blanca, one of the most worthless of Spanish currency, a stark reminder of the continuing monetary deflation during the Trastámara dynasty of the fourteenth and fifteenth centuries.[37] Alfonso XI had already devalued the currency in the early fourteenth century, and the Trastámara wars continued to deplete the treasury. After Pedro's death, Enrique devalued coinage to pay his troops, and in 1370 he again devalued the new coinage to one-third its worth.[38] By alluding to the economic difficulties caused by Pedro's rash actions and which had obliged increased taxation, the romances attempted to distract the audience from the abuses of the Trastámaras, whose own taxes were prompting bitter complaints from the peasants.[40] Blanca de Borbón's reification in the romances as both blanco and blanca, as the target of the king's ire on one hand and unwanted species on the other, reduces her to an entirely submissive position, subjected to Pedro's anger and final rejection. Forced to give up her specificity as wife and queen, she is instead transmuted into a sign of Franco-Castilian relations at their basest level.

We have seen how critics have commented on the romances' capacity for reinterpreting historical events by transforming them into philosophical abstractions. Mirrer speaks of the ballads' "human interest" that warrants their durability far beyond the historical moment, and gives as an example the *canto aguinaldero*, whose children's verses reappropriate for folklore a dehistoricized María de Padilla pleading every Christmas holiday for Fadrique's head. Recently, Sánchez Ortega has confirmed the identity of the María de Padilla invoked in the conjurations of sorceresses processed by the Inquisition, as that of Pedro's mistress.[40] Recalling María's reputed sexual powers, the following conjuration, one of the most well known taken from Inquisition records, demonizes her memory by linking her with popular devil figures such as *el diablo cojuelo*, Beelzebub, and Satan:

> "No bengo a quemar sal
> ni bengo a abrasar sal
> el coraçon de fulano
> bengo a quemar y abrasar
> con mi amor
> conjúrote sal
> con Satanas, con Barrabas
> con Bercebú, con Lucifer
> con el diablo Cojuelo
> con doña Maria de Padilla
> y con cuantos diablos
> están en el infierno . . .

Translation:

> "I come not to burn salt
> nor to consume it in fire,
> It is [lover's name's] heart
> that I come to burn and consume
> with my love.
> I conjure you, salt
> with Satan, with Barrabas
> with Beelzebub, with Lucifer

with the Lame Devil
with Lady María de Padilla
and with all the devils
that are in Hell . . . "[41]

The conjurations utilize the ballads' representation of María de Padilla as witch for their own purposes of "love magic," since the spells are usually recited over candles, chickpeas, or even bodily fluids to secure the return of wayward lovers.[42]

In her excellent study of another popular romance, *La muerte ocultada*, Beatriz Mariscal reminds us that ballad variations reflect different contexts, and shows how these poems' open-endedness allows for the expression of new social realities.[43] One striking illustration of just such a contextual change is the appropriation in 1609 by the *moriscos* of the ballad *En triste prisión y ausencia* as a means of lamenting their expulsion from Spain.[44] Here, the historical figure of Blanca de Borbón stands for a cultural group whose otherness is identified in the feminized terms of a rejected lover. The romance lends its poignancy to the moriscos' plight, as they are reflected in the abject figure of the scorned queen, her foreignness made all the more conspicuous by the Castilian king's repudiation.

In these three examples, the female protagonists are transformed and projected beyond the historical time frame of the ballad cycle to serve different social realities. The appropriations, moreover, confirm that the ballads' feminine presence can never be completely repressed and thus results in its supplementarity within other cultural contexts. Nonetheless, by fictionalizing women's roles, the romances effect a political agenda precisely at women's expense. Like María de Padilla in the children's canto aguinaldero and in the incantations, and like Blanca de Borbón in the morisco ballad, the female characters are infantilized, demonized, and objectified as "other."

Whether for or against the Trastámara dynasty, therefore, the ballads of the "Pedro the Cruel" cycle restrict their female characters to the binary subject positions of the good wife or the evil mistress in order to rally support for or to incite the audience against contemporary political situations. Yet by confining the female characters to oppositional categories (good/evil, rational/emotional, public/private, wife/mistress, virgin/whore) the romances exploit the tensions that these dichotomies create. Accordingly, they elicit an emotional response from the audience that rationalizes the exclusion of the historical feminine through its final transformation into literary convention. What we witness in the "Pedro el Cruel" romancero is the eradication of woman's historicity as she is instead displaced, commodified, and objectified as a circulating metaphor. Historical agency disappears once the female figure becomes literary *figura*.[45]

NOTES

1. See William J. Entwistle, "The *Romancero del Rey don Pedro* in Ayala and the *Cuarta crónica general*," *Modern Language Review* 25 (1930), 307–326. Pero López de Ayala's account remains an indispensable source even though, as Entwistle confirmed, his indictment of Pedro is based on the fictional ballads. See López de Ayala, "Crónica del rey don Pedro" in Cayetano Rosell, ed., *Crónicas de los reyes de Castilla* (Madrid: Biblioteca de Autores Españoles, 1875–1877), 66. For representations of the monarch in literature, see José Lomba y Pedraja, "El rey don Pedro en el teatro," in *Homenaje a Menéndez y Pelayo en el año vigésimo de su profesorado*, vol. 2 (Madrid: V. Suárez, 1899), 2:257–339.

2. Historian J. N. Hillgarth blames the Trastámaras for mounting an anti-Petrine campaign through legends, apparitions, and pseudo-prophesies repeated in historical chronicles and ballads alike. J. N. Hillgarth, *The Spanish Kingdoms: 1250–1516,* vol. 1 (Oxford: Clarendon Press, 1976), 372–375.

3. Louis Mirrer-Singer, *The Language of Evaluation: A Sociolinguistic Approach to the Story of Pedro el Cruel in Ballad and Chronicle*, Purdue University Monographs in the Romance Languages (Amsterdam: John Benjamins, 1986).

4. See Arleen B. Dallery, "The Politics of Writing (the) Body: *Ecriture féminine*," in Alison Jaggar and Susan Bordo, eds., *Gender/Body/Knowledge: Feminist Reconstructions of Being and Knowing* (New Brunswick and London: Rutgers University Press, 1989), 52–67.

5. See Hans Robert Jauss, "The Alterity and Modernity of Medieval Literature," in *New Literary History* 10 (Win. 1979), 181–117; and Angus MacKay, *Society, Economy and Religion in Late Medieval Castile* (London: Variorum Reprints, 1987).

6. See José Angel García de Cortázar, *La época medieval,* vol. 2 of *La historia de España,* Miguel Artola, director (Madrid: Alianza Editorial, 1988), 218; and Heath Dillard, *Daughters of the Reconquest: Women in Castilian Town Society, 110–1300* (Cambridge: Cambridge University Press, 1984). Despite their historical agency, however, noblewomen in medieval Hispanic oral literature are generally presented in relation to male figures. For an evaluation of women's roles in the Spanish epic as projections of knights' missions, see Juan Victorio, "La mujer en la épica castellana," *La condición de la mujer en la edad media. Actas del coloquio celebrado en la Casa de Velázquez, del 5 al 7 de noviembre de 1984*, (Madrid: Casa de Velázquez, 1986), 75–84.

7. Antonio Pérez Gómez, "Introduction," *Romancero del Rey don Pedro* (Valencia: La fonte que mana y corre, 1954). All of the ballads cited in this study were compiled by Pérez Gómez in his edition, and are indicated by page number followed by verse numbers. Translations are my own.

8. Henrique Florez, *Memorias de las reynas catholicas. Historia genealógica de la casa real de Castilla y León*, (Madrid: Marin, 1761), vol. 2, 605–606.

9. Florez, vol. 2, 611.

10. "Mientras doña María de Portugal [se ocupa] activamente en la política del país tanto en vida de Alfonso XI como durante el reinado de su hijo Pedro I, Leonor de Guzmán permanece casi en la sombra entregada a su función de madre prolífica y compañera fiel." María Helena Sánchez Ortega, "La mujer como fuente del mal: el maleficio," in *Manuscrits* 9 (January 1991), 41–81. See also María José and Pedro Voltes, *Las mujeres en la historia de España* (Madrid: Planeta, 1986), 49.

11. Leonor de Guzmán's son Fadrique was made Maestre de Santiago at the age of ten, and Enrique, Lord of Asturias, was expected to marry the daughter of Pere III of Cataluña. Hillgarth, vol. 1, 376.

12. See Marina Warner, *Alone of All Her Sex: The Myth and Cult of the Virgin Mary* (London: Weidenfeld and Nicolson, 1976). See also Julia Kristeva's psychoanalytical perspective on the

usurpation of maternal love by the patriarchal order, "Herética del amor," in *Escandalar* 6 (1983), 68–79.

13. According to Florez (2, 625), when Pedro imprisoned Blanca in the Alcázar at Toledo, María de Portugal sided with the Toledan nobility against his treatment of the queen. When María asked her stepsons for help, the battle, which took place at Toro, resulted in the deaths of Fadrique and various other nobles.

14. Florez, vol. 2, 613.

15. Florez, vol. 2, 623.

16. Hillgarth, 236.

17. Even Pedro's staunchest apologists could not not help speculating as to why he abandoned Blanca so soon after their wedding: "The King must have found less than he expected in the Queen. Some of the few who write about this, and other actions of the King, assert that he might be bewitched . . . some say with a necklace of charms made by María de Padilla to control him, others [say] from the Queen D. Blanca to separate him from Doña María, but none who say this believe it, and I even less (Algo devio de hallar menos el Rey de lo q[ue] esperava en la Reyna. Algunos de los pocos q[ue] escriven esta, y otras acciones del Rey, assientan q[ue] estava hechizado . . . vnos dizen q[ue] con vn collar de hechizos fabricados por Doña María de Padilla para traerle asi, otros, que fabricada por la Reyna D. Blanca para apartarle de Doña María, pero ninguno de los q[ue] lo quentan lo cree y yo menos.") Juan Antonio Vera y Figueroa, *El rei d. Pedro defendido* (Madrid: F. García, 1647), 15v.

18. "The Bishop of Palencia, D. Rodrigo (who wrote a century later) states that the discord between the king and Blanca was due to bewitchment, requested by María de Padilla, his concubine, and given by a Jew, whom she came by easily for this evil, since the queen requested the king to expel all Jews from the palace and the kingdom (El Obispo de Palencia D. Rodrigo [que escribió en el siglo siguiente] dice que la discordia entre el Rey y dña. Blanca provino de maleficio, solicitado por dña María de Padilla, su Concubina y dado por medio de un Judío, a quien halló pronto para la maldad a causa de que la reyna trataba con el Rey, que echasse fuera del Palacio y del reyno a todos los Judíos.)" (Florez, 631–632).

19. Hillgarth, vol. 1, 376.

20. The Coimbra of the romance is not the Portuguese town, but an archaic placename for Jumilla, the Murcian town conquered by Fadrique; cf. Entwistle, "Romancero del rey don Pedro," 319.

21. Hillgarth, vol. 1, 377. Another variant similarly depicts María de Padilla flaunting her sexual powers over Pedro asking for his brother's head, yet ends with the mistress safely locked up in a dungeon, reinstating the king to his rightful place in the patriarchy.

22. See Julio Valdeón Baruque, *Los conflictos sociales en el reino de Castilla en los siglos XIV y XV* (Madrid: Siglo Veintiuno, 1976).

23. "[A]creçentando e enrriqueçiendo los moros e los iudios e enseñoreandolos." L. Serrano, *Cartulario del Infantado de Covarrubias* (Madrid, 1930). Qtd. by Valdeón Baruque, 131.

24. Valdeón Baruque, 133–134.

25. Ramón Menéndez Pidal, *Romancero hispánico: Teoría e historia* (Madrid: Espasa-Calpe, 1968).

26. Luis Suárez Fernández, *El Canciller Ayala y su tiempo (1332–1407)*, (Alava: Consejo de Cultura, 1962).

27. Enrique's letter, dated 11 February 1369, states: "Bien sabedes en como el traydor, herege, tirano de Pero Gil fizo estruir la ciudad de Ubeda con los moros, e la entraron, e quemaron, e estruyeron toda, e mataron muchos de los vecinos de la dicha ciudad e moradores della." *Sermones de diversis*, Sermo II ("In Consecratione Pontificis Maximi") in Migne, *Patrologia latina*, 217, cols. 657–658. Qtd. in Joaquín Gimeno Casalduero, *La imagen del*

monarca en la Castilla del siglo XIV: Pedro el Cruel, Enrique II y Juan I (Madrid: Revista de Occidente, 1972), 104.

28. Mirrer-Singer, 1–2.

29. See Valdeón Baruque, 98–l00; and Luis Suárez Fernández, *Nobleza y monarquía. Puntos de vista sobre la historia política castellana del siglo XV* (Valladolid: Departamento de Historia Medieval, Universidad de Valladolid, 1975).

30. Historians disagree as to the extent of Enrique's *mercedes* and the benefits accrued the nobility; Julio Valdeón Baruque is clear in that they had a devastating effect on the peasants. Luis Suárez Fernández has spoken glowingly of Enrique's accomplishments in restoring public order, protecting the church, seeking wide popular support in seeing justice applied, and stabilizing the currency (*Nobleza*, 29, note 20). In a recent study, however, he notes the process of "aristocratization" that ensued in Castile: "the economy, society, culture, even life itself, was organized at the service of this dominant class, whose influence descends to the bottom levels of the populace." See his *Los trastámaras y los Reyes Católicos* (Madrid: Gredos, 1985).

31. Angus MacKay, *Spain in the Middle Ages: From Frontier to Empire 1000–1500*, (London, 1983).

32. Hillgarth, vol. 1, 387–388.

33. Mirrer-Singer, 67.

34. Mirrer-Singer, 43, 47.

35. Florez blames the ballads for spreading falsehoods about Blanca: "One hears that the King hated this unfortunate lady for having allowed herself to be courted and having sexual intercourse with D. Fadrique, the king's brother, while he brought her to Spain. But if this is based on popular songs, these should hardly receive any credit for such a serious, loathsome topic (Voz hay de que el Rey aborreció a esta desgraciada Señora por haverse dejado galantear y gozar de D. Fadrique, hermano del rey al tiempo de conducirla a España. Pero si esto se funda en canciones vulgares poco credito merecen para cosa tan grave, tan execrable.)" Florez, vol. 2, 632).

36. Hillgarth, vol. 1, 387.

37. At 22 carats, the French écu would later serve as model for the Spanish escudo tariffed at 350 maravedís, or the equivalent of 700 blancas. Earl J. Hamilton, *American Treasure and the Price Revolution in Spain* (Cambridge: Harvard University Press, 1934), 55.

38. Hillgarth, vol. 1, 391.

39. Valdeón Baruque, 103.

40. According to Sánchez Ortega ("La mujer," 76–81), the conjurations that mentioned Pedro's mistress were so well known during the Early Modern period that the Inquisitors called them "conjurations of María de Padilla." See also J. Blázquez Miguel, *Eros y tanatos. Brujería, hechicería y superstición en España* (Toledo: Arcano, 1989).

41. Spanish National Archives (AHN), Inquisition leg. 90, n.9. Qtd. by Sánchez Ortega, "La mujer," 78.

42. See María Helena Sánchez Ortega, "Sorcery and Eroticism in Love Magic," Mary Elizabeth Perry and Anne J. Cruz, eds., *Cultural Encounters: The Impact of the Inquisition in Spain and the New World* (Berkeley and Los Angeles: University of California Press, 1991), 58–92.

43. Beatriz Mariscal de Rhett, *La muerte ocultada*, Seminario Menéndez Pidal (Madrid: Gredos, 1985), 332.

44. The romance was included in the *Relación del sentimiento de los moriscos por su justo destierro de España, y el número y cantidad que se han embarcado dellos, assí hombres y mugeres, y niños de todas edades hasta aora. Y de las mandas que dexan hechas á iglesias y lugares píos, y otras cosas dignas de memoria. Lleva dos romances al fin muy gustosos. . . .* (Sevilla, 1610). See Pérez Gómez, 69.

45. A variant of this essay, "The Politics of Illicit Love in the 'Pedro el Cruel' Ballad Cycle," has been published in *ARV Scandinavian Yearbook of Folklore* 48 (1992), 1–16. I gratefully acknowledge research support from the University of California, Irvine, Organized Research Unit on Woman and the Image.

6

Pious and Political Images of a Habsburg Woman at the Court of Philip III (1598–1621)

Magdalena S. Sánchez

hree women formed the core of the Austrian Habsburg diplomatic network at the Spanish court of Philip III: Empress María, daughter of Charles V, served as a key diplomatic representative for the Austrian Habsburgs from her arrival at the Spanish court in 1582 until her death in Madrid in 1603.[1] Empress María's daughter, Archduchess Margaret (usually known as Margaret of the Cross—the religious name she took when she entered the convent of the Descalzas Reales in 1588), also served as the Austrian Habsburg's diplomatic representative until her death in 1633.[2] Philip III's wife and queen, Margaret of Austria, represented the Austrian Habsburg interests at the Spanish court from 1599 until her death in 1611.[3] All three women corresponded regularly with their Austrian Habsburg relatives and met with the Austrian Habsburg diplomats who were sent to the Spanish court. The Austrian Habsburgs expected the women to pressure Philip III for financial and military assistance to Central Europe and to ensure that Austrian Habsburg interests were not overshadowed at the Spanish court by those of any other country or potentate. The influence of all three women in the political relations between the two Habsburg branches is documented in personal correspondence between the women and their Austrian relatives, in the reports of the Austrian Habsburg diplomats in Madrid, and in the writings of court chroniclers and of individuals at the Spanish court. Nevertheless, because this influence was often indirect and private, and because they and others often described their influence in the language of familial devotion and religious concerns, historians have ignored the political and diplomatic role that these women actually played.

In part, the lack of historical concern for the political role of these Habsburg women stems from historians' lack of scholarly interest in the reign of Philip III. The reign of Philip III has failed to receive much attention from historians because of its association with weak political leadership and with the beginning of Spanish decline.[4] With Philip III began what Spanish historians traditionally have called the period of the "lesser Austrian" monarchs (*Los Austrias menores*) (i.e., Philip III, Philip IV, Charles II) to distinguish these monarchs from the "great Austrians" of the sixteenth century (i.e., Charles I and Philip II).[5] Although historians have modified their negative impressions of Philip IV, Philip III still retains the reputation of a weak, dim-witted monarch who preferred hunting and travelling to governing and therefore turned over the reins of power to his royal favorite, the Duke of Lerma.[6] Historians have taken for granted the Duke of Lerma's influence and power over Philip III, and have not fully considered the influence that other individuals exercised at the court or the limits of Lerma's power.[7] The means through which Lerma exercised political control has only recently received some scholarly attention; nevertheless, court politics and factionalism during Philip III's reign remain to be studied.[8] Philip III's reign, therefore, has been ignored largely because of the traditional negative interpretation of the monarch and his *privado*.[9] This chapter analyzes one aspect of the politics of Philip III's court: the political role of Habsburg women (in particular, that of the queen, Margaret of Austria) and the manner in which women voiced their political concerns. In so doing, this chapter begins to redress the traditional interpretation of Philip III's reign by arguing that factions opposed to that of the Duke of Lerma's were active throughout the reign, and that the monarch listened to voices other than those of the Duke of Lerma and his associates.

❦

The historical image of Margaret of Austria, Empress María, and Margaret of the Cross has in large part been shaped by men whose purpose was to create a devotional and idyllic picture of these Habsburg women. This picture, presented in eulogies and biographies written after the women's deaths, set up the Habsburg women as examples of feminine virtue and proper behavior for aristocratic women. This image of Empress María, Margaret of Austria, and Margaret of the Cross did not correspond to the social reality of their lives; that is, the authors portrayed only select facets of the lives of the Habsburg women, facets which corresponded to the picture of women that men wished to portray, and even these facets were colored in a biased light. There was, for instance, little or no mention of the political sides of the Habsburg women's lives. This devotional literature was at root pedagogical because the authors aimed not only to eulogize and praise the women, but also to make them models for other generations of royal women. In fact, male relatives of the women usually commissioned the authors to write the laudatory works.

Margaret of Austria, Empress María, and Margaret of the Cross clearly transcended the roles proscribed for them by men. Despite the attempts of their biographers to depict and define them in strictly pious terms, the comments of individuals around the women demonstrate that all three women concerned themselves with political issues. Although the three Habsburg women followed seventeenth-century notions of piety and, like many Spanish aristocratic women, they patronized religious institutions, their piety did not preclude a concern for political issues, particularly those matters that affected their relatives. These women often used religious devotion and familial duties as a means to express their political concerns; that is, they consciously couched their political demands in the language of family and piety. Moreover, the reports of their piety come to us from male observers, who no doubt thought religious devotion appropriate of royal women.

The picture presented in biographies and eulogies cannot be dismissed because of its overt bias. Men perpetuated this image of royal women, an image that served to tell later generations that royal women had no political role and were supposed to spend their lives in prayer and in performing charitable deeds. This portrayal corresponded to early modern notions that women should speak only through prayer and examples. This chapter will examine the devotional representation of one of the Habsburg women, Margaret of Austria, and will then consider other, more political images of Philip III's queen. My purpose is to analyze how men wanted to perceive royal women, how they used the printed word to restrict female action and power, and how historians have been able to write the history of politics without considering the role played by royal women. We can thus ascertain the power of male images of women, for in describing women in strictly devotional terms, men attempted to marginalize these women and to obscure their political importance. In the process, however, we can also discover the real political power enjoyed by Habsburg women at Philip III's court.

🐛

Margaret of Austria, Philip III's queen from 1599 until her death in 1611, and an influential critic of the Duke of Lerma, came from the Styrian branch of the Austrian Habsburgs. Margaret had supposedly chosen the life of a nun before being betrothed to Philip III.[10] When she arrived in Spain in 1599, Margaret of Austria was only fifteen years old, but her young age did not prevent her from stating her opinions and from defending the interests of her Austrian Habsburg relatives at the Spanish court. The queen gave birth to eight children between 1601 and 1611, and she gained particular honor from giving birth to four sons, among them the future Philip IV.

When Margaret of Austria died in 1611 at the age of twenty-six, rumors abounded that she had been poisoned by the Duke of Lerma's close associate, Rodrigo Calderón (whom the queen had criticized openly).[11] This accusation eventually led to a criminal investigation of Calderón in 1621, but although he was convicted of other charges, Calderón was acquitted of having poisoned the queen. Numerous Spaniards bemoaned the great loss Margaret's death meant for the Spanish kingdoms; there were even those who claimed that Margaret of Austria had died a martyr.[12] This image of the saintly queen sacrificed for her subjects and for her rejection of the dishonest practices at the Spanish court was established at the queen's death. It was perhaps the most powerful image created of Margaret of Austria and one that eulogists and her biographer perpetuated in order to use her as an example of a virtuous wife, mother, and queen, as well as to voice their criticism of the Spanish court during the reign of Philip III.

The predominant image of Margaret of Austria fostered by male observers was that of a devout and humble queen who was submissive to males around her. In this way, the queen served as a "mirror for queens."[13] Diego de Guzmán, Philip III's royal almoner who wrote the queen's biography,[14] noted Margaret's complete obedience to her confessor, Richard Haller, a Jesuit like Guzmán.[15]

> To her confessor she was so submissive and obedient that she could tell him what she felt with complete liberty, as if she were a novice in the faith. And on certain occasions she said to him, Father tell me . . . what I am in conscience obliged to do, and I will do it, even if it costs me my life. . . . On another occasion she said that she would not be able to retain a confessor who did not tell her the simple, clear truth.[16]

Jerónimo de Florencia, a Jesuit priest and court preacher who delivered several eulogies at Margaret of Austria's death, also emphasized the queen's submission to her confessor.[17] Moreover, according to Florencia and Guzmán, Margaret of Austria treated Richard Haller (and all priests) with tremendous deference, something that a queen was not commanded to do but which was mandatory for a religious novice.[18] In this way, she exemplified the saintly, pure queen who modeled herself after a nun and thus confirmed and even surpassed the established social norms for women and for rulers. As Florencia stated, "in her person she had the purple of a queen but in her soul lay the inclination and love of the virginal state of nuns."[19]

Margaret of Austria supposedly fit the mold of obedient wife, living under her husband's orders, spending time in prayer when she could not be with him. She followed the advice given to wives of all social classes to stay in the house when ordered to do so by her husband, without attending any social functions and without speaking to anyone.[20] Diego de Guzmán recorded that when Philip III went to Valencia to attend a meeting of the Cortes (parliamentary body), he left Margaret of Austria in Madrid at the Descalzas monastery with instructions to remain there until he returned. Guzmán noted that the queen hated to be left behind, but she agreed to follow her husband's orders. "Never did a wife . . . with the great love she had for her husband, suffer so much to be away from him . . . no other [wife] was so resigned in this and in everything which he [her husband, Philip III] ordered her. She was certainly a rare example in both things."[21] While at the Descalzas, according to Diego de Guzmán, the queen did not leave the monastery except with the express consent of her husband. Guzmán indicated two such occasions, one to attend a mass presided over by Guzmán himself at the Jesuit residence in Madrid, and the other to visit orphans.[22] An aristocratic woman was expected to concern herself with piety and with charitable deeds, and thus it was acceptable for the queen to leave the monastery on the two occasions that Guzmán noted.

According to Jerónimo de Florencia, Margaret of Austria was a "brave and strong" (*valerosa y fuerte*) woman.[23] Florencia claimed that the queen thought always of her salvation, and in doing so she demonstrated masculine strength and a rational mind. In order to concentrate on salvation, according to Florencia, one needed a manly heart (*pecho varonil*), something that the queen possessed. Florencia compared a woman's (masculine) strength to that of military squadrons. "The queen showed this [manly strength] in the ease with which she conquered her desires and preferences, always giving in to reason, for which more strength is needed than that [strength] to conquer squadrons."[24] Florencia undoubtedly held the common early modern notion that women lacked rational minds and their actions were subject to everchanging humors and emotions.[25] His description of Margaret of Austria and the strength necessary to deal with matters on a rational basis reflected the assumption that reason was a masculine characteristic, and that by demonstrating rational thought Margaret of Austria had acted like a man.[26] The queen's ability to overcome her female nature, in other words, a nature dominated by passion and uncontrollable emotions, was extraordinary in Florencia's opinion, and he described this ability as masculine because only men were thought capable of conquering their emotions. In so doing, Florencia paid the ultimate male compliment to Margaret of Austria.

The image of Margaret of Austria as a strong, manly woman also appeared in the eulogy given by Fray Andrés de Espinosa in the funeral honors for the queen given at the University of Salamanca.[27] Espinosa characterized Margaret of Austria as a brave woman who possessed all possible virtues. Espinosa explained that in saying that the queen was a strong woman (*mujer fuerte*), he meant that she was "adorned with all virtues." A virtuous woman, in Espinosa's description, should be saintly, chaste, charitable, and pious.[28] But a virtuous woman who was truly brave and strong should be married and should be loyal to her husband, and demonstrate strength and justice on all occasions.[29] Espinosa succeeded in defining Margaret of Austria strictly in her position as a wife; she could be virtuous and strong because she was subordinate to a man. Following Espinosa's reasoning, an unmarried woman who was not under male authority could not be strong and completely virtuous. Association with a man provided strength to a woman, because by nature women lacked moral and physical strength.[30] Margaret of Austria, in Espinosa's eulogy, was mostly an adjunct to Philip III. According to Espinosa, the queen was the "joy to our king ... and crowned and adorned his regal head."[31] Yet Espinosa claimed that a queen gained status from her marriage to a king; as a king was supposed to be a shepherd to his people, so a queen as the king's wife could also be considered a shepherdess to his subjects.[32]

Margaret of Austria's legacy to Spain, in the opinion of her eulogist, Jerónimo de Florencia, was twofold. On the one hand, she provided a model for female conduct, particularly for other aristocratic women. By exercising her hands and not her mouth, and by controlling her emotions, she also served as an example to her female servants. On the other hand, her legacy applied to men as well as women. Florencia reminded all Spaniards that, with her death, Margaret of Austria had gone to heaven and would thereafter act as an intercessor with God for her subjects. Her death should remind all Spaniards of the imminence of their own deaths, and should cause them to pray to the queen for her assistance as well as to follow her example of a life spent in prayer and in charitable deeds. Florencia thus clearly stated what was the place of women, particularly royal women, in the secular and the divine hierarchy: on earth they were silent, industrious, and pious, good wives, mothers, and queens; in heaven they interceded on behalf of others.[33] In both cases, women played roles subordinate to men, and constantly had to sacrifice themselves and their own goals for those of others. Florencia certainly idealized the queen and held her up as an example of purity and feminine virtue. Nevertheless, his idealization of the queen, like the Catholic idealization of the Virgin Mary, gave the impression that few women ever reached the heights set for them by men, and that when they did, it was by subordinating themselves to the will and goals of men.

Jerónimo de Florencia's and Diego de Guzmán's writings about Margaret of Austria were certainly rhetorical pieces that employed the literary conventions of their genre: eulogy and biography, respectively. Nevertheless, Florencia's and Guzmán's accounts of the queen were meant to be read by other generations of royal women and men and were meant to create a model for a queen. Although royal women might deviate from this model, and although individual women's failures to live up to the model might have been widely recognized, the model remained the standard for acceptable female behavior. A royal woman's political activities were rarely if ever mentioned in such pieces as funeral sermons or biographies. These funeral sermons and biographies often entered other women's collections, and were meant to inspire similar behavior in the women who read and collected them. Margaret of Austria, for example, owned a copy of the eulogy given by Jerónimo de Florencia at Empress María's funeral in 1603. Ideally, the queen was to model herself after the image that Florencia presented of Empress María, an image that accentuated the empress's piety and familial devotion (despite the fact that she had exercised important political roles as joint regent of Castile from 1548 to 1551, and empress of Central Europe from 1564 to 1576.)[34]

Describing Margaret of Austria in terms of her piety and maternal characteristics could sometimes be a thin disguise for criticism of her influence over Philip III. Matías de Novoa, court chronicler, secretary to Philip III, and close supporter of Rodrigo Calderón and the Duke of Lerma, painted a picture of Margaret of Austria as the perfect royal wife: "a strong mother, prudent, religious, and wise . . . her palace is a house of prayer, her ladies-in-waiting and servants live in imitation of her example . . . she frees republics from vices; she desires and persuades the best and the most useful [things] for the government."[35] In his description of the queen, however, Novoa hinted at her interest in governing, although he chose to present this interest as that of a devout mother for her child. Nevertheless, Novoa criticized the queen for what he considered extreme and naive piety. This piety, according to Novoa, at times clouded Margaret of Austria's vision and made her overly susceptible to the dangerous counsel of priests and nuns.

The chronicler detailed the fall in 1618 of Lerma's close associate, Rodrigo Calderón, an event that seems to have wounded Novoa personally, and he ascribed Calderón's fall to the influence of religious figures over Philip III. This influence, according to Novoa, dated back to the time of Margaret of Austria. In his memoirs, Novoa described Margaret of Austria as a credulous woman, guided solely by her piety and her love for Philip III and therefore blind to the machinations of what Novoa considered profit-seeking nuns and priests. The chronicler had in mind the specific influence of Fray Juan de Santa María, confessor of the Infanta Doña María (daughter of Philip III and Margaret of Austria) and writer of the political treatise entitled *Tratado de república y policía christiana* that was highly critical of *privados*.[36] Novoa emphasized what he considered to be the pernicious influence exercised by Santa María over Philip III in the last few years of the monarch's life. Novoa also criticized the influence of Mariana de San José, an Augustinian nun handpicked by Margaret of Austria to serve as the first prioress of the Convent of the Encarnación.[37] If Novoa is to be believed, Santa María and Mariana de San José were responsible for Philip III's dismissal of Rodrigo Calderón, and even of the Duke of Lerma. The chronicler ultimately insinuated that these religious figures gained influence over the king through Margaret of Austria's gullibility. Novoa's praise for the queen thus hid a deeply felt criticism of the queen's supposed blind faith in nuns and priests. His criticism also demonstrates that Margaret's influence at her husband's court was often thought to be through religious individuals, and that this influence was thought to have shaped politics in the latter years of Philip III's reign, even after the queen's death in 1611.

Novoa's chronicle clearly shows that all men did not describe Margaret of Austria in such laudatory terms as Jerónimo de Florencia and Diego de Guzmán. Court chroniclers and ambassadors depicted her in a less devotional light. These authors often noted the queen's foibles, her personality, her political voice, and her personal interests. Court chronicles and diplomatic correspondence were not devotional genres, and their authors could therefore afford to speak more frankly about the political activities of women. In so doing, these male observers commented on the role that royal women actually played at the Spanish court of Philip III and gave a male opinion on how the female relatives of a monarch should act.

Venetian ambassadors noted the queen's interest in political matters and her desire to have a say in the making of decisions. The Venetian ambassador, Ottaviano Bon, reported in 1602 that Queen Margaret of Austria "is capable of great things, so much so that she would govern if she could in a manner different from that of the king [Philip III]."[38] In fact, Bon implied that the queen's political intuition was sounder than her husband's. Francesco Soranzo, Venetian ambassador in Spain from 1598 to 1600, reported that Philip III loved his queen very dearly. Soranzo described Margaret of Austria as "astute and very skillful [*grandemente artificiosa*] in securing the king's love . . . she wants to be respected and known as queen."[39] Although Soranzo implied that Margaret of Austria was an intelligent and resourceful queen, he added that she "likes to have others think that she has great authority with the king, but she does not have it [authority] except in petitions of little importance."[40] According to Soranzo, the Duke of Lerma watched the queen and ensured that she had little influence with the king. Ottaviano Bon, who noted Margaret of Austria's political acumen, also reported that she was "controlled [*circondata*] by the Duchess of Lerma and the Duke her husband . . . and the king has greater estimation of them [the Duke and Duchess of Lerma] than of her [the queen] in many things, which makes her [the queen] reticent, melancholic, and without any authority."[41] Bon thus indirectly criticized the king for not following the intelligent counsel of his wife and preferring the counsel of individuals who were obviously motivated by self-interest. The ambassador also made the connection between disapproval of the ways of the Spanish court with the rise of melancholic humors in a female.[42]

The more frequent references to Margaret of Austria center around her unhappiness at the court, an unhappiness brought on by the Duke of Lerma's influence over Philip III. Hans Khevenhüller, the imperial ambassador in Madrid, detailed a conversation he had with the queen in which Margaret of Austria expressed her discontent with the Spanish court. Khevenhüller reported that the queen was so unhappy that she had told him that she would "much rather be a nun in a convent in Goricia (Styria) than Queen of Spain."[43] Khevenhüller attributed this unhappiness to the Duke of Lerma's attempts to isolate Philip III from Margaret of Austria. According to Khevenhüller, Lerma had gone so far as to interfere in the private moments that the king and queen shared by instructing her not to speak about political matters with the king at any time, and especially not in her moments alone at night with Philip III. To ensure the queen's compliance, Lerma threatened to arrange trips for Philip III that would leave Margaret of Austria alone in Madrid. He also threatened to remove María Sidonia, the queen's lady-in-waiting and closest friend, from the court.[33] These were potent threats for a young queen who had difficulty speaking Castilian and who was far away from her family.

Margaret of Austria, however, used acceptable "feminine tools" to combat Lerma's maneuverings. Luis Cabrera de Córdoba recorded the queen's reaction to the physical absence of Philip III. In an entry from 1601, the chronicler noted that the queen was ill and that the illness was a result of her displeasure with the king's absence and the attempt to control her servants. "This illness has been attributed to the sorrow she felt in His Majesty's [Philip III's] departure because he did not take her with him as he had promised her several days before, and to the displeasure caused by not allowing her to be served by those servants she brought with her from Germany [*Alemania*], and of other [things] which go against her desires."[45] According to the court chronicler, the queen's health reflected her state of mind. Cabrera de Córdoba collected the rumors of the Spanish court in his chronicle. Thus, what he reported implied that many Spaniards believed that the queen was unhappy, and that her unhappiness and illness were directly connected to the Duke of Lerma's attempts to control her. Margaret of Austria's illness did cause Philip III to return to the royal palace and remain with her until her health improved.

Lerma's efforts to remove María Sidonia from the court failed, as did his attempts to send the queen's Jesuit confessor, Richard Haller, back to Central Europe. The latter case demonstrates the power that Margaret of Austria had over Philip III. In the original instructions that Philip II had sent to Margaret of Austria's mother detailing the conditions for the marriage between Margaret and Philip III, the Spanish king had stated that Margaret of Austria would receive a Spanish confessor upon arrival in the Spanish kingdoms.[46] Despite these instructions, and despite Lerma's open hostility toward the queen's confessor, Margaret managed to maintain her German Jesuit confessor up until her death in 1611. Lerma also did not succeed in silencing the queen. In fact, Margaret of Austria questioned Lerma's political and financial policies, and went so far as to warn Philip III that the *Junta de Desempeño*, set up by Lerma in 1603 to improve the monarchy's financial situation, had only worsened Spain's economic problems.[47]

Despite the attempts of biographers and eulogists to deny that Margaret of Austria exercised a political voice at her husband's court, and despite chroniclers' negative assessments of the impact of the queen's advice, Margaret of Austria did succeed in voicing her opinions and winning the ear and the support of Philip III. The queen consistently sought to negotiate favorable marriages for her sisters, and successfully arranged for them to marry important princes. In order to do this, she negotiated with Rudolf II for his assistance in arranging advantageous matches. Rudolf regularly wrote to Margaret of Austria asking her for assistance in negotiating issues with Philip III. Hans Khevenhüller also visited the queen regularly to convey messages from Rudolf II, and to ask her to intervene with Philip III in the Austrian Habsburgs' favor. Margaret of Austria always assured Khevenhüller that she would do her best, and that she always had Rudolf's best interests in mind. In turn, however, she expected Rudolf to meet her demands and help arrange favorable marriages for her sisters.[48]

❦

The negotiation of marriages was an area in which women were allowed to and even expected to interfere.[49] Thus it is not surprising that Philip III supported Margaret of Austria's wishes, and even got the Duke of Lerma to speak to Khevenhüller and remind him of the need to press for favorable marriages for the queen's siblings.[50] Yet the queen's forceful pursuit of the issue, and her ability to make her intervention with Philip III contingent upon Rudolf reciprocating with assistance in the marriage arrangements, shows Margaret's political astuteness and her skills as a negotiator.

Khevenhüller employed the queen's influence on numerous occasions. In requesting the queen's support, the ambassador did not confine himself to minor issues or issues traditionally thought to be feminine. Khevenhüller went so far as to ask for Margaret's help in two of the major conflicts between Philip III and Rudolf II: Spanish assistance to Rudolf in the war against the Turks, and Spanish restitution of imperial fiefs in Italy (particularly the fief of Finale.)[51] The Austrian Habsburgs certainly considered Margaret to be an essential link at the Spanish court because they consistently directed their requests to her, and asked her to take their requests to Philip III.

Margaret of Austria was particularly successful in getting Spanish aid for her brother, Archduke Ferdinand. In October, 1600, the queen convinced Philip III to give Ferdinand a monthly stipend of 5000 ducats.[52] Ferdinand valued his sister's influence, and even after Margaret's death in 1611, Ferdinand continued to use her memory to negotiate matters at the court. In his instructions to an ambassador he was sending to the Spanish court in 1613, Ferdinand listed individuals at the Spanish court on whom the ambassador could count because they had had great affection for Margaret of Austria.[53] It is noteworthy that Philip III's pursuit of his claims to the Bohemian and Hungarian thrones—claims that brought him into direct competition and conflict with Archduke Ferdinand—did not begin in earnest until after Margaret's death. Although the issue had been brought up by Guillén de San Clemente, the Spanish ambassador in central Europe, as early as 1603, and again by his successor, Baltasar de Zúñiga in 1611, it did not receive serious attention until 1612.[54] Margaret's influence with Philip III was personal and familial; they had an affectionate, close relationship, particularly after Margaret bore a son in 1605. The king listened to her requests and to her comments, as for example in 1610 when, following her advice and that of Margaret of the Cross, the king agreed to consider Rudolf

II's request to have princes treated the same as Spanish grandees at the court.[55] Although Venetian ambassadors claimed that the queen was unable to circumvent Lerma's influence, and that she remained frustrated in her attempt to have a political say, Margaret of Austria nonetheless did reach Philip III, and because of this she consistently proved to be a threat to the Duke of Lerma and his network of power and influence.

❧

Philip III did not comment upon his wife's role in politics, or at least none of his comments have survived. However, in his advice to his daughter, Ana, when she married Louis XIII of France, Philip III did note what he thought to be a queen's proper role. He first of all advised his daughter to guard her faith and devotion to God "from whose hand we receive the crown which we have."[56] After her trust in God, she was to "have faith and true love for her husband." Philip III knew that his young daughter would need councillors to advise her. He therefore recommended that she take advice from "wise, prudent, and experienced men," but he also advised her that "in no way should you interfere in matters of government or justice, because this does not concern you. [Concern yourself with these matters] only if the king, your husband, orders you to do so, and then show preference for pity and clemency [*misericordia y clemencia*]."[57] In this advice to his daughter, Philip III clearly argued that a queen should not interfere in political matters. Moreover, a queen was to be primarily a wife, obedient to her husband, and devoted to God. Her public acts revolved around charity and piety, the accepted public domain for women. Philip III believed that his own wife had fulfilled these roles, because he advised his daughter to follow her mother's example and to study Margaret of Austria's biography which Diego de Guzmán was writing.[58] At least the monarch knew that the biography that Guzmán would write would present the proper image of the queen, if not a completely accurate representation of Margaret of Austria.

In these instructions to his daughter, Philip III also warned her against people who gossiped (*parlerais*) and advised her to investigate matters secretly before believing everything that was told her.[59] The Spanish monarch knew well the ways of the court, but his advise also demonstrates that the king believed that females were too credulous and easily manipulated. The king clearly subscribed to the notion that gossip and idle talk plagued females in particular. Finally, in his letters to Ana after she married Louis XIII, Philip III consistently referred to the need to produce an heir. He went so far as to question his daughter as to how often her husband slept with her.[60] Philip III obviously thought that, to become a woman, his daughter had to become a mother. As he wrote her in November, 1616, "I am anxious that you become a woman; I could benefit from that . . . and from you giving me a grandson soon."[61] To Philip III, queen, wife, and mother were intimately connected, and all three roles were subsumed under the category of "woman."

❦

Jerónimo de Florencia, Diego de Guzmán, and other eulogists of Margaret of Austria created portraits of a virtuous Habsburg woman who was committed to her family and to her religion. Because these authors had the express purpose of writing commemorative works of a woman whose life could serve as a model for other women, they did not choose to highlight her political capacities, or to note any conflict between Margaret and the male hierarchy. Royal women, and certainly Margaret of Austria, did not always conform to these devotional models set up by men. Rumors often circulated at the Spanish court that hinted at the frustration which the Habsburg queen felt and at her attempts to voice her political concerns. Nevertheless, these rumors remained merely rumors and could not form part of the official, court-sanctioned biographies of a Habsburg royal woman. Chroniclers might mention these rumors, but then the accuracy of chronicles was generally questioned. To substantiate the rumors and to include them in literature that other generations of women would read would be to condone female discontent with the existing male political structure—a totally unacceptable occurrence in a patriarchal court.

NOTES

1. Empress María was Philip II's sister, and was Philip III's aunt and grandmother (because Philip III was the son of her daughter, and Philip II's fourth wife, Anna.) On Empress María, see Rodrigo Mendes Silva, *Admirable vida . . . de la enclarecida Emperatriz María, hija del siempre invicto Emperador Carlos V* (Madrid, 1655); María del Carmen Blas y Díaz Jiménez, *La Emperatriz Doña María de Austria*, Ph.D. diss. (Madrid: Universidad Complutense, 1950); Friedrich Edelmayer, entry on "María (de Austria)" in *Neue Deutsche Biographie*, vol. 16 (Berlin, 1990), 174–175; Elías Tormo, *En las Descalzas Reales* (Madrid: Junta de Iconografía Nacional, 1917); Magdalena S. Sánchez, "Empress María and the Making of Political Policy in the Early Years of Philip III's Reign," Alain Saint-Saëns, ed., *Religion, Body and Gender in Early Modern Spain* (San Francisco: Mellen Research University Press, 1991), 139–147; Helga Widorn, *Die Spanischen Gemahlinnen der Kaiser Maximilian II., Ferdinand III. und Leopold I.*, Ph.D. diss. (University of Vienna, 1960).

2. On Margaret of the Cross, see Fray Juan de Palma, *Vida de la serenissima infanta Sor Margarita de la Cruz, Religiosa Descalza de Santa Clara* (Sevilla, 1653). On the history of the Descalzas Reales, see Fray Juan de Carrillo, *Relación de la real fundación del Monasterio de las Descalzas Reales de Santa Cruz de la villa de Madrid* (Madrid: Luis Sánchez, 1616); Elías Tormo, *En las Descalzas Reales*, Nicolás Álvarez Solar-Quintes, *Reales cédulas de Felipe II y adiciones de Felipe III en la escritura fundacional del Monasterio de las Descalzas de Madrid* (Madrid: Instituto de Estudios Madrileños, 1962); Juan de Contreras (Marqués de Lozoya), *Las Descalzas Reales* (Madrid: Instituto de Estudios Madrileños del Consejo Superior de Investigaciones Científicas, 1970).

3. On Margaret of Austria, see Diego de Guzmán, *Reina católica. Vida y muerte de D. Margarita de Austria, Reyna de España* (Madrid: Luis Sánchez, 1617).

4. On the subject of Spanish decline, see John H. Elliott, "Self-perception and Decline in Early Seventeenth-Century Spain," *Past and Present* 74 (1977), 41–61; Elliott, "The Decline

of Spain," *Past and Present* 20 (1961), 52–75; Earl J. Hamilton, "The Decline of Spain," *Economic History Review*, 1st ser., 8 (1938), 168–79.

5. See, for example, Antonio Domínguez Ortiz, *Crisis y decadencia de la España de los Austrias* (Barcelona: Editorial Ariel, 1969); Jean-Paul Le Flem et al., *La Frustración de un imperio*, vol. 5 of *Historia de España*, Manuel Tuñón de Lara, director (Barcelona: Editorial Labor, 1982).

6. On the reevaluation of Philip IV, see R. A. Stradling, *Philip IV and the Government of Spain, 1621–1665* (New York: Cambridge University Press, 1988); John H. Elliott, *The Count-Duke of Olivares. The Statesman in an Age of Decline* (New Haven and London: Yale University Press, 1986); John Elliott and Angel García Sanz, *La España del Conde Duque de Olivares. Encuentro internacional sobre la España del Conde Duque de Olivares celebrado en Toro los Dias 15–18 de Septiembre de 1987* (Valladolid: Secretariado de Publicaciones, Universidad de Valladolid, 1990). It is interesting that although Stradling dedicates himself to improving the image that historians have of Philip IV, he insists on retaining and even emphasizing the negative impression of Philip III. Stradling describes Philip III as "that miserable monarch." *Philip IV and the Government of Spain*, 18.

7. Historians have argued that the Duke of Lerma's power decreased after 1612, and that his son, the Duke of Uceda, exercised much influence at the court in the latter years of Philip III's reign. Lerma indirectly assisted his son in his political aspirations by increasingly delegating greater authority to him. This was particularly the case during Lerma's periodic bouts of melancholy, which often occurred at times of personal crisis such as Lerma experienced in 1608 with Pedro de Franqueza's arrest and in 1612 with the accusations against Rodrigo Calderón of having poisoned the queen. Although Uceda did not immediately challenge his father directly or openly, he profited from greater authority and began to usurp the very networks that Lerma had set up. By 1615, Lerma's continued support of Rodrigo Calderón, who by then had been discredited at the Spanish court, caused the *privado*'s influence to diminish greatly and in turn caused Uceda to break with his father openly and side with Philip III's confessor, Luis de Aliaga. See Antonio Feros Carrasco, "Gobierno de corte y patronazgo real en el reinado de Felipe III," (Madrid: Tesina de Licenciatura, Universidad Autónoma, 1986), 110–123; and John H. Elliott, *The Count-Duke of Olivares*, 34.

8. Antonio Feros Carrasco, "Gobierno de corte,"; Antonio Feros Carrasco, "Felipe III," in *La Crisis del Siglo XVII*, vol. 6 of *Historia de España* (Barcelona: Planeta Editorial, 1988), 9–67.

9. Only recently have scholars begun to devote more attention to Philip III's reign. See the articles by Peter Brightwell, "The Spanish Origins of the Thirty Years' War," *European Studies Review* 9 (1979), 409–431; "Spain and Bohemia: the Decision to Intervene,"*European Studies Review* 12 (1982), 117–141; "Spain, Bohemia, and Europe, 1619–1621,"*European Studies Review* 12 (1982), 371–399; "The Spanish System and the Twelve Years Truce," *The English Historical Review* 89 (1974), 270–292. See also the articles by Patrick Williams, "Philip III and the Restoration of Spanish Government, 1598–1603," *The English Historical Review* 88 (1973), 751–769; "Lerma, Old Castile and the Travels of Philip III of Spain,"; "Lerma, 1618: Dismissal or Retirement?" *European History Quarterly* 19, 3 (July 1989), 307–332; Magdalena S. Sánchez, "Dynasty, State, and Diplomacy in the Spain of Philip III," Ph.D. diss. (Baltimore: The Johns Hopkins University, 1988). See also the promising work on the Duke of Lerma and Philip III's reign by Bernardo José García García, "El Duque de Lerma y la pax hispánica. Auge y crisis del pacifismo en la política exterior de la monarquía (1607–1615)," (Madrid: Memoria de Licenciatura, Universidad Complutense, 1991).

10. María Jesús Pérez Martín, *Margarita de Austria, Reina de España* (Madrid: Espasa-Calpe, 1961), 22.

11. On the Rodrigo Calderón trial, see Angel Ossorio, *Los hombres de toga en el proceso de D. Rodrigo Calderón* (Madrid:Biblioteca Nueva, 1918). See also Archivo General de Simancas (hereafter AGS), Diversos de Castilla, Legajos 34–36.

12. See Biblioteca Nacional (hereafter BN), Madrid, Manuscript (hereafter MS) 20.260/30, fols. 124–127.

13. Jerónimo de Florencia, "Segundo sermón que predicó el Padre Gerónimo de Florencia . . . en las honras que hizo a la . . . Reyna D. Margarita." 19 December 1612, in Micael Avellan, *Oración Funebre* . . . , BN Madrid, R/24245, fol. A2.

14. Diego de Guzmán, *Reyna católica. Vida y muerte de Doña Margarita de Austria.* Diego de Guzmán was appointed capellan mayor of the Descalzas in 1602. He became royal almoner in 1609 and for several months served in both capacities. His duties at the Descalzas officially ended in April 1609. In January 1610, Guzmán was appointed teacher of the Infanta Ana, an office he filled until the infanta went to France to marry Louis XIII. Guzmán died in January 1631, while accompanying the Infanta Mariana on her trip to Central Europe to marry the future Ferdinand II. He was buried in the Jesuit college in Avila. On Diego de Guzmán, see his "Memorias del Cardenal Diego de Guzmán," Real Academia de la Historia (hereafter RAH), Madrid, Colección Salazar, 9/476 and 9/477. See also Diego Ortiz de Zúñiga, *Anales eclesiásticos y seculares de la muy noble y muy leal ciudad de Sevilla* (Madrid: En la Imprenta Real, por I. García Infanzon, 1677), 645–659.

15. See, for example, Diego de Guzmán's entry for 29 January 1609, where he says that he ate with Richard Haller and spent the rest of the afternoon with the Jesuit fathers in their residence. "Memorias del Cardenal Diego de Guzmán," RAH, 9/476, fol. 7.

16. Guzmán, *Reyna católica*, fols. 112v–113.

17. Florencia delivered two sermons at the queen's death, the first was dedicated to Philip III and the second to the Duke of Lerma. For the first sermon, see "Sermón que predicó Gerónimo de Florencia a Felipe III en las honras de Margarita de Austria," 18 November 1611, BN Madrid, Varios Especiales (hereafter abbreviated VE), 54–93. For the second sermon, see "Segundo sermón que predicó el Padre Gerónimo de Florencia. . . . "

18. See the rules for a religious novice in Juan de la Cerda, *Vida política de todos los estados de mujeres* (Alcalá de Henares, 1599); Juan Luis Vives in Lorenzo Riber, ed., *La mujer cristiana* (1523) (Madrid, 1949). The biographies written about nuns such as Sor Margarita de la Cruz and Sor Mariana de San José emphasize their obedience to their confessors. See Juan de la Palma, *Vida de la serenisima infanta Sor Margarita de la Cruz*, and Luis Muñoz, *Vida de la venerable Sor Mariana de San José* (Madrid: En la Imprenta Real, 1643).

19. Florencia, "Segundo sermón que predicó . . . en las honras que hizo a la . . . Reyna D. Margarita," fol. 14v.

20. See, for example, the advice of Galindo, quoted in Mariló Vigil, *La vida de las mujeres en los siglos XVI y XVII* (Madrid: Siglo Veintiuno de España, 1986), 98. Galindo's book is from 1678, but the advice he gave was standard for sixteenth- and seventeenth-century Spain.

21. Guzmán, *Reyna católica*, fols. 134v–135.

22. Ibid., fols. 136v–137.

23. Florencia, "Segundo sermón que predicó . . . en las honras que hizo a la . . . Reyna D. Margarita," fol. 11.

24. Ibid., fol. 11v. For a historical discussion of early modern notions of a masculine woman, see Mary Elizabeth Perry "The Manly Woman. A Historical Case Study," *American Behavioral Scientist* 31, 1 (September/October 1987), 86–100.

25. For a discussion of early modern notions about the female character, see Ian MaClean, *The Renaissance Notion of Women* (Cambridge: Cambridge University Press, 1980); Merry E. Wiesner, *Women and Gender in Early Modern Europe* (Cambridge: Cambridge University Press, 1993), 9–38; Linda Woodbridge, *Women and the English Renaissance: Literature and*

the Nature of Womankind (Urbana and Chicago: University of Illinois Press, 1984); Theodora A. Jankowski, *Women in Power in the Early Modern Drama* (Urbana and Chicago: University of Illinois Press, 1992), 22–53; Constance Jordan, *Renaissance Feminism* (Ithaca and London: Cornell University Press, 1990), 11–64; Marilyn J. Boxer and Jean H. Quataert, eds., *Connecting Spheres. Women in the Western World, 1500 to the Present* (New York: Oxford University Press, 1987), 24–25.

26. For a discussion of reason as a male characteristic, see Theodora A. Jankowski, *Women in Power in the Early Modern Drama*, 59–60. It was also common to describe nuns who were especially fervent in their prayers as masculine. So, for example, Mariana de San José, prioress of the Monastery of the Encarnación in Madrid from 1612 to 1638, was described by her nuns as "varonil." Madre Aldonza, who succeeded Mariana de San José as prioress, described her predecessor as "a prudent, manly woman who can be called a prudent and wise woman." ("Muger baronil prudente que se le puede llamar la muger prudente y savia.") Archivo Real del Monasterio de la Encarnación, Leg. 1, tomo I: Relacion de testigos que convivieron con la Madre Mariana de San José, fol. 3. Madre Aldonza also said that Mariana de San José's tears were those of a man, not of a woman (fol. 17). These comments about Mariana de San José are found in testimonies taken from nuns who knew Mariana de San José, and were the first part of a process to beatify the prioress. Thus, the masculine qualities attributed to Mariana de San José might have been used to make her more legitimate to a masculine audience.

27. "Sermón a las honras de su Magestad de la Reyna Doña Margarita de Austria N.S. que la muy insigne Universidad de Salamanca hizo en los 9. dias del mes de noviembre del año de 1611," fols. 1–31v.

28. Ibid., fol. 16.

29. Ibid., fol. 17.

30. Constance Jordan, *Renaissance Feminism*, 29–34; Theodora A. Jankowski, *Women in Power*, 54–60.

31. "Sermon a las honras de su Magestad de la Reyna Doña Margarita de Austria N.s. que la muy insigne Universidad de Salamanca hizo en los 9. dias del mes de noviembre del año de 1611," fol. 1v.

32. Ibid., fol. 15.

33. This image of women is clearly elaborated in Juan Luis Vives, *La mujer cristiana*. The significance of a cult of female intercessors during the medieval period is discussed in Jo Ann McNamara, "A Legacy of Miracles: Hagiography and Nunneries in Merovingian Gaul," Julius Kirshner and Suzanne F. Wemple, eds., *Women of the Medieval World* (New York: Basil Blackwell, 1985), 36–52.

34. See Jerónimo de Florencia, "Sermón que predicó el Padre Gerónimo de Florencia . . . en las honras de S.C. Magestad de la Emperatriz Doña María," *Libro de las Honras para la Emperatriz María que el Colegio Jesuita . . .* (Madrid, 1603).

35. Matías de Novoa, "Memorias de Matías de Novoa," *Colección de documentos inéditos para la historia de España*, vol. 60 (Madrid: Academia de las Historia, 1895).

36. Juan de Santa María, *Tratado de repúblicas y policía christiana* (Madrid, 1615).

37. The queen founded the convent shortly before her death. Her will stipulated the construction of a convent adjacent to and connected by an underground passage with the royal palace. Philip III carried out his wife's wish, and the building was built and inaugurated in 1618. On the rules for the foundation and formation of the convent, see BN, Madrid, MS 6955, "Escritura de obligación que otorgaron la priora y monjas del Convento de la Encarnación de Madrid." For a modern study of the Convent of the Encarnación, see María Leticia Sánchez Hernández, *El Monasterio de la Encarnación de Madrid. Un modelo de vida religiosa en el siglo XVII* (Salamanca: Ediciones Escurialenses, 1986). On the prioress, see Luis Muñoz, *Vida de la venerable Sor Mariana de San José.*

38. Relazione di Ottaviano Bon, 21 December 1602, in Nicolo Barozzi and Guglielmo Berchet, *Relazioni degli stati europei. Lette al senato dagli ambasciatori veneti nel secolo decimosettimo*, Serie I: Spagna, vol. 1 (Venice: Tip di P. Naratovich, 1856), 247.

39. Relazione di Francesco Soranzo, 11 October 1602, in Barozzi and Berchet, *Relazione degli stati europei*, 162.

40. Ibid.

41. Relazione di Ottaviano Bon, 21 December 1602, in Barozzi and Berchet, *Relazioni degli stati europei.*

42. Francesco Priuli, writing in 1608, described the queen in much the same terms. Priuli reported that the queen had no influence whatsoever in the government, and no one could obtain favors through her intercession because the queen had too much reverence (*riverenza*) for the king and because Lerma kept the queen isolated. Relazione di Francesco Priuli, 1608, in Barozzi and Berchet, *Relazione degli stati europei*, 358. On women's use of melancholy and illness to influence political decisions and to express their disapproval of court politics, see Magdalena S. Sánchez, "Melancholy and Female Illness: Habsburg Women and the Court of Philip III," *Journal of Women's History*, forthcoming.

43. BN, Madrid, MS 2751, "Historia de Joan Kevenhuller de Aichelberg," 1140–1141. For the German version, see Haus-, Hof-, und Staatsarchiv, Vienna (hereafter abbreviated as HHStA), *Spanien, Diplomatische Korrespondenz*, Karton 13 (hereafter SDK 13), "Die geheime Korrespondenz des kaiserlichen Botschafters am königlichen spanischen Hof in Madrid," Graf von Frankenburg am Kaiser Rudolf II., vol. VI, 1606, fol. 331r.

44. BN, Madrid, MS 2751, "Historia de Joan Kevenhuller," 1140–1141.

45. Luis Cabrera de Córdoba, *Relaciones de las cosas sucedidas en la corte de España desde 1599 hasta 1614* (Madrid, 1847), 124, entry from 1 August 1601.

46. HHStA, Spanien Varia 3, letter from Guillén de San Clemente to Archduchess Maria, 18 September 1598. See specifically point #7: "Que podra llevar un confessor de aqui a España, mas con condicion, que se havra de bolver luego porque a las Reynas de España se suele dar alla Confessor de tales calidades como conviene."

47. Archivo Segreto Vaticano, Fondo Borghese, Ser. II, n. 272, Nunziatura di Spagna 1605–1606, fols. 58r–58v; 67r–67v. I have not seen the original letter but have consulted the transcribed copy in Bernardo José García García, "El Duque de Lerma y la pax hispánica," 163–164. On the Junta de Desempeño, see Jean-Marc Pelorson, "Para una reinterpretación de la junta de desempeño general (1603–1606) a la luz de la 'visita' de Alonso Ramírez de Prado y de Don Pedro Franqueza, Conde de Villalonga," in *Actas del IV Symposium de Historia de la Administración* (Madrid, 1983), 613–27.

48. HHStA, SDK 13, Khevenhüller to Rudolf II, letter from 22 November 1603, fol. 217v.

49. See Barbara J. Harris, "Women and Politics in Early Tudor England," *The Historical Journal* 33, 2 (1990), 259–281, especially 260–262.

50. HHStA, SDK 13, Khevenhüller to Rudolf II, letter from 20 December 1603, fol. 222r.

51. HHStA, SDK 13, Khevenhüller to Rudolf II, letter from 8 January 1605, fol. 278r.

52. HHStA, SDK 13, Khevenhüller to Rudolf II, letter from 11 October 1600, fol. 57r–57v.

53. HHStA, Familien Akten, #106, fol. 86: "con quien podreys . . . tratar con buena confianza pues cierto estoy que no dexaran de mostrar mucha afficion a esta casa por la que deven de tener a la memoria de la Reyna mi hermana."

54. On the Bohemian and Hungarian issue, see Otto Gliss, *Der Oñate Vertrag*, (Frankfurt/Main, 1934); Magdalena S. Sánchez, "A House Divided: Spain, Austria, and the Bohemian and Hungarian Successions," *Sixteenth Century Journal* 15, 4 (1994), 887–903. For San Clemente's recommendation, see AGS, Estado Alemania, Leg. 707, fol. 235, 31 January 1603. For Zúñiga's advice, see AGS, Estado Alemania, Leg. 709, fol. 152, Prague, 10 February 1611.

55. HHStA, *Spanien Hofkorrespondenz*, Karton 2, #7, fol. 155, 18 Dec. 1610: letter from Margarita de la Cruz to Rudolf II: "Pocos dias a q escrivi a VMd diciendole como el Rey dios le guarde por averselo suplicado la Reyno y yo hiciesse md a los principes de honrrar los entratarlos como a los grandes de aca esta resuelto de hacerlo solo se a testarado en algunos inconvenientes." (Rudolf II wanted this for his ambassador, the Prince of Castellon.)

56. Quoted in Gil González Dávila, *Historia de la vida y hechos del inclito monarca amado y santo D. Felipe Tercero* (Madrid, 1771), 189.

57. Ibid., 191.

58. Ibid.

59. Ibid.

60. BN, Madrid, MS 2348, Philip III to Ana, 16 November 1616, fol. 441v–442.

61. Ibid.

7

Women and Factionalism in the Court of Charles II of Spain

JoEllen M. Campbell

The reign of Charles II (1665–1700) is unique in Spanish history for a number of reasons. Principal among these is the fact that it was never genuinely the reign of Charles II. Charles, the only surviving son of Philip IV and Mariana of Austria, was the last of the Habsburgs to rule in Spain, and all the unfortunate genetic characteristics of that line were evident in his mental and physical condition. Although Charles enjoyed a surprisingly long life considering his weakness, he was never really capable of fulfilling the responsibilities of a monarch, and for most of his life he was little more than a pawn in the hands of those around him. Those hands, more often than not, belonged to his mother, Queen Mariana. Of the thirty-five years that Charles was nominally king of the various realms of the Spanish empire, his mother was regent for the first ten, and, until her death in 1696, near the end of his reign, she was engaged in the constant effort to maintain her influence over her son.

Although the political role of Spanish women of this time period was extremely limited, a function of the private sphere rather than the public, Mariana's case was unique. She was in the rare position, first, of having an overt public role as queen regent during Charles's minority. Charles's fourteenth birthday terminated her established position within the political system, however, and her influence was subsequently confined to the "private" sphere of her relationship to Charles. In practice, however, her role in Spanish government was hardly diminished, for hers was the guiding hand behind many of Charles's actions. She was confined to her role as a mother, but she was the mother of a king, and a king who was willing to follow her guidance in all matters.

The informal nature of Mariana's power after the termination of her regency left her open to challenges by other individuals and groups who resented her influence over Charles. The power struggles between the queen mother and certain factions among the nobility, as well her conflicts with Charles's ambitious half-brother Don Juan José of Austria, dominate Charles's reign. The factionalism itself, and the issues over which the different groups came into conflict, were largely shaped by the previous few decades of Spanish history. An understanding of these issues and conflicts may be facilitated by a brief overview of the context in which they occurred.

The Spain that Charles inherited from Philip IV in 1665 had suffered serious difficulties, both economic and territorial, through the first half of the century. The Thirty Years' War and the revolts of Catalonia and Portugal in 1640 had been extremely costly, especially for Castile. Economically, the situation was equally bleak. The increasing economic independence of Spain's overseas colonies, as well as smuggling and privateering activities by Spain's rivals in the Americas, led to a severe slump in transatlantic trade. The costs of fighting wars on so many fronts added to the weakness of the economy and resulted in the first suspension of payments to the bankers in 1647. Spain's military failures precipitated major trading concessions to her enemies: the Dutch in 1648, France in 1659, and the English in 1667. Added to these difficulties were the capricious oppositions of nature—the seventeenth century was one of demographic stagnation for much of Europe, but Spain suffered a loss of nearly 1.5 million people, mostly from Castile, due largely to epidemic disease.

Charles, only four years old at his accession, was far from being the heroic leader needed to restore Spanish strength and prestige. Philip IV had attempted to counteract this difficulty by declaring in his will that his widow Mariana should be regent and guardian until Charles came of age, and that she should rule in conjunction with a *junta de gobierno*, a council of government, which would meet daily. Such a *junta* was essentially an extension of the method of conciliar government prevalent in Spain in the seventeenth century. Each affair of government was dealt with by a separate council, and the councils were numerous. The absence of a strong monarch brought out many of the inherent weaknesses in this method of government. The councils functioned independently of one another; each supreme council had its own financial apparatus and its own income, and they were deliberative rather than decision-making bodies. In addition, the bureaucracy had grown to incredible size during the reign of Philip IV as a result of the practice of favoritism. Most appointments were the products of royal favor rather than merit, and there was no limitation to their number. Finally, the sale of offices had become popular during Philip's reign, and by the time Charles reached the throne even positions on the supreme councils were being sold.[1]

The bureaucracy therefore had become incapacitatingly cumbersome as an instrument of government, but still it might have functioned reasonably well under the guidance of a strong monarch. Being placed under the leadership of yet another council, however, produced near gridlock. The lack of precedents for such a circumstance, combined with the inefficiency of the bureaucracy to start with, resulted in chaos: "the machinery of the new government began to malfunction as soon as it came into existence (la máquina del flamante Gobierno empezó a rechinar apenas comenzó a existir)."[2] The government clearly could not function under such conditions; some sort of extraordinary measure was necessary. The pattern of government that developed out of these circumstances would come to characterize most of the reign of Charles II: rule by *valido*, or royal favorite, and policy-making by factionalism.

Charles's debility therefore opened up an entirely new realm of opportunity for many individuals in the court. Not only did the nobles have a greater chance at political power than ever before, but other individuals who were normally excluded from direct participation in the political process saw the door open for them as well. The latter belonged to two categories: women (whose political activity usually was restricted to the influence they exercised within their roles as mothers and wives), and individuals belonging to social ranks below the nobility. The most privileged and powerful members of the court were those who had the closest personal influence on Charles: his mother and his two successive wives, Marie Louise d'Orleans and María Ana of Neoburg. These women found themselves in a highly charged situation: both in a powerful position of influence regarding the king, and themselves the targets of manipulation by other groups who wanted to use them to influence the king. The factional conflicts that resulted are not simply a series of childish squabbles, although with 300 years of hindsight they often seem to be. They had little influence on domestic policy, and it is true that the peripheral provinces of Spain were left largely to themselves during this period. However, issues of Spanish foreign policy were heavily influenced by these contests of power, particularly those relating to alliances with France or Austria. It is in this arena that the royal women of Spain had the greatest effect.

Mariana of Austria, daughter of the Emperor Ferdinand II, had come to Spain to be Philip IV's bride in 1649, when he was forty-four and she, his niece, only fifteen. She had initially been intended to marry Philip's son, Baltasar Carlos, but the prince died the year of their betrothal at the age of seventeen. However, a marriage link between the Spanish and the Austrian Habsburgs was still a priority, as it had been for generations; so much so that Philip was willing to marry his own niece to maintain the ties. Such an attempt to maintain a connection between the two branches of the house of Austria would set the theme for the rest of the century, because of the efforts of Mariana (and later those of Charles's second wife, María Ana of Neoburg) to direct Spanish foreign policy in Vienna's favor. Conflicts over this Austrian orientation would become the hub around which court factionalism would revolve throughout Charles's reign.

As a young woman in the Spanish court, Mariana was initially little concerned with politics. She was only a few years older than Philip's daughter, María Teresa, and the two found a great deal of pleasure in each other's company, far removed from the concerns and complexities of government. Mariana's position as queen might have given her a great deal of influence in politics, had she chosen then to use it to its fullest extent. Although women who were not fortunate enough to be part of the immediate royal family had little chance to be directly involved in politics in Spain or elsewhere in Europe, a queen could command as much power and respect as a king, despite contemporary views about the "weaker sex." It was not unheard of for a Habsburg king to leave his queen at the head of government while he was away from court. Such was the case with Charles V, who entrusted the government of the Spanish empire to his wife, the Empress Isabel, upon his departure for Tunis in 1535,[3] and again the Emperor's son Philip, who chose his sister Juana, Princess of Portugal, over the two men suggested to him by his father to be regent of Spain while Philip traveled to England in 1554.[4] Queen Mariana, in contrast, chose to remain aloof from politics during most of Philip's reign. For many years, as far as the Spanish people were concerned, Mariana's only importance was determined by whether or not she could bear Philip an heir, for since the death of Baltasar Carlos the succession was again a crucial issue. The deaths of most of her children in infancy would keep this question alive for some time.

In later years, however, her attitude would change, and the roots of her later policy are clear from the outset. Despite her youth upon coming to the Spanish court, Mariana maintained a strong sense of identity with the Austrian Habsburgs, and this predilection would manifest itself in the years to come as her interest in politics emerged. After her father's death, her brother Leopold became Emperor, and the two remained in close contact. The connection is best illustrated by her relationship with her confessor, the Jesuit John Everard Nithard, whom she had brought with her from the emperor's court. The two relied heavily upon each other; she upon her confessor for counsel and advice as well as the companionship of a fellow countryman, and he upon the queen for the authority and influence her favor could bestow.[5] Their joint influence first appears in the context of choosing which course Spanish foreign policy should follow, the same context she would attempt to dominate in the years after Philip's death.

One of the reasons for Philip's creation of the *junta de gobierno* to aid Mariana during her son's minority was to avoid just such a situation. This *junta* was meant to provide Mariana with a group of experienced men upon whose advice she could rely, to make up for her inexperience in government; it also may have been intended to act as a check to keep her from having too much influence in those matters in which she might take an inappropriate personal interest.[6] Without any clearly defined powers, however, the junta became simply another tier added to the complex layers of Spanish conciliar government. Its members met daily to listen to the recommendations of all of the other principal councils; each member would register his opinion, and these would be presented to the queen every afternoon. Mariana, finding the sudden responsibility of government rather overwhelming, and not completely trusting the councillors who advised her, found herself relying more and more on the advice of her confessor to help her make decisions. Initially their discussions were simply part of the morning confessional, but they expanded to more organized afternoon sessions during which he would help Mariana prepare her answers for the junta's secretary, don Blasco de Loyola.[7]

Much has been made of the relationship between the queen and her confessor, and rightly so, for her reliance on his advice (and his consequent rise in power) came to be a major issue in court politics, and the focus of much conflict, during the first few years of her regency.[8] Some historians have portrayed Nithard as a ruthless manipulator, taking advantage of the queen to enhance his own power; others describe the two as a pair of scheming Austrian conspirators, calculating every move to bring Spain to ruin while they drained its resources away to the Empire.[9] Both of these interpretations lean more toward melodrama than realism. Admittedly, such dependence on one's confessor may not have been the ideal way to make major governmental decisions. On the other hand, circumstances made it difficult for Mariana to completely trust the members of the junta de gobierno. Spanish government had been characterized by the strong individual rule of its monarchs during the sixteenth century, but the seventeenth century saw an increasing reliance of kings on their principal councils and ministers.[10] The result was a growth in the power and influence of the nobles, particularly those at court. The court had been full of intrigue since the death of Philip's last minister, Don Luis de Haro, in 1661. The most important councillors immediately leapt into competition for the coveted position of royal *valido*, although Philip voiced his determination during the last years of his life to rule alone.[11] Philip's death created even greater opportunities for intrigue and factional struggle, as the most ambitious of the nobles sought to fill the political vacuum. Mariana's lack of political experience made her apt to rely on others for advice, yet her distrust of the grandees of the court led her to choose her advisors from outside this group: first her confessor Nithard, and later the commoner Valenzuela. Despite Philip's desire to break out of the pattern of *valimiento* by establishing the junta de gobierno for Mariana, his efforts had the opposite effect, and Mariana's rule was dominated by favorites even more than Philip's had been.

Mariana's first chosen favorite was her confessor, whom she believed she could trust more than the ministers of government. "El padre Everardo," as he was known, had come to the Spanish court with Mariana sixteen years earlier from Vienna, where he had been her confessor since her childhood; the two maintained an affinity both personal and political for the Empire. In the 1650s, for example, when the marriage of the infanta María Teresa became a political issue, Mariana favored a betrothal to Leopold, her brother and the son of the emperor Ferdinand, rather than the marriage to Louis XIV that eventually was arranged to seal the Peace of the Pyrenees in 1659. Later, in 1661, Austria was besieged by the Turks, and Emperor Leopold sought help from both France and Spain. The French agreed to help, under the condition that Spain would send an equal number of troops. Rather than approach Philip IV directly, Leopold discussed the matter with Mariana and Nithard—although the latter had not yet obtained any formal position in the government, his influence was recognized. The queen and her confessor were successful in persuading Philip to commit 12,000 infantry and 6,000 horse to Austria's defense.[12]

Historians often use instances such as this to illustrate what they see with hindsight as the folly of Spain's ties to Austria. Spain was exhausted by the years of war preceding the Peace of the Pyrenees in 1659, and Philip was determined in the early 1660s to increase his military efforts against the rebellious Portuguese despite the aid given them by England. Spanish military commanders, insufficiently equipped, poorly paid, and suffering from a lack of manpower, could barely raise large enough armies to fight in Portugal, much less send troops to fight someone else's battles. With centuries of hindsight, and with the often condescending point of view held by many nineteenth-century historians of Spain,[13] it may seem foolish for Philip to have committed troops to help Austria against the Turks. Indeed, it seemed foolish to some of his contemporaries, who had come to believe—especially since the fall of Olivares, who had favored the Austrian alliance—that such an alliance was more damaging than beneficial. However, one must keep in mind the circumstances and priorities of seventeenth-century Spain. The traditional ties with Austria were strong, and it would have been difficult for Philip to justify abandoning the Empire to the attacks of the infidel. The defense of the Catholic religion was a priority, one easily underestimated by modern readers unaccustomed to the role of religion in early modern Spain. In his correspondence with the nun Sor María de Agreda, Philip expressed his goals in maintaining close relations between Spain and Austria: "I consider it advisable to draw closer the ties between the Emperor and ourselves in this way, my principal aim being the exaltation of the faith; for it is certain that the more intimate the two branches of our house are, so much the firmer will religion stand throughout Christendom."[14] On the other hand, religious alliances were less potent in the seventeenth century than they had been in earlier times, and they often gave way to more pragmatic considerations. The common bonds of Catholicism never stood in the way of Louis XIV's invasions of Spanish territory, for example, and the subsequent alliance of Spain and Holland was not seriously hindered by the Protestantism of the latter. Consequently, Philip's decision whether or not to commit troops to the defense of the Empire was a choice between the ties of tradition, religion, and family on the one hand, and the obstacle of Spain's exhausted resources on the other. In this context Mariana clearly tipped the balance in favor of the Empire.

The fact that Leopold approached Philip through Mariana and her confessor indicates that her influence was crucial to overcoming Philip's reluctance and the protests of his ministers who wanted to avoid yet another military commitment. This would set the stage for the relationship between Spain and the Empire for the rest of the century, for Mariana would consistently favor the ties of tradition, religion, and, above all, family.

Although Nithard's influence was purely informal during Philip's lifetime, after his death Mariana took the opportunity to legitimize her confessor's authority. One of the positions on the junta de gobierno was to be occupied by the Archbishop of Toledo, and another was reserved for the Inquisitor General. Shortly after Philip's death, the archbishop of Toledo, Cardinal Sandoval, died as well. Mariana chose to name Don Pascual de Aragón, then the Inquisitor General, to the vacant see of Toledo. This left the position of Inquisitor General vacant, so she was able to give it to Nithard, who thus found himself not only with an important ecclesiastical position, but a spot on the junta de gobierno as well, all within a year after Philip's death. There was only one practical obstacle, one which Philip had in all likelihood set up to prevent such an occurrence: his will specified that positions on the high councils could not be occupied by foreigners. This created only a slight delay, though, for Mariana had Nithard naturalized as a Spanish citizen in September of 1666.[15]

Far from being accepted as a legitimate member of the court, however, Nithard was heartily resented by the nobles and ministers of government. The nobles who opposed him most strongly, of course, were those who had been in constant competition for the most influential positions in Mariana's regency government. Over the course of the seventeenth century it had become customary in the Spanish court for the monarch to have a royal favorite with the function, if not the title, of prime minister. Many in the court had come to take this for granted, and figures such as the Count of Castrillo and the Duke of Medina de las Torres were waiting in the wings to take up for Mariana the position left by Don Luis de Haro under Philip IV. When instead she chose her confessor, and made him not only a Spanish citizen but Inquisitor General and a councillor of the junta de gobierno, they perceived that move to be a usurpation of their rights and a rejection of their influence. This resentment was also provoked more by their perception of him as an outsider than because of any specific policy; the court saw him as a physical representation of the Austrian influence so many of them wished to reject. Those that opposed the Austrian ties, of course, opposed the queen as well as Nithard. However, Spanish tradition and respect for the crown forestalled any direct opposition to the queen, and although it was impossible to remove Mariana from government, Nithard was fair game.[16]

Opposition in the court to Nithard coalesced under the leadership of Don Juan José de Austria, the illegitimate son of Philip IV. Although Philip had fathered many illegitimate children, Don Juan was the only one to be officially recognized, and he was raised in the court and allowed to participate in Philip's councils.[17] The story of the personal rivalry between Don Juan and the queen is a familiar one, and well documented by the court chronicles of the period as well as the extensive correspondence between the two.[18] In addition to the simple dislike harbored by each for the other, the issue of power was a bone of contention. Don Juan resented being excluded from the junta de gobierno, yet Mariana distrusted him and intended to deny him participation in the regency government. Nithard's rise to power also provoked resentment, and Don Juan became a leader for the nobles of the court who resented the elevation of a foreigner to the position of prime minister, an issue reminiscent of the opposition to Charles V's Flemish advisers upon his arrival in Spain in 1517.

However, Don Juan's opposition to Mariana was not merely a personal issue. He, too, had clear foreign policy priorities, and they were diametrically opposed to Mariana's. For generations Spain had traditionally aligned itself with Austria, although this policy fell into disfavor after the disastrous *valimiento* of Olivares and his fall from power in 1643. Decades of war had also led some to believe that the Habsburg alliance was more damaging than beneficial. Don Juan believed that Spain's priorities needed to include a willingness to refrain from war in areas that were beyond recovery, such as Portugal, and a redirection of resources to reinforce areas like Flanders, which were valuable yet weak enough to invite invasion.[19] To this end he worked to establish good relations with the United Provinces beginning in the 1650s,[20] and opposed Philip's invasion of Portugal in 1657.[21] He also supported the cultivation of good relations with France, and helped to arrange the marriage of the infanta María Teresa to Louis XIV in 1660. In all these points he was largely supported by the Council of State and the Duke of Medina de las Torres, who had been a principal figure in government throughout Philip's reign.

Mariana, on the other hand, opposed these policies to the best of her ability. She did favor peace with Portugal, but only in order to concentrate on retaliating against France where the latter had invaded Spanish territories.[22] Although Medina de las Torres had been in charge of foreign affairs during the last years of Philip's life, she was able to keep him from being appointed to the junta de gobierno by supporting his rival, the Count of Castrillo. With the support of Castrillo and Nithard, she was able to overcome Medina's efforts for peace and persuade Philip to help Austria against the Turkish invasion in 1661,[23] and in 1666 she arranged the marriage of the infanta Margarita to her brother, the Emperor Leopold.

Opposition to the queen grew during the first years of the regency, however, and in 1669 Don Juan was able to successfully demand the removal of Nithard, although his position was not sufficiently strong to take over the government himself. Mariana again chose a favorite from outside the noble elite whom she believed she could trust; the subsequent rise of Fernando de Valenzuela provoked even more outrage than had the ministry of Nithard. Valenzuela was an ambitious young man, the son of a lesser army officer, and the chaotic circumstances of the court opened up a great deal of possibility for people with ambition. His friendship with Nithard seems to have been the key to his entry in court politics, for the confessor was impressed with his talent and discussed with him many important issues of government. In 1661 Valenzuela married Doña María Eugenia de Uceda, who happened to be one of the queen's favorite servants; through her he gained the queen's attention and eventually the appointment of *caballerizo*, or equerry. The skill that would gain for him the position of valido was simply finding out what went on in the palace. Valenzuela's position as caballerizo gave him unrestricted access to the royal household and acquaintance with people in high places, but was not important enough for the grandees to consider him a threat. He paid close attention to unguarded conversations, collecting various tidbits of information, and offered them to the queen. She found his talents extremely useful, and began to confer with him regularly; when it became apparent that she was aware of things the courtiers thought they kept secret, the joke spread that there was a palace ghost floating about. Later, as Valenzuela rose to a more visible position of power and it became clear that he had been the informer, the nickname stuck, and he was known from then on as the *duende del palacio*—the "palace ghost."

Although Valenzuela lent more attention to currying favor with parties and bullfights in Madrid than to foreign policy,[24] Mariana continued her efforts to support the Empire and oppose France. In 1672, Louis XIV invaded the United Provinces, and the governor of the Netherlands (the count of Monterrey, who was a partisan of Mariana) sent troops to its defense and precipitated another war with France.[25] After this incident, both the count of Peñaranda (one of the members of the *junta de gobierno*) and Don Juan advocated ceding Flanders to France.[26] This idea was strongly opposed by Mariana, who joined the Empire in its alliance with the United Provinces against France rather than giving up the valuable province. At the same time, she had Spain provide 50,000 reales a month for the emperor's army on the Rhine.[27]

During the years of Valenzuela's valimiento, Don Juan had held the viceroyalty of Aragon, waiting for his chance to move in again against Mariana. He maintained a number of strong supporters in the court, among them the Duke of Medina Sidonia and Don Antonio de Toledo. His real advantage, however, lay with his association with the king's confessor, Montenegro. Although Montenegro had been chosen by Nithard, he retained his post after the Jesuit's exile, and became more and more displeased with the rule of Valenzuela. Montenegro expressed this opinion subtly during his relationship with Charles, and the king, who was highly susceptible to suggestions made on religious grounds, was coaxed into "a belief that God wished him to save Spain from Valenzuela, using his brother as the instrument."[28] 1675, the year Charles attained his majority, gave Don Juan his opportunity. Although up until this point Charles had been too young to be a factor in court politics, he now became the prime target of factionalism, as Don Juan and Mariana did their best to manipulate him. And once he was involved, Mariana's position as Charles's mother was every bit as important as her title of queen, for Charles was easily swayed by those closest to him. Although Don Juan was successful in having his supporters in the palace convince Charles to summon him to be his prime minister, Mariana discovered the plot just before its completion. One brief session with Charles enabled her to undo all of Don Juan's plans, for she was quickly able to convince Charles to send his ambitious half-brother away again. The comments of a contemporary writer clearly illustrate the extent of Mariana's advantage in the realm of psychological domination over Charles: "combining the gentle tears of a woman and the affectionate persuasions of a mother with the commands of a queen, she was able to obtain everything she wanted of him (mezclando entre los imperios de Reyna, los halagos cariñosas de madre, y las lágrimas tiernas de muger, alcanzó quanto pretendía de él)."[29] During this episode, Charles reached his fourteenth birthday and technically became king in his own right. However, Mariana remained firmly in control even though she no longer held the post of regent; the Count of Monterrey reported to an acquaintance that she ruled with the same authority that she had maintained during her son's minority.[30]

One mother was not enough to overcome the combined efforts of Don Juan's supporters in the court, however, and a year later he was again successful in persuading Charles to call him into Madrid. This time Mariana was banished to Toledo, to neutralize with distance the psychological influence she had over her son. The queen did send a flurry of letters to Charles warning him of his brother's hypocrisy and the danger of letting him take over. The level of reasoning she used with Charles is indicative of his naiveté and the nature of her influence; rather than explaining Don Juan's motives or the inappropriateness of such a political coup, she concludes simply by reminding Charles "that I love you more than he does (que yo te quiero más que él)."[31] However, Don Juan prevented all of her correspondence from reaching her son, and her efforts to reach him were unsuccessful.

Having at last attained the position of prime minister, Don Juan was free to pursue his francophile policy. He believed that the constant wars with France were the principal obstacle facing the Spanish monarchy. After Louis's invasion of the United Provinces and the consequent rekindling of hostilities between Spain and France in 1673, things had gone poorly for Spain, and Louis began to make offers of peace in 1677. This coincided with Don Juan's rise to power, and at his very first session of the Council of State he argued for a peace settlement.[32] Flanders had been the battleground for the two nations for the last decade, and Don Juan had come to believe that it was no longer worth the cost of defending it. Popular opinion no longer supported Spain's defense of the Dutch; it was widely felt that the United Provinces and the Empire had exploited

Spanish resources for their own benefit, despite the success of Dutch aid in the retention of Sicily.

The result of Don Juan's negotiations (and of the exhausted condition of the monarchy) was the Peace of Nijmegen in 1678. The terms of this treaty were harsh for Spain, for it included the loss of Franche-Comté, yet it was celebrated with relief in Madrid as the end to a long and painful war, and even boosted the prince's popularity for a short time. Particularly important for Don Juan was the fact that the negotiations for the peace treaty came about at the same time that plans were being made for Charles's marriage. The sickly boy had managed to survive to the age of seventeen, old enough to begin planning for the succession of the Spanish crown. During her regency, Mariana had already begun the diplomatic preparations necessary for a match with a king. She, of course, planned to continue the tradition of intermarriage between the two branches of the house of Austria. Her hope was to marry Charles to the Archduchess María Antonia, who was his cousin on his mother's side (her father was Leopold, Mariana's brother) and his niece on his father's (since her mother was Charles's sister Margarita). Although the archduchess was only six years old when these arrangements were being made in 1674, Mariana began negotiations for the betrothal despite a majority opinion to the contrary in the Council of State.[33] Her preparations, however, were interrupted by Don Juan's coup and her subsequent exile to Toledo. The prince promptly broke off all her negotiations, for he had no intention of marrying Charles to the emperor's daughter, as this would significantly weaken his own position. Instead, Don Juan took advantage of the negotiations of the Peace of Nijmegen to propose a marriage with Louis's niece, Marie Louise d'Orléans. This match would serve a number of purposes. First, it was simply a more practical arrangement, since the French princess was healthy and of marriageable age. It would also hopefully ensure better relations between Spain and France, and avoid the warfare that had so weakened Spain over the past few decades. Finally, the match would strengthen Don Juan's own position, for he hoped to befriend the princess and use her as a means to manipulate Charles. Such a connection would not only increase his influence over the king, but also strengthen his position against Mariana, whose influence he still feared despite her confinement in Toledo. Had Don Juan lived a few more years, his efforts combined with those of the young queen might have resulted in greater rapprochement with France; as it was, Charles's first act after Don Juan's death was to summon his mother back from Toledo, and the Austrian faction would again become dominant in the court.

Although Louis XIV hoped that his niece would be an aid to French influence in the Spanish court (Colbert had even drawn up state papers for her outlining the French interests that were to be served),[34] Marie Louise had little interest in politics. During the ten years that she was Queen of Spain, she occasionally supported French interests (for example, by granting favorable economic concessions and ensuring that Spain would not seek new alliances against

French interests in 1680).[35] For a time she did show an interest in the debates over which individuals would be chosen for vacant governmental posts, such as the governorships of Milan and Sardinia. The other ministers strongly opposed this, however; they resented her influence, as it frustrated their own efforts to manipulate the choices for the posts.[36] On the whole, though, she remained aloof from matters of government. It is ironic that she did not choose to become involved in the factionalist quarrels, for she was in the position of greatest power in relation to Charles. He was extremely fond of his young wife, and was eager to indulge her every whim. Marie Louise's whims did not extend far beyond horseback riding and palace theater, however, so Mariana was left with the direction of Spain's foreign policy. Mariana's influence as a mother may have given way to Marie Louise's charms as a wife, but the queen mother kept a core of supporters in the court, and she was not through with politics.

Her policy continued along the same lines that it had before the interlude of Don Juan de Austria's brief rule. Mariana, along with her principal supporters Medinaceli, the Constable of Castile, and her advisor Portocarrero, immediately resumed support of Vienna in its defense against the Turkish attacks. In a situation nearly identical to that of 1672, the Marquis of Grana, a partisan of Mariana, precipitated military action against Louis in the Netherlands, and Spain once again joined the Empire in its war against France.[37]

From 1680 on, then, the Austrian faction was predominant in the Spanish court. However, it would soon have a new element: after the death of Marie Louise in 1689, Mariana and the emperor arranged a new marriage for Charles with María Ana of Neoburg, the sister of the empress. By this time it was clear that Charles was impotent, and María Ana was chosen more for her potential to influence and manipulate him than for any hope of bearing children. Although Charles was now nearly thirty years old, he was still weak of body and mind, and rarely evinced any real interest in government. His new wife, in sharp contrast to Marie Louise, was very interested in politics, and immediately began to exert her influence. Her tactics had to be different, however: where Charles had been clearly in love with his first wife, he did not have such a close bond with María Ana. Not having the weapon of affection, she had to resort to external pressure; when she felt her influence was not having the weight that it should, she used the influence of the emperor, who suggested to the king that, in the interest of domestic harmony, he should listen to his wife.[38] Her personal influence on Charles combined with her alliances within the court soon put her in a position superior even to the queen mother's. She worked closely with the king's confessor Pedro Matilla, and the *secretario del despacho*, Manuel de Lira, to have Oropesa, Charles's effective prime minister since 1685, removed from office in 1690. María Ana then dominated the selection of Charles's new Council of State, removing Oropesa's supporters and filling the council with her own followers.[39] Although Charles preferred to keep Oropesa in power, the combined efforts of his wife and confessor were too powerful for him, and he was only able to respond "They wish it, and I must comply (eso quieren, y es preciso que yo me conforme)."[40]

María Ana's faction was just as Austrian in its priorities as the queen mother's had been. She too worked with Portocarrero, as well as the Imperial Ambassador Harrach. By this time, in the 1690s, the succession was the principal question about which court factionalism revolved, since Charles was not likely to live much longer. The battles over the succession to the Spanish throne are a familiar story, but the outcome reflects the popular reaction to the Austrian faction that had dominated for so long. Although Charles's mother and his second wife had kept the Austrian group on top within the palace itself, so many years of their dominance had provoked resentment among the people, similar to that which had brought Don Juan to power in 1675. A growing number of nobles at court began to favor a French succession as an alternative. After a series of altercations during 1696 and 1697, in which María Ana's faction and the French faction alternately prevailed in their domination of Charles, popular resentment of the queen helped tip the balance in favor of the French candidate Philip of Anjou, whom Charles named as his successor in 1700 shortly before his death.

These maneuvers during the last two decades of Charles's reign were nearly meaningless in the long run, however, for Spain's fate rested in the hands of the rest of Europe more than in the hands of the court factions. Since 1668, only three years after the death of Philip IV, Louis had been quietly arranging in a series of treaties with the English, the Dutch, and even the Emperor for the partition of the Spanish empire upon Charles's death. The legacy of Spanish factionalism was essentially one of neglect. In acts of revenge similar to those of Don Juan upon his arrival to power, the ministers of the last years of Charles's reign had to spend all of their energy consolidating their own position against opposing factions, and any efforts they attempted at economic reform were likely to be reversed by their successors. As Cánovas argues, there were only three things that prevented the collapse of Spain after the end of Charles's minority: the Catalan frontiers fighting for themselves against France, the support from England, Holland, and the Empire to protect Flanders, and Louis XIV's long-term plans to keep Spain in one piece for himself.[41]

Thus ended the Austrian faction in the Spanish court, and the leading role played by women in Spanish factionalism. Given the unusual circumstances of Charles's long minority rule and his weakness throughout his life, women in the court were given a much greater opportunity to play overt political roles than they otherwise would. This was not, however, a clearly defined role; it depended entirely on the circumstances and the ambitions of the individuals involved. Although Charles's mother and his two successive wives obtained access to as much power as they desired, their lack of political experience and training often led them to rely on others for support, increasing the divisions of factionalism. In addition, the lack of any real place for women in the political system of Spain meant that the influence of these women was not lasting. As in the case of Mariana, once she was physically isolated from Charles, her power over him was neutralized. The story of women and factionalism in the court of Charles II therefore ends with María Ana of Neoburg's exile to France; but it is a fascinating chapter in Spanish history about the appropriation of power by those who would not normally have access to it.

NOTES

The author gratefully acknowledges the assistance of Magdalena Sánchez, whose suggestions were very helpful in the revision of this chapter.

🦂

1. John Lynch, *Spain under the Habsburgs*. Vol. II: *Spain and America, 1598–1700* (New York: Oxford University Press, 1969), 268.

2. Gabriel Maura y Gamazo, *Vida y reinado de Carlos II*, vol. I (Madrid: Espasa-Calpe, 1954), 54.

3. "Instrucciones que dejó Carlos V a la emperatriz Isabel para la gobernación de estos reinos," *Colección de documentos inéditos para la historia de España* (hereafter CODOIN), vol. III, 538.

4. M. J. Rodríguez Salgado, *The Changing Face of Empire: Charles V, Philip II and Habsburg Authority, 1551–1559* (Cambridge: Cambridge University Press, 1988), 85.

5. Maura, *Vida y reinado*, vol. I; see also Mariana's correspondence in CODOIN, vol. LXVII, "Relación histórica de la menor edad de Carlos II," 3–68; and BN MSS 2034, "Papeles pertenecientes a la Reyna Madre y Don Juan José."

6. Hume and other historians of his generation were often sharply critical of the role women played in Spanish politics, suggesting that women were not really capable of effective government. However, although they did not always agree with her particular choices, Mariana's contemporaries in the court never questioned her ability or her right to govern. See Sotomayor, *Semanario erudito*, vol. XIV, "Memorias históricas de la monarquía de España . . . desde los tiempos de Enrique IV hasta los del Rey Carlos II" as well as the correspondence between the Duke of Montalto and Don Pedro Ronquillo, CODOIN, vol. 79.

7. Maura, *Vida y reinado*, vol. I, 84.

8. It was not unusual for royal confessors to serve as political councillors under the Habsburgs, particularly under Philip II and Philip III. However, Nithard's influence was viewed by contemporaries as inappropriate, probably because he was a foreigner and his influence was resented by the nobles who disagreed with his priorities.

9. Donald Pennington, for example, says that Mariana was "exploited by the power-seekers of the court" and "came under the control of . . . Father Nithard," *Europe in the Seventeenth Century*, 2nd ed. (London: Longman, 1989), 401. Hume, on the other hand, is the strongest supporter of the interpretation that the two collaborated to the detriment of Spain; see especially *Queens of Old Spain* and *Spain: Its Greatness and Decay* (London: Cambridge University Press, 1898). Hume's judgments admittedly should be taken with a grain of salt; he belonged to the nineteenth-century historical tradition that not only distrusted women in politics, but painted Spain's relationship with the Holy Roman Empire in an undeservedly negative light.

10. The reigns of Ferdinand and Isabella and the Emperor Charles V are classic examples of government by strong monarchs; Philip II developed the system of bureaucracy to a greater extent but still guided it with a strong hand. Philip III began the practice of valimiento with his reliance on the Duke of Lerma, which was continued by Philip IV and the Count-Duke of

Olivares. An excellent examination of this phenomenon is Francisco Tomás y Valiente, *Los validos en la monarquía española del siglo XVII* (Madrid: Instituto de Estudios Políticos, 1963).

11. Principal among these contenders for royal favor were the Count of Castrillo, who expected to be named minister upon Haro's death but was disappointed, and the Duke of Medina de las Torres, upon whom Philip did come to rely more and more toward the end of his reign.

12. Don Modesto Lafuente, *Historia general de España*, vol. 12 (Barcelona: Montaner y Simon, 1889), 91; Hume, *Queens of Old Spain*, 382.

13. See especially Hume, *Spain: Its Greatness and Decay, 1479–1788*, and *The Court of Philip IV: Spain in Decadence* (London: Eveleigh Nash, 1907).

14. Philip IV to Sor María de Agreda, quoted in Hume, *Queens of Old Spain*, 362.

15. Maura, *Vida y reinado*, vol. I, 54–56.

16. Antonio Valladares de Sotomayor, ed., *Semanario erudito* (Madrid: Blas Roman, 1788) vol. IV: "Grandes ruidosas controversias acaecidas en la menor edad del señor Don Carlos II, entre la Reyna Madre Doña María Ana, . . . D. Juan de Austria y el P. Juan Everardo"; also vol. 14, "Memorias históricas de la monarquía de España...desde los tiempos de Enrique IV hasta los del rey Carlos II."

17. Antonio Cánovas del Castillo, *Bosquejo histórico de la Casa de Austria en España* (Madrid, 1911), 337.

18. Antonio Valladares de Sotomayor, ed., *Semanario erudito* (Madrid: Blas Roman, 1788) vol. 4: "Grandes ruidosas controversias acaecidas en la menor edad del señor Don Carlos II, entre la Reyna madre Doña María Ana, . . . D. Juan de Austria y el P. Juan Everardo" 3–288; see also CODOIN, vol. 48, "Relación histórica de la menor edad de Carlos II," 3–68; and BN MSS 2034, "Papeles pertenecientes a la Reyna madre y Don Juan José."

19. The differences between Don Juan's and Mariana's positions on this matter mirror an earlier conflict on the same subject. During the reign of Philip III, the Duke of Lerma, like Don Juan, supported a break from the Austrian Habsburgs and a focus on internal recovery, while Philip III's queen, Margaret of Austria, hoped to maintain the Austrian ties, as did Mariana a generation later.

20. Henry Kamen, *Spain 1469–1714: A Society of Conflict* (London: Longman, 1983), 262.

21. R. A. Stradling, *Europe and the Decline of Spain* (London: George Allen & Unwin, 1981), 158.

22. Sotomayor, *Semanario erudito*, vol. 14, "Memorias históricas de la monarquía de España . . . desde los tiempos de Enrique IV hasta los del rey Carlos II," 14.

23. Hume, *Queens of Old Spain*, 382.

24. Sotomayor, *Semanario erudito*, vol. 14, 27.

25. Eduardo Ibarra y Rodríguez, *España bajo los Austrias* (Madrid: Editorial Labor, 1955), 425.

26. Kamen, *Spain 1469–1714*, 62.

27. Stradling, *Europe and the Decline of Spain*, 153.

28. John Landon-Davies, *Carlos: The King Who Would Not Die* (Englewood Cliffs, NJ: Prentice-Hall, 1962), 82.

29. Sotomayor, *Semanario erudito*, vol. 14, 30.

30. Monterrey to the Duke of Villahermosa, 20 November 1675, "Correspondencia del Duque de Villahermosa," BN MSS 2410, 242.

31. Mariana to Charles, quoted in Fernando Díaz-Plaja, *La historia de España en sus documentos: el siglo XVII* (Madrid: Instituto de Estudios Políticos, 1957), 419. This argument might well have been effective, as it was ten years earlier when Don Juan attempted to enter Madrid and she convinced her son to send him away; this time, however, he successfully isolated Charles from his mother and intercepted all correspondence between them. Maura, *Vida y reinado*, 270.

32. Stradling, *Europe and the Decline of Spain*, 163.

33. Langdon-Davies, *Carlos: The King Who Would Not Die*, 89. Only three councillors supported the marriage; the rest opposed it, either because of the girl's youth or because (like Peñaranda and Don Juan) they preferred a French match.

34. Hume, *Queens of Old Spain*, 417.

35. Stradling, *Europe and the Decline of Spain*, 186–187.

36. See the correspondence between the Duke of Montalto and Don Pedro Ronquillo, CODOIN, vol. 79, 338.

37. Stradling, *Europe and the Decline of Spain*, 187.

38. "Correspondencia de la Marquesa de Gudannes," in *Viajes de extranjeros por España y Portugal*, 210.

39. Cánovas del Castillo, *Bosquejo histórico*, 380.

40. Sotomayor, *Semanario erudito*, vol. 14, 71.

41. Cánovas del Castillo, *Bosquejo histórico*, 359–360.

Part III

FEMALE IDENTITY

8

Images and Realities of Work: Women and Guilds in Early Modern Barcelona

Marta V. Vicente

*B*etween 9:00 and 10:00 on the morning of 31 March 1628, during a meeting of the city council, a group of more than forty women spinners broke into the city hall of Barcelona. The spinners shouted insults at the councilors and demanded that they prevent master drapers from sending wool to be spun outside the city. The drapers' actions, the spinners complained, left them without work. The councilors instead called the guards. Some women were arrested while others escaped. The event was recorded in the council minutes as a great offense against the city and remembered as "the great popular riot" (lo gran avalot del poble).[1]

The spinners' action took place in the context of the European-wide economic crisis of the seventeenth century. By 1628, Catalonia had been inundated by foreign goods, exports had declined, and the Barcelona wool textile industry was depressed. Drapers had transferred some of their activities outside the city to reduce labor costs and maintain their competitiveness in relation to foreign cloths. But the practice affected women spinners in the city who depended on the raw wool from the drapers to make thread.[2] This was, then, the context in which the spinners decided to assault city hall and demand an end to the drapers' practices.

What do we know about these women spinners? In general, women artisans were known only as the daughters, wives, and widows of masters. Guild records never listed them as apprentices, daily workers, or masters.[3] In fact, women workers in Barcelona were rarely recorded in guild documents as independent producers. Nor do these records make reference to the spinners who protested in 1628. Although they worked for drapers spinning raw wool, women spinners rarely appear in guild and municipal records.

What accounts for this absence? The answer to this question lies in the nature of Barcelona's guilds. Only masters could be members of a guild.[4] Women could not become masters and thus could not have a workshop of their own, hire journeymen, have apprentices, or enjoy the privilege of producing and selling manufactures.[5] As women they could not be masters; as non-masters they were formally restricted in their labor activities. And yet the participation of women in the city's economy was accepted and encouraged. Women worked in a variety of jobs inside and outside the household. Moreover, masters depended on women who usually performed unskilled and semi-skilled tasks, such as the preparation of raw materials, the polishing of finished products, the carding, combing, and washing of wool, and the retail sale of some finished products.

Guilds' records thus do not reflect the variety of women's work but, rather, account only for a small part of documented activities. Women's work tended to be much more complex than the image presented by guilds, which most historians have accepted as a reflection of reality. Whether historians can ever use images to explain one "reality" is not an issue that I want to address in this chapter. Instead, I want to discuss the relation between images and these documented activities and experiences of women that constituted the reality of women's work.

The spinners' case helps us to rethink the traditional image of women's work. Here we have a group of women who worked with the approval of masters and the city government. They engaged in activities that were not formally part of a guild and where the household and the work of women were central. The spinners' case also reveals the multiplicity of images of women's work. For instance, during their protest women spinners described themselves as poor workers who needed to spin wool to support themselves and their families; master drapers, on the other hand, claimed that their work was of poor quality; for their part, the city councilors saw the spinners as troublesome women who nonetheless deserved protection from the guilds. Only by recognizing, first, that the masters' image of women's work accounted only for part of it; second, that women participated in the formal and informal economies of the city; and third, that their acts were described by multiple images, can we begin to understand the complexities of women's work in early modern Barcelona.

GUILDS' IMAGES OF WOMEN'S WORK

To Barcelona's guilds the basic distinction among workers was between masters and non-masters.[6] This distinction also presupposed a subordination of all non-masters, such as apprentices and journeymen, to the authority of masters.[7] Similarly, guilds saw women, whether wives, daughters, or widows, as subordinate to their masters. Moreover, women were rarely referred to as masters (*mestresses*), daily workers (*fadrines*), or even apprentices (*aprenentes*). Guilds only gave formal recognition to women's work through their relation to a master. According to the guilds' ordinances, women's work was intrinsically different from men's work. Male artisanal work was generally constrained by limits stipulated by guild ordinances, as well as in contracts. The ideal of women's work was, instead, customarily described in terms of duty, instead of privilege.

In general, Spanish and Catalan medieval and early modern writers shared the guilds' conception of women's work as an obligation adaptable to the particular needs of their families. The work of a woman and her capacity to carry out multiple and nonspecialized tasks thus responded to a view of women as individuals devoted to their families and communities. For example, in 1405, the Catalan humanist thinker Francesc Eiximenis stated, "a wife at home cannot stay without an occupation. She has to work in a job useful to the community or to her family."[8] Eiximenis implied, of course, that women could perform tasks useful to the household while remaining at home. A century later, Juan Luis Vives echoed this idea in his famous treatise, *On the Education of the Christian Woman* (1540). Vives imagined that perfection for women consisted of a state of constant activity in which they should do "anything necessary in the household."[9] Similarly, in 1572, Fray Luis de León described the "perfect wife" as one who was totally dedicated to the care of the family.[10] Two centuries later the Catalan Antonio de Capmany similarly believed that the wives and daughters of artisans should assist their husbands and fathers "in easy and sedentary tasks" so that the family could live "in prosperity."[11] Therefore, women's work was formally limited by the fact that a woman could not become a master, and was morally prescribed as "subordinate," "easy," and "sedentary."

Not surprisingly, given these images, masters were suspicious of women who worked on their own. One of their explanations was that these women were unfair economic competitors who did not conform with guild ordinances; another reason was that they were simply liars and troublemakers.

This attitude toward independent women artisans was widespread in the case of women retailers. A 1649 ordinance of the retailers' guild stated that women bought chickens and fruit and sold them illegally. Unless prohibited, the ordinance went on, such illegal activities would "encourage them [these women] to fall into bad habits," and added that by monopolizing the sale of those items, women were forcing up prices.[12] This tendency to judge women's work under two lenses, one economic and the other moral, is also exemplified in the treatment of women fishmongers.

Male fishmongers regarded women who sold fish as liars and troublemakers who would attempt, whenever possible, to monopolize the sale of fish. For example, in 1654 fishmongers protested to the city council that their livelihood was being hurt by women who secretly sold fish at lower prices.[13] Twelve years later, in 1666, they again complained about women's sales practices: "they [women] do not bring the larger and better fish [to the market] but hide them inside their houses, selling them secretly to convents at prices well below those set by the *mostaçaf* [the officer who supervised public markets]."[14] Likewise, in 1717 the *Audiencia* or Royal Court of Appeals stated that women fishmongers increased prices solely out of greed. In 1734 the same tribunal denounced them again for acting selfishly and for being uncontrollable.[15]

Although these complaints against female fishmongers were rooted in an image of independent women artisans as troublemakers, male fishmongers were responding to a real economic problem: These women were effective competitors. As we will see next, despite the image of subordination and dependence ascribed to most women artisans in general, as well as the negative description of the more independent ones, women's work was in reality more flexible and versatile than masters' images would ever suggest.

REALITIES OF WOMEN'S WORK

The household, with the participation of all of its members, contributed to artisanal production in a way that is hardly reflected in the records.[16] In early modern Barcelona, artisanal production and household work were hardly distinguished. The work of artisans was, moreover, part of family and community life. Workshop, store, and home thus coexisted in one. This was well reflected in the arrangement of the artisan house, where most workshops opened to the streets without any transition between interior and exterior spaces.[17] Thomas Platter, a Swiss traveller who arrived in Barcelona in 1599, described one such arrangement as follows: "As for the surgeons and barbers, their shops look out on the street with no more than a simple curtain over the door and when a costumer is to be shaved, they put the chair on the doorstep, throwing the curtain behind out of the way."[18]

The physical fluidity characteristic of work and family activities in Barcelona hardly changed until the end of the eighteenth century. Only then did the artisan house begin a gradual separation from the "public" domain of the street as municipal authorities prohibited the placement of workshops in front of the houses.[19] Yet many older practices remained. In 1779, for instance, despite municipal prohibitions, smiths continued to have anvils outside the doors of their houses, and in 1807 needle-makers (*agullers*) still worked in the street outside their homes. As late as 1845, city tanners asserted that they had to dry leather out in the street because it would not dry inside their shops, suggesting that their workshops were still in their homes.[20]

Guilds filled the lives of masters and their families with multiple social events, notably numerous religious festivities honoring guild patron saints.[21] In artisan neighborhoods, such as La Ribera, which faced the port, guild allegiance could be even stronger than that of the parish or neighborhood.[22] These links among artisans' work, household, and the community gave work a social significance that is barely reflected in the records. Likewise, masters' productive activities depended on the work of women, for whom artisanal activities and more "domestic" tasks were hardly distinguished.

Household and artisanal production, therefore, were closely interrelated. Let us now look at the nature of women's work in this artisanal household.

Women's work in early modern Barcelona is best expressed in terms of versatility and "flexibility." A woman's work was flexible because she could work at a craft and at the same time carry on household tasks. It was also variable because it changed whenever her social or economic condition changed.[23] When a woman married, she assisted her husband in his trade, even if it was different from the one she had previously done. When her husband died, a widow became solely responsible for the shop and her family's survival. Her work presumably changed once again when she became a widow because she would have to perform many tasks previously carried out by her mate in order to keep the family business going.

It is not possible for early modern Barcelona to classify and analyze all of the jobs that artisan women performed at the various stages in their lives since only glimpses of their activities appear in the city's archives. For instance, few documents have survived illustrating girls' training and work. We know, though, that despite the guilds' refusal to admit women as masters, some women were formally taught crafts.[24] In 1578, Bartomeu Gener, a *tapiner* (a master who made *tapins* or cork shoes for women), wanted his daughter Ana to learn his trade. For that purpose Bartomeu Gener hired a master *tapiner* to live in his house and teach Ana his craft. The contract they signed even included a clause which stipulated that after one year of training two masters of the shoemakers' guild would evaluate the quality of Ana's work.[25]

The example of Ana Gener reflects the special nature of women's training in a guild. For one thing, it reveals one master's preoccupation with having his daughter learn his trade, probably for the purpose of assisting him in his workshop. Gener's case also tells us about the limited training that a young woman in early modern Barcelona could expect to receive.

Despite her formal training, Ana Gener could not become a master. Likewise, other women in early modern Barcelona confronted this situation: Though many possessed skills equal to those of men, guilds barred them from becoming masters. In the fifteenth century women weavers could practice their trade following a brief apprenticeship and an informal examination conducted by the weavers' guild, but they could not become masters.[26] Yet women could not become masters because they did not receive the full training reserved for men. In the seventeenth century, Barcelona's silk guilds still used women's lack of a full formal training to justify a policy of denying them the authority to have their own workshops.[27]

Records illustrating the work of unmarried female artisans are as rare as those about girls. Women who married master artisans are better documented, though by no means in any adequate way. Wives and widows of masters are the most "visible" women in surviving records largely because of their links to their husbands' own work. This is especially true in the many cases where these women represented their husbands' "business" (*negoci*) before guild officers. We find masters' wives carrying out tasks in their husbands' name and running their workshops when masters were ill or absent. In 1701, Theresa Salvat ran the shop of her missing husband, as did Mariangela Miralles in 1786, who was also in charge of the vineyard she and her husband owned outside the city.[28] Many women understood work in these activities as a privilege they had achieved as wives. For instance, a carter's spouse from the late eighteenth century made this clear when she reminded guild officers (*prohomes*) that carters' wives had the privilege to transport goods inside and outside the city while their husbands were away.[29]

This capacity of masters' wives to perform different tasks was generally taken for granted. For instance, in a lawsuit dating from 1737 it was asserted that "Clara Ribas did the kitchen and so on, because, since she ate, it was fair that she worked."[30] Yet the reality was much different: Women's work consisted not only of "doing the kitchen." Wives made important contributions to the household economy, and in many instances they even supported families on their own.[31] For instance, in 1717, Joan Cussó, a master baker, stated that being seventy years old and unable to work, "I could not support myself if my wife, though old, would not work so hard to feed the two of us." In the same year Felipe Alonso, a cobbler, affirmed that he lived thanks to his wife's work.[32]

In the case of masters' widows, women temporarily enjoyed more control over their deceased husbands' workshops. Guilds usually allowed widows with children to keep the late husbands' workshops open until a son could take over the business. A childless widow, however, could only work in her husband's workshop for the year following the death of the master, which was known as *l'any de plor* or "the year of weeping."[33] Widows could therefore act as independent workers only temporarily. However, their situation still raised concerns within the guilds, which feared competition from working widows whose children were still very young and who did not immediately remarry. Mainly for this reason widows were subjected to controls until they remarried or their children reached adulthood.[34] For instance, few guilds allowed widows to have apprentices, and only under special circumstances; this prevented widows from having recourse to one of the cheapest forms of labor force available to masters.

Yet widows were not the only women artisans to work on their own. There is evidence that both married and unmarried women worked independently, particularly in activities connected to the distribution of goods and services.[35] Some women carried out commercial activities in their own right; among them we find the women in the mid-seventeenth century who made a living providing the city council with paper, candles, and ink.[36] The city council also contracted women to supply food to some convents, while many women who sold in the market obtained a city license without joining the retailers' (*revenedors*) guild.[37] Some women, however, simply worked without the approval of either the city or the guilds; such were the women hagglers (*regatonas*) who sold food illegally in the streets and in public markets.[38]

The examples shown thus far describe one central aspect of women's relation to their work: They needed to be flexible in order to adapt to changes in their social status. We must now turn briefly to the relation between this flexibility and the city's informal economy.

The flexibility of women's work benefitted both the city and the guild, since together women represented a work force adaptable to changing economic circumstances. The female labor force in early modern Barcelona worked in a way very similar to today's "informal economy"; that is, it was complementary to, and functioned alongside, the city's formal economy, the work as outlined in the ordinances of the guilds.[39] The extent of this "informal economy" is by its nature difficult to determine, but women's work adapted relatively easily to changes in demand for casual workers. In comparison, work in the formal economy, regulated by ordinances and guild restrictions, was far more rigid, unable to adapt quickly to either economic fluctuations or technological changes. The informal economy was therefore essential to the city's well-being, and the women who comprised it made a far more valuable contribution to the local economy than existing guilds' records reveal.

In short, whereas guilds described an image of women's work as subordinate, easy, and sedentary, the surviving documentation suggests that instead it was flexible, adaptable, and in some cases independent from masters' authority. No wonder women's work was crucial to their families, to artisan production, and even to the city economy.

COMPETING IMAGES OF WOMEN'S WORK

We first saw masters' images of women's work, and then how the reality of women's work contradicted those very images. This, however, does not mean that masters' images were not important. Their importance becomes clear when we look at how such images tried to influence the regulation of artisanal activities in Barcelona. Let us therefore examine again masters' images and how the city government challenged them with their own.

Thus far we have focused on the guilds' authority over artisanal production. However, the organization of work in Barcelona was not the exclusive turf of the guilds. The city council also played a role in regulating labor activities, as the spinners' riot of 1628 reveals. The spinners, for instance, demanded that the city council prohibit the drapers' illegal practices. Even the royal government claimed authority over guild activities: The women arrested during the spinners' riot were freed by the viceroy, the king's "alter ego" in Catalonia. The viceroy's action provoked protests from the city councilors, who regarded it as a violation of their prerogatives.[40] The spinners' riot, therefore, not only shows the variety of competing participants in the organization of work in Barcelona, but also how women's work was as much a political as an economic issue in the city.

As in the case of the spinners, women's work had political implications for women in silk clothing manufacture. Fortunately, documentation for the latter is more abundant. But before we discuss the differences involving women in the silk industry, let us look at the organization of that industry in Barcelona.

In the late Middle Ages women played an important role in the manufacture of silk, one of Barcelona's most important textile industries.[41] During the fifteenth century, however, following the emergence of the guild of masters silk weavers women were gradually barred from weaving silk clothing.[42] Yet during the sixteenth and seventeenth centuries, women retained the privilege to produce and sell certain small silk cloths.

These "silk women" (*sederes*), as they were called, represented an important labor force that the guild and the city government attempted to control. Apparently, silk-producing women were found engaged in illegal activities. Some silk-producing women had been privately hired by various silk masters, and some appear to have been selling surplus goods on their own. Silk women represented a double threat to silk masters: On the one hand, they could legally produce silk items; on the other, they engaged in illegal practices. The city council tolerated these women partly because taxes on Barcelona's growing silk industry represented a substantial source of income. Yet it also recognized that silk women were "poor women" who needed the earnings from silk manufacture to support themselves and their families. Based on this argument, in 1636 the city council passed an ordinance allowing women to make small hand-made silk items and sell them in public markets.[43]

Differences over the image of silk women as poor women needing protection from masters versus that of the fierce and illegal competitors argued by the guilds had wide implications. Despite its modest provisions, the 1636 "Ordinance in Favor of Women" threatened one of the principles of guild corporatism: the exclusive privilege of masters to produce and sell manufactured silk cloths.[44]

Silk masters' guilds described these silk women as unwelcome competitors and generally sought to limit the scope of their activities. As a result, and for more than fifty years, the silk masters' guilds attempted without success to persuade the city council to rescind the 1636 ordinance or at least impose greater limitations on what women could produce and sell. In 1656, the veil-makers asked the city council to restrict the 1636 ordinance to poor women who had no other means of subsistence. In their view, so many women were taking advantage of the ordinance that masters' livelihood was at risk.[45] In a later document, the silk masters claimed that prior to 1636 women had done little more than card silk and produce hand-made taffeta, for [silk] masters. Women earned with their work an important wage, with which they supported their homes and families. They felt happy just working with their hands and nothing more, which was legal and allowed. Time passed and some women who made fortune bought silk themselves, benefiting from making taffeta and selling wholesale the remaining pieces.[46]

The silk masters further claimed that women owned looms and hired workers, even though the 1636 ordinance strictly prohibited such practices. Women, they affirmed, also sold wholesale in front of their houses in violation of the ordinance.[47] In 1672, the master hat-makers (*barreters*) again complained that women represented an unfair source of competition and a threat to their existence.[48] These complaints continued during the eighteenth century. In 1745, for instance, an ordinance of the "silk twisters" (*torcedors de seda*)—the artisans who twisted silk threads—stipulated that masters could only give work to journeymen and to their own wives, but not to other women. Silk women also sold silk pieces similar to those made by masters. This practice was illegal and, according to silk masters, it also favored cheap and low-quality goods. As late as 1782, Joseph Ponsico, a silk master, claimed that women were selling hair nets similar to the ones he produced but at a lower price.[49]

These competing images reflected a basic difference between city government and masters' guilds. For one thing, the city council and the guilds had a different understanding of who had the privilege to work silk. The city regarded women's work as necessary to the city's economy and the survival of women and their families, while the guilds considered it a threat to their interests. Whereas the guilds argued that only masters could produce and sell silk items, and that women could only make items that silk masters did not manufacture, the city insisted on the legitimacy of poor women to make a modest living through their own work. In the end, the city council's image won, so that despite continuous protests from masters, the privileges provided to silk women by the 1636 ordinance remained in place.

In conclusion, the battles carried out by spinners and the silk women to defend their work illuminate some of the basic characteristics of women's work in early modern Barcelona. First, they show the complex relationship between the informal economy, where women's work was common, and the formal economy, described by the guild records, where women were hardly ever present. Second, we have seen how competing images of women's work had a political significance regarding the activities that women artisans could and could not do. It is true that the documentation often remains incomplete, and that additional research is necessary. But at least one final conclusion is certain: We cannot understand the actions of the spinners of Barcelona in 1628 unless we look for a reality beyond the masters' image of women's work; otherwise, we might as well believe that those forty women spinners never existed.

NOTES

I am grateful to Luis R. Corteguera and Richard L. Kagan for their comments and suggestions.

❦

1. Arxiu Històric de la Ciutat de Barcelona (AHCB): Consellers, Registre de deliberacions (minutes of the city council), fols. 44–50, 31 March 1628.

2. Pierre Vilar, *La Catalogne dans l'Espagne moderne. Recerche sur les fondements economiques des estructures nationales*, 3 vols. (Paris, 1962), vol. I, 588–633.

3. In some guilds in medieval Barcelona (such as the weavers'), women could become apprentices and masters. See Teresa Vinyoles, "Actividad de la mujer en la industria del vestir en la Barcelona de finales de la edad media," *El trabajo de las mujeres en la edad media hispana* (Madrid:Asociación Cultural AL-MUDAYNA, 1988), 255–273.

4. Luis R. Corteguera, "Artisans and Politics in Barcelona 1550–1650," Ph.D. dissertation (Princeton University, 1992), chap. 1. Until the eighteenth century, Barcelona craft organizations were known as craft confraternities. In the eighteenth century, the term "guild" became more common. See Pedro Molas Ribalta, *Los gremios barceloneses del siglo XVIII: La estructura corporativa ante el comienzo de la revolución industrial* (Madrid: Confederación Española de Cajas de Ahorros, 1970), 70–71.

5. Exceptions applied to masters' widows. See, for example, the ordinances of the tanners' guild. The tanners' guild conferred the privilege of having workshops and storage to those widows of master tanners who had living children from their husband and did not remarry; AHCB: Consell de Cent, Registre de deliberacions, fol. 2, 8 January 1711.

6. Pierre Bonnassie, *La organización del trabajo en Barcelona a fines del siglo XV* (Barcelona: C.S.I.C., 1975), 65. The history of guilds in Barcelona is, at least in its general features, similar to that of most Western European cities. See, among others, Samuel K. Cohn, *The Laboring Classes in Renaissance Florence* (New York: Academic Press, 1980); Henry Hauser, *Ouvriers du temps passés* (Paris: Flammarian, 1907); Maurice Garden, *Lyon et les lyonnais au XVIIIe siècle* (Paris, 1975); and Mack Walker, *German Home Towns: Community, State, and General Estate, 1648–1871* (Ithaca, NY: Cornell University Press, 1971).

7. This is well exemplified by many Catalan contemporaries who described the guilds' hierarchic nature. In 1778, the Catalan historian Antonio de Capmany offered a contemporary description of the guild system where he emphasized the social and economic dependency of all male non-master artisans to their masters. See Antonio de Capmany y Montapalau, *Memorias históricas sobre la marina, comercio y artes de la ciudad de Barcelona*, vol. II (Barcelona: Camara Oficial de Comercio y Navegación de Barcelona, 1961–1963 [1778]), 1079.

8. Francesc de Eiximenis, *Regiment de la cosa pública* (Barcelona: Imprenta Varias, 1927 [1405]), 33.

9. Juan Luis Vives, *Instrucción de la mujer cristiana* (Buenos Aires: Espasa-Calpe Argentina, 1927 [1540]), 16.

10. Fray Luis de León, *La perfecta casada* (Madrid: J. Pérez del Hoyo, 1972 [1572]).

11. Capmany, *Memorias históricas . . .* , vol. I, 477. Capmany wanted to preserve the guilds' existence, contrary to the wishes of many enlightened thinkers. He was thus idealizing the artisan family in the guilds.

12. AHCB: Documentació Gremial Particular, Revenedors, Registre d'ordinacions, 3 February 1649.

13. Jaime Carrera Pujal, *Historia política y económica de Cataluña* 3 vols. (Barcelona: Bosch, 1946–1947), vol. I, 575.

14. AHCB: Consellers, Bosses de deliberacions, 25 February 1666.

15. Jaime Carrera Pujal, *La Barcelona del segle XVIII*, 2 vols. (Barcelona: Bosch, 1951), vol. II, 337.

16. See Joan Scott and Louise Tilly, *Women, Work & Family* (New York: Routledge, 1987); Natalie Zemon Davis, "Women in the Crafts in Sixteenth–Century Lyon," *Feminist Studies* 8, 1 (Spring, 1982), 47–80; Barbara Hanawalt, ed., *Women and Work in Preindustrial Europe* (Bloomington: Indiana University Press, 1986).

17. Teresa Vinyoles, *La vida quotidiana a Barcelona vers 1400* (Barcelona: R. Dalmau, 1985), 69; Albert Garcia i Espuche, "Barcelona a principis del segle XVIII: La ciutadella i els canvis de l'estructura urbana," Ph.D. diss. (University of Barcelona, 1987).

18. Thomas Platter, *Journal of a Younger Brother*, S. Jennett, tr. (London: F. Muller, 1963), 203. Platter was a young medical student in Montpellier travelling around Catalonia.

19. See Albert Garcia i Espuche and Manuel Guàrdia i Bassols. *Espai i societat a la Barcelona pre-industrial* (Barcelona: Edicions de la Magrana, Institut Municipal d'Història, 1986).

20. AHCB: Documentació Gremial Municipal, Ferrers 1779; Agullers 1807; Blanquers 1845. In 1811, the needle–makers claimed that they needed to work outside because their houses did not have enough light; ibid., agullers 1811.

21. Corteguera, "Artisans and Politics . . . ;" and for a similar situation in other European cities, see James R. Farr, *Hands of Honor: Artisans and Their World in Dijon, 1550–1650* (Ithaca, NY: Cornell University Press, 1988).

22. James S. Amelang, "People of the *Ribera*: Popular Politics and Neighborhood Identity in Early Modern Barcelona," in B. Diefendorf and Carla Hesse, eds., *Culture and Identity in Early Modern Europe (1500–1800): Essays in Honor of Natalie Z. Davis* (Ann Arbor: University of Michigan Press, 1993), 119–137.

23. Marta V. Vicente "Mujeres artesanas en la Barcelona moderna," *Las mujeres en el antiguo régimen: Imagen y realidad* (Barcelona: Icaria, 1994), 59–90; for the case of early modern Lyon, see Natalie Davis, "Women in the Crafts . . . ," 49–53.

24. During the fifteenth century, guilds in Barcelona gradually forbade women from becoming apprentices. See Teresa Vinyoles, *Les barcelonines a les darreries de l'edat mitjana* (Barcelona: Fundació Salvador Vives Casajana, 1976); Manuel Riu, "Aportación a la organización gremial de la industria textil Catalana en el siglo XIV," *VII Congreso de la Corona de Aragón* (Barcelona, 1962); David Herlihy, "Women's Work in the Towns of Traditional Europe," *La donna nell'economia secc. XIII–XVIII: atti della "Ventunesima Settimana di Studi," 10–15 aprile 1989* (Florence: Le Monnier, 1990), 119–122.

25. AHCB: Fons Notarials, notary Onofre Rialb, lligall 14, llibre 2. Capítols i sentències 1573–1589. Quoted in Agustí Duran i Sanpere, *Barcelona i la seva història: La societat i l'organització del treball*, (Barcelona: Curial, 1973), vol. 2, 374, note 8.

26. Bonnassie, *La organización del trabajo*, 107.

27. Biblioteca de Catalunya (B.C.): Fullets Bonsoms, no. 2759, fol. 4, "Allegacio en fet, dels medis, entre altres, que justifiquen la instancia de la causa que les confrarias dels mestres perxers, velers y velluters, proseguieren contra algunas donas" (no date or place). In this document, the silk guilds petitioned the city to stop the activities of women who sold silk products in shops and markets because they did not have proper masters' training.

28. AHCB: Documentació Gremial Municipal, Corders de cordes de viola, fol. 170; Barreters d'agulla, 1786.

29. Her husband had gone to Cadiz and left her in charge of the "business"; AHCB: Documentació Gremial General, carreters (carters), fols. 21–23, 1786.

30. Arxiu de la Corona d'Aragó (ACA): (Reia) Audiència, plets civils (civil lawsuits), no. 39, fol. 42, 1737–1746.

31. In 1716, for instance, Margarita Mensa claimed to support with her own work three great-grandchildren, one granddaughter, and "other relatives." AHCB: Documentació Gremial Municipal, Carreters, 1716. For other European cities, see also Angela Groppi, "Le travail des femmes a Paris a L'époque de la revolution française," *Bulletin d'Histoire Economique et Sociale de la Revolution Française* 46 (1979), 27–46. The fragility of the household economy in difficult times has been studied for eighteenth-century Barcelona by Montserrat Carbonell, "Pobresa i estrategies de supervivència a Barcelona a la segona meitat del segle XVIII," Ph.D. diss. (Universitat de Barcelona, 1993); and for eighteenth-century France by Olwen Hufton, "Women and the Family Economy in Eighteenth-Century France," *French Historical Studies* 9 (1975), 1–22. According to Hufton, the importance of women as breadwinners was essential; their death or incapacity could drive the family to abject poverty.

32. AHCB: Cadastre, Llibre d'informacions de pobresa, absencia, mort i altres causes d'alguns individuos d'aquesta ciutat (Reports on poverty, absence, death, and other causes of some individuals of this city), 25 July and 12 August 1717.

33. AHCB: Documentació Gremial Municipal, lletra C, Corders de viola, ordenances del segle XVIII, cap. 10.

34. AHCB: Consell de Cent, Registre de deliberacions, fol. 169, 8 January 1657; also AHCB: Documentació Gremial General, Carnissers, fol. 14.

35. For other European cities, see Jean H. Quataert, "The Shaping of Women's Work in Manufacturing: Guilds, Household, and the State in Central Europe, 1648–1870," *The American Historical Review*, 90, 5 (December 1985), 1122–1148; Martha Howell, *Women, Production and Patriarchy in Late Medieval Cities* (Chicago: Univeristy of Chicago Press, 1986); Merry Wiesner, "Paltry Peddlers or Essential Merchants? Women in the Distributive Trades in Early Modern Nüremberg," *The Sixteenth Century Journal* 12, 2 (Summer, 1981), 3–14.

36. In 1655, the city offered several payments to Estasia Benavayre, widow of Pere Benavayre, for candles she sold to the councilors. AHCB: Consell de Cent,. registre de deliberacions, fol. 139, 4 July and 24 September 1665. Similarly, Heather Swanson has documented that fifteenth-century English women played an essential part in the making of candles; "The Illusion of Economic Structure: Craft Guilds in Medieval English Towns," *Past and Present* 121 (November, 1980), 29–48.

37. According to Carrera Pujal *Historia política*, vol. II, 323, the city council supplied free meat and bread to the General Hospital and the convents of penitents (*apenedides*) and Capuchins. In 1677, Paula Font, a widow, was paid for delivering daily bread to the convent of Capuchins from September 1676 to January 1677. AHCB: Consell de Cent, Registre de deliberacions, fols. 65–66, 10 March 1677. Retailers in Barcelona markets needed to be members of the retailers' guild as well as to purchase a license from the city. See Gloria Mora and M. Reyes Pasqual, "El proveïment de carn a la Barcelona del set-cents: Comerç i sanitat," *Manuscrits* 2 (December, 1985), 115–128.

38. .The city council worked hard to eliminate these women. In 1734, women hagglers were invited to enter as confreres of the retailers' (*revenedors*) guild, but it is not known how many accepted. AHCB: Documentació Gremial Particular, Revenedors, súplicas, instancias y certificados [cridas de revenedors], 1734. Women retailers were especially concerned about these illegal competitors. For instance, in 1769, fifteen women retailers protested that any problem was blamed on them and that authorities were not concerned about hagglers. AHCB: Documentació Gremial Particular, Revenedors, súplicas, instancias y certificados, cuadern 46, 1769.

39. The terminology of "formal" and "informal" economy has been borrowed from Lauren A. Benton, *Invisible Factories: The Informal Economy and Industrial Development in Spain* (Albany: State University of New York Press, 1990).

40. After 1714, the royal government took over direct control of guild matters in the city; see Molas, *Los gremios*, 133–145.

41. Pedro Voltes Bou, "Notas sobre el personal de los talleres sederos barceloneses. Siglos XIII–XVIII," *Boletín de Estudios Económicos* 26, (1971), 1005–1029. See also Teresa Vinyoles "La mujer bajomedieval a través de las ordenanzas municipales de Barcelona," *Las mujeres medievales y su ámbito jurídico* (Madrid: Universidad Autónoma de Madrid, 1983), 138.

42. Vinyoles, ibid.

43. AHCB: Consell de Cent, Registre de deliberacions, fol. 124, 1636.

44. Molas, *Los gremios*, 71. One could always manufacture goods for domestic use but not to be sold.

45. AHCB: Consell de Cent, Registre de deliberacions, fol. 68, 1656.

46. BC: Fullets Bonsoms, no. 2759 (no place or date), fol. 4.

47. Ibid.

48. By that time, the silk guilds had already appealed to the *Audiencia*, but they were ignored if they won their case. See Carrera Pujal, *Historia política*, vol. II, 216.

49. AHCB: Consell de Cent, Registre de deliberacions, fol. 4, 21 August 1782.

9

Conversions of the Woman Monarch in the Drama of Calderón de la Barca

Mary Lorene Thomas

If in their education they were given books and preceptors rather than fine linen, working cases, and sketches for embroidery frames, then they would be as capable as men of filling official posts and university chairs.[1]

Don Pedro Calderón de la Barca (1600–1681) was the leading dramatist of the late Spanish Golden Age; his fame is attributed to his authorship of more than 120 *comedias* and 70 one-act religious plays known as *autos sacramentales*. Following the rich Spanish theatrical tradition, Calderón's *comedias* conform in structure and content to the pattern established during the previous century and given its definitive form by the renowned dramatist Lope de Vega.[2] In the seventeenth century, the term *comedia* referred to any three-act play written for public performance. Its meaning was not restricted to that of "comedy" as used today, but encompassed a wide variety of dramas, including both tragedy and comedy, as well as a blending of the two in tragicomedy, a frequent tendency in seventeenth century Spanish theater.[3] The subtitles of the plays frequently incorporated descriptive adjectives that modified the general term comedia; these provided supplementary information about the milieu of the protagonists, the narrative outcome, and the degree of comic relief present. The classical dichotomy of tragedy/comedy was replaced by a wider range of dramatic categories that allowed for possibilities such as "comedias palaciegas" (palace plays), "comedias de capa y espada" (cloak and sword plays), "comedias de enredo" (plays of high intrigue), and "tragicomedias" (tragicomedies).[4]

Polymetric structure was common to all comedias; the function of the passage, whether it provided action, narrative, or mere transition between scenes, and its emotional overtone were the determining factors in the choice of verse form. Legend, mythology, history, and Biblical narratives provided material for the conflicts of the plots; frequently the dramatists selected their material from Spanish sources close at hand, including the "romanceros," "canciones," and contemporary events in Spain.

During the first fifty years of his life Calderón wrote comedias for perform-ance in small public theaters that would play to a heterogeneous urban audience as well as for private theaters with nobility and royalty in attendance. Once ordained, Calderón's theatrical production was more limited in scope; when called upon by royal petition and after receiving permission from the religious hierarchy, he continued, albeit less frequently, to write comedias for perform-ance during royal celebrations; these same plays were performed later in public theaters. In spite of his somewhat diminished output of comedias, his acknow-ledged expertise in writing *autos sacramentales* called for him to write two of these plays a year for the Villa de Madrid until his death in 1681.[5]

The *autos sacramentales* are short allegorical presentations designed to instruct the public on issues central to Catholic doctrine and, during Calderón's time, to explain the mysteries of the Eucharist. They were performed before a vast audience during the Corpus Christi celebrations and were staged on movable platforms, frequently placed in front of a cathedral. Their didactic purpose was carried out through allegory. In this way, abstract theological concepts relating to the fall and redemption of mankind were presented. Consequently, characters such as the world, sin, lust, guilt, desire, faith, grace, knowledge, peace, and justice abounded, each to impede or further the progress of the lead character toward salvation and the final scene in which the protago-nist partook of the Eucharistic meal.

❦

In both genres, Calderón manifested unequalled ability in versification, imagery, and the production of a tightly woven plot. But distinctions between the two genres, the comedia and the auto sacramental as practiced by Calderón, extend beyond their purpose, content, and structure, as outlined above, to differences in their roles as objects of literary criticism. The comedia has attracted the attention of scholars and critics during the last four centuries and its critical history reflects the ever-changing literary perspectives from López Pinciano to the feminist approaches at the forefront of today's literary criticism.[6] On the other hand, the limited group of Golden Age scholars who have devoted their work to the autos sacramentales have mainly studied their dramatic structure, and have viewed the allegorical characters, for the most part, as simple personifications assigned traditional attributes. Legendary or historical figures who appear in the autos sacramentales have only been summarily treated, and this usually to provide evidence about the possible date of composition of the play. The female characters of the autos sacramentales, whether based on mythological, historical, or religious personages, have been entirely ignored as sources of information about the perception of women in seventeenth-century Spanish theater.

An analysis of the depiction of the female protagonists in two of Calderón's plays, the comedia *Afectos de odio y amor* and the auto sacramental *La protestación de la fe*, offers some insights that will further our understanding of the construction of female identity in Golden Age drama. This chapter is not meant to provide a definitive account of the seventeenth-century perception of the status and role of women. Hopefully, however, it will elucidate Calderón's portrait of a fictional queen as she confronted issues inherent to the governance of a political state, and explain how one author suggested a woman leader might or should resolve such issues.

The protagonist of each play is loosely based on the historical personage of Queen Christina of Sweden. During the seventeenth century, Queen Christina had an extraordinary reputation in Europe, and particularly in Spain, where her conversion to Roman Catholicism was of extreme interest to the church's hierarchy as well as to the practicing faithful.[7] When her father, King Gustavus Adolphus, died at the battle of Lutzen, one of several battles waged against the Spaniards in 1632, Christina inherited the throne at the age of six. She was guided by Chancellor Oxenstierna, who gave her political instruction until she attained the throne in 1644 at age eighteen. Reputed to be an intelligent and valorous leader and a scholar, she was said to have favored the arts and sciences. During her reign she brought Descartes to her scholarly court; credit for her conversion to Roman Catholicism is frequently attributed to him. Her anti-Protestant views and her refusal to marry led to her abdication in 1654 and her eventual move to Rome where she participated in an active intellectual life. Her reputation for being an able horsewoman, an agile thinker, and a passionate lover always preceded her.[8]

In the comedia *Afectos de odio y amor* and its counterpart, the auto sacramental *La protestación de la fe*, the historical personage of Queen Christina is represented by a fictional northern queen who is a leader in the religious wars in Europe.[9] The similarity of their names (Cristerna in the comedia and Cristina in the auto sacramental), both plays' reference to the continuing battles between Catholics and the northern heretics, and the conversion that both protagonists experience at the conclusion of each play contribute to the assumption that Queen Christina serves as the historical referent for the two fictional queens.

A brief summary of the setting of the conflict in the comedia will facilitate our understanding of the portrait of Cristerna. The action takes place in the courts of Russia, Gocia, and the imaginary Suevia between the years 1646 and 1655. Casimiro, the Duke of Russia, has waged war with the Suevians and killed Cristerna's father, Adolfo. During this same battle, Casimiro witnessed

Cristerna in action and immediately fell in love with her, even though she led the enemy camp. Struck by the pangs of love, he gives up the reins of government and, in the disguise of a common soldier of the Suevian forces, Casimiro makes his way to the enemy camp, determined to persuade Cristerna to accept his love. Cristerna, at the same time, plans revenge for the death of her father, promising her hand in marriage to the noble who accomplishes such a feat. After numerous court intrigues, disguises, impersonations, deceptions, and duels, Cristerna and Casimero are eventually brought together in marriage and wedded bliss.

When Cristerna first appears on stage, at the sound of the trumpets and the beat of the drums, she paces around the military camp wielding the royal staff, surrounded by numerous women, each with a feathered pen and a sword in hand. As soon as Cristerna speaks, she shows that she is in command and that she can rise to the challenge of running a kingdom. She declares:

> quiero empezar a mostrar
> si tiene o no la mujer
> ingenio para aprender,
> juicio para gobernar
> y valor para lidiar.[10]

Translation:
> I want to begin to show
> whether woman has
> the mind to learn,
> judgment to govern
> and valor to fight.

Even by the campfire, she rewrites the laws by which the kingdom inherited from her father, Gustavus Adolphus, will be governed:

> dispone que la mujer
> que se aplicare, inclinada
> al estudio de las letras
> o al manejo de las armas,
> sea admitida a los puestos
> públicos. (1762A)

Translation:
> [Queen Cristerna] orders that the woman
> who applies herself, inclined to
> the study of letters
> or to the wielding of arms,
> be admitted to public office.

Cristerna is not only the declared ruler of the northern kingdom, but also a militant feminist, for within a few hours of gaining control she has declared the

Salic laws invalid, outlawed duels, and provided women the opportunity to wage war and distribute justice.

Confronted by this early portrait of the northern queen, the reader's initial response is to question her previous assumptions about the presentation of women in Golden Age comedia. This early evidence at first suggests a radical position in Calderón's construction of female characters and their motivations. Perhaps this dramatist has provided a female lead who will be able to carry a pen and a sword to the end. And maybe exception can be made to Sandra Foa's idea that the sixteenth-century concern for the position of women in society, expressed in words like those of María de Zayas y Sotomayor in the epigraph of this chapter, has, in the seventeenth century, succumbed to the traditional view of women as subordinate.[11]

As a contemporary of Philip IV, a possible marriage between Queen Christina and the Spanish king was suggested, and, in this light, the delineation of Cristerna's pretender in the comedia, Casimiro, takes on new significance. At the beginning of the play and, in spite of victory over Cristerna's father, lovestruck Casimero recites a lengthy description of Cristerna to his sister, Auristela, while bemoaning his fate as the impossible lover. His first description of Cristerna should put us on guard immediately:

> Es Cristerna tan *altiva*
> que la sobra la belleza.
> Mira si la sobra poco
> para ser *vana y soberia...*
> No sólo, pues, de Diana
> en la venatoria escuela
> discípula creció; pero
> aun en la *altivez* severa
> con que de Venus y Amor
> *el blando yugo desprecia.*
> No tiene príncipe el Norte
> que no la idolatre bella,
> ni príncipe tiene que
> sus *esquiveces* no sienta,
> diciendo que ha de quitar,
> sin que a sujetarse venga,
> del mundo el infame abuso
> de que las mujeres sean
> acostumbradas vasallas
> del hombre, y que *ha de ponerlas*
> *en el absoluto imperio*
> *de las armas y las letras.* (1757B–1758A, emphasis my own)

Translation:
> Cristerna is so haughty
> that her beauty is superfluous.
> No wonder that she is on the verge

of being vain and proud.
Not only was she educated
in Diana's hunting school
but even [in the school of] severe haughtiness
with which she scorns
the soft yoke of Venus and Love.
The North has no prince
who does not idolize her beauty,
nor does it have a prince
who does not feel her disdain,
[for she says] that [she] has to abolish from the world,
without succumbing herself,
the vile abuse
that makes women
habitual vassals
of men, and that she has to place them [women]
in absolute command
of arms and letters.

In spite of being lovestruck and in awe of Cristerna, Casimiro's earliest description of the queen forecasts her eventual submission. In his first lines she is described as "altiva," "vana," and "soberbia." In spite of her royalty, her vanity and arrogance automatically classify her as the stock character of the "mujer esquiva" as described by Melveena McKendrick in *Women and Society in the Spanish Drama of the Golden Age*, a book that has provided the standards and determined the direction of feminist studies of the comedia for the last twenty years.[12] In her extensive analysis of the multitude of female characters that populated the stage in Golden Age comedias, McKendrick divided the major female roles into six main groups: bandits, huntresses, scholars, warriors, avengers, and the "mujer esquiva." It is difficult to translate the term "mujer esquiva" but disdainful, elusive, distant, shy, cold approximate the meaning. Melveena McKendrick has described her as "the woman who, for some reason, is averse to the idea of love and marriage" and who is "usually, but not invariably, averse to men as well" (p. 142).

The physical description of Cristerna, also provided early by Casimiro, concurs with the picture of a woman who has stepped outside the norm, in this case the pattern of feminine dress. Describing a tremendous battle fought with the still unseen female protagonist, Casimiro pauses to recall Cristerna's abrupt arrival in the heat of battle.

traía
sobre las doradas trenzas
solo una media celada,
a la borgoñeta puesta;
una hungarina o casaca
en dos mitades abierta,

de acero el pecho vestido
mostraba, de cuya tela
un tonelete, que no
pasaba de media pierna,
dejaba libre el batido
de la bota y de la espuela. (1759A)

Translation:
   She wore
only a Burgundian helmet
over her golden braids;
a military coat
open down the middle,
revealing her chest
covered by a steel plate,
a skirt of armor of the same material
which only reached mid calf
gave freedom of movement
to the boot and spur.

Throughout the first two acts, descriptions and references to Cristerna abound; but only rare mention of the queen is made without adding the terms "esquiva," "arrogante," "vana," or "soberbia." Nobles and servants alike often reiterate her "esquivez."

Soberbia, esquiva, (1760B) (Arrogant, cold)
hermosa fiera (1761A) (Beautiful wild beast)

Not only do others portray her as such, but her own words and actions leave little doubt that her desire for independence and her feminism are not attributable to any positive character trait but instead to pure arrogant pride. Her work as a lawmaker and a distributor of justice at first warrant admiration, as when she allows for women to hold public positions:

sea admitida a los puestos
públicos, siendo en su patria
capaz del honor que en guerra
y paz más al hombre ensalza. (1762A)

Translation:
[that the woman] be admitted to public office,
affording her in her own country
the same benefits that grace men in war and peace.

and she forbids duels:

manda también que se borren
duelos que notan de infamia

al marido que sin culpa
desdichado es por desgracia. (1762A)

Translation:
it is ordered that duels be forbidden
for they dishonor
the husband who, blameless,
is unfortunately disgraced.

and when she legislates in women's favor by expurgating the Salic law, although no longer in practice, from the books of governance.

Her fourth and final law forbids women to marry out of love beneath their station in life on pain of death. She adds that this law should be stamped in bronze:

el amor
no es disculpa para nada.
Porque ¿qué es amor? ¿Es más
que una ciega ilusión vana,
que vence, porque yo quiero
que venza? (1762B)

Translation:
Love
isn't an excuse for anything.
Because, what is love?
Is it anything but a blind, vain illusion
which conquers at will?

It is this fourth law, against marriage based on love, its supporting rationale, that love is only a figment of the imagination, and the harsh punishment promised to those women who break the law, which finally confirms that Cristerna is operating contrary to natural law and brings into question all of her previous decrees. As Malveena McKendrick states, the "mujer esquiva," and here we may read Cristerna, exemplifies one aspect of the traditional seventeenth-century Spanish perception of women. "In the eyes of the dramatist the 'mujer esquiva' is not, ultimately, rebelling against man-made rules which, given the weakness of human nature, may be misguided ones. Her defiance, whatever the motive, whatever the incitement, is directed against the natural order of things as decreed by God." (p. 143)

Cristerna must be converted to the natural law of female subordination as argued by seventeenth-century moral thinkers. The conversion process is accomplished in several steps that call for the breakdown of her initial aversion to love, her gradual yielding to the laws of nature, the pretended disdain by her suitor, her susceptibility to jealousy, and a final crisis in which Cristerna recognizes that her beloved suitor is indeed her avowed enemy whose death she has called for. By the beginning of the third act, the women of Cristerna's court realize that she is in love with the disguised soldier, Casimiro, the Prince of Russia, her sworn enemy, and the fourth law that she decreed, that love not be used as an excuse, a "disculpa para nada," will be the first to be invalidated by her own actions. Cristerna recognizes the errancy of her former ways, looses her "altivez" and "ánimo varonil," and subjugates herself to the bland yoke of marriage. By the conclusion of the comedia, the law against marriage for love has been annulled and all other laws designed to protect women's rights have been declared equally invalid. (1796A)

At the end of the comedia love has won. The binary opposition of love and hatred reflected by the bimembral structure of the verses,[13] the secondary conflict between Auristela and her suitor Segismundo, which duplicated the primary dramatic situations between Cristerna and Casimiro, the doubling of disguises and entanglements have come to an end and the singular natural order takes precedence:

> Y pues que mis vanidades
> se dan a partido, puedes,
> Lesbia, borrar de aquel libro
> las exenciones. Estése
> el mundo como se estaba,
> y sepan que las mujeres,
> vasallas del hombre nacen;
> pues en sus afectos, siempre
> que el odio y el amor compiten
> es el amor el que vence. (1796A)

Translation:

> And since my vanities
> are giving way,
> Lesbia, you can erase
> the exemptions from that book.
> Let the world be like it was,
> and let it be known that women
> are born vassals of man;
> for in their emotions, whenever
> hatred and love compete,
> it is always love which wins.

Cristerna is a prime example of the "mujer esquiva"; her crises were limited to the choice between love and hatred of an individual, as is consistent with many personal struggles in the *comedia palaciega*. She is not necessarily representative of Calderón's thoughts of women as regents, either in disapproval or acceptance; several of his serious dramas, including *La Gran Cenobia*,[14] for example, deal more directly with this issue. Nor should one use the play to analyze Calderón's evaluation of the monarchy. The choice of Cristerna as protagonist seems largely predetermined by the standardized portrait of the "mujer esquiva," a literary convention behind which all but the most liberated dramatist could hide his own misgivings about women as equals and as independent thinkers.

In *Afectos de odio y amor*, the northern queen was used to portray a female leader caught by birth and historical situation in a kind of heresy, the subversion of the law of nature, but who, through love and careful guidance from another, is eventually persuaded to conform to the norm, to accept the laws of society and her own biological nature. Cristerna passes through a conversion, she has become a believer in the natural law, and subsequently become the submissive and faithful vassal of man.

In the auto sacramental the protagonist's conversion process takes quite a different turn. Calderón's autos sacramentales rarely include legendary or historical women; those of the Old Testament, like Ruth, Rachel, Deborah, and Jael, in *¿Quién hallará mujer fuerte* usually serve as a prefiguration of the Virgin Mary.[15] Of the eighty *autos* by Calderón, according to the classification of Valbuena Prat,[16] nine are based on legends or historical events, and in only one the main character is a woman, Queen Christina of Sweden. In *La protestación de la fe* Cristina portrays a heretic converted to the Roman Catholic faith.

Because of internal and external evidence, *La protestación de la fe* has been assigned a date of composition of 1656.[17] As in other autos sacramentales written early in Calderón's career, in *La protestación de la fe*, the personification of evil, depicted by the character Herejía (Heresy), stands alone as Cristina's potentiality to turn away from the Holy Faith. Herejía's positive counterpart, that is to say, Cristina's predilection to turn toward God, is Sabiduría (Wisdom). Sabiduría is accompanied by the four virtues: Fe, Oración, Penitencia, and Religión (Faith, Prayer, Penitence, Religion), each a willing and necessary accomplice to Cristina's conversion.

The comparison of just a few descriptions of Cristina with those of Cristerna will elucidate the conversion process. As in the comedia, Cristina does not immediately appear on stage, but is first described to Wisdom by her sympathetic guardian, Heresy.

> ¿qué más poder, que más armas
> que aquella beldad, que aquella
> heroica heredera, hija
> del que en la más dura guerra,
> que vió del sol la campaña,
> murió sin que borrar pueda
> lo grande de la osadía,
> lo infeliz de la tragedia?[18]

Translation:
> What greater power, what greater arms
> than that beauty, than that

heroic heiress, daughter
of he who in the harshest war
which the battlefield ever revealed
died without diminishing
the enormity of his audacity,
the misfortune of the tragedy.

Apparently Cristina is not to be characterized by the reprehensible trait of arrogant pride. Whereas Cristerna was repeatedly alluded to in terms of her vanity and "esquivez," Cristina's defect is one of omission; her failure is symbolized by the missing letter in her name. Separately, Herejia, Sabiduria, and Religion all make reference to the missing "A," which would transform her from Cristina to Cristiana:

> *Sabid*
> Quizá Cristina, que el nombre
> hoy imperfecto conserva
> de Cristiano, mal viciado
> por la falta de una letra
> (siendo la A la que falta,
> que es la Alfa en frase griega
> significación de Dios,
> pues Dios es Alfa y Omega)
> podrá ser que se le añada
> algún día y que a ser venga
> Cristiana perfectamente
> quien hoy lo es mente imperfecta. (734A)

> *Relig.*
> Como ya Cristina
> (tú lo dijiste), a quien falta
> una letra para ser
> perfectamente Cristiana,
> siendo Alfa la letra, viene,
> buscando a Dios, a buscarla. (742A)

Translation:
> *Sabid*
> Perhaps Cristina, whose name
> is but an imperfect rendering
> of Christian, vitiated
> by the lack of a letter
> (the one missing being the A,
> which is Alpha in Greek,
> signifying God,
> since God is the Alpha and Omega),
> it could be that some day
> it might still be added
> and that she who today is imperfect

becomes perfectly
Christian.

Relig.
Since Cristina,
as you said, who is missing
a letter to be
a perfect Christian,
Alpha being the letter,
looking for God comes to find it [the letter].

The second attribute of Cristerna, that of being a scholar, lawmaker, and soldier, is characteristic of Cristina as well. Her entrance on stage could have been taken directly from the comedia but for one important difference. Rather than women wielding pens and swords, a group of male soldiers accompanies Cristina. She appears "vestida de corto, armada" and once center stage, begins to disarm and receive the other accoutrements of her office, the "plumas, espadas" (735B). After the soldiers shout "long live victorious Cristina, long live our heroic queen," she asks to be left alone with her books. She makes no pronouncements and declares no laws. In a speech reminiscent of that by Cristerna on the value of both arms and letters to the monarch:

de que letras y armas son
los polos, que han mantenido
la máquina de reinar,
me han ayudado a vencer,
pues no menos el poder
estriba en la singular
toga que en la militar túnica de Marte. (735B)

Translation:
that letters and arms are
the poles that have supported
the machinery of rule,
[these books] have helped me to conquer,
for no less is power
built upon the professorial
cloak than on the military tunic of Mars.

Cristina shows the extent of her wisdom; she is a worthy and balanced leader, not led astray by her knowledge. Her scholarship becomes the guide to her eventual salvation.

Throughout the auto, Cristina is described as a "mujer fuerte" and a "mujer constante," and because her reading of the texts of Saint Augustine on free will has opened her eyes to the possibility of personal religious choice, it comes as no surprise that her inner strength (*fuerza*) allows her to reject the heretical religion of her youth and seize the opportunity for salvation by becoming a vassal of the true faith:

> sujeta hoy, como vasalla
> de su Imperio, la que ayer
> era Reina de su Patria. (745A)

Translation:
> subject today, as a vassal
> of its empire, she who yesterday
> was queen of her nation.

The "mujer esquiva" of the comedia has ceased to exist in the auto sacramental. The adjectives that qualified Cristerna such as "docta," "altiva," and "arrogante," have now become attributes attached to the personifications of death, doubt, fortune, and, most frequently, the miserable condition of man. Few favorable descriptive terms remain for female protagonists, these being "fuerte" (strong) and "constante" (constant).

Whereas the texts read by Cristerna in *Afectos de odio y amor* are the new laws that she has just proclaimed throughout the northern kingdom, in the auto sacramental Cristina is seen reading a passage from Saint Augustine on free will. Her scholarship is not a demonstration of arrogant female pride, but instead provides the rationale for her desire to give up the reins of her kingdom:

> ¿Qué interior música . . .
>   . . .
> me está sonando al oído,
> cuya ilusión ha podido
> mi espíritu arrebatar
> tanto, que llegando a dar
> toda la rienda al cuidado
> de saber, casi he llegado
> a aborrecer el reinar? (735B)

Translation:
> What interior music . . .
> always sounds in my ears
> whose illusion has been able
> to stir my spirit
> so much that giving into my thirst
> for knowledge, I have almost come
> to detest ruling?

In the auto sacramental the northern queen was used to portray a leader caught by birth or historical situation in a heretical religion, but who, through reading and careful guidance from Sabiduria and the ambassadors from the courts of Felipe IV, could eventually be brought to the true faith.

In both of Calderón's plays, the female protagonists have been converted, in the comedia, to the natural law, and therefore to God, and in the auto sacramental to the Roman Catholic faith. Each protagonist has had qualifications and attributes built into her character—"esquivez," arrogance, and vanity in the comedia, strength and constancy in the auto—but since each attribute was called for by the plot, few generalizations about Calderón's feminism can be based solely on these two protagonists. But yet, since both plays are works of popular literature, performed before a heterogeneous Spanish audience, they might be seen as purveyors of popular opinion, and we must acknowledge the call for the conversion of the female protagonist from imperfection to perfection, from independent woman to perfect wife, from heresy to Roman Catholicism, from leader to vassal.

NOTES

1. From María de Zayas y Sotomayor, *Novelas amorosas y ejemplares*, vol. I (Madrid: Biblioteca Selecta de Clásicos Españoles, 1948), 22. Sandra M. Foa has given the English translation for this passage as well as for several others from *Novelas amorosas y ejemplares* in her article "María de Zayas y Sotomayor: Sibyl of Madrid (Spanish, 1590–1661?)," J. R. Brink, ed., *Female Scholars: A Tradition of Learned Women Before 1800* (Montreal: Eden Press Women's Publications, 1980), 65. For a complete translation of the *Novelas amorosas y ejemplares* see *Enchantments of Love. Amorous and Exemplary Novels*, tr. and ed. by H. Patsy Boyer (Berkeley: California University Press, 1990).

2. In 1609, Lope de Vega defined the new comedia in a short treatise entitled *Arte nuevo de hacer comedias en este tiempo*. It was first published by Alonso Pérez in Lope's *Rimas humanas*, Parte II (Madrid: Imprenta del Reino, 1634). I have consulted the edition by Juan de José Prades (Madrid: CSIC, 1971).

3. Numerous articles and books about the birth, history, and structure of the Spanish Golden Age comedia are available in English. For more information the reader might consult the following: Sturgis E. Leavitt, *Golden Age Drama in Spain* (Chapel Hill, University of North Carolina Press, 1972); A. A. Parker, *The Approach to the Spanish Drama of the Golden Age* (London: Hispanic and Luso-Brazilian Councils, 1957); Norman D. Shergold, *A History of the Spanish Stage from Medieval Times until the End of the Seventeenth Century* (Oxford: Clarendon Press, 1967); Edward M. Wilson and Duncan Moir, *A Literary History of Spain: The Golden Age Drama* (New York: Barnes and Noble, 1971); and Henryk Ziomek, *A History of Spanish Golden Age Drama* (Lexington: University of Kentucky Press, 1984.

4. The second term applies to a comedia in which the protagonists, either members of the middle class or peasants, meet an unfortunate outcome at the conclusion of the dramatic conflict.

5. See Emilio Cotarelo y Mori's biography of Calderón in "Ensayo sobre la vida y obras de don Pedro Calderón de la Barca," *Boletín de la Real Academia Española* (1922), 624–649.

6. With respect to Calderón's theater, three relatively recent feminist studies of the comedia are noteworthy for their insights. These are Anita K. Stoll and Dawn L. Smith's edition of a collection of articles on women in the comedia in *The Perception of Women in Spanish Theater of the Golden Age* (Lewisburg: Bucknell University Press, 1991), Frederick de Armas' book *The Invisible Mistress* (Charlottesville: Biblioteca Siglo de Oro, 1976), and Melveena McKendrick's book *Women and Society in the Spanish Drama of the Golden Age* (Cambridge:

Cambridge University Press, 1974), which provided the foundation and set the standards for more recent work in this field.

7. See Georgina Masson, *Queen Christina* (New York: Farrar, Straus & Giroux, 1968). Several texts have provided information about the depiction of Christina by her contemporaries. See Susanna Akerman, *Queen Christina of Sweden and Her Circle* (Leiden: E. J. Brill, 1991); the Stockholm National Museum catalog for the 11th Exhibition of the Council of Europe intitled *Christina, Queen of Sweden* (Stockholm: Egnellska Boktryckeriet, 1966); Per Bjurstrom, *Feast and Theatre in Queen Christina's Rome* (Stockholm: Bengtsons litografiska, 1966). Earlier Swedish histories prepared for North American audiences include Carl Grimberg, *A History of Sweden* (Rock Island, IL: Augustana Book Concern, 1935); Victor Nilsson, *Sweden* (New York: The Cooperative Publication Society, 1899); and Paul Lewis, *Queen of Caprice* (New York: Holt, Rinehart and Winston, 1962).

8. See Ruth Lundelius, "Queen Christina of Sweden and Calderón's *Afectos de odio y amor*," *Bulletin de Comediantes* 38, 2, 231–248, for a careful analysis of the distinction between the historical figure and her theatrical representation in the comedia. R. Lundelius provides excerpts from contemporary Spanish documents that show how the portrayal of Christina fluctuates with the political tide. Initially admired as a wise and prudent leader, her portrait grows increasingly negative as the Spaniards became aware of her diminishing ability to restore Roman Catholicism in Sweden.

9. There is insufficient evidence to establish the date of composition of the comedia; conjectures range from 1652 to 1658. J. Weiner has chosen the early date, basing this assumption on Calderon's desire to promote Christina's conversion, "Cristina de Suecia en dos obras de Calderón de la Barca," *Bulletin de Comediantes* 31 (1970), 25–31. Others have proposed a date closer to its first known performance late in 1657 or 1658. See Document 153 of Cristóbal Pérez Pastor's *Documentos para la biografía de D. Pedro Calderón de la Barca* (Madrid: Establecimiento Tipográfica de Fortanet, 1905), in which Francisco García justifies his absence from a public performance on 28 February 1658, stating that he was taken to Buen Retiro for a rehearsal of *Afectos de odio y amor* to be performed on 5 March (Shrove Tuesday) of that year. According to Emilio Cotarelo y Mori, "Ensayo sobre la vida y obras de don Pedro Calderón de la Barca," *Boletín de la Real Academia Española* 9 (December, 1922), 638, the performance was cancelled due to the queen's illness and the play was presented to the general public at a later date.

10. Pedro Calderón de la Barca, *Afectos de odio y amor*, *Obras completas*, Vol. II (Madrid: Aguilar, 1973), 1761B. All subsequent textual references are to page and column in this edition. As with all but a few of Calderón's most famous comedias, this play has not yet been translated into English. The prose translations of all quotations from the comedia are my own.

11. Sandra Foa, "María de Zayas y Sotomayor: Sybil of Madrid" J. R. Brink, ed., *Female Scholars: A Tradition of Learned Women before 1800* (Montreal: Eden Press Women's Publications, 1980), 54–67.

12. Melveena McKendrick, *Woman and Society in the Spanish Drama of the Golden Age. A Study of the "Mujer Varonil"* (London: Cambridge University Press, 1974). Although McKendrick's conclusions have recently been characterized as "somewhat tentative" by Dawn L. Smith, "Introduction: The Perception of Women in the Spanish Comedia," in Stoll and Smith, *The Perception of Women in the Theater of the Spanish Golden Age* (see note 6), her significant research on the female characters of the comedia and her considerable effort to draw attention to the need for further scholarly criticism in this area have made a positive impact on feminist studies of the Spanish Golden Age.

13. See Dámaso Alonso, "La correlación en la estructura del teatro calderoniano," *Seis calas en la expresión literaria española* (Madrid: Gredos, 1970), 111–175. In this benchmark essay, Alonso discusses Calderón's use of parallelism and correlation within dramatic dialogue.

Because drama usually involves a conflict between two principal characters, dramatic dialogue often takes the form of bi-membered parallelism. Many exchanges between Cristerna and Casimiro are built on this structure; in Act 3, when Casimiro's origins are about to be revealed, both his and Cristerna's internal conflicts are revealed in a bi-membered correlation:

Cris.	[Aparte] En fin, fortuna, has logrado . . .	
Casim.	[Aparte] En fin, fortuna, has sabido . . .	
Cris.	[Aparte] hacer que el que he aborrecido . . .	
Casim.	[Aparte] hacer que la que he adorado . . .	
Cris.	[Aparte] haya a mi vista llegado.	
Casim.	[Aparte] haya de saber quién soy.	
Cris.	[Aparte] ¡Muerta llego!	
Casim.	[Aparte]	¡Ciego voy!
Cris.	[Aparte] ¡Qué temores!	
Casim.	[Aparte]	¡Qué recelos!

14. Based on late Roman history, *La gran Cenobia* recounts the defeat of Zenobia at the hands of Lucius Domitius Aurelius. Calderón assigned the qualities of intelligence and courage to the Assyrian queen. The play was first presented by the company of Andrés Varga in 1625. It is included in the edition of A. Valbuena Briones, ed., *Obras completas*, vol. 1 (Madrid: Aguilar, 1969).

15. Pedro Calderón de la Barca, *¿Quién hallará mujer fuerte?* Angel Valbuena Prat, ed., *Obras completas*, vol. III (Madrid: Aguilar, 1952), 655–676.

16. Volume III of Calderón's *Obras completas* included seventy-four autos sacramentales as well as second versions of three of the included plays. The editor, Angel Valbuena Prat, categorized the autos into seven groups according to theme or narrative source; *¿Quién hallará mujer fuerte* is listed as one of thirteen based on themes taken from the Old Testament, 32–35. Although the reliability of the edition has been challenged because of errors in transcription, it remains the most complete and frequently cited source for the autos sacramentales.

17. *La protestación de la fe*, originally written for the Corpus Christi celebrations of 1656, was cancelled "bajo decreto del Rey al Presidente que no se hiciese, porque las cosas de esta señora no estaban en aquel primer estado que tuvieron al principio, cuya casa y servicio de criados se compone ahora de sólo franceses" (by the king's decree to the President, that [the play] not be performed because things relating to this lady were not in the same situation as they were at the beginning, for her house and servants now only consist of the French) See *Avisos de don Jerónimo de Barrionuevo* (Madrid, 1892, II, 423), quoted by Emilio Cotarelo y Mori, *Ensayo*, 629.

18. Pedro Calderón de la Barca, *La protestación de la fe*, in Obras completas, vol. III, 734A. All subsequent textual references are to page and column in this edition. The translations are mine.

10

Rhetorical Canons and Female Portraits in Pastoral Romances

Sylvia Trelles

*T*he ancient discipline of rhetoric remains the source of basic literary practices during the renaissance and baroque periods. Authors were well-acquainted with both rhetoric and poetics as part of their training in the *studia humanitatis*. It is thus valuable in literary analysis to find the rhetorical and poetical canons underpinning literary texts. If, as López Grigera states, we accept the fact that for two millennia rhetoric was the fundamental code from which every text was generated and that it established many of the basic precepts of literary production, then we do not need to reconstruct, but rather to rediscover which of its systems was operating as a canon at a specific moment.[1] This is precisely what I intend to do, specifically in the area of description of women in Spanish Golden Age pastoral romances, for it is my belief that rhetorical prescriptions were influential in the creation of images of women in the literature of that period. In order to better understand some aspects of the portrayal of women in renaissance literature, I will analyze female portraits in two pastoral works, searching to rediscover which rhetorical systems have been used, and how.

I will first provide a synopsis of the section of classical rhetoric pertaining to portraiture and a brief background of female literary portraiture during the Middle Ages as a needed introduction to the analysis of female descriptions in various Spanish pastoral romances. Although reference will be made to Jorge de Montemayor's *Diana*, this study will center on Gaspar Gil Polo's *Diana enamorada* and Luis Gálvez de Montalvo's *Pastor de Fílida*.

Cicero distinguishes between three categories of subjects: epideitic, deliberative, and judicial. The first, "devoted to the praise or censure of a particular individual,"[2] is particularly pertinent in literary characterization. Of all five parts of rhetoric: invention, arrangement, expression, memory, and delivery, I will be concerned only with that of invention, defined by Cicero as "the discovery of valid or seemingly valid arguments to render one's cause plausible."[3] These arguments can be of two types: person or action.[4]

The *De inventione*, however, is not the only classical treatise that is influential to portraiture. Quintillian, in his *Institutions of Oratory*, takes up Cicero's theories relative to portraiture, eliminates the circumstance "nature," but includes individually as other attributes the elements found within that category in Cicero. From the *Rhetorica ad Herennium* comes the division between a physical and a moral portrait; and Horace supplies us with the concept of decorum whereby a character must act in accordance to age, profession, and nationality.[5]

During the Middle Ages something rather peculiar occurred: poets and rhetoritians began following classical precepts so closely that portraits became isolated, static, and lacking in individuality. Moreover, as Faral points out, there was a much greater split between moral and physical portraits. The latter, and referring most specifically to female portraits, centered almost exclusively on highly detailed physical characteristics that followed a descending order from hair to forehead, to eyes, nose, and so on, and then went on to the description of clothing.[6] The models for these descriptions were found in twelfth- and thirteenth-century medieval poetical treatises such as the *Ars versificatoria* of Mathieu de Vendôme and the *Poetria nova* of Geoffroi de Vinsauf, rather than in classical rhetorics. In Spanish literature we find this static physical description in, for example, *Santa María Egipciaca*, in the portrait of the ideal lady lover in the *Book of Good Love*, and in Calixto's famous description of Melibea, where we begin to see a shift toward the detailing of other attributes of person.

The first known edition of the *Celestina* appeared in 1499. We might or might not detect a parodic intent in Melibea's portrait,[7] but when we read Don Quijote's detailed physical description of the illusory Dulcinea, we have no doubt that Cervantes, in the first book of the *Quijote* published in 1605, is discrediting through parody the paradigm of the static female portrait. But Cervantes uses that same static medieval description in his pastoral romance *La Galatea*. Why, we may wonder, is this static physical image of women acceptable in his pastoral work of 1585 and not in the *Quijote*? It is true that this type of description of women is particularly prevalent in some works of this genre. The question, of course, is why. I believe the answer lies in the confluence of several literary traditions in the pastoral. The static medieval descriptions of women are vestiges of a continuing Petrarchan tradition found more or less prominently in these pastoral works.

Montemayor's *Los siete libros de la Diana*, published in 1558 or 1559, is the first of its kind in Spain, and was to be followed by a series of continuations and imitations, among which is Gil Polo's *Diana enamorada* (Valencia, 1564). Avalle-arce points to another type of pastoral romance, distinct because the story line is based almost exclusively on the matrix of the anecdotal personal life of the writer[8]; in other words, the characters have their origin in real people whose anecdotal stories are portrayed in a pastoral setting. Such is the case with Gálvez de Montalvo's *Pastor de Fílida* (Madrid, 1582). Cervantes' *Galatea* is more in line with Montemayor's tradition while Lope de Vega's *Arcadia* (1598) follows the anecdotal one. It should be pointed out that these pastoral novels, or romances, using Blair's terminology,[9] were very popular in Spain through the first quarter of the seventeenth century.

The arrangement of Montemayor's *Siete libros de la Diana* consists of a main plot (the unrequited loves of Sireno and Sylvano for the unhappily married Diana), to which are added a series of subplots, all on the theme of unrequited love, as the characters make their way to the enchanted castle of Felicia where they will find the solutions to their love problems. In addition to several secondary and alluded ones, there are six main female characters, including the protagonist, Diana. The traditional medieval female portrait is found only once in the presentation of Diana. It is a song by Sylvano in the Petrarchan tradition.[10]

Montemayor basically follows the descending order of the medieval canon, describing the color of Diana's hair, face, lips, and neck. This is the only instance where such a pattern is seen almost in its entirety in this *Diana*. There are also frequent descriptions of the eyes and hair along with even more frequent references to her beauty. Overall, however, a more complete and dynamic portrait is done following Cicero's attributes of person and expanding on more than just the physical description falling under the category of nature.

But let us now look more closely at Gil Polo's *Diana enamorada*, which, unlike Montemayor's work, was to be preserved without changes in the inquisition of Don Quijote's library as "if it were by Apollo himself,"[11] for resolution of the love conflicts comes more through reason and will on the part of the characters than by way of Felicia's magical powers. Gil Polo's work is composed of five rather than seven books. Just as in Montemayor's *Diana*, characters make their way to Felicia's castle where happiness awaits in the fourth book; the fifth one being reserved for celebration and moralizing. There are three main plots based on the love conflicts of Diana/Sireno, Alcida/Marcelio, and Ismenia/Montano, out of which only the second is not a continuation of Montemayor's invention. I will analyze the portrait of Diana, a truly pastoral character inherited from the previous romance, and that of Alcida, Gil Polo's exclusive creation in a story that follows the pattern of Greco-Byzantine romances.[12]

Contrary to Montemayor's protagonist, Gil Polo's Diana, unhappily married to a jealous man she does not love, suffers from the impossible and unrequited love for Sireno who was left loveless by Felicia's magical potion in the first romance. Only the death of her husband, Delio, will allow the resolution of love and marriage for Diana and Sireno. Although still a relatively passive character due to her limitations within the pastoral tradition, Diana now does seek Sireno and makes her way to Felicia's castle, sure to find him there.

Diana's total portrait, expressed by the narrator, other characters, and the protagonist herself, is distributed in fragments throughout the entire work. Referring to Cicero's attributes of person, the initial presentation centers on feeling, as is to be expected in a work whose main theme is love.[13]

Two other circumstances are apparent: name and accident. Her name, inherited from Montemayor's work, relates to the chaste hunter and goddess of the forests, to whose temple the first Diana was denied entrance after breaking the promise of chastity and constancy in love by marrying Delio. Thus, her married state, part of the fourth attribute, fortune, plays an important role, as do the circumstance accidents with Cupid's accurate aim at Diana's heart, since they set the stage for the development of the love plot.

Of the second attribute, nature, her sex is emphasized once in a song by Berardo who calls her "la luz de perfectíssimas mujeres"[14] ("the glorie of the fairest women"[15]). Contrary to Montemayor, who states it at the outset, at no point does Gil Polo declare either race or place of birth of his protagonist. Not much is said of family. Her father is mentioned in relation to the obedience owed him in the choice of her spouse: "Mas la Fortuna, que pervierte los humanos intentos, quiso que, obedesciendo más a mi padre que a mi voluntad, dexasse de casarme con él"[16] ("Fortune, which overturneth humane intents, married me to Delius [enforced more by the hard commandement of my parents, then by mine own will]"[17]). Reference is made to Diana's age when she introduces herself to Alcida: "Pues no aprovechará para mas de lastimarte, viendo mi tierna juventud en tanta fatiga"[18] ("since thou shalt profit thee no more, then to make thy selfe compassionate and condolent for my tender yeeres, seeing them oppressed with so many cares and troubles"[19]). This statement is destined to move the listener by accentuating the tragedy of extreme sadness begun at an exceptionaly early age. Diana's qualities of body are repeatedly described in general terms with the words "hermosura" (fairness), "belleza" (beauty), "gentileza" (gentleness), "gracia" (gracefulness), and "perfición" (perfection).

We are reminded, of course, that beauty is at the source of platonic love since it reflects internal virtue.[20] Moreover, physical beauty elicits desire and amorous contemplation. Thus beauty, as Cirurgiao states for Montemayor's work, is substantial rather than accidental since it is the reflection of the universal soul in matter and love is the absolute desire to possess that beauty.[21] However, the fact is that Montemayor stresses Diana's beauty more than Gil Polo, and that physical description in general is markedly reduced in the latter. At no point in Gil Polo does the static physical description of Diana that we saw in Montemayor's work appear. Furthermore, Montemayor's detailed descriptions of individual parts of the body are greatly reduced in Gil Polo, who depicts Diana's hair only on two occasions and in the traditional manner as "las hebras de oro fino / cubiertas con un velo"[22] ("A vaile of Lawne upon her golden haire"[23]). Her eyes are "aquellas dos claríssimas estrellas" ("Of those cleere stars"[24]) and "aquellos ojos claros soberanos" ("those clear and unsurpassed eyes"[25]), while her hands are "las delicadas manos / de aquel marfil para mi muerte hechas"[26] ("In such ill time I sawe those daintie handes / Of whitest Ivorie, fram'd for thousand smartes"[27]). These descriptions are part of an amabeic song, traditional in pastoral poetry, where two characters compete in singing the praises of their loved ones. Diana's qualities of mind are described differently according to the moment and the character speaking. The rejected lover Tauriso complains of her "dureza" (harshness)[28] while Belisa admires her "discreción" (discretion).[29]

Continuing now with the third of Cicero's attributes of person, manner of life, Diana's profession as a shepherdess is often mentioned by the narrator and other characters. Compared with Alcida, whose portrait we will study next, Diana legitimately belongs in the pastoral setting in which she finds herself.

Of fortune, the fourth circumstance, it is her married state to the unloving and jealous Delio that is accentuated, for it is only through his death and Diana's subsequent change of state to that of widow that a happy resolution and harmony can be restored ultimately with her marriage to Sireno. Alcida makes this clear to Sireno, informing him of "la viudez de tu Diana, y pienses si te conviene mudar intento, pues ella mudó el estado"[30] ("thou shouldest understand of Dianas widowhood, and consider with thy selfe, if now it were good for thee to change thine intent, since she hath changed her condition and estate"[31]). "Fame" falls under this circumstance. When Diana introduces herself to Alcida, saying, "Sabe que yo me llamo Diana, por estos campos harto conoscida"[32] ("Yet know (Gentle Shepherdesse) that I am called Diana, knowen too well in all the fields and villages hereabouts"[33]), she lets us know that she is vividly aware of how well she and her sad story are known. Diana's dexterity in singing and playing the reed flute, traditional habits of pastoral characters, are exalted by the cleverness of her verses.[34]

Conscious of the fault in decorum of his protagonist, Gil Polo excuses Diana's unusual abilities for a shepherdess with love's transformations of a person. But Diana's acute memory, knowledge, and mental abilities are displayed again in the series of enigmas that she is asked to solve and where everyone can admire "el aviso, la gala, la criança y comedimiento de Diana"[35] ("the fine wit, the comely grace, the passing behaviour, and sweete actions of Diana"[36]). Unlike Montemayor, Gil Polo gives much importance to the mental capabilities of his female protagonist.

The sixth attribute, feeling, is at the root of all pastoral works. Just as its predecessor, the *Diana enamorada* is composed of a series of cases of love to be resolved at Felicia's castle. Diana's "pena" (sorrow) is, of course, caused by unrequited love for she is "maltratada del mal" (tormented with grief)[37] because of Sireno's lack of love. Diana, however, no longer suffers from lovesickness. She is terribly saddened by an unhappy marriage and a loved one who ignores her, but is resigned to what "Fortuna" gave her. On the other hand, she actively attempts to see and speak with Sireno. There has been a reversal of roles from the pursued to seeker. Gil Polo's Diana is a more active and self-determining character.

Nothing is said of the seventh circumstance, interest. But of purpose, we know that Diana's current suffering results from a change of constancy in love since she obeyed her father rather than her heart in agreeing to marry Delio. She blames her state on Fortune, constituting the tenth circumstance, accidents. Lacking in purpose, she gave in too easily to fate.

Achievements and speech are the actions, dialogues, and songs that make up the essence of the novel and do not need to be analyzed in detail. We see that including these latter two circumstances, Gil Polo has used ten of the eleven attributes of person prescribed by Cicero: name, nature (and of this one sex, family, age, and qualities of body and mind), manner of life, fortune, habit, feeling, purpose, achievements, accidents, and speech. We note also that there is less emphasis than in Montemayor on detailed physical description and that the medieval static female portrait is not present. Moreover, Gil Polo emphasized Diana's knowledge and mental dexterity in solving enigmas.

As we look at the other character selected from Gil Polo's *Diana enamorada*, Alcida, we need to keep in mind that her story, full of adventures, shipwrecks, and abductions, follows the pattern of Greco-Byzantine works, just as the Felismena/Felis one does in Montemayor's work. Contrary to Felismena, who very actively seeks out Felis, Alcida is saught by Marcelio. However, by no means a passive character, Alcida is constantly eluding Marcelio's pursuit and then forcefully rejects Delio's love advances. Furthermore, it should be noted that, as was said before, Alcida does not appear in Montemayor's romance.

From the outset it is made clear to the reader that Alcida is "extranjera, y por aquellas partes nunca vista"[38] ("a stranger and never seene in those parts before"[39]) in the pastoral world of Diana. She declares her name upon Diana's request after they have been conversing for some time. Through the portrait of her father, we discover some elements of the nature of Alcida: place of birth, family, age, and qualities of body.[40] The nouns "hermosura," "gracia," and "gentileza" are often used in the general description of Alcida, as they were with Diana. A description of a specific part of the body is found only once in a letter written to her by Marcelio where he mentions her "gentil y angélico semblante"[41] ("but yet thy gentle, and sweete Angels face"[42]). Sex is alluded to twice when she is referred to as "donzella" and "dama." In both cases the word connotes other meanings, *donzella* alluding to her unmarrried state, and *dama* to her noble and urban background. But it is in the qualities of mind where the emphasis rests in the portrait of Alcida. Diana, after hearing the enigma that Alcida presents to her, calls attention to Alcida's "gentileza" and "discreción."[43] However, Marcelio, distraught over his bride's rejection, repeatedly points to her cruelty: "Busco la más cruel, la más áspera y despiadada donzella que se puede hallar"[44] ("I seeke the most cruell and pitilesse Damsell that lives on earth"[45]).

Alcida is called "pastora" (shepherdess) several times since she is disguising herself as such, but her manner of life is not that, for we know that her estate, under the fourth circumstance, fortune, is one of nobility, and that her attire of shepherdess is only a disguise in her attempt to elude Marcelio.

Alcida's cruel condition is justified by her disillusionment with love. As in Diana's case, feeling constitutes the most important element of her portrait. In her "desamorada condición" (loveless condition) Alcida's character contrasts with Diana's: "He sido muchos años captiva, y agora me veo libre"[46] ("For I my selfe have beene manie yeeres a captive in like bondage, but now am free"[47]), she states, opposing her assessment of Diana's feelings "que lo que agora quieres, en otro tiempo lo has aborrescido"[48] ("since now thou lovest him, whom thou hast heeretofore hated"[49]). After finding out the truth about Marcelio's and Clenarda's story, she becomes "captiva del amor de Marcelio"[50] ("wounded afresh with the love of my betrothed Marcelius"[51]).

As to purpose, we see her with a deliberative plan not to "amar hombre nascido"[52] ("that love I will not any man that's borne"[53]) and to forever run away from Marcelio. This determination, as mentioned, changes after hearing the truth from her sister Clenarda at Felicia's castle.

Achievements constitute the adventure-filled story of Alcida. Called "fugitiva pastora" (fugitive shepherdess[54]) by Marcelio, she is the typical protagonist of Greco-Byzantine novels in her activity and decisiveness. It is Fortune, under the tenth attribute, accidents, which causes her to "aborrescer su esposo, que más que a su vida la quería"[55] ("ensued the hating of her husband, who loved her deerer then his owne life"[56]) and evade him. Speech once again completes the portrait with the dialogues in which Alcida participates.

Thus, nine of the eleven attributes are used in Alcida's portrait: name, nature, manner of life, fortune, feeling, purpose, achievements, accidents, and speech. Within nature, qualities of mind are emphasized over those of body, as are place of birth and family since Alcida is not a true pastoral character but rather a noble lady from urban regions in pastoral disguise. At no time do we see the medieval detailed physical description of these women or, in fact, of any other in Gil Polo's *Diana enamorada*. What we have are portraits composed of Cicero's attributes, more or less emphasized according to the type of character concerned.

Luis Gálvez de Montalvo's *Pastor de Fílida* is rooted in history despite its fictional setting. Francisco Rodríguez Marín has concluded that the story of Fílida and Siralvo's love is based on the author's unhappy love for Magdalena Girón.[57] Other characters in the book represent Don Enrique de Mendoza y Aragón and other friends of Gálvez de Montalvo, including poets, musicians, and other members of the nobility.[58] What Avalle-Arce has called the double process of "pastoralizing reality and socializing the pastoral"[59] is influential in the portrayal of female characters.

We find a proliferation of characters, some of them making only brief appearances, and secondary plots in the *Pastor de Fílida*. Elisea and Fílida are the most prominent female protagonists; of the secondary plots, Finea, Silvera, and Andria are the most salient ones. I have chosen to analyze the portraits of Fílida and Andria because they are the most closely related to Diana and Alcida. Fílida, the object of Silverio's unrequited love, has devoted herself to the goddess Diana and to chastity rather than marry the man her father has chosen. As such, she parallels Montemayor's Diana by being the unattainable love pursued by Silverio. Marriage, and not a commitment to chastity, interferes with Diana's and Sireno's love.

Upon encountering Fílida, we learn that Siralvo "andaba furiosamente herido de los amores de Fílida, Fílida que por lo menos en hermosura era llamada sin par, y en suerte no la tenía" ("was furiously wounded by the love of Filida, Filida, who, at least in beauty was called unequalled, and in fortune, she had none").[60] Her name gets its prefix from that of the nymph Filis. Two other attributes are immediately brought to our attention: nature, with the traditional topic of unequaled beauty in an epithet that will be repeated often, and accidents, for she is a woman without luck. Both of these are critical in her characterization. As we begin with nature, Siralvo's explanation to Alfeo partially fills this section of her portrait: "Bien habrás oído nombrar á Fílida, . . . y sabrás que dexó las aguas de su pequeño río, anchas y felicíssimas por su nacimiento, y engrandeció con su presencia las del dorado Tajo en los ricos albergues de Vandalio" (You must have heard Filida's name mentioned, . . . and must know that she abandoned the waters of her small river, made wide and joyous by her birth, and she enlarged by her presence the waters of the golden Tajo river in the rich refuges of Vandalio).[61] Thus, although her place of birth is not specified, we are informed that she is not from where she finds herself at the time.

Gálvez de Montalvo has followed very closely the model of the traditional static female portrait in detailing the nature of Fílida.[62] He mentions age, then proceeds to the qualities of body: face, hair, forehead, cheeks, teeth ("finas perlas"), mouth, and eyes; to be followed, as the paradigm dictates, by qualities of the mind: judgment, verve, and valor. The attribute fortune follows with her noble estate among the "ilustríssimas." In the physical description there is one element that does not follow the medieval pattern: her dark hair. Gálvez de Montalvo uses this isolated and static physical description, more or less complete, a total of seven times in the characterization of Fílida. He has also dedicated one entire poem to her face ("rostro divino") and two to her eyes : "Son ojos verdes, rasgados; / en el revolver suaves, / apacibles sobre graves, / mañosos y descuidados" (Green eyes, almond shaped; / soft as they move, / peaceful more than grave, / crafty and unworried).[63] Among the adjectives used to qualify Fílida's physical traits in general terms, "hermosura" and "belleza" are the most commonly employed, but we also find "gracia" and "perfección." The qualities of mind depicted in Fílida's portrait include "valor" (valor), "bondad" (goodness), "dignidad" (dignity), "donaire" (verve), "gala" (charm), and "discreción" (discretion).

The third of Cicero's circumstances, manner of life, is depicted in an unusually detailed and dynamic description of both Fílida and Florela. Consecrated now to the goddess Diana, they are deer hunting.[64]

Llegaron dos gallardas cazadoras, que con presuroso vuelo le venían siguiendo. Descalzos traían los blancos pies y desnudos los hermosos brazos; sueltos los cabellos que, como fino oro, al viento se esparcían; blanco cendal y tela de fina plata cubrían sus gentiles cuerpos, las aljabas abiertas, y los arcos colgando.

Translation:
Two graceful women hunters arrived, who were following him with great speed. Their white feet were uncovered, and so their beautiful arms. Their hair was loose, and like fine gold, was scattered by the wind. A white veil and fine silver material covered their gentle bodies, while their quivers were open and their arches hanging.

The dynamism we witness in this description by Gálvez de Montalvo appears in Montemayor's *Diana*, but is infrequent in Gil Polo.

Gálvez de Montalvo, who, we must remember, with his protagonist is praising the noble lady Magdalena Girón, stresses Fílida's high social standing, part of the fourth attribute, fortune, with qualifiers such as "ilustre" (illustrious) and "sin par nacida" (of unequaled birth).[65] Her lineage and economic level are measured against that of another character for "aunque Albana no es de menos suerte y de más hacienda, Fílida es muy aventajada en hermosura y discreción" ("even though Albana is of no less condition and is of greater wealth, Fílida is far superior in beauty and discretion").[66] The attributes of habit and purpose are exemplified in Florela's description of Fílida.[67]

Her dedication to the goddess Diana, along with her constancy, indicate strength in purpose, while "profundidad en las artes," "limpieza," "aseo," "liberalidad," and "trato" do so in habit. As with other characters, Fílida's actions in the story comprise the ninth attribute, achievements, but in her case one action marks a change in purpose, a new determination, and rests as the catalyst for the story of unrequited love.

Fílida left earthly goods, family, and independence to enter the world of the goddess Diana, in other words, to enter a convent.[68] Fortune, part of the circumstance accidents, had been adverse, as we saw earlier, for, just like the character Diana, she was being forced to marry a man she did not love. This is all that is known about the attribute feeling, which is significantly unaccentuated in Fílida's characterization.

Ten of Cicero's attributes are used in Fílida's portrait: name, nature (and within it place of birth, age, and qualities of body and of mind), manner of life, fortune, habit, feeling, purpose, achievements, accidents, and speech. Gálvez de Montalvo uses the static medieval portrait seven times in the characterization of Fílida. Once Siralvo calls it a "retrato en verso . . . que cuando a Fílida no se parezca, menos habrá quien se parezca á [él]" ("portrait in verse that if it were not to resemble Filida, then even less could anyone else resemble it"),[69] and proceeds to paint the medieval pattern describing hair, forehead, eyes, nose, cheeks, mouth, neck, chest, hand, and then attributes of the mind. The model is followed even in the strict descending order. In another instance, the same type of isolated portrait is accomplished with twelve different characters singing in praise of Fílida's individual physical and spiritual traits, disposed in equally strict descending order. Without a doubt, nature is the most underlined circumstance, and physical traits, with the exception of the dark hair, are repeatedly described in traditional patterns dating back to the Middle Ages. Fortune is stressed in a manner not seen in Gil Polo, while feeling is markedly deemphasized.

Andria, the inconstant woman pursued by Alfeo, is a nonpastoral character in Gálvez de Montalvo's *Pastor de Fílida*. She appears as such as Alfeo tells of his unhappy love story and his reason for escaping from the court into the life of a shepherd. However, Andria later appears disguised as the shepherdess Amarantha, resolute to find Alfeo and rekindle their love. The roles have now changed and she actively persues Alfeo. The latter's new love, Finea, appears now as the opposing force to her love.

Gálvez de Montalvo has followed closely Cicero's prescription and has included the medieval static physical description in a most traditional manner.[70] In Alfeo's representation of Andria he includes the attributes name, nature, fortune ("clara generación" and "caudalosos parientes"), habit ("habilidad raríssima"), and feeling ("ligero corazón"). Within nature, family, age, and qualities of body are detailed. Once again we find the old topic of unequaled beauty and a step by step repeat of the static female portrait. This same traditional portrait is used, with even greater detail, one more time in Andria's characterization.

The circumstance purpose comes through as her lack of constancy when Andria is called "varia mujer" (inconstant woman)[71] by Siralvo. Whereas Andria's nature is underscored and her physical beauty is contrasted with her harsh qualities of mind: "intratable" (unsociable), "dessabrida" (surly), "pujante" (strong), "soberbia" (proud), "dura" (harsh), and "violenta" (violent), among others,[72] it is the attribute feeling that gains primary importance in her role as Amarantha, since "todo para Amarantha era tristeza y desconsuelo" ("everything for Amarantha was sadness and desolation").[73] Her new manner of life as shepherdess completes the portrait of Andria disguised as Amarantha.

Including achievements and speech which, as previously stated, constitute the adventures and dialogues of the character, a total of nine of Cicero's eleven attributes are used in Andria's presentation: name, nature, manner of life, fortune, habit, feeling, purpose, achievements, and speech.

In the portrayal of both characters, Fílida and Andria, Gálvez de Montalvo emphasized the attribute nature and in particular the descriptions of qualities of body. We have seen that Gil Polo and Gálvez de Montalvo follow rhetorical canons in their portrayal of women. Both of them use the Ciceronian prescription for the arguments of person, but only Gálvez de Montalvo uses the female portrait model found in medieval poetics and carried over particularly in poetry of Petrarchan tradition. Of each work I purposely selected a character ensuing from a more pastoral tradition and one following the pattern of Greco-Byzantine romances.

In his *Diana enamorada*, Gil Polo has dispersed the portrayal of his characters throughout the work in fragments, each of which details several circumstances of person: ten were used in Diana's portrait and nine in Alcida's. In neither characterization are qualities of body accentuated, contrasting with Montemayor's depiction of Diana and those of the two characters studied of the *Pastor de Fílida*. I believe that two elements are at play here. On the one hand, there is the Greco-Byzantine inclination of Gil Polo's work, including the Diana/Sireno story. As was mentioned earlier, Diana is less passive and more assertive than her counterpart in the first romance, and the entire *Diana enamorada* has the faster pace of Byzantine romances. This is partially achieved through less descriptive detailing in the portraits. On the other hand, there is the distinction in the philosophical concepts of love studied by Avalle-Arce, who indicates that Montemayor, because of his neoplatonic interest, gives love absolute primacy, whereas Gil Polo's stoicism brings love down, making it firmly subordinate to reason.[74] Supporting his neoplatonic ideas, Montemayor amplifies the descriptions of the qualities of body of his protagonist, whereas Gil Polo centers on Diana's qualities of mind and attribute habit, that is, her mental dexterity and knowledge. Alcida could be compared with Montemayor's Felismena as protagonist of a Greco-Byzantine inset story. In both cases, qualities of mind are stressed over those of body, and place of birth and family are underlined pointing to their foreignness in the pastoral world. Thus, Gil Polo's stoic philosophical attitude toward love and the "Byzantinism" of his work call for the absence of excessive detailing of physical traits and for an emphasis on Cicero's other attributes of person. Moreover, in his female portraiture, Gil Polo follows rhetorical prescriptions consistent with Aristotelian concepts granting importance to action, verisimilitude, and decorum. It might be well to remember that Aristotle's *Poetics* was rediscovered at the end of the fifteenth century and by the middle of the following century had gained much prestige and popularity.[75]

Gálvez de Montalvo, however, purposely places all of his characters in a pastoral plane. Solé-Leris has indicated that even the Greco-Byzantine story of Andria and Alfeo is not dealt with as an inset story, but is fitted into that same pastoral world and developed as the others.[76] This is reflected in portraiture. The importance given to the attribute nature, with the repeated use of the isolated and static female portrait of medieval origin in both types of characters, the pastoral Fílida and the courtly Andria, points to this single plane. In his aim of placing historical individuals in a fictional pastoral setting, Gálvez de Montalvo has created set characters portrayed in a composite of often isolated and decorative descriptions that often seem solely a display of poetic dexterity. There is no theorizing of either neoplatonic or stoic concepts of love, but instead, as Solé-Leris states, "the underlying attitude . . . harks back to the medieval conception of a love service which is its own reward."[77] Gálvez de Montalvo's ornamental use of the medieval pattern of portraiture in female characterization parallels this vision of love. He persists in a model of portraiture that Cervantes will use in high mockery only a few years later.

We have rediscovered two fundamental systems operating in the portrayal of female characters in these pastoral romances of the Golden Age. One amplifies and distributes throughout the work the arguments of person found in Cicero's *De inventione*. The other, exemplified in medieval poetical treatises, creates static and often isolated portraits detailing physical traits in descending order. Not surprisingly, in the *Pastor de Fílida*, where Gálvez de Montalvo seeks to immerse historical beings into the fictional realm of a pastoral romance, the superficially decorative is enhanced, and the traditional static canon often found in Petrarchan pastoral poetry becomes another embellishment for his pastoral stage. In contrast, by reducing physical description and integrating the Ciceronian attributes of person of his female characters well into the fiber of the text, Gil Polo is making use of classical rhetorical canons in a manner consistent with emerging paradigms of literary fiction emphasizing action and verisimilitude.

NOTES

1. Luisa López Grigera, "La retórica como código de producción y de análisis literario." *Teorías literarias en la actualidad* (Madrid: El Arquero, 1989), 136.

2. Marcus Tullius Cicero, *De inventione. De optimo genere oratorum, Topica* (London: W. Heinemann, 1949), 17.

3. Ibid., 19.

4. The attributes of persons are: name, nature, manner of life, fortune, habit, feeling, interests, purposes, achievements, accidents, speeches made. Ibid., 71–75.

5. Edmond Faral, *Les Arts poétiques du xiie et du xiiie siècle* (Paris: Champion, 1971), 76–78.

6. Ibid., 80.

7. Pierre Heugas, "Variation sur un portrait: de Melibée à Dulcinée," *Bulletin Hispanique* 71 (1969), 12.

8. Juan Bautista Avalle Arce, *La novela pastoril española* (Madrid: Revista de Occidente, 1959), 119.

9. Hugh Blair, *Lectures on Rhetoric and Belles Lettres*, vol. 2 (Carbondale: Southern Illinois University Press, 1965), 303–310.

10. Jorge de Montemayor, *Los siete libros de la Diana* (Madrid: Espasa Calpe, 1970), 67.

11. Miguel de Cervantes, *Don Quixote*, J. M. Cohen, tr. (Middlesex, UK: Penguin, 1977), 61.

12. The Greco-Byzantine romance or Milesian tale is "a tale of romantic adventures dealing with distant travels, shipwrecks, pirates, the separation and miraculous reunion of lovers, etc. The type first occurs in late Greek fiction; e.g., *Teágenes y Clariclea* (third century) by Heliodorus." Maxim Newmark. *Dictionary of Spanish Literature* (New York: N.Y. Philosophical Library, 1956), 239–240.

13. Gaspar Gil Polo, *Diana enamorada* (Madrid: Espasa Calpe, 1953), 15–16. The source for most translations of Gil Polo's work appearing in this chapter is Judith M. Kennedy's 1968 edition of Yong's sixteenth-century English version unless there was a need for me to provide my own translation, in which case no reference to Yong appears in the notes. See Judith M. Kennedy, ed., *A Critical Edition of Yong's Translation of George of Montemayor's Diana and Gil Polo's Enamoured Diana* (Oxford: Clarendon Press, 1968). In the notes I refer to Kennedy's edition of Yong's translation as Gil Polo, *Enamoured Diana*.

14. Gil Polo, *Diana enamorada*, 67.

15. Gil Polo, *Enamoured Diana*, 282.

16. Gil Polo, *Diana enamorada*, 81–82.

17. Gil Polo, *Enamoured Diana*, 293.

18. Gil Polo, *Diana enamorada*, 21.

19. Gil Polo, *Enamoured Diana*, 248.

20. Bruce W. Wardropper, "The Diana of Montemayor: Revaluation and Interpretation," *Studies in Philology* 48 (1951), 140.

21. Antonio A. Cirurgiao, "O papel de la beleza na Diana de Jorge de Montemor," *Hispania* 51 1968), 402.

22. Gil Polo, *Diana enamorada*, 67.

23. Gil Polo, *Enamoured Diana*, 282.

24. Ibid., 279.

25. Gil Polo, *Diana enamorada*, 63.

26. Ibid.

27. Gil Polo, *Enamoured Diana*, 279.

28. Gil Polo, *Diana enamorada*, 65.

29. Ibid., 229.

30. Ibid., 202.

31. Gil Polo, *Enamoured Diana*, 374–375.

32. Gil Polo, *Diana enamorada*, 21.

33. Gil Polo, *Enamoured Diana*, 248.

34. Gil Polo, *Diana enamorada*, 77.

35. Ibid., 233.

36. Gil Polo, *Enamoured Diana*, 396.

37. Gil Polo, *Diana enamorada*, 81.

38. Ibid., 20.

39. Gil Polo, *Enamoured Diana*, 247.

40. Gil Polo, *Diana enamorada*, 42.

41. Ibid., 44.

42. Gil Polo, *Enamoured Diana*, 264.

43. Gil Polo, *Diana enamorada*, 231.

44. Ibid., 40.

45. Gil Polo, *Enamoured Diana*, 261.

46. Gil Polo, *Diana enamorada*, 21.

47. Gil Polo, *Enamoured Diana*, 248.

48. Gil Polo, *Diana enamorada*, 22.

49. Gil Polo, *Enamoured Diana*, 249.

50. Gil Polo, *Diana enamorada*, 199.

51. Gil Polo, *Enamoured Diana*, 372.

52. Gil Polo, *Diana enamorada*, 57.

53. Gil Polo, *Enamoured Diana*, 275.

54. Gil Polo, *Diana enamorada*, 82.

55. Ibid., 73.

56. Gil Polo, *Enamoured Diana*, 286.

57. Magdalena Girón was the daughter of the Countess of Ureña and chief lady-in-waiting of Elizabeth of Valois. She was greatly admired at the court for her beauty, talents, and grace. Philip II fell in love with her, as did Gálvez de Montalvo. Both their loves remained unrequited. *Diccionario de la historia de España*, vol. 2, German Bleiberg, ed. (Madrid: Alianza, 1986), 209.

58. Avalle Arce, *La novela pastoril española*, 122–123.

59. Ibid., 123.

60. Luis Gálvez de Montalvo, *El pastor de Fílida*, M. Menendez Pelayo, *Orígines de la novela* (Madrid: Bailly/Bailliere, 1907), 406. All translations of the *Pastor de Fílida* are mine.

61. Ibid., 429.

62. Ibid., 459.

63. Ibid., 462.

64. Ibid., 449.

65. Ibid., 448.

66. Ibid., 433.

67. Ibid., 426.

68. Ibid., 448.

69. Ibid., 426.

70. Ibid., 428.

71. Ibid., 429.

72. Ibid., 430.

73. Ibid., 452.

74. Avalle Arce, *La novela pastoril española*, 109.

75. Bernard Weinberg, *A History of Literary Criticism in the Italian Renaissance*, vol. 1 (Chicago: University of Chicago Press, 1961), 349.

76. Amadeu Solé-Leris, *The Spanish Pastoral Novel* (Boston: Twayne Publishers, 1980), 119.

77. Ibid.

11

The Gendered Context of Melancholy for Spanish Golden Age Women Writers

Teresa S. Soufas

In a poem entitled "Romanze melancólico" ("Melancholic ballad"), the seventeenth-century writer Marcia Belisarda's poetic voice addresses her own thought and locates its speaker within the long tradition of melancholy thinkers and scholars:

> Thought, if you think about providing
> a remedy for my illness,
> you think mistakenly, because it is a sickness
> caused by thoughts.[1]

This is an association rich in implications for both traditional and unorthodox Renaissance views of female capabilities and the biological determinants of humoral medicine that contributed to literary conventions and societal assumptions about the weakness, irrationality, and passivity of the female mind. As is the case with literature on many topics by and about women from that time period, the works considered here record their own polemical tone in the discourse on gender during the sixteenth and seventeenth centuries throughout Europe. Due to their engagement of arguments raised in the contemporary medical, cultural, and literary tenets, the works chosen expand the limits of contention. In addition, they can be understood as part of the diffuse body of Renaissance works informed by melancholia that itself was a subject of study and debate among the medical and philosophical writers considered authoritative.

The women writers of artistic literature make use of these ambiguities and tensions in order to articulate a variety of challenges to the proscriptive and prescriptive notions about the female mind and body. As coproducers of the literature of the period, these authors join with their male colleagues in examining and critiquing the value of the melancholic mind that came to represent the medium of brilliant but dangerously independent, if not pathological, thought. For these women authors and thinkers, however, their sex is a starting point of the transgressive examination of the appropriate use of knowledge and its public voice that patriarchy had for so many centuries attempted to deny women.

The medical, philosophical, literary, and popular fascination with melancholy is a phenomenon easily traced in the artistic and scientific writings of many European nations during the Renaissance and the Baroque. The humoral theory of health and disease that had figured prominently in medicine since antiquity posits the basis of health as a systemic equilibrium maintained among the amounts of the so-called liquids or humors blood, choler, melancholy, and phlegm. Humoral medicine still held its authority during the sixteenth and seventeenth centuries even as the newer, empirical scientific methods were rendering it obsolete. Its longevity can, in part, be attributed to the usefulness of humoral typing and characterization in folklore and literary portrayals, such that melancholy—with what had become its nearly all-encompassing list of extreme symptoms and behavior patterns—is a widely depicted humoral character type in literature of the period.[2] Melancholia was a convenient diagnosis from the Renaissance medical standpoint also because, by then, it covered such a broad range of physical and mental disorders of which patients complained.[3]

The medical literature evinces this unique place enjoyed by melancholy from among the four humors. Entire treatises and books are devoted to its etiology and symptoms: in Spain, for example, Andrés Velásques's *Libro de la melancholia* (1585) (*Book about melancholy*) and in England Robert Burton's *Anatomy of Melancholy* (1620) are but two of the many works written on melancholy.[4] In these medical writings generally, the term *melancholy* is used in multiple ways. It names the humor itself; it also denotes the natural systemic condition of individuals whose humoral makeup is dominated by the supposedly cold, dry substance melancholy; it likewise identifies a distemper brought on by the predominance of this humor that produces numerous negative symptoms, including obsessive thought, emotional instability, despondency, mental and physical weakness, lovesickness, excessive fear, hallucinations, exaggerated passivity, and insomnia as well as criminal violence, jealousy, and a shortened life expectancy. Many such characteristics are also associated with female physiology and psychology from antiquity onward, and have underlain the gender stereotyping that structures much cultural, political, and literary discourse about women. Sander Gilman's examination of the representation of mental and physical diseases includes his insights on the connection between melancholia, madness, and women. Pondering the states of imbalance that are subsumed under the broader title of melancholy and the frequency with which they have appeared as female images, Gilman contends: "The female is per-ceived as being especially prone to the exaggeration of emotional states; thus she becomes the icon of melancholia."[5]

The connection of women to the purely physical as well as the aberrant emotional qualities of melancholy is challenged by female writers in Renais-sance Spain who stress in various ways their association with their male peers' claims about a link between melancholia and scholarly achievements, a link that also rests on ancient authority. The first-century Greek physician Rufus, the Arabian Rhazes from the ninth century, and Constantinus Africanus two centuries later are all among the early authors of passages about melancholy scholars. The renowned medieval medical text *Regimen sanitatis salerni* like-wise contains the following caveat: "he that desireth health of body, must eschew and avoide . . . thought and care. For thought dryeth up mans body."[6] The Renaissance inherited such notions about melancholy scholars. Among the reiterations of them is Levinus Lemnius's sixteenth-century *The Touchstone of Complexion*, in which he writes about scholarly types who "at unseasonable times sit at their Bookes and Stuedies."[7] Timothy Bright, another physician of the same century, also warns that studies "have great force to procure melan-cholie: if they be vehement, and of difficult matters, and high misteries."[8]

Spanish physicians of the late sixteenth and early seventeenth centuries also concur. Two such doctors are Alonso de Freylas and Juan Huarte de San Juan, though the latter expounds praise of the melancholy mind that is based on fifteenth-century reinterpretations of pseudo-Aristetolian ideas.[9] The early Ren-aissance interest in melancholy as a contributing factor for the mental brilliance of artistic and literary minds is promoted by the Florentine Neoplatonists, in particular Marsilio Ficino, a phenomenon that can be understood as part of the ongoing recognition of scholars' tendency toward melancholia. Their sedentary routine, deep contemplation, and isolation supposedly foster the right physi-ological and mental conditions for predominance of the cold, dry melancholy humor in the system which, in reciprocal fashion, inclines one to sedentary, thoughtful undertakings.[10]

Among the ideological impediments to assigning melancholic woman un-questionably to the category of melancholic scholars is the common medical description that attributes a cold, wet system to the female body. Such designa-tions are nevertheless part of a confused and contradictory medico-philosophi-cal tradition that, by the Renaissance, had been manipulated to allow for numerous versions of the ancient theories so as to be made compatible with contemporary notions and ideology. The natural physical properties of moisture and low temperature in the female body were themselves ambiguously dis-cussed from antiquity, but as Ian Maclean points out, "[n]early all . . . ancient texts can be interpreted to indicate that woman is colder and moister in dominant humours."[11] By the sixteenth century, the cooler temperature of female physi-ology was generally accepted as a functional element for metabolism and childbearing, and many commentators articulate the view that "woman, in her own sex, is as perfect as man."[12] Female coldness, nevertheless, is linked to many anatomical observations that strengthen the physiological justification for ethical arguments about her exclusion from public life and her relegation to the privacy of the home and domestic duties.[13]

In her very recent book on the psychoanalytic implications of Renaissance literary representations of gender, melancholia, and loss, Juliana Schiesari traces the hierarchical discourse on melancholic women. Her sources are numerous and span many centuries, and they lead her to thoughtful conclusions about the culturally constructed relegation of women to the negative range of melancholy:

> women . . . appear more afflicted by [melancholia's] negative or patho-logical effects than creatively inspired by the potential for "eminence" it seems to encode in men. . . . Although, of course, both women and men can be depressed, the *discourse* of melancholia has historically designated a topos of expressibility for men and has accordingly given them a means to express their sorrows in a less alienated way, while relegating women to an inexpressive babble whose only sense (at least for the doctors of melancholia) is their need for a good man . . . melancholia is at best made available to woman as a debilitating disease and certainly not as an enabling ethos.[14]

Several early women authors, however, contemplate alternative values to these commonplaces. In her poem "Un fin, una esperanza, un cómo, un cuándo" ("An end, a hope, a question of how, a question of when"), the sixteenth-century poet Luisa Sigea writes, for example, of her emotional and intellectual discom-fort which includes such symptoms of melancholia as sleeplessness, fear, sadness, and mental agitation. It is precisely thought, however, that the poetic voice identifies as the greatest burden, one that the persona does not purport to be incapable of bearing, but rather one that brings to her the same melancholic condition that conventional male thinkers claim:

> For this occasion alone I linger
> and with unhappiness so near,
> I count the mournful nights, and I can never
> find an end to the suffering that I recount;
> I now fear myself in this matter
> because of the threat my thought poses to me;
> but let life go on this way, and let it proceed quickly,
> since my cause can have no end.[15]

Such women writers articulate both overt and covert opposition to the accepted arguments against their mental capabilities.[16] Sigea thus incorporates her assertions of mental agency into declarations about the pain of thinking in a piece of literature that symbolizes scholarly creativity. In another poem, "Habui menses vacuos et noctes laboriosas, et numeravi mihi" ("I had vacant months and wearisome nights, numerous to me"), her poetic voice recounts the discomfort of nights, days, and even months of uncertain hopefulness, motivated by thoughts about an unhappy life and the "avara estrella" (cruel star) that seems to influence it. Concerning this "estrella," the poet writes: "muriera el poder de ella" ("let its power die"), adding further, "con el de la razón que es más terrible" ("with that of my reason which is more terrible").[17] The terrible power of thought, nevertheless, is the force of energy that represents continuity. albeit the means of prolonging her pain:

> I will have to think constantly day and night about
> the wearisome nights
> foreign to happiness
> the days, months and years
> full of grave dangers.[18]

In her poetry, Sigea reveals that, far from experiencing an absence of mental activity, her mind is engaged in incessant thought, self-consciously celebrated in the verses she composes that are her means of expression and the product of her melancholic creativity.

A century after Sigea wrote, Catalina Clara de Guzmán articulates a complaint about the vacuity of an unwanted "vida tan oziosa" ("so empty a life") in which the memory, like women's other mental faculties, remains unstimulated due to societal restrictions upon her opportunities for intellectual pursuits: "Nothing occupies my memory, since above all I have a vacuum in each mental faculty."[19] The consequences are dire, and the pessimistic message and tone of the poem build to what ultimately becomes a declaration of a preference for deep sadness—a pessimistic validation of melancholia's principle symptom: "just to have something I would enjoy having pain."[20] Guzmán's is an implication of injustice against limitations imposed upon women, and her charge of deprivation and lack is directed externally rather than at the female mind and its composition.

The functionalism argument, however, allows "Renaissance doctors to salvage from ancient writings whatever details fit into their modified conceptual scheme, and, in using them, still to claim the authority of philosophers whose justificatory structures of thought they have rejected."[21] In particular, the Renaissance medical commentators base themselves on Galenic principles and invoke belief in the stultifying psychological effects of cold upon women. According to these theories, the cold humors do not generate enough energy for mental activity, and thus the imperfection of the female mental faculties is accepted in spite of the partial abandonment of theories that promote woman as an imperfect male.[22] Such medico-philosophical authors argue "not only that woman is equally perfect in her sex as the male is in his, but also that she is inferior to him for physiological reasons."[23] The dichotomous arguments can thus insist on woman's unbalanced melancholic characteristics but deny to her the properties that are linked to melancholic brilliance. Schiesari asserts:

> The parameters of a tradition are staked out in terms of a gendered set of values: when melancholia is considered undesirable it is stereotypically metaphorized as feminine or viewed as an affliction women bring onto men; when melancholia is valued as a creative condition, however, its privilege is grounded on an implicit or explicit exclusion of women.[24]

The women authors, nevertheless, can modify the "conceptual scheme," too. In concert with the variety of theoretical explanations and cultural assumptions, one finds literary representations of female characters and personae by seventeenth-century Spanish women authors to be rich in their linguistic and ideological manipulation of the contradictions and challenges offered not only by popular beliefs but also by the more formal scientific and philosophical notions. As Alison Weber points out, for instance, St. Teresa of Ávila protects the ecstatic nuns in her convents from charges of demonic possession by describing them as melancholics whose pathological condition is brought on and exacerbated by exaggerated asceticism. The connection between religious rapture and humoral melancholy antedates St. Teresa, but: "Teresa's originality lies in her ability to use the theory as a defensive weapon."[25]

Examples of other women's invocations of the association of melancholy with their sex can also be interpreted as strategic subversions of the medical, social, and literary tenets. In what is ultimately a classist defense of the female intellect by a woman of comfortable economic means and education, María de Zayas's narrative voice complains about women's lack of education because of normative restrictions and argues against limiting their intellectual and literary development. The concept of obtaining an education is, of course, only within the purview of seventeenth-century women with enough social and economic privilege to take advantage of the free time to study and cultivate one's mind. But, like the privileged, educated male writers who comment upon scholarly melancholy in the process of studying and writing about it, so Zayas claims her place among these intellectuals whose chosen path of endeavor is either the cause or the symptom of the more positive manifestation of melancholia. Taking issue with the common devaluation of the moist, cold physiology of the female, Zayas effects a reversal that deprivileges the hot, dry male's system and supposed mental acuity: "la verdadera causa de no ser las mujeres doctas no es defecto del caudal, sino falta de la aplicación, porque si . . . nos dieran libros y preceptores, fuéramos tan aptas para los puestos y para las cátedras como los hombres, y quizá más agudas por ser de natural más frío, por consistir en humedad el entendimiento" ("the real cause for the lack of scholarly women lies not in a defect in intellectual capactiy, but rather a lack of mental application, because if . . . they were to give us books and teachers we would be as suitable for the positions and the professorships as men, and perhaps more clever by dint of our colder nature and our moist intellect").[26]

Such a restatement of the commonplace hierarchy of characteristics does not in and of itself effect a widely accepted revision in the traditional biological essentialist notions that dismiss women's intellectual capacities because of her coldness and moisture. Instead, like St. Teresa's politically convenient dependence upon melancholia as an explanation, Zayas's claims imply an educated recognition of the conflicting explanations about melancholy and can be understood as a contribution to the ongoing questions about it. In the process, Zayas also challenges the associated notions about faculty psychology, theories that posit a strong memory in woman because of her moistness.[27]

For women, the notions about the melancholy mind present uneasy overlaps. On the one hand, her supposedly inferior mental faculties render her unstable and prone to suffer melancholia's most passive and despondent symptoms. On the other, in the more positive interpretation of the melancholic mentality, the insistence is upon the presence of systemic heat as a contributing factor in melancholy brilliance, a condition that would seem to exclude the physiologically cold woman. In Spain, a medical author such as the widely read Huarte, who does accept the positive connection between melancholy and scholarly intelligence, can reiterate the misogynistic theories about women's minds and bodies by invoking convenient interpretations of myriad well-known materials, including the Bible. He writes, for instance, of Eve's lesser mental strengths; his argument depends upon biological essentialist tenets:

> The truth of this doctrine seems clear upon consideration of the wits of the world's first woman: for once God made her with his own hands, so sound and perfect in her sex, it is obvious that she knew much less than Adam . . . the reason that the first woman did not have great wit is that God made her cold and moist, which is the systemic makeup for fertility and childbearing and that which contradicts knowledge.[28]

Huarte as well makes a distinction between the moist and soft physiology of women and children and the drier, harder physical characteristics of men. He concludes: "y con todo eso, los hombres en común tienen mejor ingenio que las mujeres" ("and with all that, men commonly have better minds than women").[29]

In her "Romance burlesco" ("Comic ballad"), however, Marcia Belisarda recounts controlled mental processes and the act of purposeful forgetting through the rejection of an unfaithful lover's mementos and gifts. She begins with the description of Leonida and her destruction of presents and letters from "un ausente descortés" ("a discourteous absentee lover") named Lisardo. Instead of giving account of a sad and nostalgic complaint about despondency and emotional loss, the poet turns away from the stereotypically melancholic expression, and her poem continues through a section narrated in first person discourse. The female voice complains not only about the communicative powers of males, but likewise about a woman's inability to take men seriously. Attacking men's speech—the very evidence of men's education and their public activities authorized by gender ideology—the poet reverses the stereotypical roles. On the one hand, "if he is stupid, there is no one who listens to him." On the other, "if he is sensible and speaks well, he satirizes, prattles on and gossips, about things said, done and yet to happen." She ends by proclaiming her intention to break with tradition and/or societal values in order to love many men: "They all seem fine to me and I intend to love them all."[30] The tables are turned, and men function here as the objectified targets of female desire.

The final declaration of this "Romance burlesco" is: "but to subjugate myself to one, God deliver us," a statement that implies a sense of female community through the plural accusative and a rebuttal to the fate of many abandoned or neglected and unloved female characters of literature and folkloric tradition. The latter lovesick figures are like a conventionally passive woman described in another of Marcia Belisarda's poems: She suffers melancholy because the husband with whom she lives does not return her affection. The poet makes much of the physical beauty of this "señora" ("lady"), a suggestive acknowledgment of the traditional superficial basis for social and literary judgments concerning women and their suitability as loveable partners. The poetic voice raises a question, however: Appealing to faculty psychology in her critique of the described situation, the poet challenges the notion of the male's rational soul which should seek the good and which is prized in masculinist tradition as a male strength. In this instance, the conventional assumption is overturned; the poet says of the man: "Without doubt he has an irrational soul, since he does not aspire to a heaven."[31]

The latter poem exemplifies some of the apsects raised in the Renaissance discourse on love and the melancholic ailment lovesickness that also pertain to an examination of gender and melancholy. Recognized since antiquity as a somatic disorder, lovesickness became a much discussed condition in the Middle Ages and identified by the term "heroic love" or *amor hereos*.[32] Wack offers a summary of the historical developments of notions about and treatments for lovesickness, noting that numerous medical writers and practicing physicians of the Middle Ages considered *amor hereos* to be a disease of aristocratic males and one located in the brain rather than in the genital organs. In these earlier concepts, such a disorder thus "resided at the top of physical, social, and sexual hierarchies."[33] The medieval physician Peter of Spain, however, wrote passages on lovesickness, and his focus on the importance of sexual physiology in generating the disorder led to a gradual conceptual shift " 'downward' . . . in the estimation of some later writers" such that *amor hereos* was eventually thought of as "an illness of the sexual organs and of women, thus preserving the homology between the corporal and social place' of the disease."[34] Wack points out differences of opinion in this regard, but notes that "the shift in localization from brain to testes is thus apparent even before the end of the Middle Ages in some writers. Such a gradual decline' in the localization of *amor hereos* may help account for the replacement of heroic' by hysteric' in descriptions of this sort of love."[35] The seventeenth-century physician Jacques Ferrand, who devoted an entire book to lovesickness, indeed claims that women are its primary sufferers.[36] Ferrand, nevertheless, places great emphasis upon the physical heat and dryness of love melancholy, an assertion that, when coupled with his contentions about females' susceptibility to it, demonstrates the flexibility exercised by doctors in their explanations.

Lovesickness as a cause and not merely a symptom of distorted thought processes is of particular concern to many who describe melancholy conditions that often entail the passions' influence over thought processes. Within this context, Marcia Belisadra's contemporary Leonor de la Cueva y Silva contributes her own challenges to the conventional thought about and representation of women in love. Often these challenges involve a poetic description of the female lover whose intellectual dominance over her passions is clearly articulated. In some examples, such a woman guards herself from the amorous experience by refusing to fall in love with an appealing youth who himself is cast in the role of the observed and critiqued individual though not the desired love object:

> but now that I am acquainted
> with his deceits and cunning,
> in order not to become ensnared in his traps,
> I will close my soul's portal.[37]

Sentiments like these suggest a reevaluation of the usual representation and critical interpretation of the *esquiva* (disdainful woman) figure. Near the end of Cueva's *romance*, the poetic voice proclaims her victory over the god of love: "but I am free, lasses / from his torments and pains." Her ability to resist the passions and her conscious, intellectual recognition of the duplicitous behavior of the youth in question, evince a rational mind not in danger of becoming confused and uncontrolled due to love and melancholy lovesickness. The references to "zagalas" ("lasses" or "shepherdesses") echo not only other ballad-like compositions of the Siglo de Oro, but also imply the sisterhood of women in the face of romantic experiences, regardless of class.

In another *décima* (ten-line stanza), Cueva describes a carefully planned test administered surreptitiously to a woman's new lover:

He who in two days of love
might reveal so much fickleness
should have no hope
of deserving my favor;
my harshness was feigned
to better find out if the devotion
that you proclaimed as a lover was constant;
the plan turned out well,
since at the first sign of disdain
you show yourself so fickle.[38]

The firm resolution and intellectual composure articulated here are a direct challenge to the charges of female inconstancy, a socio-literary convention that is often a target of complaint in female-authored poetry. Cueva contradicts the repeated notions about man's ability to discern truth, and she devalues the tensions of courtly love by showing men to be vulnerable to the ruses of an independent woman who seems not to need the traditional support of a male protector.[39]

Cueva provides further rejoinders to the conventional notions about female inferiority through other poems also narrated from the female's point of view. It is precisely the act of forgetting that is foregrounded in several of these works, but with an insistence upon the conscious intent to expel the image of the ungrateful or deceitful lover from the memory of the female mind that shows itself capable of much more complicated thought processes than the simple storing of past images and events. In a sonnet that begins with the lines "Alcindo, a true love died in your deceit," Cueva's poetic persona ends by renouncing her memories of this man, saying "my forgetting from now on obscures memory of you."[40] The poet replaces the mournful discourse of loss that patriarchy relegates to female melancholia with a validation of her preference for autonomy.

In general, the melancholic mind is depicted in Spanish male-authored works of the Siglo de Oro as a dangerous source of independent thought that promotes separation of the individual from the social and intellectual community. The highly active melancholic mind's self-contemplation can be a means to baroque *desengaño*, but its isolation is depicted by many canonical authors such as Cervantes, Tirso de Molina, Lope de Vega, Calderón de la Barca, Quevedo, and others as disruptive for social well-being and universal harmony. The very medium of literary and scholarly brilliance is also the agent of implied destruction of epistemological order premised on universal connections and hierarchies of authority and being that lead to God. The individual intellect that gained preeminence with the hegemony of the Cartesian *cogito ergo sum* was anticipated with suspicion and resisted openly by Spanish intellectuals who frequently sought to reassert the more medieval conceptual framework that located human beings and their intellectual faculties within a great interrelated universal network. But, at the same time, the recognition of the newer mode of thought that prizes the individual intellect and that is celebrated elsewhere in Europe did not go unnoticed in Spain. Spanish thinkers understood its implications and affirmed its power (in spite of their reluctance to do so) by the very presence of its negative treatment in their literature.

The women writers of sixteenth- and seventeenth-century Spain are part of this intellectual posture, but in a way that further transvalues the melancholic mind. Asserting her powers of thought, a woman author may also acknowledge the unpleasant effects of the intellectual life that society makes specific to her gender. Marcia Belisarda's "Romanze melancólico," referred to at the beginning of this chapter, describes precisely "un mal / causado de pensamientos" ("a sickness / caused by thoughts"). There is no ready context for her intellectual activity. What emerges is the woman writer's acknowledgement of the two aspects of melancholia that she experiences: the one a brilliant, creative type that enables her to write and express herself in a learned manner; the other a despondent, passive sort that afflicts one such as she whose restricted life and lack of outlets for articulation constrain and stifle that brilliant mind.

The passages considered here do not contain complaints against the weight of melancholia in and of itself, but rather against socially imposed restraint, enclosure, and silence. Claiming the ability to think and write educated works, however, did not necessarily validate a woman's claim to the right to do so within the prevailing gender ideology. Paul Julian Smith's observations about Juan de Espinosa's sixteenth-century arguments concerning the superiority of female biology, for example, reveal that "attempts to reverse a prevailing hierarchy . . . are always doomed to failure. The difference of view' can never displace its more potent rival, and the female term remains negative and inferior."[41] Similarly, in a study of the debate about reason and gender in Europe from the mid-sixteenth century through the seventeenth century, Timothy J. Reiss considers the positive aspects associated with women's reason that, unlike men's violent and active reason, was considered by some to foster "tranquil passion, calm emotion, depth of sentiment, nurturing instinct, and . . . a return to a belief in traditionally asserted female attributes."[42] As Reiss points out, however, the positive value acquired by such characteristics did not bring about an end to the polemics over reason and gender. He says: "The dominant culture thus found the means to *coopt* the strong arguments about women's reason, leaving it as a positive' characteristic, but making it gender specific and thus able to be subordinated to what was then given as men's more powerful reason. This reason has to do, then, first with what was said about women and women's status, and second with what that *saying* established as a consequence."[43]

There is thus a feeling of unresolved identity communicated in much of the writing by the female intellectuals who articulate a profundity of unhappiness and discontent that expresses a feeling of melancholy about being melancholy since the outlets for scholarly creativity are not easily accessible to them. These limitations which inspire the vagueness, restlessness, and despondency that are otherwise considered typical of the female mind are frequently invoked in the female scholar's writings. In literary and artistic composition, the female poet articulates the melancholy sentiments of a sad, distressed woman whose inability to focus consistently upon one extreme of feeling or another communicate her efforts to contribute to the debate about melancholy and gender that lead the woman writer to a conscious confrontation with the difficulty of her place in the societal paradigm.

NOTES

1. Marcia Belisarda, "Romance melancólico," 367. Marcia Belisarda is the pseudonym of Sor María de Santa Isabel. All translations into English of the literary passages quoted are mine.

2. Bridget Gellert Lyons, *Voices of Melancholy* (New York: Norton, 1971), vi–viii, 17–18.

3. Lawrence Babb, *The Elizabethan Malady* (East Lansing: Michigan State University Press, 1951), 36. Babb notes: "It looks somewhat as if melancholy embraces all irrationality, for there is hardly a mental disease which is not associated with melancholic humors by one author or another."

4. Among other treatises and books from the same time period that include substantial information on melancholy are: Cristóbal Acosta, *Tratado en contra y pro de la vida solitaria* (Venice, 1592); Gaspar Bravo de Sobremonte, *Resolutionum, & Consultationum Medicarum* (Lyon, 1671); Dionisio Daza Chacón, *Practica y teorica de cirugia en romance y en latin* (Valencia, 1673); André Du Laurens, *A Discourse of the Preservation of the Sight: of Melancholike diseases; of Rheumes, and of Old Age*, Richard Surphlet, tr. (London: Shakespeare Association, 1938); Pedro Foresto, *Observationum et Curationum Medicinalium sive Medicinae Theoricae & Practicae* (Frankfurt, 1611); Pedro García Carrero, *Disputationes medicae super sen primam* (Madrid, 1612); Juan Gutiérrez de Godoy, *Disputationes Phylosophicae, ac Medicae super libros Aristotelis de memoria, & reminiscentia, physicis utiles, medicis necesarie duobus libris contentae* (Madrid, 1629); Francisco López de Villalobos, *Sumario de la Medicina*, Luis S. Granjel, ed. (Salamanca: Real Academia de Medicina de Salamanca, 1977); Luis Mercado, *Opera*, 2 vols. (Frankfurt, 1619–1920); Christóbal Pérez de Herrera, *Proverbios morales y consejos christianos muy provechosos para concierto, y espejo de vida* (Madrid, 1733); Alfonso de Santa Cruz, "Diagnostio et cura affectuum melancholicorum," in *Antonio de Ponce de Santa Cruz, Opuscula Medica* (Madrid, 1624); Thomas Wright, *The Passions of the Minde in Generall* (London, 1621).

5. Sander L. Gilman, *Disease and Representation: Images of Illness from Madness to AIDS* (Ithaca, NY: Cornell University Press, 1988), 19. The interchangeability of terms like "melancolía," "furor," "insania," and "mania" in Spanish medical tracts is characteristic of the general lack of precision found in European medical commentaries on melancholy. An example of the many works that exhibit such usage is found in Velásquez's *Libro de la melancholia*, fol. 55v. Echoing Gilman's observations on melancholy and madness, Babb notes, "[t]here is, indeed, no discoverable line of distinction in the old psychiatry between melancholy and madness," Babb, *The Elizabethan Malady*, 36.

6. Babb, *The Elizabethan Malady*, 24–25.

7. Levinus Lemnius, *The Touchstone Complexion*, Thomas Newton, tr. (London: 1576), fol. 136v.

8. Timothy Bright, *A Treatise of Melancholie* (London, 1586), 243.

9. Alonso de Freylas' work is *Conocimiento, curacion y preservacion de la peste y un tratado de arte de descontagiar las ropas de sedas y un discurso si los melancolicos pueden saber lo que esta por venir con la fuerza de la imaginacion* (Jaen, 1605). Juan Huarte de San Juan, *Examen de ingenios para las ciencial*, Esteban Torre, ed. (Barcelona: Promociones y Publicaciones Universitarias, 1988). Among other works in which considerable attention is given to the melancholy condition of students and scholars, Babb lists the following: Jason Van der Valde, *De cerebri morbis* (1549); Thomas Lorkyn, *Recta regula & victus ratio pro studiosis & literatis* (1562); Thomas Cogan, *The Haven of Health* (1589); and Burton, *The Anatomy of Melancholy*.

10. Spain's polemical response to the European intellectual currents that produced different evaluations of the autonomous mind is generally a negative one during the sixteenth and early seventeenth centuries. Spanish authors who articulate this response depict their melancholy, thoughtful characters in ways that show the danger of their separation from the epistemological system that hierarchizes the universe and locates the individual in relation to all other objects and elements. In my book *Melancholy and the Secular Mind in Spanish Golden Age Literature* (Columbia: University of Missouri Press, 1990), I discuss Spanish Golden Age literary figures and literary issues within this context. They include: Cervantes's Don Quixote; Tirso de Molina's despairing monk Paulo in *El vergonzoso por desconfiado*; Lope de Vega's knight from Olmedo; Calderón's wife-murderers; the rogues of the picaresque works; and the poetics of Góngora.

11. Ian Maclean, *The Renaissance Notion of Woman. A Study in the Fortunes of Scholasticism and Medical Science in European Intellectual Life* (New York: Cambridge University Press, 1980), 34.

12. Ibid., 31.

13. Ibid., 34–35.

14. Juliana Schiesari, *The Gendering of Melancholia. Feminism, Psychoanalysis, and the Symbolics of Loss in Renaissance Literature* (Ithaca, NY: Cornell University Press, 1992), 14–15.

15. Clara Janés, *Las primeras poetisas en lengua castellana* (Madrid: Editorial Ayuso, 1986), 39.

16. As Joan Kelly argues concerning early feminist notions, these women imply "a sure sense that the sexes are culturally, not just biologically formed. . . . They directed their ideas against the notions of an inherently defective sex that flowed from the misogynous side of the debate, and against the societal shaping of women to fit those notions." Joan Kelly, *Women, History and Theory: The Essays of Joan Kelly* (Chicago: University of Chicago Press, 1984), 67.

17. Janés, *Las primeras poetisas*, 37.

18. Ibid.

19. Manuel Serrano y Sanz, *Apuntes para una biblioteca de escritoras españolas* (Madrid: Biblioteca de Autores Españoles, 1975), vol. 269, 489.

20. Ibid.

21. Maclean, *The Renaissance Notion of Woman*, 35.

22. Ibid.

23. Ibid.

24. Schiesari, *The Gendering of Melancholia*, 18.

25. Alison Weber, *Teresa of Ávila and the Rhetoric of Femininity* (Princeton: Princeton University Press, 1990), 139.

26. María de Zayas y Sotomayor, *Novelas amorosas y ejemplares* (Madrid: Aldus, 1948), 22.

27. The model of the human mind that St. Thomas Aquinas provides is generally followed by later scholars, such as Juan Luis Vives. See Vives, *Obras completas*, Lorenzo Riber, ed., vol.

2 (Madrid: Aguilar, 1948), 1170. See also the discussions of Renaissance faculty psychology by Babb, *The Elizabethan Malady*, 2–5; and Stanley W. Jackson, *Melancholia and Depression: From Hippocratic Timess to Modern Times* (New Haven: Yale University Press, 1986), 89–90.

28. Huarte, *Examen de ingenios para las ciencias*, 320.

29. Ibid., 143.

30. Serrano y Sanz, *Apuntes para una biblioteca*, vol. 270, 367–368.

31. Ibid., 368.

32. For a fuller examination of the history of the term *amor hereos*, see the classical article by John Livingston Lowes, "The Loveres Maladye of *Hereos*," *Modern Philology* 11 (1914), 491–546.

33. Mary Frances Wack, "The Measure of Pleasure: Peter of Spain on Men, Women, and Lovesickness," *Viator* 17 (1986), 195.

34. Ibid.

35. Ibid.

36. Ferrand writes that "woemen are farre more subject to this passion, and more cruelly tormented with it, then men are," *Erotomania or a Treatise Discoursing of the Essence, Causes, Symptomes, Prognosticks, and Cure of Love, or Erotique Melancholy*. Edmund Chilmead, tr. (Oxford, 1640). Gilman's arguments about the feminization of madness and melancholia also follows this ideological shift. He says: "If the roots of the disease [of lovesickness] are corporeal, it must most directly influence the female, the epitome of the physical." Gilman, *Disease and Representation*, 100. The association of women and melancholic disorders such as lovesickness is more clearly defined in later Renaissance medical texts. A case history of the sixteenth-century Petrus Forestus, for example, recounts the attention given to a young woman suffering from the malady of love due to separation from her beloved. See Wack, "The Measure of Pleasure," 192–193; See also Jackson, *Melancholia and Depression*, 359; Lyons, *Voices of Melancholy*, 25.

37. Leonor Cueva y Silva, original ms. 4127 (Madrid: Biblioteca Nacional, n.d.), 219.

38. Ibid., 216.

39. In another of Cueva's poems, for instance, she writes from a male narrator's perspective with complaints about the time he must spend away from the woman he loves. He also bemoans his suspicions about his beloved's faithfulness. Ibid., 226.

40. Ibid., 257.

41. Paul Julian Smith, *The Body Hispanic: Gender and Sexuality in Spanish and Spanish-American Literature* (Oxford: Clarendon Press, 1989), 18.

42. Timothy J. Reiss, "Corneille and Cornelia: Reason, Violence, and the Cultural Status of the Feminine. Or, How a Dominant Discourse Recuperated and Subverted the Advance of Women," *Renaissance Drama* 18 (1987), 4–5.

43. Ibid., 5.

Bibliography

Agreda, Sor María de Jesús de. *Escala para subir a la perfección*, edited by Carlos Seco Serrano, 109. Madrid: Biblioteca de Autores Españoles, 1958.

Akerman, Susana. *Queen Christina of Sweden and Her Circle: The Transformation of a Seventeenth-Century Philosophical Libertine*. Leiden: E. J. Brill, 1991.

Alba, Ramón, ed. *Leyendas moriscas*. Madrid: Miraguena, 1984.

Allchin, A. M., ed. *Solitude and Communion. Papers on the hermit life given at Saint David's Wales*. Oxford: S.L.G. Press, Fall, 1977.

Alonso, Dámaso. "La Correlación en la Estructura del Teatro Calderoniano," in *Seis Calas en la Expresión Literaria Española*, 111–175. Madrid: Gredos, 1970.

Alvar, Manuel. *Vida de Santa María Egipciaca. Estudios. Vocabulario. Edición de los textos*, 2 vols. Madrid: Consejo Superior de Investigaciones Científicas, 1970–1972.

Alvarez de Araujo, Angel. *Las Ordenes militares de Santiago, Calatrava, Alcántara y Montesa*. Madrid: Fernando Cao y Domingo de Val, 1891.

Alvarez Santaló, C., María Jesús Buxó, and S. Rodríguez Becerra, eds. *La religiosidad popular*, 3 vols. Barcelona: Anthropos, 1989.

Alvarez Solar-Quintes, Nicolás. *Reales cédulas de Felipe II y adiciones de Felipe III en la escritura fundacional del Monasterio de las Descalzas de Madrid*. Madrid: Instituto de Estudios Madrileños, 1962.

Amarie, Dennis. *Philip III: The Shadow of a King*. Madrid: Sucesores de Rivadeneyra, 1985.

Ambrogetti, Michela. "La fortuna dell' ermitaño nel teatro del Siglo de Oro," in *Actas del coloquio "Teoría y realidad en el teatro español del siglo XVII. La influencia italiana,"* edited by Francisco Ramos Ortega, 463–470. Roma: Instituto Español de Cultura y Literatura de Roma, 1981.

Amelang, James, et al., eds. *Culture and Identity in Early Modern Europe*. Ann Arbor: University of Michigan Press, 1993.

Amelang, James S. "People of the *Ribera*: Popular Politics and Neighborhood Identity in Early Modern Barcelona." Paper presented at the Conference on "Dialogues with the Past: A Cultural History in honor of Natalie Zemon Davis," Boston, November 1990, 119–137.

Ames, Debra Collins. "Love Melancholy in *La Quinta de Florencia*." *Bulletin of the Comediantes* 44, 1(1992), 45–58.

Andrés Martín, Melquiades. "En torno al estatuto de la mujer en España en la crisis religiosa del Renacimiento: observantes, beatas, alumbradas." *NORBA. Revista de Historia* 10 (1989/90), 155–171.

Andrist, Diane Debra. "Love, Honor and the Male-Female Relationship in Representative Authors of the Spanish Comedia.' " Ph.D. diss., State University of NewYork-Buffalo, 1986.

Arenal, Electa. "The Convent as Catalyst for Autonomy. Two Hispanic Nuns of the Seventeenth Century," in *Women in Hispanic Literature. Icons and Fallen Idols*, edited by Beth Miller. Berkeley: University of California Press, 1983.

Arenal, Electa, and Stacey Schlau. *Untold Sisters: Hispanic Nuns in Their Own Works*. Albuquerque: University of New Mexico Press, 1989.

Armas, Frederick Alfred de. *The Invisible Mistress: Aspects of Feminism and Fantasy in the Golden Age*. Charlottesville, VA: Biblioteca Siglo de Oro, 1976.

Asín Palacios, Miguel. *Vidas de santones andaluces: La "epístola de la santidad" de Ibn Arabi de Murcia*. Madrid: Estanislao Maestre, 1933.

Avalle-Arce, Juan Bautista. *La novela pastoril española*. Madrid: Ediciones Istmo, 1974.

Avila, Juan de. *Obras completas*, edited by Luis Sala Balust. Madrid: Biblioteca de Autores Cristianos, 1952.

Avila, Teresa de. *Libro de la vida*. Madrid, Biblioteca de Autores Cristianos, 1986.

Azcona, Tarsicio de. "Reforma de las clarisas de Cataluña en tiempos de los Reyes Católicos." *Collectanea Franciscana* 27(1957), 5–51.

Azcona, Tarsicio de. "Reforma de Religiosas Benedictinas y Cistercienses en Cataluña en tiempo de los Reyes Católicos." *Studia Monástica* 9(1967).

Aznar Cardona, Padre. *Expulsión justificada de los moriscos españoles y suma de las excelencias christianas de nuestro Rey D. Felipe Tercero deste nombre*. Huesca, 1612.

Babb, Lawrence. *The Elizabethan Malady*. East Lansing: Michigan State College Press, 1951.

Barbeito Carneiro, María Isabel. *Escritoras madrileñas del siglo XVII (Estudio Bibliográfico-Crítico)*, 2 vols. Madrid: Universidad Complutense, 1986.

Barghahn, Barbara von. *Philip IV of Spain: His Art Collection at the Buen Retiro Palace. A Hapsburg Versailles*. Lanham, MD: University Press of America, 1982.

Barghahn, Barbara von. "The Pictorial Decoration of the Buen Retiro and the Court of Philip IV." Ph.D. diss., New York University, 1979.

Barozzi, Nicolo, and Guglielmo Berchet. *Relazioni degli stati europei. Lette al senato dagli ambasciatori veneti nel secolo decimosettimo*. Serie I, Spagna, vol. 1. Venice: Tip. Di P. Naratovich, 1856.

Barrionuevo, Jerónimo de. *Avisos de Don Jerónimo de Barrionuevo*, edited by A. Paz y Melia. Biblioteca de Autores Españoles, vol. 221. Madrid: Ediciones Atlas, 1968.

Barth, Fredrik. *Introduction to Ethnic Groups and Boundaries*, edited by Fredrik Barth. Boston: Little, Brown and Company, 1969.

Bataillon, Marcel. *Erasmo y España. Estudios sobre la historia espiritual del siglo XVI*. Mexico/Buenos Aires: Fondo de Cultura Económica, 1966.

Beltrán de Heredia, Vicente. "Directrices de la espiritualidad dominicana durante las primeras decadas del siglo XVI," *Miscelánea Beltrán de Heredia*, vol. 3. Salamanca: Universidad de Salamanca, 1972.

Beltrán de Heredia, Vicente. *Historia de la reforma de la provincia de España (1450–1550)*. Rome: Istituto Storico Domenicano, 1939.

Benito Domenech, Fernando. *Catálogo Los Ribalta y la pintura valenciana de su tiempo*. Madrid: Museo del Prado, 1987.

Bennassar, Bartolomé, ed. *Histoire des espagnols*, 2 vols. Paris: Armand Colin, 1985.

Bennassar, Bartolomé, ed. *L'Inquisition espagnole. XVe–XIXe siècle*. Paris: Hachette, 1979.

Benton, Lauren A. *Invisible Factories: The Informal Economy and Industrial Development in Spain*. Albany: State University of New York Press, 1990.

Berg, Charles. *The Unconscious Significance of Hair*. Washington, DC: Guild Press, 1951.

Bertelli, Sergio. *Rebeldes, libertinos y ortodoxos en el barroco*. Barcelona: Ediciones Península, 1984.

Bilinkoff, Jodi. *The Avila of Saint Teresa: Religious Reform in a Sixteenth-Century City*. Ithaca: Cornell University Press, 1989.

Bilinkoff, Jodi. "Confessors, Penitents, and the Construction of Identities in Early Modern Avila," in *Culture and Identity in Early Modern Europe: Essays in Honor of Natalie Zemon Davis*, edited by Barbara B. Diefendorf and Carla Hesse, 83–100. Ann Arbor: University of Michigan Press, 1993.

Bilinkoff, Jodi. "Establishing Authority: A Peasant Visionary and Her Audience in Early Sixteenth-Century Spain." Paper presented at Western Michigan University, March 1994.

Bilinkoff, Jodi. "The Holy Woman and the Urban Community in Sixteenth-Century Avila," in *Women and the Structure of Society*, edited by Barbara J. Harris, and JoAnn K. McNamara, 74–80. Durham, NC: Duke University Press, 1984.

Bilinkoff, Jodi. "The Social Meaning of Religious Reform: The Case of St. Teresa and Avila." *Archiv für Reformationsgeschichte* 79 (1988): 340–357.

Bilinkoff, Jodi. "A Spanish Prophetess and Her Patrons: The Case of María de Santo Domingo." *Sixteenth Century Journal* 23, 1(1992), 21–34.

Bilinkoff, Jodi. "Woman with a Mission: Teresa of Avila and the Apostolic Model," in *Modelli de santità e modelli di comportamento: Contrasti, intersezioni, complementarità*, edited by Guilia Barone, Marina Caffiero, Francesco Scorza Barcellona, 295–305. Turin: Rosenberg and Sellier, 1993.

Bjurstrom, Per. *Feast and Theatre in Queen Christina's Rome*. Stockholm: Bengtsons litografiska, 1966.

Blair, Hugh. *Lectures on Rhetoric and Belles Lettres*, vol. 2. Carbondale: Southern Illinois University Press, 1965.

Blas y Díaz Jiménez, María del Carmen. "La Emperatriz Doña María de Austria." Ph.D diss. Madrid: Universidad Complutense, 1950.

Blázquez Miguel, J. *Eros y tanatos. Brujería, hechicería, y superstición en España*. Toledo: Editorial Arcano, 1989.

Blecua, José Manuel, ed. *Libro de la oración de Sor María de Santo Domingo*. Madrid: Hauser and Menet, 1948.

Blecua, José Manuel, ed. *Poesía de la Edad de Oro. I. Renacimiento*. Madrid: Castalia, 1984.

Bleda, Jaime. *Coronica de los moros de España*. Valencia: Felipe May, 1618.

Bleiberg, German, ed. *Diccionario de la historia de España*, vol. 2. Madrid: Alianza, 1986.

Bolton, Brenda. "Mulieres Sanctae," in *Women in Medieval Society*, edited by Susan Stuard, 141–158. Philadelphia: University of Pennsylvania Press, 1976.

Bonnassie, Pierre. *La Organización del trabajo en Barcelona a fines del siglo XV*. Barcelona: Consejo Superior de Investigaciones Científicas, 1975.

Borja de Medina, Francisco de. "La Compañía de Jesús y la minoría morisca (1545–1614)." *Archivum Historicum Societatis Iesu* 57(1988), 69–73.

Bornstein, Diane, ed. *Distaves and Dames. Renaissance Treatises for and about Women*. Delmar, NY: Scholars' Facsimiles and Reprints, 1978.

Boronat y Barrachina, Pascual. *Los moriscos españoles y su expulsión: Estudio histórico-crítico*, 2 vols. Valencia: Francisco Vives y Mora, 1901.

Bosch Vilá, Jacinto. *La sevilla islámica*. Seville: Universidad de Sevilla, 1984.

Boureau, Alain. *La légende dorée. Le système narratif de Jacques de Voragine*. Paris: Editions du Cerf, 1984.

Boureau, Alain. "Vitae fratrum, vitae patrum. L'Ordre Dominicain et le modèle des pères du désert au XIIIème siècle." *Mélanges de l'Ecole Française de Rome* 99 (1987), 79–100.

Boxer, Marilyn J. and Jean H. Quataert, eds. *Connecting Spheres. Women in the Western World, 1500 to the Present*. New York: Oxford University Press, 1987.

Boyer, H. Patsy, ed. and tr. *Enchantments of Love. Amorous and Exemplary Novels*. Berkeley: University of California Press, 1990.

Bridenthal, Renate, and Claudia Koonz, eds. *Becoming Visible: Women in European History*. Boston: Houghton Mifflin, 1977.

Bright, Timothy. *A Treatise of Melancholy*. New York: Classics of Psychiatry and Behavioral Sciences Library, 1586 and 1995.

Brightwell, Peter. "Spain and Bohemia: the Decision to Intervene." *European Studies Review* 12(1982), 117–141.

Brightwell, Peter. "Spain, Bohemia, and Europe, 1619–1621." *European Studies Review* 12(1982): 371–399.

Brightwell, Peter. "The Spanish Origins of the Thirty Years' War." *European Studies Review* 9(1979), 409–431.

Brightwell, Peter. "The Spanish System and the Twelve Years Truce." *The English Historical Review* 89(1974), 270–292.

Brink, Jean R., Allison P. Coudert, and Maryanne C. Horowitz, eds. *The Politics of Gender in Early Modern Europe*. Kirksville, MO: Sixteenth Century Journal Publishers, 1989.

Brock, Sebastian P., and Susan Ashbrook Harvey, eds. and trs. *Holy Women of the Syrian Orient*. Berkeley: University of California Press, 1987.

Broida, Equipo. "La Viudez, ¿Triste o feliz estado? (Las últimas voluntades de las barcelonesas en torno al 1400)," in *Las Mujeres en las ciudades medievales*, 27–42. Madrid: Seminario de Estudios de la Mujer, Universidad Autónoma de Madrid, 1984.

Brooten, Bernadette J. "Paul's Views on the Nature of Women and Female Homoeroticism," in *Immaculate and Powerful: The Female in Sacred Image and Social Reality*, edited by Clarissa W. Atkinson, Constance H. Buchanan, and Margaret R. Miles. Boston: Beacon Press, 1985.

Brown, Jonathan, and John H. Elliott. *A Palace for a King. The Buen Retiro and the Court of Philip IV*. New Haven and London: Yale University Press, 1980.

Brown, Judith C. *Immodest Acts: The Life of a Lesbian Nun in Renaissance Italy*. Oxford: Oxford University Press, 1986.

Burgos García, Palma Martínez. *Idolos e imágenes. La controversia del arte religioso en el siglo XVI español*. Valladolid: Secretariado de Publicaciones, Universidad de Valladolid, 1990.

Burns, Robert I., S.J. *Muslims, Christians, and Jews in the Crusader Kingdom of Valencia: Societies in Symbiosis*. Cambridge: Cambridge University Press, 1984.

Buser, Thomas. "The Supernatural in Baroque Religious Art." *Gazette des Beaux-Arts* 108 (July-August 1986), 38–42.

Bynum, Caroline Walker. *Fragmentation and Redemption: Essays on Gender and the Human Body in Medieval Religion*. New York: Zone Books, 1991.

Bynum, Caroline Walker. *Holy Feast and Holy Fast: The Religious Significance of Food to Medieval Women*. Berkeley: University of California Press, 1987.

Bynum, Caroline Walker. "Women Mystics and Eucharistic Devotion in the Thirteenth Century." *Women's Studies* 11(1984), 179–214.

Bynum, Caroline Walker, Stevan Harrel, and Paula Richman, eds. *Gender and Religion: On the Complexity of Symbols*. Boston: Beacon Press, 1986.

Cabrera de Córdoba, Luis. *Relaciones de las cosas sucedidas en la corte de España, desde 1599 hasta 1614*. Madrid: J. Martín Alegria, 1957.

Cairasco de Figueroa, Bartolomé. *Definiciones poéticas, morales y cristianas*, edited by Alfonso de Castro, 42. Madrid: Biblioteca de Autores Españoles, 1951.

Calderón de la Barca, Pedro. *Obras completas*, edited by Angel Valbuena Prat, 3 vols. Madrid: Aguilar, 1952–1973.

Calvin, Jean. *L'Institution de la religion chrétienne*, 32. Francfort: Corpus Reformatorum, 1964.

Cánovas del Castillo, Antonio. *Bosquejo histórico de la casa de Austria en España*. Madrid: V. Suarez, 1911.

Capmany y Montapalau, Antonio de. *Memorias históricas sobre la Marina, comercio y artes de la ciudad de Barcelona (1778)*, vol. 2. Barcelona: Cámara Oficial de Comerico y Navegación de Barcelona, 1961.

Carande, Ramón. *Sevilla, fortaleza y mercado: Las tierras, las gentes y la administración de la ciudad en el siglo XIV*. Seville: Diputación Provincial de Sevilla, 1982.

Carrera Pujal, Jaime. *La Barcelona del segle XVIII*, vol. 2. Barcelona: Bosch, 1951.

Carrera Pujal, Jaime. *Historia política y económica de Cataluña*, vol. 1. Barcelona: Bosch, 1946–1947.

Carrillo, Fray Juan de. *Relación de la real fundación del Monasterio de las Descalzas Reales de Santa Cruz de la villa de Madrid*. Madrid: Luis Sánchez, 1616.

Casalduero, Gimeno. *La imagen del monarca en la Castilla del siglo XIV: Pedro el Cruel, Enrique II y Juan I*, 104. Madrid: Revista de Occidente, 1972.

Castillo, Álvaro. "La Coyuntura de la Economía valenciana en los siglos XVI y XVII." *Anuario de Historia Económica y Social* 2 (1969), 254–270.

Castillo, Enríquez de. *Crónica del Rey Don Enrique IV*. Madrid: Biblioteca de Autores Españoles, 1875.

Cerda, Juan de la. *Vida política de todos los estados de mujeres*. Alcalá de Henares, 1599.

Cervantes, Miguel de. *Don Quixote*, J. M. Cohen, tr. Harmondsworth, Middlesex, England: Penguin Books, 1977.

Cervantes, Miguel. *Don Quijote de la Mancha*, edited by B. Carlos Arribau, 1. Madrid: Biblioteca de Autores Españoles, 1943.

Cervantes, Miguel. *Persiles y Sigismunda*, edited by B. Carlos Arribau, 1. Madrid: Biblioteca de Autores Españoles, 1943.

Christian, William, Jr. *Local Religion in Sixteenth-Century Spain*. Princeton: Princeton University Press, 1989.

Christian, William A., Jr., "Provoked Religious Weeping in Early Modern Spain," in *Religious Organization and Religious Experience*, edited by J. Davis. London: Academic Press, 1982.

Christina, Queen of Sweden. Stockholm: Egnellska Boktryckeriet, 1966.

Ciammitti, Luisa. "One Saint Less: The Story of Angela Mellini, Bolognese Seamstress (1667–17[?])," in *Sex and Gender in Historical Perspective*, edited by Edward Muir and Guido Ruggiero. Baltimore: Johns Hopkins University Press, 1990.

Cicero, Marcus Tullius. *De inventione, De optimo genere oratorum, Topica*. London: W. Heinemann, 1949.

Cirurgiao, Antonio A. "O papel da beleza na Diana de Jorge de Montemor." *Hispania* 51 (1968), 402–407.

Clavería, Carlos. "Gustavo Adolfo y Cristina de Suecia, vistos por los españoles de su tiempo," in *Estudios Hispano-Suecos*, 101–156. Granada: Universidad de Granada, 1954.

Clavería, C. "Notas sobre la caracterización de la personalidad en generaciones y semblanzas." *Anales de la Universidad de Murcia* 10(1951–1952).

Clavero, Bartolomé. "Delito y pecado. Noción y escala de transgresiones," in *Sexo barroco y otras transgresiones premodernas*, edited by F. Tomás y Valiente, 57–90. Madrid: Alianza Editorial, S.A., 1990.

Coakley, John. "Friars as Confidants of Holy Women in Medieval Dominican Hagiography," in *Images of Sainthood in Medieval Europe*, edited by Renate Blumenfeld-Kosinski and Timea Szell, 222–246. Ithaca: Cornell University Press, 1991.

Coakley, John. "The Representation of Sanctity in Late Medieval Hagiography: Evidence from *Lives* of Saints of the Dominican Order." Ph.D. diss. Cambridge: Harvard Divinity School, 1980.

Cohn, Samuel K. *The Laboring Classes in Renaissance Florence*. New York: Academic Press, 1980.

Colby, A. M. *The Portrait in 12th Century French Literature: An Example of the Stylistic Originality of Chrétien de Troyes*. Geneva: Droz, 1965.

Collante de Terán Sánchez, Antonio. *Sevilla en la baja edad media: La ciudad y sus hombres*. Seville: Ayuntamiento, 1977.

Comas, Antonio. "Espirituales, letrados, y confesores en Santa Teresa de Jesús," in *Homenaje a Jaime Vicens Vives*, edited by J. Maluquer de Motes, 85–99. Barcelona: Universidad de Barcelona, 1967.

Constituciones del arcobispado de Sevilla. Seville: Alonso Rodríguez Gamarra, 1609.

"Constituciones synodales loaysa de 1596," edited by Ricardo Saez. *Mélanges de la Casa de Velázquez* 22(1986), 251.

Contreras, Juan de (Marqués de Lozoya). *Las Descalzas Reales*. Madrid: Instituto de Estudios Madrileños del Consejo Superior de Investigaciones Científicas, 1970.

Corteguera, Luis. "Artisans and Politics in Barcelona, 1550–1650." Ph.D. diss. Princeton: Princeton University, 1992.

Cotarelo y Mori, Emilio. "Ensayo sobre la vida y obras de Don Pedro Calderón de la Barca." *Boletín de la Real Academia Española* (1922), 624–649.

Cousin, Bernard. *Le miracle et le quotidien*. Ph.D. diss., Université d'Aix-En-Provence, 1981.

Coussemacker, Sophie. "Les femmes hiéronymites," in *Les Religieuses dans le cloitre et dans le monde des origines a nos jours: actes du deuxième colloque internationale du C.E.R.C.O.R., Poitiers, 29 septembre–2 octobre 1988*. Saint-Etienne: Publications de l'Université de Saint-Etienne, 1994.

Crowther, J. D. "Narrative Technique in the Legend of Saint Mary of Egypt." *Neuphilologische Mitteilungen* 85(1984), 76–91.

Cruz, Anne. " 'La bella malmaridada': Lessons for the Good Wife," in *Culture and Control in Counter Reformation Spain*, edited by Anne J. Cruz and Mary Elizabeth Perry, 145–170. Minneapolis: University of Minnesota Press, 1992.

Cruz, Anne. "The Princess and the Page: Social Transgression and Marriage in the Spanish Ballad 'Gerineldos.' " *Scandinavian Yearbook of Folklore* 46(1990), 33–46.

Cruz, Anne J., and Mary Elizabeth Perry, eds. *Culture and Control in Counter-Reformation Spain*. Minneapolis: University of Minnesota Press, 1992.

Cueva y Silva, Leonor. *Autograph Manuscript of Poetic Works*. Madrid: Biblioteca Nacional.

Curtius, Ernst Robert. *Literatura europea y edad media latina*, 2 vols. Mexico: Fondo de Cultura Económica, 1955.

Dallery, Arleen B. "The Politics of Writing (the) Body: *Ecriture féminine*," in *Gender/Body/Knowledge: Feminist Reconstructions of Being and Knowing*, edited by Alison Jaggar and Susan Bordo, 52–67. New Brunswick, NJ: Rutgers University Press, 1989.

Damisch, Hubert. "Un outil plastique, le nuage." *Revue d'Esthétique* 11(1958), 104–148.

Damisch, Hubert. *Théorie du nuage. Pour une histoire de la peinture.* Paris: Edition du Seuil, 1972.

Davis, Natalie Zemon. *Society and Culture in Early Modern France.* Stanford: Stanford University Press, 1975.

Davis, Natalie Zemon. "Women in the Crafts in Sixteenth-Century Lyon." *Feminist Studies* 8, 1(Spring 1982): 47–80.

Declaración del bando que se a publicado de la·expulsión de los moriscos. Sevilla: Alonso Rodríguez Gamarra, 1610.

Delumeau, Jean. *Le péché et la peur: La culpabilisation en occident, XIIIe–XVIIIe siècles.* Paris: Fayard, 1983.

Dembowski, Peter F. *La vie de sainte Marie l'Egyptienne, versions en ancien et moyen français.* Genève: Droz, 1977.

Deneuville, Dominique. *Sainte Thérèse d'Avila et la femme.* Lyon: Edition du Chalet, 1964.

Devroede, Maurice. "Erémitisme et instruction dans les Pays-Bas autrichiens et la principauté de Liège au XVIIIe siècle." *Revue d'Histoire Ecclésiastique* 86, 3–4 (July-December 1991).

Díaz-Plaja, Fernando. *La historia de España en sus documentos: El siglo XVII.* Madrid: Instituto de Estudios Políticos, 1957.

Dillard, Heath. *Daughters of the Reconquest: Women in Castilian Town Society, 1110–1300.* Cambridge: Cambridge University Press, 1984.

Domínguez Ortiz, Antonio. *Orto y ocaso de Sevilla. Estudio sobre la prosperidad y decadencia de la ciudad.durante los siglos XVI y XVII.* Seville: Diputación Provincial de Sevilla, 1946.

Domínguez Ortiz, Antonio. *Crisis y decadencia de la España de los Austrias.* Barcelona: Editorial Ariel, 1969.

Domínguez Ortiz, Antonio, and Bernard Vincent. *Historia de los moriscos: Vida y tragedia de una minoría.* Madrid: Revista de Occidente, 1978.

"Les dones a l'antic regim: imatge i realitat," *L'Avenç,* 142 (November 1990): 29–47.

Douglas, Mary. *Purity and Danger: An Analysis of Concepts of Pollution and Taboo.* New York and Washington: Frederick A. Praeger, 1966.

Duran i Sanpere, Agustí. *Barcelona i la seva història: La societat i l'organització del treball.* Barcelona: Curial, 1973.

Echániz, María. "Espiritualidad femenina en la Orden Militar de Santiago (siglos XII–XV)," in *Religiosidad femenina: expectativas y realidades (ss. VIII-XVIII),* edited by Angela Muñóz and María del Mar Graña. Madrid: Asociación Cultural AL-MUDAYNA, 1991.

Echániz, María. "María de Zúñiga. La Definición de un modelo de vida espiritual dirigido a una comunidad de mujeres," in *La Voz del silencio,* edited by Cristina Segura, 207–218, vol. 1 (siglos VIII–XVIII). Madrid: Asociación Cultural AL-MUDAYNA, 1992.

Echániz, María. "El Monasterio de Sancti Spiritus de Salamanca. Un espacio monástico de mujeres de la Orden Militar de Santiago (siglos XIII–XV)." *Studia Historica* 9 (1991).

Echániz, María. "Las mujeres de la Orden Militar de Santiago. El monasterio de Sancti Spiritus de Salamanca (1268–1500)." Ph.D. diss., University of Barcelona, 1990.

Edelmayer, Friedrich. "María (de Austria)," in *Neue Deutsche Biographie,* 174–175. Berlin: Duncker & Humblot, 1990.

Eiximenis, Francesc de. *Regiment de la cosa pública* (1405). Barcelona: Imprenta Varias, 1927.

Elizalde, Ignacio. "Teresa de Jesús, protagonista de la dramática española del siglo XVII." *Letras de Deusto* 12, 24 (1982), 173–198.

Elliott, Alison Goddard. *Roads to Paradise: Reading the Lives of the Early Saints.* Hanover and London: Cambridge University Press, 1987.

Elliott, John H. *The Count-Duke of Olivares. The Statesman in an Age of Decline.* New Haven: Yale University Press, 1984.

Elliott, John H. *The Revolt of the Catalans. A Study in the Decline of Spain (1598–1640).* New York: Cambridge University Press, 1963.

Elliott, John H., and Angel García Sanz. *La España del Conde Duque de Olivares. Encuentro Internacional sobre la España del Conde Duque de Olivares celebrado en Toro los Dias 15–18 de Septiembre de 1987.* Valladolid: Secretariado de Publicaciones, Universidad de Valladolid, 1990.

En la España medieval. Madrid: Universidad Complutense, 1990.

Entwistle, William J. *European Balladry.* Oxford: Clarendon, 1969.

Entwistle, William J. "The *Romancero del Rey don Pedro* in Ayala and the *Cuarta crónica general.*" *Modern Language Review* 25 (1930), 307–326.

Espinosa, Fray Andrés de. "Sermon a las honras de su Magestad de la Reyna Doña Margarita de Austria N.S. que la muy insigne Universidad de Salamanca hizo en los 9. dias del mes de noviembre del año de 1611." Fols. 1–31v.

Establecimiento of Chapter of Mérida in 1249. New York: The Hispanic Society of America, HC Mss, 380/834, fols. 2v–3r.

Evans, Robert John Weston. *The Making of the Habsburg Monarchy (1550–1700).* New York and London: Oxford University Press, 1985.

Faral, Edmond. *Les arts poétiques du XIIè et du XIIIè siècle.* Paris: Champion, 1971.

Farr, James R. *Hands of Honor: Artisans and Their World in Dijon, 1550–1650.* Ithaca: Cornell University Press, 1988.

Ferguson, Margaret, Maureen Quilligan, and Nancy Vickers, eds. *Rewriting the Renaissance. The Discourse of Sexual Differences in Early Modern Europe.* Chicago: University of Chicago Press, 1986.

Fernández, Fidel. *Fray Hernando de Talavera: Confesor de los reyes católicos y primer arzobispo de Granada.* Madrid: Biblioteca Nueva, 1942.

Fernández Baytón, Gloria Fernández. *Inventarios reales. Testamentaria del Rey Carlos II (1701–1703),* vol. 2. Madrid: Museo del Prado, 1981.

Fernández Minaya, Fray Lope. *Tratado breve de penitencia,* edited by Fernando Rubio, 171. Madrid: Biblioteca de Autores Españoles, 1964.

Feros Carrasco, Antonio. "Felipe III," in *Historia de España,* vol. 6, *La crisis del siglo XVII.* Barcelona: Planeta Editorial, 1988.

Feros Carrasco, Antonio. "Gobierno de corte y patronazgo real en el reinado de Felipe III." Tesina de Licenciatura, Universidad Autónoma, Madrid, 1986.

Ferrara, Orestes. *Un pleito sucesorio: Enrique IV, Isabel de Castilla y la Beltraneja.* Madrid: Editorial La Nave, 1945.

Ferrazzi, Cecilia. *Autobiografia di una santa mancata 1609–1664,* edited by Anne Jacobson Schutte. Bergamo: Pierluigi Lubrina, 1990.

Ferrer Vidal, María Soledad. "Los monasterios femeninos de la Orden de Santiago en la edad media," in *Las Ordenes Militares en el Mediterráneo Occidental,* 41–50. Madrid: Casa de Velázquez: Instituto de Estudios Manchegos, 1989.

Ferrer Vidal, María Soledad. "La mujer en la Orden Militar de Santiago," in *Las Mujeres medievales y su ambito jurídico,* 201–215. Madrid: Servicio de Publicaciones de la Universidad Auutónoma de Madrid, 1983.

Ferrer Vidal, María Soledad, and Díaz del Reguero. "Santa Eufemia de Cozuelos: un monasterio femenino de la Orden Militar de Santiago," in *En la España medieval. Estudios en memoria del profesor Salvador de Moxó,* vol. 1, 337–348. Madrid: Universidad Complutense, 1982.

Florencia, Jerónimo de. "Segundo sermón que predicó el Padre Gerónimo de Florencia . . . en las honras que hizo a la . . . Reyna D. Margarita," 19 December 1612, in Micael *Avellan, Oración Funebre. . . .* Madrid, 1612.

Florencia, Jerónimo de. "Sermón que predicó Gerónimo de Florencia a Felipe III en las honras de Margarita de Austria," 18 November 1611, Biblioteca National Madrid, Varios Especiales, 54–93.

Florencia, Jerónimo de. "Sermón que predicó el Padre Gerónimo de Florencia . . . en las honras de S.C. Magestad de la Emperatriz Doña María," in *Libro de las Honras para la Emperatriz Maria que el Colegio Jesuita. . . .* Madrid, 1603.

Florez, Henrique. *Memorias de las reynas católicas. Historia genealógica de la Casa Real de Castilla y León.* Madrid: Marin, 1761.

Flynn, Maureen. "Mimesis of the Last Judgment: The Spanish Auto de fe." *The Sixteenth Century Journal* 22, 2 (1991), 289–291.

Foa, Sandra M. "María de Zayas y Sotomayor: Sibyl of Madrid (Spanish, 1590–1661?)," in *Female Scholars: A Tradition of Learned Women Before 1800,* edited by J. R. Brink, 54–67. Montreal: Eden Press Women's Publications, 1980.

Fonseca, Damián. *Justa expulsion de los moriscos de España: con la instrvccion, apostasia, y traycion dellos: y respvesta á las dudas que se ofrecieron acerca desta materia.* Rome: Iacomo Mascardo, 1612.

Forey, Alan. *The Military Orders from the Twelfth to the Early Fourteenth Centuries.* Toronto: University of Toronto Press, 1992.

Forey, Alan. "Women and the Military Orders in the Twelfth and Thirteenth Centuries." *Studia Monastica* 29, 1(1987), 63–92.

"Fray Luis de León, 1591/1991." *Ciudad de dios. (Número homenaje)* 204, 2/3 (1991).

Freed, John. "Urban Development and 'Cura Monialium' in Thirteenth Century Germany." *Viator* 3 (1972): 311–327.

Gaeto, Enrique. "Inquisición y censura en el Barroco," in *Sexo barroco y otras transgresiones premodernas,* edited by F. Tomás y Valiente, 153–173. Madrid: Alianza Editorial, S.A., 1990.

Galerstein, Caryn L., and Kathleen McNervey. *Women Writers of Spain: An Annotated Bio-Bibilographic Guide.* Westport, CT: Greenwood Press, 1986.

Gallego Blanco, Enrique. *The Rule of the Spanish Military Order of St. James (1170–1493).* Leiden: E. J. Brill, 1971.

Galmés de Fuentes, Alvaro. "La literatura aljamiado-morisca, literatura tradicional," in *Les morisques et leur temps: Table Ronde Internationale 4–7 juillet 1981, Montpellier.* Paris: Centre National de la Recherche Scientifique, 1983.

Gálvez de Montalvo, *Luis. El pastor de Fílida,* in Menéndez Pelayo, M. *Orígenes de la novela.* Madrid: Bailly/Bailliere, 1907.

García Arenal, Mercedes. *Los moriscos.* Madrid: Editora Nacional, 1975.

García Ballester, Luis. *Los moriscos y la medicina: Un capítulo de la medicina y la ciencia marginada en la España del siglo XVI.* Barcelona: Editorial Labor, 1984.

García Cárcel, Ricardo. *Herejía y sociedad en el siglo XVI. La inquisición de Valencia, 1530–1609.* Barcelona: Península, 1980.

García de Cortázar, José Angel. *La época medieval,* vol. 2 of *La historia de Espána,* directed by Miguel Artola. Madrid: Alianza Editorial, 1988.

Garcia i Espuche, Albert. "Barcelona a principis del segle XVIII: La ciutadella i els canvis de l'estructura urbana." Ph.D. diss., University of Barcelona, 1987.

Garcia i Espuche, Albert, and Manuel Guàrdia i Bassols. *Espai i societat a la Barcelona pre-industrial.* Barcelona: Edicions de la Magrana, Institut Municipal d'Història, 1986.

García Garcia, Bernardo José. "El Duque de Lerma y la pax hispánica. Auge y crisis del pacifismo en la política exterior de la monarquía (1607–1615)." Memoria de Licenciatura, Universidad Complutense, Madrid, 1991.

García Hernández, *Carta al Rey don Felipe II*, edited by Eugenio de Ochoa, 62. Madrid: Biblioteca de Autores Españoles, 1952.

Garden, Maurice. *Lyon et les lyonnais au XVIIIe siècle*. Paris: Flammarian, 1975.

Gibb, Hamilton Alexander Rosskeen, and Johannes Hendrik Kramers, eds. *Shorter Encyclopaedia of Islam*. Ithaca: Cornell University Press, 1961.

Gil Polo, Gaspar. *Diana enamorada*. Madrid: Espasa-Calpe, 1953.

Gilbert, Sandra M. "What do Feminist Critics Want? A Postcard from the Volcano," in *The New Feminist Criticism: Essays on Women, Literature and Theory*, edited by Elaine Showalter. New York: Pantheon, 1985.

Giles, Mary E. *The Book of Prayer of Sor María of Santo Domingo: A Study and Translation*. Albany: State University of New York Press, 1990.

Gilman, Sander L. *Disease and Representation: Images of Illness from Madness to AIDS*. Ithaca: Cornell University Press, 1988.

Gliss, Otto. *Der Oñate Vertrag*. Frankfurt/Main, 1934.

Gobry, Ivan. *De Saint Antoine à Saint Basile*, vol. 1. Paris: Armand Colin, 1985.

Goffen, Rona. *Piety and Patronage in Renaissance Venice: Bellini, Titian, and the Franciscans*. New Haven and London: Yale University Press, 1986.

Gombrich, Ernst Hans. *The Image and The Eye. Further Studies in the Psychology of Pictorial Representation*. London: Phaidon, 1982.

González, Tomás, ed. *Censo de población de las provincias y partidos de la corona de Castilla en el siglo XVI, con varios apéndices para completar la del resto de la peninsula en el mismo siglo, y formar juicio comparativo con la del anterior y siguiente, segun resulta de los libros y registros que se custodian en el Real Archivo de Simancas*. Madrid: Imprenta Real, 1829.

González Dávila, Gil. *Historia de la vida y hechos del inclito monarca, amado y santo D. Felipe Tercero*. Madrid: J. Ibarra, 1771.

Gossy, Mary S. *The Untold Story: Women and Theory in Golden Age Texts*. Ann Arbor: University of Michigan Press, 1989.

Gramsci, Antonio. *Letters from Prison*. New York: Harper and Row, 1973.

Gramsci, Antonio. *Selections from the Prison Notebooks of Antonio Gramsci*. New York: International Publishers, 1972.

Granada, Fray Luis de. *Los libros de la retórica eclesiástica*, in *Obras*, vol. 2. Biblioteca de Autores Españoles, 3. Madrid: Atlas, 1945.

Granada, Fray Luis de. *Memorial de la vida cristiana*, edited by B. Carlos Aribau. Madrid: Biblioteca de Autores Españoles, 8, 1945.

Greer, Margaret Rich. *The Play of Power. Mythological Court Dramas of Calderón de la Barca*. Princeton: Princeton University Press, 1991.

Greimas, Algirdas Julien. *Sémantique structurale*. Paris: Larousse, 1966.

Grimberg, Carl. *A History of Sweden*. Rock Island, IL: Augustana Book Concern, 1935.

Groppi, Angela. "Le travail des femmes a Paris a l'époque de la revolution française." *Bulletin d'Histoire Economique et Sociale de la Revolution Française* 46 (1979): 27–46.

Guilhem, Claire. "L'Inquisition et la dévaluation des discours féminins," in *L'Inquisition espagnole, XVe–XIXe*, edited by Bartolomé Bennassar, 197–229. Paris: Hachette, 1979.

Guillén Robles, Francisco. *Leyendas de José hijo de Jacob y de Alejandro Magno sacadas de dos manuscritos moriscos de la Biblioteca Nacional de Madrid*. Zaragoza: Hospicio Provincial, 1888.

Gutiérrez Pastor, Ismael. *Ermitas de la Rioja*. Logroño: Caja de Ahorros de Zaragoza, Aragón y Rioja, 1985.

Gutton, Francis. *L'Ordre de Santiago*. Paris: P. Lethielleux, 1972.

Guzmán, Diego de. *Reina católica. Vida y muerte de D. Margarita de Austria, Reyna de España*. Madrid, 1617.

Hamilton, Earl J. *American Treasure and the Price Revolution in Spain*. Cambridge: Harvard University Press, 1934.

Hamilton, Earl J. "The Decline of Spain." *Economic History Review*, 1st ser., 8 (1938), 168–179.

Hanawalt, Barbara, ed. *Women and Work in Preindustrial Europe*. Bloomington: Indiana University Press, 1986.

Harris, Barbara J. "Women and Politics in Early Tudor England." *The Historical Journal* 33, 2 (1990), 259–281.

Hauser, Henry. *Ouvriers du temps passés*. Paris, 1907.

Herlihy, David. "Women's Work in the Towns of Traditional Europe," in *La donna nell'economia secc. XIII–XVIII: atti della "Ventunesima Settimana di Studi," 10–15 aprile 1989*. Florence: Le Monnier, 1990.

Hernández, Ramón. "Actas de los capítulos provinciales de la provincia de España del siglo XVI (II)." *Archivo Dominicano* 7 (1986), 5–28.

Hesse, Everett W. *Theology, Sex, and the "Comedia," and Other Essays*. Potomac, MD: Studia Humanitatis, 1982.

Heugas, Pierre. "Variation sur un portrait: de Melibée à Dulcinée." *Bulletin Hispanique* 71 (1969), 5–30.

Hillgarth, J. N. *The Spanish Kingdoms: 1250–1516*. Oxford: Clarendon Press, 1976.

Himes, Norman E. *Medical History of Contraception*. New York: Schocken Books, 1970.

Horowitz, Maryanne Cline, Anne J. Cruz, and Wendy A. Furman, eds. *Renaissance Rereadings: Intertext and Context*. Urbana: University of Illinois Press, 1988.

Howell, Martha J. *Women, Production and Patriarchy in Late Medieval Cities*. Chicago: University of Chicago Press, 1986.

Huarte de San Juan, Juan. *Examen de ingenios para las ciencias*, edited by Esteban Torre. Barcelona: Promociones y Publicaciones Universitarias, 1988.

Huerga, Alvaro. "Los Pre-Alumbrados y la Beata de Piedrahita," vol. 18 of *Historia de la Iglesia*. Valencia: EDICEP, 1974.

Huerga, Alvaro. *Santa Catalina de Siena en la historia de la espiritualidad hispana*. Rome: n.p., 1969.

Huerga, Alvaro. "Santa Catalina de Siena, precursora de Santa Teresa," *Cuadernos de Investigación Histórica* 10(1986), 197–214.

Hufton, Olwen. "Women and the Family Economy in Eighteenth-Century France." *French Historical Studies* 9 (1975), 1–22.

Hume, Martin. *The Court of Philip IV: Spain in Decadence*. London: Eveleigh Nash, 1907.

Hume, Martin. *Queens of Old Spain and Spain: Its Greatness and Decay*. London: Cambridge University Press, 1898.

Ibarra y Rodríguez, Eduardo. *España bajo los Austrias*. Madrid: Editorial Labor, 1955.

Imirizaldu, Jesús de. *Monjas y beatas embaucadoras*. Madrid: Nacional, 1977.

Jackson, Stanley W. *Melancholia and Depression: From Hippocratic Times to Modern Times*. New Haven: Yale University Press, 1986.

Jacobus, Mary L. "Incorruptible Milk: Breast-Feeding and the French Revolution," in *Rebel Daughters. Women and the French Revolution*, edited by Sara E. Melzer and Leslie W. Rabine, 54–75. New York: Oxford University Press, 1992.

Janés, Clara. *Las primeras poetisas en lengua castellana*. Madrid: Editorial Ayuso, 1986.

Jankowski, Theodora A. *Women in Power in the Early Modern Drama.* Urbana and Chicago: University of Illinois Press, 1992.

Jauss, Hans Robert. "The Alterity and Modernity of Medieval Literature." *New Literary History* 10 (Winter 1979): 117–181.

Jedin, Huber. *Geschichte des Konzils von Trient,* 4 vols. Freiburg: Verlag Herder, 1949–1975.

Jimeno Casalduero, Joaquín. *La imagen del monarca en Castilla del siglo XIV.* Madrid: Ediciones J. Porrúa Turanzas, 1972.

Jones, Ann Rosalind. "Surprising Fame: Renaissance Gender Ideologies and Women's Lyric," in *The Poetics of Gender,* edited by Nancy Miller, 74–95. New York: Columbia University Press, 1986.

Kagan, Richard L. *Lucrecia's Dreams. Politics and Prophecy in Sixteenth-Century Spain.* Berkeley: University of California Press, 1990.

Kamen, Henry. *Inquisition and Society in Spain in the Sixteenth and Seventeenth Centuries.* Bloomington: Indiana University Press, 1985.

Kamen, Henry. *Spain. 1469–1714. A Society of Conflict,* 2d ed. London and New York: Longman, 1991.

Kelly, Joan. "Did Women Have a Renaissance?" in *Becoming Visible,* edited by Renate Bridenthal and Claudia Koonz, 175–201. Boston: Houghton Mifflin, 1977.

Kelly, Joan. *Women, History and Theory: The Essays of Joan Kelly.* Chicago: University of Chicago Press, 1984.

Kennedy, Judith M., ed. *A Critical Edition of Yong's Translation of George of Montemayor's Diana and Gil Polo's Enamoured Diana.* Oxford: Clarendon Press, 1968.

Kinder, Gordon A. "Le livre et les idées réformées en Espagne," in *La Réforme et le livre,* edited by Jean-Francois Gilmont, 301–326. Paris: Cerf, 1988.

King, Margaret L. *Women of the Renaissance.* Chicago: University of Chicago Press, 1991.

King, Margaret L., and Albert Rabil, Jr., eds. *Her Immaculate Hand. Selected Works by and about the Women Humanists of Quattrocento Italy.* Binghamton, NY: Medieval and Renaissance Texts and Studies, 1983.

King, Margot H. *The Desert Mothers: A Survey of the Feminine Anchorite Tradition in Western Europe.* Saskatoon, Sask.: Peregrina, 1985.

Kristeva, Julia. "Herética del amor." *Escandalar* 6 (1983), 68–79.

Kuhn, Annette. "Passionate Detachment," in *Women's Pictures: Feminism and Cinema.* Boston: Routledge and Kegan Paul, 1982.

Kunze, Konrad. *Die Legende der heiligen Maria Aegyptiaca. Ein Beispiel hagiographischer Überlieferung in 16 unveröffentlichten deutschen, niederländischen und lateinischen Fassungen.* Berlin: E. Schmidt, 1978.

Labarge, Margaret Wade. *A Small Sound of the Trumpet: Women in Medieval Life.* Boston: Beacon Press, 1986.

Lafond, Jean, and Augustin Redondo, eds. *L'Image du monde renversé et ses représentations littéraires et para-littéraires de la fin du XVIe siècle au milieu du XVIIe siècle.* Paris: Librairie Philosophique J. Vrin, 1979.

Lafuente, Don Modesto. *Historia general de España,* vol. 12. Barcelona: Montaner y Simon, 1889.

Lammens, H. *Islam. Beliefs and Institutions,* tr. Sir E. Denison Ross. London: Methuen & Co., 1968.

Langdon-Davies, John. *Carlos: The King Who Would Not Die.* Englewood Cliffs, NJ: Prentice-Hall, 1962.

Le Flem, Jean Paul, et al. *La frustración de un imperio,* vol. 5 of *Historia de España,* directed by Manuel Tuñón de Lara. Barcelona: Editorial Labor, 1982.

Lea, Henry Charles. *The Moriscos of Spain: Their Conversion and Expulsion*. New York: Burt Franklin, 1968.

Leach, Edmund. "Late Medieval Representations of Saint Mary Magdalene." *The Psychoanalytic Review* 75 (1988), 95–109.

Leach, Edmund. "Magical Hair." *Journal of the Royal Anthropological Institute* 88 (1958), 147–164.

Leavitt, Sturgis, E. *Golden Age Drama in Spain*. Chapel Hill: University of North Carolina Press, 1972.

Lecercle, Francois. "Le regard détourné: l'aveuglement à l'image en théologie et en peinture, au XVIe siècle," in *Les fins de la peinture*, edited by René Démoris, 221–231. Paris: Desjonquères, 1990.

Leclercq, Jean. "La vie et la prière des Chevaliers de Santiago d'après leur règle primitive." *Liturgica* 2 (1958), 347–357.

Lecoy, F. *Recherches sur le Libro de Buen Amor*. Paris: Droz, 1938.

Lemnius, Levinus. *The Touchstone of Complexions*, tr. Thomas Newton. London: Thomas Marsh, 1576.

León, Fray Luis de. *La perfecta casada* (1572). Madrid: J. Pérez del Hoyo, 1972.

Les mentalités dans la péninsule ibérique et en Amérique Latine aux XVIe et XVIIe siècles. Tours: Publications de l'Université de Tours, 1978.

Lewis, Paul. *Queen of Caprice*. New York: Holt, Rinehart and Winston, 1962.

Linage Conde, Antonio. "Tipología de la vida monástica en las Ordenes Militares." *Yermo* 12 (1974), 73–115.

Lisón Tolosana, Carmelo. *La imagen del rey: monarquía, realeza y poder ritual en la Casa de los Austrias. Discurso de recepción en la Real Academia de Ciencias Morales y Políticas*. Madrid: Espasa-Calpe, 1991.

Llorca, Bernardino. *La inquisición española y los alumbrados (1509–1667)*. Salamanca: Universidad Pontificia, 1980.

Lomax, Derek W. *La Orden de Santiago (1170–1275)*. Madrid: Consejo Superior de Investigaciones Científicas, Escuela de Estudios Medievales, 1965.

Lomax, Derek. "The Order of Santiago and the Kings of León." *Hispania* 18 (1958).

Lomba y Pedraja, José. "El rey don Pedro en el teatro," in *Homenaje a Menéndez y Pelayo en el año vigésimo de su profesorado*. 2 vols., 257–339. Madrid: V. Suárez, 1899.

Longás, Pedro. *Vida religiosa de los moriscos*. Madrid: Ibérica, 1915.

López, Carmelo Luis. *La comunidad de villa y tierra de Piedrahita en el tránsito de la edad media a la moderna*. Avila: Institución "Gran Duque de Alba," 1987.

López, Juan. *Quinta parte de la historia de Santo Domingo y de su orden de predicadores*, Bk. I. Valladolid: Juan de Rueda, 1621.

López de Ayala, Pedro. "Crónica del Rey Don Pedro," in *Crónicas de los Reyes de Castilla*, edited by Cayetano Rosell, vol. 66 of Biblioteca de Autores Españoles. Madrid: M. Rivadeneyra, 1875–1878.

López Estrada, F. "La retórica en las generaciones y Semblanzas de Fernán Pérez de Guzmán." *Revista de Filología Española* 30 (1946), 310–352.

López Grigera, Luisa. "La retórica como codigo de producción y de análisis literario. Teorias literarias en la actualidad." Madrid: El Arquero, 1989.

López de Úbeda, Francisco. *La pícara Justina*, edited by Eustaquio Fernández Navarrete, 33. Madrid: Biblioteca de Autores Españoles, 1950.

Lovett, A. W. *Early Habsburg Spain (1517–1598)*. New York: Oxford University Press, 1986.

Loyola, Ignacio de. *Obras completas*, edited by Ignacio Iparraguire and Cándido de Dalmases. Madrid: Biblioteca de Autores Cristianos, 1982.

Luna, J., ed. *Catálogo Claudio de Lorena y el ideal clásico de paisaje en el siglo XVII*. Madrid: Museo del Prado, 1984.

Lunas Almeida, Jesús G. *La historia del señorío de Valdecorneja, en la parte referente a Piedrahita*. Avila: Tip. Senén Martín, 1930.

Lundelius, Ruth. "Queen Christina of Sweden and Calderón's *Afectos de Odio y Amor.*" *Bulletin de Comediantes* 38, 2 (1986), 231–248.

Lynch, John. *Spain under the Habsburgs. Vol. 2, Spain and America, 1598–1700*. New York: Oxford University Press, 1969.

Lyons, Bridget Gellert. *Voices of Melancholy*. New York: Norton, 1971.

MacKay, Angus. *Society, Economy and Religion in Late Medieval Castile*. London: Variorum Reprints, 1987.

MacKay, Angus. *Spain in the Middle Ages: From Frontier to Empire 1000–1500*. London, MacMillan Education Ltd., 1985.

Maclean, Ian. *The Renaissance Notion of Woman*. New York: Cambridge University Press, 1980.

MacNamara, JoAnn. "Sexual Equality and the Cult of Virginity in Early Christian Thought." *Feminist Studies* 3 (1976), 145–158.

Madre de Dios, Efrén de la. "La escisión de Pastrana," in *Actas del Congreso Internacional Teresiano I*, 389–407. Salamanca: Universidad, 1983.

Madre de Dios, Efrén de la, and Otger Steggink. *Tiempo y vida de Santa Teresa*. Madrid: Biblioteca de Autores Cristianos, 1968.

Madrid, I. de. "La bula fundacional de la Orden de San Jerónimo." *Yermo* 2 (1973), 5–7.

Madrid, I. de. "Jerónimos," in *Diccionario de historia eclesiástica de España*, vol. 2, 1229–1231. Madrid: Instituto Enrique Flórez, Consejo Superior de Investigaciones Científicas, 1972.

Maier, John R. "Sainthood, Heroism and Sexuality in the Estoria de santa María Egipciaca." *Revista Canadiense de Estudios Hispánicos* 8, 3 (1984), 424–435.

Malón de Chaide, Pedro. *La conversión de la Madalena*. Madrid: Biblioteca de Autores Españoles, 1948.

Malvern, Marjorie M. *Venus in Sackcloth: The Magdalen's Origins and Metamorphoses*. London: Cambridge University Press, 1975.

Marcos Martín, Alberto. "Religión 'predicada' y religión 'vivida.' Constituciones sinodales y visitas pastorales: ¿Un elemento de contraste?" in *La religion popular*, edited by C. Álvarez Santaló, vol. 2, 45–56. Barcelona: Anthropos/Editorial del Hombre, 1989.

Mariscal de Rhett, Beatriz. *La muerte ocultada*. Seminario Menéndez Pidal. Madrid: Gredos, 1985.

Marshall, Sherrin, ed. *Women in Reformation and Counter-Reformation Europe*. Bloomington: Indiana University Press, 1989.

Martín Rodríguez, José Luis. *Orígenes de la Orden Militar de Santiago (1170–1195)*. Barcelona: Consejo Superior de Investigaciones Científicas, 1974.

Martínez Arancón, Ana. *Geografía de la eternidad*. Madrid: Edición Technos, 1987.

Martínez Cuesta, Juan. "San Antonio Abad y San Pablo, primer ermitaño," in *Velázquez y el arte de su tiempo*, 127–133. Madrid: Departamento de Historia del Arte "Diego Velázquez," CSIC, V Jornadas de Arte, Editorial Alpuerto, S.A., 1991.

Martínez-Burgos García, Palma. "Ut pictura natura: La imagen plástica del santo ermitaño en la literatura espiritual del siglo XVI," in *Norba Arte*, vol. 9, 15–27. Cáceres: Universidad de Extremadura, 1989.

Martínez-Burgos García, Palma. "Los tópicos del paisaje en la pintura española del siglo XVI." *Fragmentos* 7 (1986), 66–83.

Martír de Angleria, Pedro. *Epistolario*, vol. 2, tr. José López de Toro. Madrid: Gongora, 1953–1957.

Masson, Georgina. *Queen Christina*. New York: Farrar, Straus & Giroux, 1968.

Maura y Gamazo, Gabriel. *Vida y reinado de Carlos II*, vol. 1. Madrid: Espasa-Calpe, 1954.

McDannell, Colleen, and Bernhard Lang, *Heaven. A History*. New York: Vintage Books, 1989.

McKendrick, Melveena. *Theater in Spain: 1490–1700*. New York: Cambridge University Press, 1989.

McKendrick, Melveena. *Woman and Society in the Spanish Drama of the Golden Age. A Study of the "Mujer Varonil."* New York: Cambridge University Press, 1974.

McNamara, Jo Ann. "A Legacy of Miracles: Hagiography and Nunneries in Merovingian Gaul," in *Women of the Medieval World*, edited by Julius Kirshner and Suzanne F. Wemple, 36–52. New York: Basil Blackwell, 1985.

Medina de Vargas, Raquel. *La luz en la pintura. Un factor plástico en el siglo XVII*. Barcelona: PPU, 1988.

Mélanges Kurt Reichenberger. Estudios sobre Calderón y el teatro de la Edad de Oro. Barcelona: Promociones y Publicaciones Universitarias, 1989.

Mendes Silva, Rodrigo. *Admirable vida . . . de la enclarecida Emperatriz María, hija del siempre invicto Emperador Carlos V*. Madrid, 1655.

Menéndez Pidal, Ramón. *Romancero hispánico: Teoría e historia*. Madrid: Espasa-Calpe, 1968.

Mercé Costa, María. "Un conflicte monàstic: Valldonzella i Jonqueres." *Estudis Cistercencs* IX (1973), 5–24.

Mercé Costa, María. "Les dames nobles de Jonqueres," in *II Colloqui d'Història del Monaquisme Català*, 253–309. Abadía de Poblet, 1974.

Mercé Costa, María. "Les eleccions priorals en el Monasterio de Santa Maria de Jonqueres." *Anuario de Estudios Medievales* 11 (1981), 419–433.

Meyer, Albertus de, ed. *Registrum litterarum Fr. Thomae de Vio Caietani O.P. Magistri ordinis, 1508–1513*. Rome: Institutum Historicum Praedicatorum Historica, 1935.

Meyerson, Mark D. *The Muslims of Valencia in the Age of Fernando and Isabel. Between Coexistence and Crusade*. Berkeley: University of California Press, 1991.

Michel, Albert. *Les décrets du Concile de Trente*. Paris: Letouzey et Ane, 1939.

Migiel, Marilyn, and Juliana Schiesari, eds. *Refiguring Woman: Perspectives on Gender and the Italian Renaissance*. Ithaca: Cornell University Press, 1991.

Miller, Beth, ed. *Women in Hispanic Literature: Icons and Fallen Idols*. Berkeley: University of California Press, 1983.

Minh-ha, Trinh T. "Not you/ Like you: Post-Colonial Women and the Interlocking Questions of Identity and Difference," *Inscriptions* 3–4 (1988).

Mirrer-Singer, Louis. *The Language of Evaluation: A Socio-linguistic Approach to the Story of Pedro el Cruel in Ballad and Chronicle*. Purdue University Monographs in the Romance Languages. Amsterdam: John Benjamins, 1986.

Molas Ribalta, Pedro. *Los gremios barceloneses del siglo XVIII: La estructura corporativa ante el comienzo de la revolución industrial*. Madrid: Confederación Española de Cajas de Ahorros, 1970.

Montaner López, Emilia. "Piadosas significaciones en la devoción postridentina." *Cuadernos de Arte e Iconografía* 2, 4 (Madrid, 2nd Semester, 1989).

Montemayor, J. de. *Los siete libros de la Diana*. Madrid: Espasa-Calpe, 1970.

Mora, Gloria, and M. Reyes Pasqual, "El proveïment de carn a la Barcelona del set-cents: comerç i sanitat." *Manuscrits* (Bellaterra) 2 (December 1985), 115–128.

Moral, Tomás. *Otras aportaciones al eremitismo peninsular*. Pamplona: Diputación Foral de Navarra, Dirección de Turismo, Bibliotecas y Cultura Popular, 1970.

Morán Suárez, Isabel. "La influencia de Oriente en el eremitismo cristiano," in *Lecturas de Historia del Arte*, 60–66. Vitoria-Gasteiz: Ephialte. Instituto de Estudios Iconográficos, 1990.

Morel, Philippe. "Le Cardinal Ricci et Philippe II: cadeaux d'oeuvres d'art et envoi d'artistes." *Revue de l'Art* 88 (1990), 52–63.

Moreno, Francisco. *San Jerónimo. La espiritualidad del desierto.* Madrid: Biblioteca de Autores Cristianos, 1986.

Moreto y Cabaña, Agustín. *Yo por vos, y vos por otro,* edited by L. F. Guerra y Orbe, 39. Madrid: Biblioteca de Autores Españoles, 1950.

Morgado, Alonso. *Historia de Sevilla.* Seville: Andrea Pescioni y Juan de León, 1587.

Muir, Edward and Guido Ruggiero, eds. *Sex and Gender in Historical Perspective.* Baltimore: The Johns Hopkins University Press, 1990.

Mujica, Barbara, ed. *Texto y Espectáculo: Selected Proceedings of the Symposium on Spanish Golden Age Theater.* Lanham, MD: University Press of America, 1989.

Muñoz, Angela, ed. *Las mujeres en el cristianismo medieval.* Madrid: Laya, 1989.

Muñoz, Angela and María del Mar Graña, eds. *Religiosidad feminina: Expectativas y realidades (siglos VIII–XVIII).* Madrid: Asociación Cultural AL-MUDAYNA, 1991.

Muñoz, Carolos. *La vida de Santa María Egipciaca, mujer pecadora en Egipto, y la conversión y penitencia que tuvo; con un villancico a Nuestra Señora,* 35. Madrid: Biblioteca de Autores Españoles, 1945.

Muñoz, Luis. *Vida de la venerable Sor Mariana de San José.* Madrid: En la Imprenta Real, 1643.

Muñoz Jiménez, José Miguel. *La arquitectura carmelitana (1562–1800).* Avila: Mijan, Artes Gráficas, 1990.

Muraro, Luisa. *Guglielma e Maifreda. Storia di un'eresia femminista.* Milano: La Tartaruga, 1985.

Nalle, Sara T. "Literacy and Culture in Early Modern Castile." *Past and Present* 125 (November 1989), 65–95.

Nash, Manning. *The Cauldron of Ethnicity in the Modern World.* Chicago and London: University of Chicago Press, 1989.

Neel, Carol. "The Origins of the Beguines." *Signs* 14, 2 (1989).

Newmark, Maxim. *Dictionary of Spanish Literature,* 239–240. New York: N.Y. Philosophical Library, 1956.

Nieremberg, Juan Eusebio. *De la diferencia entre lo temporal y eterno,* edited by Eduardo Zépeda Henríquez, 104. Madrid: Biblioteca de Autores Españoles, 1957.

Nieremberg, Juan Eusebio. *Del aprecio y estima de la gracia divina,* edited by Eduardo Zépeda-Henríquez, 103. Madrid: Biblioteca de Autores Españoles, 1957.

Nilsson, Victor. *Sweden.* New York: The Cooperative Publication Society, 1899.

Novo Cazón, José Luis. *El priorato santiaguista de Vilar de Donas en la edad media (1194–1500).* La Coruña: Fundación "Pedro" de las Maza, 1986.

Novoa, Matías de. "Memorias de Matías de Novoa," in *Colección de documentos inéditos para la historia de España,* vol. LX. Madrid: Academia de la Historia, 1842, 1895.

O'Callaghan, Joseph. "The Affiliation of the Order of Calatrava with the Order of Cîteaux." *Analecta Sacri Ordinis Cisterciensis* 16 (1960).

Olmeda, Sebastián de. *Nova chronica ordinis praedicatorum.* Rome, 1936.

Oostendorp, Mélanges Henk. *España, teatro y mujeres.* Amsterdam: Rodopi, 1989.

Orlandis, José. "La disciplina eclesiástica española sobre la vida eremética," *Ius Canonicum* 4 (1964), 147–163.

Orlandis, José. "Sobre la elección de sepultura en la españa medieval," *Anuario de Historia del Derecho Español* 20 (1950), 5–49.

Orlandis, José. "Traditio corporis et animae en las iglesias y monasterios de la alta edad media," *Anuario de Historia del Derecho Español* 24 (1954), 95–279.

Ortiz de Zúñiga, Diego. *Anales eclesiásticos y seculares de la muy noble y muy leal ciudad de Sevilla*. Madrid: En la Imprenta Real, por I. Garcia Infanzon, 1677.

Ossorio, Angel. *Los hombres de toga en el proceso de D. Rodrigo Calderón*. Madrid: Biblioteca Nueva, 1918.

Palma, Fray Juan de. *Vida de la serenissima infanta Sor Margarita de la Cruz, religiosa descalza de Santa Clara*. Sevilla, 1653.

Panofsky, Erwin. *Le Titien: Questions d'iconologie*. Paris: Hazan, 1990.

Papa, Cristina. " 'Tra il dire e il fare': Búsqueda de identidad y vida cotidiana," in *Religiosidad femenina: Expectativas y realidades (ss. VIII–XVIII)*, edited by Angela Muñoz and María del Mar Graña, 73–91. Madrid: Asociación Cultural AL-MUDAYNA, 1991.

Para que lo cotenido en la nueva Pragmática de los Moriscos se pueda mejor en execución, y se preuenga y disponga a este effecto lo necessario, han de guardar las justicias y personas a cuyo cargo esto ha de ser, la orden siguiete. Madrid: Biblioteca Nacional, Varios Especiales, 26–39.

Parker, Alexander A. *The Approach to the Spanish Drama of the Golden Age*. London: Hispanic and Luso-Brazilian Councils, 1957.

Peinado Santaella, Rafael G. "La Orden de Santiago en Granada (1494–1508)." *Cuadernos de Estudios Medievales* 6–7 (1978–1979), 179–228.

Pelorson, Jean-Marc. "Para una reinterpretación de la Junta de Desempeño General (1603–1606) a la luz de la 'visita' de Alonso Ramírez de Prado y de Don Pedro Franqueza, Conde de Villalonga," in *Actas del IV Symposium de Historia de la Administración*, 613–627. Madrid: Instituto Nacional de Administración Publica, 1983.

Pennington, Donald H. *Europe in the Seventeenth Century*, 2d ed. London: Longman, 1989.

Pérez Gómez, Antonio. Introduction to *Romancero del Rey don Pedro*. Valencia: La Fonte que Mana y Corre, 1954.

Pérez Martín, María Jesús. *Margarita de Austria, Reina de España*. Madrid: Espasa-Calpe, 1961.

Pérez Pastor, Cristóbal. *Documentos para la biografía de D. Pedro Calderón de la Barca*. Madrid: Establecimiento Tipográfica de Fortanet, 1905.

Pérez Villanueva, Joaquín. "Sor María de Agreda y Felipe IV: Un epistolario en su tiempo." *Historia de la Iglesia en España*. Madrid: Biblioteca de Autores Cristianos Maior, 1979.

Perry, Mary Elizabeth. "Delusions, Assimilation, and Survival: A Christianized Muslim Holy Woman in Seventeenth-Century Spain." Paper presented at the annual meeting of the American Historical Association, Washington, DC, 1992.

Perry, Mary Elizabeth. *Gender and Disorder in Early Modern Seville*. Princeton: Princeton University Press, 1990.

Perry, Mary Elizabeth. "The Manly Woman. A Historical Case Study." *American Behavioral Scientist* 31, 1 (September/October 1987), 86–100.

Perry, Mary Elizabeth. "The Manly Woman: A Historical Study Case," in *New Gender Scholarship: Breaking Old Boundaries*, edited by Harry Brod and Walter Williams. Newbury Park, CA: Sage Publications, 1987.

Perry, Mary Elizabeth. "The 'Nefarious Sin' in Early Modern Seville." *Journal of Homosexuality* 15, 3–4 (Spring, 1988), 63–84.

Perry, Mary Elizabeth. "Schools of Conquest: Christian Pedagogy and Muslim Resistance in Sixteenth-Century Spain." Paper presented at the annual meeting of the Western Association of Women Historians, June 1991.

Perry, Mary Elizabeth, and Anne J. Cruz, eds. *Cultural Encounters: The Impact of the Inquisition in Spain and the New World*. Berkeley: University of California Press, 1991.

Phillips, William, Jr. *Enrique IV and the Crisis of Fifteenth-Century Castile, 1425–1480*. Cambridge, MA: The Medieval Academy of America, 1978.

Pineda, Juan de. *Diálogos familiares de la agricultura cristiana*, edited by Juan Meseguer Fernández, 170. Madrid: Biblioteca de Autores Españoles, 1964.

Platter, Thomas. *Journal of a Younger Brother*, tr. by S. Jennett. London: F. Muller, 1963.

Poggioli, Renato. "The Oaten Flute." *Harvard Library Bulletin* 11 (1957).

Poutrin, Isabelle. "Le voile et la plume. Mystique et sainteté féminines." Thèse de Doctorat, Paris-Sorbonne, 1993.

Poutrin, Isabelle. "Souvenires d'enfance: l'apprentissage de la sainteté dans l'Espagne moderne." *Mélanges de la Casa de Velázquez* 23 (1987), 331–354.

Pragmática y declaración sobre los moriscos del reyno de Granada. Madrid: Alonso Gómez, 1572.

Quataert, Jean H. "The Shaping of Women's Work in Manufacturing: Guilds, Household, and the State in Central Europe, 1648–1870." *The American Historical Review* 90, 5 (December 1985), 1122–1148.

Quevedo, Francisco. *Doctrina de epicteto puesta en español, sin consonantes*, edited by Florencio Janer, 69. Madrid: Biblioteca de Autores Españoles, 1953.

Quevedo, Francisco. *Epistolario*, edited by Aureliano Fernández Guerra y Orbe, 48. Madrid: Biblioteca de Autores Españoles, 1951.

Quevedo, Francisco. *Introducción a la vida devota*, edited by Aureliano Fernández Guerra y Orbe, 48. Madrid: Biblioteca de Autores Españoles, 1951.

Quevedo, Francisco. *El Parnaso español*, edited by Florencio Janer, 69. Madrid: Biblioteca de Autores Españoles, 1953.

Quintanadueñas, Antonio. *Serenísima infanta gloriosa virgen doña Sancha Alfonso*. Madrid: P. de Val, 1651.

Redondo, Augustin, ed. *Amours légitimes, Amours illégitimes en Espagne (XVIe–XVIIe siècles)*. Paris: Publications de la Sorbonne-Nouvelle, 1985.

Redondo. Augustin, ed. *Le corps dans la société espagnole des XVIé et XVIIe siècles*. Paris: Publications de la Sorbonne-Nouvelle, 1990.

Reglà, J. "El comercio entre Francia y la Corona de Aragón en los siglos XIII y XIV, y sus relaciones con el desenvolvimiento de la industria textil catalana," in *Primer Congreso de Pireneistas*. Zaragoza: Consejo Superior de Investigaciones Científicas, 1950.

Reiss, Timothy J. "Corneille and Cornelia: Reason, Violence, and the Cultural Status of the Feminine. Or, How a Dominant Discourse Recuperated and Subverted the Advance of Women." *Renaissance Drama* 18 (1987), 3–41.

Relación del sentimiento de los moriscos por su justo destierro de España, y el número y cantidad que se han embarcado dellos, assí hombres y mugeres, y niños de todas edades hasta aora. Y de las mandas que dexan hechas á iglesias y lugares píos, y otras cosas dignas de memoria. Lleva dos romances al fin muy gustosos. . . . (Seville, 1610).

Relación muy verdadera sacada de vna carta que al Illustre Cabildo y regimiento desta ciudad. Seville: Alonso de la Bar, 1569.

Ribera, Julián, and Miguel Asín. *Manuscritos árabes y aljamiados de la biblioteca de la junta*. Madrid: Junta para Amplicación de Estudios é Investigaciones Científicas, 1912.

Ribera, Julián, and Mariano Sánchez. *Colección de textos aljamiados publicada por Pablo Gil*. Zaragoza: Comas Hermanos, 1888.

Rincón García, Wifredo. *Monasterios de España*, 2 vols. Madrid: Espasa-Calpe, 1991.

Riu, Manuel. "Aportación a la organización gremial de la industria textil catalana en el siglo XIV," in *VII Congreso de la Corona de Aragón*. Barcelona, 1962.

Rivera, Milagros. *La encomienda, el priorato y la villa de uclés en la edad media (1174–1310)*. Madrid: Consejo Superior de Investigaciones Científicas, 1985.

Robertson, Duncan. "Poem and Spirit. The Twelfth-Century French 'Life of Saint Mary the Egyptian.' " *Medioevo Romanzo* 7(1980): 305–327.

Rodríguez Blanco, Daniel. "La reforma de la Orden de Santiago." *En la España Medieval* V, 2 (1986), 935–937.

Rodríguez Salgado, M. J. *The Changing Face of Empire: Charles V, Philip II and Habsburg Authority, 1551–1559*. Cambridge: Cambridge University Press, 1988.

Rodríguez de la Flor, Fernando. *De las batuecas a las hurdes*. Mérida: Junta de Extremadura, 1989.

Rodríguez de la Flor, Fernando. "La ciudad de Yahve." *Caracola* 3 (1989): 46–51.

Röthlisberger, Marcel. "Some Early Clouds." *Gazette des Beaux-Arts* 111 (May-June 1988), 284–292.

Rose, Mary Beth. "Gender, Genre, and History: Seventeenth-Century English Women and the Art of Autobiography," in *Women in the Middle Ages and the Renaissance: Literary and Historical Perspectives*, edited by Mary Beth Rose. Syracuse: Syracuse University Press, 1986.

Rosof, Patricia. "The Anchoress in the Twelfth and Thirteenth Centuries," in *Medieval Religious Women, II. Peaceweavers*, edited by Lilian Shank and John Nichols, 123–144. Kalamazoo: Cistercian Publications, 1984.

Sainseaulieu, Jean. *Etudes sur la vie érémitique en France de la contre-réforme à la restauration*. Lille: Ateliers de Thèses, 1974.

Saint-Saëns, Alain. "Antón de la Fuente, ermite-pélerin de Castille au XVIIème siècle." *Histoire, Economie et Société* (1987-1).

Saint-Saëns, Alain. "Apología y denigración del cuerpo del ermitaño en el Siglo de Oro." *Hispania Sacra* 42, 85 (1990), 169–180.

Saint-Saëns, Alain. "Contraintes et libertés du sculpteur espagnol après le Concile de Trente," in *Figures, Images religieuses baroques*, edited by Didier Souillier, 109–126. Dijon: Centre de Recherches sur l'Image, le Symbole, le Mythe, 1990.

Saint-Saëns, Alain. "Ignace de Loyola devant l'érémitisme: la dimension cartusienne." *Mélanges del'Ecole Française de Rome. Italie et Méditerranée* 102, 1 (1990), 191–209.

Saint-Saëns, Alain. *La nostalgie du désert. L'idéal érémitique en Castille au Siècle d'Or*. San Francisco: Edwin Mellen Research University Press, 1992.

Saint-Saëns, Alain. "Une nouvelle approche de l'ermitage du XVIIème siècle," *Mélanges de la Casa de Velázquez* 26 (1990), 56–61.

Saint-Saëns, Alain, ed. *Religion, Body and Gender in Early Modern Spain*. San Francisco: Mellen Research University Press, 1991.

Saint-Saëns, Alain. "Saint ou coquin. Le personnage de l'ermite dans la littérature espagnole du Siècle d'Or." *Revista Canadiense de Estudios Hispánicos* 16 (1991), 123–135.

Saint-Saëns, Alain. *In the Service of the Faith. A Study of Post-Tridentine Spanish Religious Art*, tr. by Garrett McLuthan. San Francisco: Mellen Research University Press, 1993.

Saint-Saëns, Alain. "Thérèse d'Avila ou l'érémitisme sublimé." *Mélanges de la Casa de Velázquez* 25 (1989), 121–143.

Sainz de la Maza, Regina. "El Monasterio Santiaguista de San Pedro de la Piedra en Lérida," *Anuario de Estudios Medievales* 11 (1981), 383–418.

Sainz de la Maza, Regina. *La Orden de Santiago en la Corona de Aragón*, 2 vols. Zaragoza: Institución "Fernando el Católico," 1980–1988.

Salstad, M. L. *The Presentation of Women in Spanish Golden Age Literature: An Annotated Bibliography*. Boston: G. K. Hall, 1980.

San Bartolomé, Ana de. *Autobiografía*. Madrid: Editorial de Espiritualidad, 1969.

San Francisco, María de. *Escritos*, edited by Vicente de la Fuente, 55. Madrid: Biblioteca de Autores Españoles, 1952.

Sánchez, Magdalena S. "Confession and Complicity: Margarita de Austria, Richard Haller, S.J., and the Court of Philip III." *Cuadernos de Historia Moderna* 4 (1993), 133–149.

Sánchez, Magdalena S. "Dynasty, State, and Diplomacy in the Spain of Philip III." Ph.D. diss., The Johns Hopkins University, Baltimore, 1988.

Sánchez, Magdalena S. "A House Divided: Spain, Austria, and the Bohemian and Hungarian Successions." *Sixteenth Century Journal* 25, 4 (1994), 887–903.

Sánchez, Magdalena S. "Melancholy and Female Illness: Habsburg Women and Politics at the Court of Philip III." *Journal of Women's History*, forthcoming.

Sánchez Hernández, María Leticia. "El Monasterio de la Encarnación: Una fundación real en el siglo XVII." *Reales Sitios* 89 (1986), 21–28.

Sánchez Hernández, María Leticia. *El Monasterio de la Encarnación de Madrid. Un modelo de vida religiosa en el siglo XVII.* Salamanca: Ediciones Escurialenses, 1986.

Sánchez Lora, José Luis. *Mujeres, conventos y formas de la religiosidad barroca.* Madrid: Fundación Universitaria Española, 1988.

Sánchez Ortega, María Helena. *La inquisición y las gitanas.* Madrid: Taurus, 1988.

Sánchez Ortega, María Helena. "La Mujer como fuente del mal: el maleficio." *Manuscrits* 9 (January 1991), 41–81.

Sandoval, Fray Prudencio de. *Historia de la vida y hechos del Emperador Carlos V*, edited by Carlos Seco Serrano, 92. Madrid: Biblioteca de Autores Españoles, 1956.

Santa María, Juan de. *Tratado de repúblicas y policía christiana.* Madrid, 1615.

Sargent, Anne-Maria. "The Penitent Prostitute: The Tradition and Evolution of the 'Life of Saint Mary the Egyptian.' " Ph.D. diss., University of Michigan, Ann Arbor, 1977.

Sastre Santos, Eutimio. "El martirologio de Uclés y los orígenes de la Orden de Santiago." *Hispania Sacra* 34 (1982), 217–252.

Sastre Santos, Eutimio. "La Orden de Santiago y su Regla." Ph.D. diss., Universidad Complutense, Madrid, 1981.

Saxer, Victor. *Le culte de Marie-Madeleine en occident des origines à la fin du moyen age.* Auxerre: CNRS, 1959.

Schiesari, Juliana. *The Gendering of Melancholia. Feminism, Psychoanalysis, and the Symbolics of Loss in Renaissance Literature.* Ithaca: Cornell University Press, 1992.

Schiesari, Juliana. "In Praise of Virtuous Women? For a Genealogy of Gender Morals in Renaissance Italy." *Annali d'Italianistica* 7 (1989), 66–87.

Scott, Joan, and Louise Tilly. *Women, Work & Family.* New York: Routledge, 1987.

Serrano, L. *Cartulario del Infantado de Covarrubias.* Madrid, 1930.

Serrano y Sanz, Manuel. *Apuntes para una biblioteca de escritoras españolas*, 4 vols. Madrid: Biblioteca de Autores Españoles, 1975.

Shergold, Norman D. *A History of the Spanish Stage from Medieval Times until the End of the Seventeenth Century.* Oxford: Clarendon Press, 1967.

Showalter, Elaine. "Towards a Feminist Poetics," in *The New Feminist Criticism: Essays on Women, Literature and Theory*, edited by Elaine Showalter. New York: Pantheon, 1985.

Sicroff, Albert A. *Los estatutos de limpieza de sangre: Controversias entre los siglos XV y XVII.* Madrid: Taurus, 1985.

Smith, Margaret. *Rabi'a the Mystic and Her Fellow-Saints in Islam: Being the Life and Teachings of Rabi'a al-Adawiyya Al-Qaysiyya of Basra together with Some Account of the Place of the Women Saints in Islam.* Cambridge: Cambridge University Press, 1984.

Smith, Paul Julian. *The Body Hispanic: Gender and Sexuality in Spanish and Spanish American Literature.* Oxford: Clarendon Press, 1989.

Solé-Leris, Amadeu. *The Spanish Pastoral Novel.* Boston: Twayne Publishers, 1980.

Sor María del Espíritu Santo. *Escritoras españolas*, edited by Manuel Serrano y Sanz, 269. Madrid: Biblioteca de Autores Españoles, 1975.

Soufas, Teresa S. "Carnival, Spectacle, and the *Gracioso*'s Theatrics of Dissent." *Revista Canadiense de Estudios Hispánicos* 14, 2 (1990), 315–327.

Soufas, Teresa S. *Melancholy and the Secular Mind in Spanish Golden Age Literature.* Columbia, MO: University of Missouri Press, 1989.

Souriau, E. *Les deux cent mille situations dramatiques.* Paris: Flamarion, 1950.

Stoll, Anita K., and Dawn L. Smith, eds. *The Perception of Women in Spanish Theater of the Golden Age.* Lewisburg, PA: Bucknell University Press, 1991.

Stradling, R. A. *Europe and the Decline of Spain.* London: George Allen & Unwin, 1981.

Stradling, R. A. *Philip IV and the Government of Spain, 1621–1665.* New York: Cambridge University Press, 1988.

Suárez Fernández, Luis. *El Canciller Ayala y su tiempo (1332–1407).* Alava: Consejo de Cultura, 1962.

Suárez Fernández, Luis. *Nobleza y monarquía. Puntos de vista sobre la historia política castellana del siglo XV.* Valladolid: Departamento de Historia Medieval, Universidad de Valladolid, 1975.

Suárez Fernández, Luis. *Los Trastámaras y los Reyes Católicos.* Madrid: Editorial Gredos, 1985.

Surtz, Ronald E. *The Guitar of God. Gender, Power, and Authority in the Visionary World of Mother Juana de la Cruz (1481–1534).* Philadelphia: University of Pennsylvania Press, 1990.

Surtz, Ronald E. "The 'Sweet Melody' of Christ's Blood: Musical Images in the 'Libro de la Oración' of Sister María de Santo Domingo." *Mystics Quarterly* 17 (1991), 94–101.

Surtz, Ronald E. *Writing Women in Late Medieval and Early Modern Spain: The Mothers of Saint Téresa of Ávila.* Philadelphia: University of Pennsylvania Press, 1995.

Swanson, Heather. "The Illusion of Economic Structure: Craft Guilds in Medieval English Towns." *Past and Present* 121 (November 1980), 29–48.

Teresa de Jesús, *Obras completas*, edited by Efrén de la Madre de Dios and Otger Steggink. Madrid: Biblioteca de Autores Cristianos, 1986.

Tinto Sala, Margarida. *Els gremis a la Barcelona medieval.* Barcelona: Ajuntament, Delegacio de Cultura, 1978.

Tomás y Valiente, Francisco, ed. *Sexo Barroco y otras transgresiones premodernas.* Madrid: Editorial Alianza, 1990.

Tomás y Valiente, Francisco. *Los validos en la monarquía española del siglo XVII.* Madrid: Instituto de Estudios Políticos, 1963.

Tomizza, Fulvio. *Heavenly Supper: The Story of María Janis*, tr. Anne Jacobson Schutte. Chicago: University of Chicago Press, 1991.

Tormo, Elías. *En las Descalzas Reales.* Madrid: Junta de Iconografía Nacional, 1917.

Trexler, Richard. "Habiller et déshabiller les images: esquisse d'une analyse," in *L'image et la production du sacré*, edited by Francoise Dunand, Jean-Michel Spieser, and Jean Wirth. Paris: Méridiens Klincksieck, 1991.

Usener, Hermann. "Legenden der Pelagia." *Vorträge und Aufsätze.* Leipzig: B. G. Teubner, 1907.

Valdeón Baruque, Julio. *Los conflictos sociales en el reino de Castilla en los siglos XIV y XV.* Madrid: Siglo Veintiuno, 1976.

Vallardes de Sotomayor, Antonio, ed. *Semanario Erudito.* Madrid: Blas Roman, 1788.

Vega Carpío, Lope de. *Rimas humanas*, edited by Juan de José Prades. Madrid: Consejo Superior de Investigaciones Científicas, 1971.

Vendôme, M. of. *The Art of Versification.* Ames: Iowa State University Press, 1980.

Vera y Figueroa, Juan Antonio de. *El Rei d. Pedro defendido.* Madrid: F. García, 1648.

Vespertino Rodríguez, Antonio, ed. *Leyendas aljamiadas y moriscas sobre personajes bíblios.* Madrid: Editorial Gredos, 1983.

Vicente, Marta. "Mujeres artesanas en la Barcelona moderna," in *Las mujeres en el Antiguo Régimen: Imagen y realidad*, 59–90. Barcelona: Icaria, 1994.

Victorio, Juan. "La mujer en la épica castellana," in *La condición de la mujer en la edad media. Actas del Coloquio Celebrado en la Casa de Velázquez, del 5 al 7 de noviembre de 1984*, 75–84. Madrid: Casa de Velázquez, 1986.

Vigier, Françoise. "La folie amoureuse dans le roman pastoral espagnol (deuxième moitié du XVIe siècle)," in *Visages de la folie (1500–1650)*, edited by Augustin Redondo and André Rochon, 117–130. Paris: Publications de la Sorbonne, 1981.

Vigil, Mariló. *La mujer en la historia de España (Siglos XVI–XIX)*. Madrid: Universidad Autónoma, 1984.

Vigil, Mariló. *La vida de las mujeres en los siglos XVI y XVII*. Madrid: Siglo Veintiuno de España, 1986.

Vilar, Pierre, *La Catalogne dans L'Espagne moderne*. Paris: Flammarion, 1977.

Vincent, Bernard. *Minorías y marginados en la España del siglo XVI*. Granada: Diputación Provincial, 1987.

Vinsauf, G. of. *The New Poetics*, in *Three Medieval Rhetorical Arts*, edited by J. J. Murphy, 27–108. Berkeley: University of California Press, 1971.

Vinyoles i Vidal, Teresa María. "Actividad de la mujer en la industria del vestir en la Barcelona de finales de la edad media," in *El trabajo de las mujeres en la edad media hispana*, 255–273. Madrid: Asociación Cultural AL-MUDAYNA, 1988.

Vinyoles i Vidal, Teresa María. *Les barcelonines a les darreries de l'edat mitjana*. Barcelona: Fundació Salvador Vives Casajana, 1976.

Vinyoles i Vidal, Teresa María. "La Mujer bajomedieval a través de las ordenanzas municipales de Barcelona," in *Las mujeres medievales y su ambito jurídico*, 137–154. Madrid: "Seminario de Estudios de la Mujer," Universidad Autónoma de Madrid, 1983.

Vinyoles i Vidal, Teresa María. *La Vida quotidiana a Barcelona vers 1400*. Barcelona: R. Dalmau, 1985.

Vives, Juan Luis. *Instrucción de la mujer cristiana* (1540). Buenos Aires: Espasa-Calpe Argentina, 1943.

Vives, Juan Luis. *La mujer cristiana*. (1523), edited by Lorenzo Riber. Madrid: Aguilar, 1949.

Vives, Juan Luis. *Obras completas*, vol. 2, edited by Lorenzo Riber. Madrid: Aguilar, 1948.

Voltes, María José and Pedro. *Las mujeres en la historia de España*. Madrid: Planeta, 1986.

Voltes Bou, Pedro. "Notas sobre el personal de los talleres sederos barceloneses. Siglos XIII–XVIII." *Boletín de Estudios Económicos* 26 (1971), 1005–1029.

Voragine. Jacques de. *La Légende Dorée*, 2 vols. Paris: Garnier-Flammarion, 1967.

Wack, Mary Frances. "The Measure of Pleasure: Peter of Spain on Men, Women, and Lovesickness." *Viator* 17 (1986), 173–196.

Walker, Mack. *German Home Towns: Community, State, and General Estate, 1648–1871*. Ithaca: Cornell University Press, 1971.

Ward, Benedicta. *Harlots of the Desert: A Study of Repentance in Early Monastic Sources*. Kalamazoo: Cistercian Publications, 1987.

Wardropper, Bruce W. "The Diana of Montemayor: Revaluation and Interpretation." *Studies in Philology* 48 (1951), 126–144.

Warner, Marina. *Alone of All Her Sex: The Myth and Cult of the Virgin Mary*. London: Weidenfeld and Nicolson, 1976.

Warren, Ann Kosser. *The Anchorite in Medieval England. 1100–1539*. Cleveland: Case Western Reserve University, 1980.

Watt, H. Montgomery. *A History of Islamic Spain*. Edinburgh: Edinburgh University Press, 1965.

Weber, Alison. "The Paradoxes of Humility: Santa Teresa's *Libro de la Vida* as Double Mind." *Journal of Hispanic Philology* 9 (1985), 211–230.

Weber, Alison. *Teresa of Avila and the Rhetoric of Femininity*. Princeton: Princeton University Press, 1990.

Weinberg, B. *A History of Literary Criticism in the Italian Renaissance*, vol. 1. Chicago: University of Chicago Press, 1961.

Weiner, Jack. "Cristina de Suecia en dos obras de Calderón de la Barca." *Bulletin of the Comediantes* 31 (1979).

Widorn, Helga. "Die Spanischen Gemahlinnen der Kaiser Maximilian II., Ferdinand III. und Leopold I." Ph.D. diss., University of Vienna, 1960.

Wiesner, Merry E. "Paltry Peddlers or Essential Merchants? Women in the Distributive Trades in Early Modern Nüremberg." *Sixteenth Century Journal* 12, 2 (Summer 1981), 3–14.

Wiesner, Merry E. *Women and Gender in Early Modern Europe*. Cambridge: Cambridge University Press, 1993.

Wiesner, Merry E. *Working Women in Renaissance Germany*. New Brunswick, NJ: Rutgers University Press, 1986.

Wilk, Sara. "The Cult of Mary Magdalen in Fifteenth Century Florence and its Iconography." *Studi Medievali* 26 (1985), 685–698.

Williams, Patrick. "Lerma, Old Castile and the Travels of Philip III of Spain." *History* 73, 239 (October 1988), 379–397.

Williams, Patrick. "Lerma, 1618: Dismissal or Retirement?" *European History Quaterly* 19, 3 (July 1989), 307–332.

Williams, Patrick. "Philip III and the Restoration of Spanish Government, 1598–1603." *The English Historical Review* 88 (1973), 751–769.

Wilson, Edward M., and Duncan Moir. *A Literary History of Spain: The Golden Age Drama*. New York: Barnes and Noble, 1971.

Woodbridge, Linda. *Women and the English Renaissance: Literature and the Nature of Womankind*. Urbana and Chicago: University of Illinois Press, 1984.

Wright, L. P. "The Military Orders in Sixteenth and Seventeenth Century Spanish Society. The Institutional Embodiment of a Historical Tradition." *Past and Present* 43 (1969).

Zahareas, A. *The Art of Juan Ruiz Archpriest of Hita*. Madrid: Estudios de Literatura Española, 1965.

Zálama Rodríguez, Miguel Angel. *Ermitas y santuarios de la provincia de Valladolid*. Valladolid: Diputación de Valladolid, Editora Provincial/Publicaciones Gráficas Andrés Martín, S.A., 1987.

Zarri, Gabriella. "Le sante vive: per una tipologia della santità femminile nel primo cinquecento." *Annali dell'Istituto Storico Italo-Germanico in Trento* 6 (1980), 371–445.

Zayas y Sotomayor, María de Zayas. *Novelas Amorosas y Ejemplares*, Biblioteca Selecta de Clásicos Españoles. Madrid: Aldus, 1948.

Ziomek, Henryk. *A History of Spanish Golden Age Drama*. Lexington: University of Kentucky Press, 1984.

Index

Action, in Polo's *Diana enamorada*, 167–168

Adolfo, 144

Adultery, 72, 81

Afectos de odio y amor, 143, 150, 153

Agrarian economy, 79

Agrarian workers, 38

Agreda, Sor María de, 114

Agullers, 130

Alba, Duke of, 24–25, 28

Albaladejo, 58

Albana, 165

Alberit, María and Pascual, 11

Albernáez, Clara, 12

Albuquerque, Juan Alfonso de, 72–73

Alcalá, 56

Alcalá, Pedro de, 39

Alcántara, Peter of, 56

Alcida, 159–163, 167

Alcida/Marcelio, 159

Alcindo, a true love died in your deceit, 180

Aldeanueva, 23, 25, 31

Alexander III, Pope, bull of, 4, 7

Alexander VI, 15; papal brief of, 15

Alfaquíes, 42, 44–45

Alfeo, 164, 166, 168

Alfonso, Inés, 12

Alfonso, Martín, Infant, 13

Alfonso, Sancha, Infanta, 13; brother of, 13

Alfonso IV, King of Portugal, 71

Alfonso VIII, King, 13

Alfonso XI of Castile, King, 70–71; authoritarian rule of, 70; ban on usury of, 76; devaluation of the currency by, 83

Alfonso de Valdevieso, Martín de, 12; widow of, 12

Alhambra, 39

Aljama, 38

Aljamía, 37, 45–46

Aljamiado literature, 37, 45

Allegory, 142

Alonso, Felipe, 132

Alpujarras, 42, 45

Amarantha, 166–167; as shepherdess, 167

Americas, 110

Amorous contemplation, 160

Amulet, 46

Ana of Austria, Queen of France, 101

Anatomy of Melancholy, 172

Anchoresses, 5, 56–57; modern, 57

Anchorite model, 57, 59

Anchorite penances, 55

Anchorite vocations, 55

Andria, 164, 166–168

Anglesola, Guillem d', 13; widow of, 13

Anglo-Portuguese alliance, 82

Anthony the Abbot, 55
Antisemitic sentiment, 77
Apollo, 159
Apostasy, 47
Apostolate, 30
Apprentices, 128
Aprenentes, 129
Aquinas, Thomas, 30
Arabic, 39, 41, 43, 46–47; books, 41–42; dialects, 38; medicine, 46; vocabulary, 39
Aragón, 6, 14; kingdom of, 38, 40
Aragón, Pascual de, Don, Archbishop of Toledo, 115
Arcadia, 159
Archbishop of Toledo, 115
Archiepiscopal chancellery, registers of, 57
Aristocracy, 78
Aristocratic women, 71, 93, 95–96
Aristotelian concepts, 167
Aristotle, 167
Ars versificatoria, 158
Artisanal activities, regulation of, 133
Artisan neighborhood, 130
Artisans, 39, 130; house of, 130
Artistic literature, 171
Ascetic exploits, 55
Asceticism, 28, 30; extreme, 30
Ascetic life, 55
Ascetic standards, 28
Audiencia, 130
Auñón, 55
Aurembiaix, 12
Auristela, 145, 149
Austria, 111, 114, 116
Austrian conspirators, 113, 115
Austrian Habsburg diplomatic network, 91, 111–112, 120–121
Austrian Habsburg interests, 91, 93, 111–112, 115, 120–121
Austrian Habsburgs, 91, 100; relatives at the Spanish court, 93, 111–112, 120–121; Styrian branch of, 93
Autos sacramentales, 141–142, 150; allegorical characters of, 142; dramatic structure of, 142; female characters of, 143; historical figures in, 142; legendary figures in, 142
Avalle–Arce, Juan Bautista, 163; philosophical concepts of love, 167
Ave/Eva, 72

Avellaneda, Isabel de, 16
Avila, 23; bishopric of, 23; Dominican house, 24
Avila, Damián de, 25
Avila, Juan de, 60
Avila, Teresa of, 55–57; hagiographer of, 56–57
Azcona, Juan de, 25–26

Bacon, dietary prohibitions against, 41
Ballads, 69–85; anti-Petrine, 70, 73, 79; metaphoric language of, 83; pro-Petrine, 81
Baltasar Carlos, 111
Barbers, 130
Barcelona, 13, 129–135; city council, 127–128, 132–133; city councilors, 127–128, 134; city government, 128, 134; city hall, 127; city ordinance, 134; early modern, 128, 130; guilds, 128; municipal authorities, 130; port of, 130; wool textile industry, 127
Baroque, 172
Barreters, 135
Beata, 23–31
Beelzebub, 84
Beguines, 5
Belisa, 161
Belisarda, María, 171, 177–179, 181
Beltrán de Heredia, Vicente, 26, 30
Benedictus Deus, Alexander III, 7
Benito Domenech, Fernando, 59
Ben Muzahim, Isa, 38
Berardo, 160
Berbery, 48
Bible, 177
Biblical narratives, 142
Biographers, 93–94, 99
Biography, 96; court-sanctioned, 101–102
Bishop, 58, 60; Portuguese, 71; of Toledo, 79
Black Plague, 77
Blair, Hugh, 159
Blanca, coin, 82–83
Blanco, 83
Blasco de Loyola, Don, 113
Blood, and humoral theory, 172
Bodily fluids, 85
Bohemian throne, 100
Bon, Ottaviano, 98
Book of Good Love, 158

Book of pastoral visits, 57
Book of remedies, 46
Borbón, Blanca de, 70, 72–73, 75–76, 79–85; reification of, 84; repudiation of, 85
Bricklayers, 39
Bright, Timothy, 173
Brothels, 46
Bullfights, 117
Bureaucracy, 110; as an instrument of government, 110–111; inefficiency of, 111
Burgos, 25
Burton, Robert, 172

Cabalistic signs, 46
Caballerizo, 117
Cabrera de Córdoba, Luis, 99
Cáceres, fraternity of, 4
Cajetan, Thomas, 24–25, 30
Calderón, Rodrigo, 93, 97; criminal investigation of, 94
Calderón de la Barca, Pedro, Don, 141–154; evaluation of the monarchy, 150; feminism of, 154; as leading dramatist, 141; on melancholy, 180; portrait of a fictional queen by, 143; thoughts of women as regents, 149
Calixto, 158
Campo, Ynés de, 58
Canciones, 142
Candles, 85, 132
Canons, 4, 9, 15; Augustinian, 4–5
Cánovas del Castillo, Antonio, 121
Canto aguilnadero, 78, 84–85
Capitulation, 39
Capmany, Antonio de, 129
Cara, Isabel, 58
Cárdenas, Alonso de, 3, 9, 15
Cárdenas, Iñigo de, 16
Carding, 128, 134
Cardona, Catalina de, 56–57
Caretakers, 57
Carmelite, 56–57
Carter, 132
Casimiro, Duke of Russia, 143–146, 149
Castile: of Charles II, 110; financial woes of, 80; late medieval and early modern, 23; medieval, 3, 6, 14, 39, 70, 72–73, 78–79; premodern, 25
Castile-León, 5
Castilian Cortes, 79
Castilian hegemony, 70

Castilian Kingdom, 14
Castilian society, 15
Castilian throne, 70
Castilian values, 79
Castrating woman, archetype of, 74
Castrillo, Count of, 115–116
Casual workers, 133
Catalan frontiers, 121
Catalonia, 110, 127
Catherine of Siena, 30
Catherinist tradition, 30
Catholic doctrine, 142
Catholic Kings, 9, 12, 15–16, 39; program of reforms, 15–16; religious reforms of, 15–16; terms of capitulation, 39
Catholic Reformation, 59
Catholic religion, defense of, 114
Catholicism, 37, 150, 154
Catholics, 143
Caxtigo para lax gentex, 45
Ceballos, Juan de, 28
Celestina, 158
Celibacy, 7
Central Europe, 91, 99–100
Centralizing policy, 70
Cercada tiene a Baeza, 77
Cervantes, Miguel, 58, 69, 158; on melancholy, 180; mockery, 168; pastoral work, 158
Chacón, Gonzalo, Commander, 12; wife of, 12
Charismatic spirituality, 30–31
Charitable deeds, 93, 95–96
Charles II, 92, 109–122; death of, 121–122; debility of, 111; marriage of, 119
Charles V, 40, 91, 112, 115
Chastity, 29; complete, vow of, 5, 7, 9–10, 15–16; conjugal, vow of, 4–5, 7, 9–10
Chasuble, 59
Childbearing, 174
Child-marriage, 45
Choler, 172
Christ, 83
Christendom, 114
Christian canon laws, 41
Christian culture, 38
Christian doctrine, 39–40
Christian instruction, 43; lack of, 43
Christianity, aversion to, 47
Christian lands, 48
Christian rule, 38

Christian schools, 40, 42

Christian values, 79

Christina of Sweden, Queen, 143; abdication, 143; able horsewoman, 143; agile thinker, 143; anti-Protestant views, 143; conversion to Catholicism, 143; main character of an auto, 150; move to Rome, 143; passionate lover, 143; patroness of arts and sciences, 143; possible marriage with Philip IV, 145; refusal to marry, 143; reputation in Spain, 143

Chronicles, 37, 99

Church, 60

Cicero, 157–163, 165–168

Ciceronian prescription, 167

Circumciser, 42

Cisneros, Francisco Jiménez de, Cardinal, 25, 39

City regulations, 37

City tanners, 130

Civil strife, 73

Civil war, 69, 77–79

Clairvaux, Bernard of, 4

Clenarda, 163

Clergy, 5, 15; clerical census, 46; clerics, 39–40, 43, 45, 47–48

Cloister, 5

Cobbler, 132

Cogito ergo sum, 180

Colbert, 119

Collapse of Spain, 121

Comedias, 141; end of, 149; female characters of, 146; female protagonist, 146, 154; feminist studies of, 146; *mujer esquiva* of, 153; polymetric structure of, 142; presentation of women in, 145

Comedias de capa y espada, 141

Comedias de enredo, 141

Comedias palaciegas, 141, 149

Comendadoras, 6

Comic ballad, 177

Commercial activities, carried out by women, 132

Commissioners, 42

Common life, women, 8, 15

Common property, 15

Communion, 28

Conceptual scheme, 176

Conciliar government, 110, 112

Confession, 27

Confessor, 60, 94, 99; political role of, 112–115, 117, 120

Consanguinity, degrees of, 41

Consolidation of state power, 15–17

Constable of Castile, 120

Constantinus Africanus, 173

Constanza, 13

Constitution of a religious community, 16

Contemplative life, 4

Contreras, Fernando de, 58

Convent, 5–6, 11–14, 60, 72, 130, 133

Conventual life, 9

Conversion sermons, 39

Conversos, 24

Convivencia, 38–39

Cordero, María del, 29

Córdoba, 38

Corpus Christi, 142; celebrations, 142

Correspondence, 116; between Don Juan and Mariana, 116

Cortes, 94

Cotton, 38

Councillors, 101, 113

Council of government, 110

Council of State, 116, 118–120

Council of the Thirteen, 6, 10

Council of Trent, 10, 16, 59

Countess of Urgel, 12

Countryfolk, 69

Court chroniclers, 91, 97, 101–102

Court chronicles, 97, 99, 101–102, 116

Courtly love ideal, 72

Courtly love tradition, 83

Court politics, 113, 117–118

Court preacher, 94

Crafts, 131

Cristerna, 143–150, 152–153; declared ruler of the northern kingdom, 145; descriptions of, 147; distributor of justice, 147; eventual submission, 146; lawmaker, 147, 152; militant feminist, 145; "mujer esquiva," 149; operating against natural law, 148; pure arrogant pride, 147; scholar, 152; soldier, 152; susceptibility to jealousy, 148; vanity and "esquivez" of, 151; yielding to the laws of nature, 148

Cristiana, 151

Cristina, 143, 150–153; arrogant pride, 151; balanced leader, 152; eventual salvation, 152–153; extent of her wisdom,

152; lawmaker, 152; scholar, 152–153; soldier, 152
Crusade: against Pedro of Castile, 76; against Muslims, 3
Cruz, Lucia de la, 44
Cuenca, 11; diocese of, 60
Cueva y Silva, Leonor de la, 179–180, 182
Cussó, Joan, 132

Dalarun, Jacques, 55
Dama, 162
Dance, 26–29; Muslim, 45
Daymiel, 58
Deborah, 150
Décima, 179
Decorum, 161, 167
De Inventione, 158, 168
De laude novae militiae, 4
Delio, 160–161
Demonic possession, 176
Descalzas Reales, 91, 94–95
Descartes, 143
Desert, 60
Desert Fathers, 55, 57
Desire, 142
Destriana, 13
Desventurada, 81
Devil, 55, 78
Devotional literature, 92, 98
Devotional model, 102
Devotional representation, 93
Diana, goddess, 165
Diana, pastoral romance protagonist, 159–165, 167
Diana enamorada: Montemayor's, 157–158; Polo's, 157–158, 161–163, 167
Diana/Sireno, 159, 167
Dietary prohibitions, 41; against wine and bacon, 41
Diplomatic correspondence, 97
Discipline, 28
Distribution of goods and services, 132
Divine gifts, 29
Doctors, 38
Dominican friars, 25, 31
Dominican history, 30
Dominican house, 24, 31
Dominican life, 30
Dominican Order, 25; schism within, 25
Dominican province of Spain, 23

Dominicans, 23, 28; new master general, 24, 30
Dominican spirituality, 30; catherinist tradition of, 30
Dominican Third Order, 24
Dominican tradition, 23, 28
Doña María, Infanta, 97; confessor of, 97
Doña María de Padilla, 75
Don Quixote, 58, 158; library of, 159; physical description of Dulcinea, 158
Don Quixote, 58, 158
Donzella, 162
Dowry, 40, 45, 81; usurpation of Blanca's, 75
Dramas, 149
Dramatic categories, 141
Dramatists, 142, 145
Drapers, 127–128, 133; master, 128
Duels, 145
Dulcinea, 158
Dutch, 110, 118, 121

Ecclesiastical reports, 37
Ecija, 15
Economic problems, 99, 110, 114, 119
Economic reform, 121
Ecstasy, 23, 27–29; false, 25
Ecu, 83
Edict of Grace, 40
Effeminate nature, of Pedro el Cruel, 77
Egypt, 55
Eiximenis, Francesc, 129
"El cruel," 70
El diablo cojuelo, 84
Elias, 56
Elisea, 164
El parnaso español, 58
Emperegilados, 77
Emperejilado, 77
Encarnación, Convent of, 97
Enclosure, 10, 15; complete, 15–16
England, 72–73, 112, 114, 121
English, 110, 121
Enguera, Juan de, 25
Enrique of Trastámara, 69, 73, 76–78; devaluation of the coinage by, 84; right to the Castilian throne of, 79; son of, 80; support of the *mesta* by, 78
Enríquez, Enrique, 12; wife of, 12
En triste prision y ausencia, 82–83, 85
Epidemic disease, 110

Episcopal jurisdiction, 6
Epistemological order, destruction of, 180
Epistolario, 60
Eremitical ideal, 55
Eremitical life, 55
Eremitical models, 56, 59
Ermitaña, 57–58
Ermitaño femenino, 57
Espinosa, Andrés de, Fray, 95–96
Espinosa, Jerónimo Jacinto de, 59
Espinosa, Juan de, 181
Espíritu, Margarita de, Sor, 56
Establecimientos, 6, 14
Eucharist, 28; mysteries of, 142
Eucharistic meal, 142
Eufemia de Cozuelos, santa, 7, 13, 15
Eulogists, 99, 101–102
Eulogy, 96
Europe, 30; late medieval, 30; early modern, 30, 112, 121, 181
European economic crisis, 127
European nations, 172
Eusebia, 58
Exaltation of the military ideal, 9
Exotic clothing, 37
Exposuerunt Nobis, 15

Factional conflicts, 111, 113, 120
Factionalism, 110–122
Fadrines, 129
Fadrique of Trastámara, 69, 72–74, 77, 80–81, 84; death of, 73–74
Faith, 142; character of an auto, 150
Faith and Peace, order of, 13
False Christians, 39
Familial devotion, 91, 96
Familiaritas, 11
Familiars, 11
Fasting, 28; Islamic days of, 41–43
Favoritism, 110
Felicia, 161; magical powers of, 159
Felis, 162
Felismena, 162, 167
Felismena/Felis, 162
Female action, restriction of, 93
Female asceticism, 28
Female behavior, 96
Female body, 171; low temperature in, 173, 177; moisture in, 173,177
Female characters, 85; oppositional categories of, 85

Female coldness, 174
Female credulity, 101
Female discontent, 102
Female disenfranchisement, 72
Female figures: binary representation of, 75; depictions of, 69, 83; as literary *figura*, 85, 157; as martyrs, 70; repression of, 71; as seductresses, 70
Female inconstancy, 180
Female intellectuals, 181
Female lover, poetic description of, 179
Female mind, 171
Female model, 96
Female monasticism, 16
Female physiology, 172
Female power, restriction of, 93
Female psychology, 172
Female servants, 96
Female stereotypes, 70
Feminine victimization, 69
Feminine virtues, 92
Feminist criticism, 38
Ferdinand II, Holy Roman Emperor, Archduke of Styria, 100, 111
Ferran, Aragon prince, 73
Ferrand, Jacques, 179
Fernández, García, 12; widow of, 12
Fernández, Pedro, 4
Fernández, Sancho, Master, 13
Fernández Serrano, Luis, 58
Fernando, King of Aragón, 15, 24, 39; confessor of, 25
Fernando II, King of León, 4
Feudal violence, 15
Ficino, Marsilio, 173
Fílida, 163–165, 168; characterization of, 166–167
Filis, 164
Finale, imperial fief of, 100
Finea, 164, 166
First cousins, marriage between, 40
Fishmongers, 129–130
Flanders, 116–118, 121
Flax, 38
Flemish advisers, 116
Fleur-de-lis, 83
Florela, 165
Florence, 59
Florencia, Jerónimo de, 94–97, 102
Florentine Neoplatonists, 173
Flores, 14

Florez, Henrique, 71, 73
Foa, Sandra, 145
Folklore, 84, 172
Fonseca, María de, 15
Foreign cloths, 127
Fortune, 160–163, 165
France, 72–73, 79–82, 110–111, 114, 116–118, 121
Franche-Comté, loss of, 119
Franco-Castilian relations, 84
Francophile policy, 118
Fraternal correction, 27
Fraternity, of Cáceres, 4
Fratrissa, 12–13
Fratrum of Canceris, 4
Free will, 152, 153
Freilas, 3, 5–10, 12, 14–17; conventual, 10, 12–13, 15–16; secular, 10, 12, 16
Freiles, 7–9, 12, 16; daughters of widows of, 8; married couple, 11, 16
Freiles caballeros, 5
Freiles clérigos, 5
French, 76, 81
French faction, 121
French influence, 119, 121
French interests, 119–121
French succession, 121
French support, 82; loss of, 83
Freylas, Alonso de, 173
Friars, 24–27, 29, 31
Frontier, 12
Frontier society, 11, 16
Fuente, 58
Funeral, 96
Funeral sermons, 96
Funes, Agustín de, 25–26

Gaetano Filangieri Museum, 56
Gaibol, Lope de, 26
Galatea, 159
Galenic principles, 175
Galicia, 10
Galleys, 46
Gallinas, 58
Gálvez de Montalvo, Luis, 157, 159, 163–166; emphasis on qualities of body, 167; follower of tradition, 164, 166; pastoral plane in his work, 168
García, Juan de, 58
Garsenda de Bearn, Countess, 13

Gaunt, John of, Duke of Lancaster, 79–80; claim to the Castilian throne, 79–80
Gender: behavior, 69; beliefs, 45; codification of behavior, 69, 71; definitions, 38; discourse on, 171; expectations, 69; roles, 23; system, 48; and melancholy, 178, 182; and reason in Europe, 181
Gendered eremitical inheritance, 55
Gendered misconduct, 57
Gendered process, 60
Gendered rejection, 55–60
Gener, Bartolomeu, 131
Germanía, 39
Germany, 99
Gil, Pero, 77
Gilman, Sander, 172–173
Giotto, disciple of, 59
Girls' training and work, 131
Girón, Magdalena, 163, 165
Gocia, 143
God, 78–79, 96, 101, 117, 150, 154
Gold, 41, 48
Golden Age drama, 143; construction of female identity in, 143
Golden Age literature, 58
Golden Age scholars, 142
Góngora, 69
González, Catalina, 14
Goricia, 98
Grace, 142
Gramsci, Antonio, hegemonic theory of, 38
Grana, Marquis of, 120
Granada, 15, 38–39, 42–43, 45; archbishop of, 39; Muslims of, 39
Grandes letrados, 28
Greco-Byzantine novels, 163, 168
Greco-Byzantine romances, 159, 167
Greco-Byzantine works, 162
Grotto, 55
Guilds, 127–135; authority over artisanal production, 133; corporatism, 134; documents, 127; masters, 127–128; of retailers, 133; officers, 132; ordinances, 129; patron saint, 130; protection from, 128; recognition of women's work, 129; records, 127–128, 131; refusal to admit women as masters, 129–131; women's training in, 131
Guilt, 142
Gustavus Adolphus, King of Sweden, 143–144

Guzmán, Catalina Clara de, 175
Guzmán, Diego de, 94–97, 101–102
Guzmán, Leonor de, 70–72, 75

Habsburg alliance, 116
Habsburg Empire, 113–114, 117–118, 120–121
Habsburg king, 112
Habsburgs, 109; last of, 109
Habsburg Spain, 55, 59
Habsburg women: piety of, 93; political role of, 92, 112
Haller, Richard, 94, 99
Haro, Luis de, Don, 113, 115
Harrach, Imperial Ambassador, 121
Hat-makers, 135; masters, 135
Healing, 45–46
Heaven, 58, 96
Heresy, 154; character of an auto, 150–151
Heretical movements, 5
Hermit, 56–58
Hermitage, 55, 57–58
Hermitess, 55–61; guilt of, 59; repulsion for, 57–60
Hernández, Leonor, 44
Hernández, Ramón, 28
Herod, 74
Heroic love, 178–179
Heroic virtues, 70
Hidalgo, 14
High Mass, 59
Hispanic military orders, 4–5
Historical documents, 49
Holiness, 60
Holland, 114, 121
Holy Faith, 150
Holy Land, 4
Holy mystic, 25
Holy Thursday, 59
Holy Virgin, 43
Holy wars, 4, 10
Holy water, 39
Holy woman, 23, 27–29, 31; male followers of, 31
Horace, 158
Horseback riding, 120
Hospitals, 7, 11
Host, 26; consecrated, 26, 59; unconsecrated, 26
Household, 129–131; artisanal production of, 130

Huarte de San Juan, Juan, 173, 177
Humility, 29
Humoral medicine, 171; theory of health and disease, 172
Humoral melancholy, 176
Humors, 172; cold, 175, 177
Hundred Years' War, 73
Hungarian throne, 100
Hurtado de Mendoza, Juan, 24–27, 29
Hypocrites, 60

Iberian peninsula, 4, 38
Idealized models, 55
Imagery, 142
Imperial ambassador, 98
Imperial fiefs, Spanish restitution of, 100
Informal economy, 133
Infused wisdom, 23, 28, 30
Innocent VI, 73
Inquisition, 24, 40, 42–44, 46–47, 84; case, 37; prosecution against Muslims, 43, 48; secret prisons of, 39; against sorcery, 46; trial records, 37, 57, 59, 84
Inquisitor, 44, 57
Inquisitor General, 40, 115
Institutions of Oratory, 158
Intermarriage, 38, 41
Invention, 158
Iron workers, 39
Irrigation, 38
Isabel, Empress, 112
Isabel, Queen, 12, 15, 39
Isidoro, Mayor, 11
Isidro, saint, 57
Islam, 4, 37, 44
Islamic burial, 41; Christian prohibitions against, 41
Islamic law, 40
Islamic rites, 40, 43–44
Islamic rituals, 41, 48; of death, 41
Islamic tradition, 44
Ismenia/Montano, 159
Italy, 59, 100

Jael, 150
Jerome, 56
Jesuit, 47, 94; morisco, 47; residence in Madrid, 95
Jewish community, 76
Jewish neighborhood, looting of, 77

Jews, 41, 73, 76, 78–79; adultery with, 70; attacks against, 77; marginalization of, 79; mistreatment of, 79
Joan, Aragon Prince, 73
Journeymen, 128, 135
Juana, Princess of Portugal, 112; Regent of Spain, 112
Juan José de Austria, Don, 110, 115–118; attempt to be prime minister, 118; death of, 119; francophile policy, 118; leader for the nobles, 116; negotiations with France, 119; prime minister, 118, 120; Vice-Roy of Aragón, 117
Juan Manuel, 71
Juglares, 73
Julius II, 15, 25
Jumilla, 73
Junta de desempeño, 99
Junta de govierno, 110, 112–113, 115–117
Junta meeting, 40
Jurisdictional rights, 78
Justice, 142

Kelly, Joan, 17
Khevenhüller, Hans, imperial ambassador, 98–100
Knight, 4–5, 14–15; daughters of, 8; of Santiago, 5; widows of, 8
Koran, 41, 45
Koranic law, 45

Labor costs, 127
Laborers, 39, 43, 69
La Cabrera, hermitage, 57
Ladies-in-waiting, 97, 99
La Galatea, 158
La Goda, Sara, 38
La Gran Cenobia, 149
Laity, 5, 9; participation in the religious life, 5
La Mancha, 58
La muerte ocultada, 85
Lancaster, Duke of, 79, 82
La protestación de la fe, 143, 150
La Ribera, 130
Las Casas, Ignacio de, 47
Lasciviousness, 27
Last Communion of Magdalene, 59
Last Rites, 41
Latina, 15
Laudatory works, 92

Lawsuit, 132
Lay fraternity, 9
Laymen, 4, 15; married, 4
Lay sheriffs, 40
Lay sisters, 24
Laywomen, married, 4
Legend, 142
Legistas, 78
León, 13
León, King of, 4
León, Lucia de, 44
León, Luis de, Fray, 129
León, María de, 44
Leonida, 177
Leopold, Emperor, 112, 114–115
Lérida, 13
Lerma, Duchess of, 98
Lerma, Duke of, 92–93, 97–98, 100–101; maneuverings against the Queen, 98–99; network of power and influence, 101
Levinus Lemnius, 173
Libro de dichox marabilloxox, 46
Libro de la Melancholia, 172
Libro de la Vida, 55
Libro de las Fundaciones, 56–57
License, 58
Licentiousness, 37, 45
Life in prayer, 93
Lira, Manuel de, 120
Lisardo, 178
Lisbon, 13
Literary analysis, 157
Literary characterization, 157
Literary conventions, 96, 150, 171
Literary criticism, objects of, 142
Literary fiction, paradigms of, 168
Literary portrayals, 172; of female characters, 176
Lives of the Fathers, 56
Local ordinances, 45
Looms, 135
Lope de Vega, 69, 141, 159; on melancholy, 180
López de Ubeda, Francisco, 60
López Grigera, 157
López Pinciano, 142
Los siete libros de la Diana, 158
Louis XIII, King of France, 101
Louis XIV, King of France, 114, 116–117, 119; diplomacy, 121; invasion of the United Provinces by, 118

Love magic, 46, 85
Lovesickness: and melancholy, 178; focus on sexual physiology, 178–179
Lucía, 11
Luna, María de, 12; preserving morisca medical tradition, 46
Lust, 142
Lutzen, battle of, 143
Luz, Sancha, 12

Madness, as alibi for gendered misconduct, 57
Madre de Dios, Efrén de la, 56–57
Madrid, 16, 91, 94–95, 98, 117–119, 142
Magic, 46, 159
Magical potion, 159
Maldonado, 14
Male dominance, 72
Male hierarchy, 102
Male images of women, 93, 101–102
Male monasticism, 16
Male political structure, 102
Mankind: fall of, 142; redemption of, 142
Manly heart, 95
Manly woman, 95
Manufactures, 128
Maravedí, 82
Marcelio, 162–163
Margaret of Austria, Queen, 91–102; brave and strong, 95; committed to her family, 102; death of, 94, 97, 100; funeral honors for, 95; gullibility, 97; illness of, 99; image as humble and submissive, 94; influence over Philip III, 97; intercessor with God, 96; interest in political matters, 98; legacy to Spain, 96; masculine strength of, 95; maternal characteristics, 97; model for female conduct, 96, 101–102; perfect royal wife, 97; piety of, 97, 102; political intuition, 98, 100, 102; political voice, 97–99, 101–102; rational mind of, 95; skills as a negotiator, 100; submission to her confessor, 94; unhappiness at the court, 98; virtuous Habsburg woman, 102
Margaret of the Cross, 91–93, 100
María, doña, 13
María, Empress, 91–93, 96; familial devotion of, 96; funeral of, 96; joint regent of Castile, 96; piety of, 96

María Antonia, Archduchess, 119
Mariana of Austria, Queen, 109–122; daughter of the emperor, 111; diplomatic preparations of her son's marriage, 119; exile to Toledo, 118; guardian, 110; mother of a king, 109, 118; Queen regent, 109–110, 116; role in Spanish government, 109; termination of her regency, 110
María Teresa, Infanta, 112–113; Queen of France, 116
Mariology, 72
Mariscal, Beatriz, 85
Marriage, 7, 45; "a la morisca," 45
Marseilles, 55
Martín, Alonso, 43
Martín, Diego, 44
Martín de la Chica, widow of, 11
Martínez, Catalina, 59–60
Mary Magdalene, 25, 56–57, 59
Mary of the Head, 57
Mary the Egyptian, 56–57
Masons, 39
Mass, 40, 95
Master drapers, 127; authority of, 128
Masters, 130; baker, 132; productive activities of, 131; widows of, 132; wives of, 132
Masters/non-masters, 128
Maternal characteristics, 97; grief, 81; sovereignty, 72
Matilla, Pedro, 120
Mayor commanders, 6
Mayordomo mayor, 12
McKendrick, Melveena, 146, 148
Mecca, 41
Medicine, 46; Arabic, 46; Christian, 46; domestic, 46
Medico-philosophical authors, 176
Medieval Castile, 3
Medieval culture, 3
Medieval gender system, 6
Medieval poetical treatises, 158, 167
Medieval women, 5
Medina de la Torres, Duke of, 115–116
Medina Sidonia, 72, 75
Medina Sidonia, Duke of, 117
Medinaceli, 120
Melancholia, 171, 173, 176, 181; discourse of loss, 180; link with scholarly achievements, 173, 181; mental disor-

der, 172; physical disorder, 172; subject of study and debate, 171
Melancholic ballad, 171
Melancholic expression, 178
Melancholic humors, 98
Melancholic mind, 180–181; self-contemplation of, 180
Melancholic women, 174
Melancholy, 98, 172, 182; as humoral character type, 172; women's unbalanced characteristics, 176
Melancholy scholars, 173, 181–182
Melibea, 158
Méndez, María, 13
Mendoza y Aragón, Enrique de, Don, 163
Mérida, 15
Mesta, 78
Mestresses, 129
Middle Ages, 10, 16, 55, 166, 178–179
Midwifery, 45
Milan, governorship of, 120
Military squadrons, 95
Miralles, Mariangela, 132
Mirrer, Louise, 70, 78–80, 84
Miscarriage, prevention of, 46
Molina, 59–60
Monastery, 10, 40
Monastic life, 5
Monetary deflation, 83
Monks, 28
Monroy, 14
Montalbán, commandery of, 11
Montemayor, Jorge de, 157–162, 164–165, 167; Neoplatonic ideas, 167; tradition, 159
Montenegro, king's confessor, 117
Monterrey, Count of, 117–118
Moorish witch, 71
Moors, 76–77
Mora de Ubeda, la, 45
Morales, Leonor de, 44
Moras de allende, 46
Morerías, 38
Moreto y Cabaña, 58
Morisca, 37–49; child-rearing, 41; cleanliness, 41; domestic seclusion, 48; experiences, 37, 49; fertility of, 45; food preparation, 41; resistance, 48; silent submission, 38; subcultures, 38; subversion, 38, 48; survival, 48; voice, 37
Morisca, Magdalena, 43

Morisco home, 39
Moriscos, 39, 42–44, 85; assimilation, 41; ballad, 85; baptism of, 40; beliefs, 46; community, 41–42; dispersion, 42, 47; enslavement, 42, 46–47; expulsion of, 48; families, 43, 47; immorality, 45; incantations, 85; infants, 47–48; outlaw groups, 46; particularism, 40; persecution of, 45; population, 40; rebellion, 42; religious traditions, 41, 44
Morocco, bishop of, 47
Mortification of the flesh, 28, 56
Mosques, 41
Mostaçaf, 130
Motherhood, 72
Mother of the Church, 72
Mudéjares, 38–39
Muhammed, 41–42; "sect of," 44
Mujer esquiva, 146, 148–150, 153; defiance, 148; as perception of women, 148; reevalution of, 179; standardized portrait, 150
Municipal authorities, 130
Municipal prohibitions, 130
Municipal records, 128
Muslim-Christian conflicts, 37
Muslims, 3, 5, 38, 40–41; alms, 42; baths, 42–43, 46; book, 46; children, 39–40, 47; circumcision, 42; clothing, 44–46; cultural practices, 40, 44, 46, 48; diet, 42, 44; doctrines, 48; family rituals, 43; festivals, 43; food, 43–44; holy leaders, 42, 44; musical instruments, 42–43; prayers, 42, 44; presence, 40; religious freedom of, 38–39; stronghold, 39; traditional ceremonies, 41–43; women, 38; women religious leaders, 44
Mystical experience, 30
Mystical literature, 28
Mystics, 28; female, 28; Sufi, 45
Mythology, 142

Natural law, 41, 154
Nature, 158, 163
Needle-makers, 130
Negoci, 132
Neoburg, María Ana of, 111; exile to France, 122; faction of, 121; Queen of Spain, 120
Neoplatonic ideas, 167
Netherlands, 117, 120

New Castile, 57
New Testament, 83
New World, evangelization of, 31
Nieto, 14
Nithard, John Everard, 112, 114–116; "el padre Everardo," 113; exile of, 117; Inquisitor General, 115; legitimization of his authority, 115; opposition in the court to, 115–116; as a ruthless manipulator, 113; Spanish citizen, 115
Nobility, 14, 47, 69–70, 111, 113, 142, 163; Castilian high, 15; factions among, 110; lower, 70, 78; new titles of, 78
Noble status, 76; of sheepowners, 79
Non-masters, subordination of all, 128
Normative narratives, 69
North Africa, 38, 42, 45, 48
Novoa, Matías de, 97
Nuns, 10, 28, 48, 93, 97; Augustinian, 97; virginal state of, 94
Nurueña, Isabel de, 12

Obedience, 29, 31; vow, 4, 10
Ocaña, 7, 9; General Chapter of, 12
Olalla, santa, 15
Old Christians, 40–43, 47–48
Old Testament, 150
Olivares, Count Duke of, 114; disastrous *valimiento* of, 116
Olives, 38
On the Education of the Christian Woman, 129
"Ordinance in favor of women," 134; violation by women, 135
Organ, 27
Orleans, Marie Louise d', Queen, 111, 119; death of, 120
Oropesa, prime minister, 120
Our Lady of the Valley, hermitage, 59
Oxenstierna, Swedish Chancellor, 143

Padilla, María de, 70, 72–75, 77–79, 84–85
Palace theater, 120
Palencia, 13
Papacy, 7
Papal brief, 15
Papal bull, 16
Papal permission, 40
Paper, 132
Pareja, 58

Parish, 40, 43
Parish priest, 59
Parra y Carvajal, Angela Teodora, 55
Passion, 28; bodily imitation of Christ's, 30; of Christ, 28, 30, 83
Pastoral disguise, 163
Pastoralizing reality, 164
Pastoral romances, 157–168
Pastoral setting, 159
Pastor de Fílida, 157–158, 163–164, 167–168
Pastrana, 57–58
Pastry makers, 45
Patria potestas, 71
Patriarchal authority, 72
Patriarchal model, 72
Patriarchal society, 70
Patriarchal systems of power, 69
Patriarchal systems of values, 70
Patriarchy, 172
Patronage, 93
Patroness, 13
Paul, 26
Paul, the First Hermit, 55
Paula the Roman, 56
Paz, 14
Peace, 142
Peace of Nijmegen, 119
Peace of the Pyrenees, 114
Peasants: abandonment of their lands by, 79; forced emigration of, 79
Pecadora, 56
Pedro, Archbishop of Santiago de Compostela, 4
Pedro el Cruel, ballad, 69–85
Pedro of Castile, King, 60; daughter of, 79; death of, 84; family of, 80; overthrow of, 81; reputed Jewish origins of, 76
Peña, Antonio de la, 24, 29–30
Penances, 56
Peñaranda, Count of, 117
Penitence, 31; character of an auto, 150; model of, 57
Penitential practices, 23
Pérez, Leonor, 14
Pérez, Pelay, Master, 12; tenure of, 12–13
Pérez de Azagra, Sancha, 12
Pérez Gómez, Antonio, 71
Persecution, 42; against Muslims, 42
Persiles y Sigismunda, 58

Peter of Spain, 178
Petrarchan smile, 83
Petrarchan tradition, 158–159, 167–168
Picaresque Justina, 60
Pictorial representations, 59
Phallocentric assumptions, 48–49
Phallocentric symbolization, 70
Philip II, King, 92
Philip III, King, 48, 91–101
Philip IV, King, 92, 109–111, 114, 145,
    153; death of, 113, 115, 121; invasion
    of Portugal, 116
Philip of Anjou, 121
Phlegm, and humoral theory, 172
Physical beauty, 160
Piedrahita, 23; beata de, 23, 25, 30; charis-
    matic movement of, 31; Dominican
    monastery, 25; inn of, 27
Piety, 29, 93, 95–96
Platonic love, 160; reflection of internal
    virtue, 160
Platter, Thomas, 130
Podestà, 59
Poetical canons, 157
Poetics, 69
Poetics, 167–168
Poetic voice, 179
Poetria nova, 158
Poetry, female-authored, 180
Pogroms, 77
Political allegory, 82
Political alliances, 79
Political factions, 69, 73, 92, 110
Political issues, women concerned with, 93
Political propaganda, 69
Polo, Gaspar Gil, 157–163, 166–167;
    Greco-Byzantine inclination, 167; stoi-
    cism, 167
Polygamy, 45
Polymetric structure, 142
Ponsico, Joseph, 135
Pope, 5–6, 16, 25, 73, 76
Popular culture, 38, 154
Popular opinion, 118, 154
Por los campos de Xerez, 79
Portocarrero, 120–121
Portraits, 158
Portugal, 13, 79, 110, 116
Portugal, María of, 70–72, 77
Poverty, vow, 4, 10
Prado Museum, 56

Pragmatic, Royal, 43
Prayer, 30–31, 93–94, 96–97; character of
    an auto, 150; for the dead (Islam), 42
Preachers, order of, 23, 30
Precaution, 42
Prejudices, 45; racial, 45; religious, 45
Priest, 59, 97
Prioress, 6, 25, 97
Privado, 92, 97
Privateering activities, 110
Procurator of the Royal Councils, 57
Prohomes, 132
Promiscuity, 45, 58
Prophecy, 23, 26, 28–29
Prophetess, 25
Protestantism, 114
Prudence, 28
Pseudo-Aristotelian ideas, 173
Public apostolate, 27
Public markets, 130
Public theaters: private, 142; small, 142
Purity of Blood statutes, 41

Queen, as a shepherdess, 96
Queen of Heaven, 72
Queen of Spain, 98
Queen regent, 109
Queenship, 81
Quevedo, Francisco de, 58; on melancholy,
    180
¿Quién hallará mujer fuerte?, 150; prefigu-
    ration of the Virgin Mary, 150
Quinteria, 58
Quintillian, 158

Rachel, 150
Ramadan, 43
Ramírez de Guzmán, María de, 12
Raptures, 25, 27–29
Reconquest, 4, 11, 15, 38, 71
Rectors, 40
Redemption of Christian captives, 11
Regatonas, 133
Regimen sanitatis salerni, 173
Regular observance, 30
Regulations, 40; ecclesiastical, 40; local,
    40; royal, 40
Reiss, Timothy J., 181
Religion, character of an auto, 150–151
Religious alliances, 114
Religious concerns, 91

Religious figures, 97
Religious institutions, 93
Religious life, 30; new ways of, 5
Religious novice, 94
Religious rapture, 176
Religious reform, twelfth century, 4
Renaissance, 172–173; discourse on love, 178; interest in melancholy, 173; melancholic lovesickness, 178
Renaissance doctors, 175
Renaissance medical commentators, 175
Renaissance Spain, 173
Renato, 58
Repentence, 30
Requiem mass, 12
Retailers, 133
Retail sale, 128; by women, 133
Revenedors, 133
Revolts: of Catalonia, 110; of Portugal, 110, 114
Rhazes, 173
Rhetoric, 157; source of literary practices, 157
Rhetorica ad Herennium, 158
Rhetorical canons, 157, 167–168
Rhetorical pieces, 96
Rhetorical strategies, 71
Rhine, 117
Ribas, Clara, 132
Ribera, José, 56
Rice, 38
Río, Nicolás del, Fray, 47
Ritual ablution, 41
Ritual of novitiate, 14
Ritual of profession, 14
Rodríguez de Guiomar, Hieronymo, 44
Rodríguez Marín, Francisco, 163
Rojo, Juan, 58
Role of the priest, 27; appropriation by a woman, 27
Romance de doña Blanca, 80
Romancero, 69, 142
Romances, 69–85, 179; anti-Petrine, 75, 77; pro-Petrine, 70, 82
Romances noticieros, 69
Rome, 23
Royal almoner, 94
Royal celebration, 142
Royal Court of Appeals, 130
Royal donations, 14
Royal family, 112

Royal favor, 110
Royal liaisons, 71
Royal petition, 142
Royal pragmatics, 39
Royal privileges, 14
Royal women, 102; models for, 92, 95–96, 101–102
Royalty, 142
Rudolf II, Holy Roman Emperor, 99–100
Rufus, 173
Ruling class, 16–17; Castilian women from, 16–17
Russia, 143
Ruth, 150

Sabadell, 13
Sacrament, 59; of order, 59
Sacristy, 58
Saint Anne, feast day of, 43
Saint Augustine, 152–153; on free will, 152–153
Saint-John of the Hospital, order of, 4
Saint Mary the Egyptian: Gaetano Filangieri Museum, 56; Prado Museum, 56
Salamanca, 3, 7, 9, 12, 14; University of, 95
Sale of fish, 129
Sale of offices, 110
Salic laws, 145, 148
Salome, 74
Salvat, Theresa, 132
Salvation of the soul, 11, 95
Sanbenito, 47
Sánchez, Lope and Juan, 12
Sánchez Ortega, María Helena, 71, 84
Sancho I of Portugal, King, 13
San Clemente, Guillén de, 100
Sancti Spiritus, 3, 7, 9, 12, 14–15; commanders of, 12; freilas of, 10; puebla of, 13
Sanctity, example of, 55; new model of, 60
Sandoval, Cardinal, 115
San José, Mariana de, 97
San Marcos de León, prior of, 11
San Mateo de Avila, hospital of, 13
San Pedro, Diego de, 24
San Salvador, 58
Santa Catalina, beatorio of, 24
Santa Cruz, monastery, 15–16
Santa María, Juan de, Fray, 97

Santa María Egipciaca, 158
Santera, 57, 60; house of, 57; insulting sexual insinuations against, 58; marginalization of, 58; *officio de*, 58; rejection of, 58–60
Santero, 58
Santiago, Apostol, 4
Santiago, Knights of, 5, 12, 15
Santiago, Order of, 3–6, 10, 13–17; donations to, 10, 12–14; General Chapter of, 7, 9–10, 15; house of, 11; ideal of spiritual life, 7; mayor commander, 6, 8; Master of, 3, 5–6, 8–11; foundation of, 3, 14–15; property tenure, 5, 9; rituals of profession and novitiate, 14; rule of, 6–7, 9–10, 12, 15; soror of, 12; visitors, 6, 10
Santiago de Compostela, Archbishop of, 4
Santiago de Dorra, monastery, 12
Santiago de la Madre de Dios, monastery, 15–16
Santiago el Mayor, monastery, 16
Santo Domingo, Dominican monastery, 24
Santo Domingo, María de, 23–31; confessor of, 25, 27, 29; reform movement of, 30
Santos, 13
Santos-o-Velho, 13
Santo Tomás, Dominican house, 24
Sardinia, governorship of, 120
Satan, 84
Schiesari, Juliana, 174, 176
Scholarly women, 177
Scholastic theology, 31
Seclusion of women, 37
Secretario del despacho, 120
Sederes, 134
Segismundo, 149
Segovia, 78
Seignorial regime, 70
Seminaries, 47
Sensuality, 45
Sepúlveda, 15; bachelor of, 15
Servants, 97, 99, 117
Setiembre, Juan de, 24, 28
Seville, 38, 40, 43, 45–46, 73
Sex/gender roles, 3
Sexual alliance, 72
Sexuality, 80
Sheepowners, 79
Shoemakers, guild of, 131

Sidonia, María, 99
Siena, Catherine of, 30
Siete Libros de la Diana, 158–159
Sigea, Luisa, 174–175
Signa, Joan of, 55
Silk cloth, 41
Silk clothing manufacture: city taxes on, 134; ordinance by the city, 134; women in, 134; women barred from, 134; women engaged in illegal practices, 134
Silk guilds, 131
Silk masters, 134–135
Silk twisters, 135
Silk worms, 38
Silver, 41, 48
Silvera, 164
Silverio, 164
Simon Peter, 83; first bishop of Rome, 83
Sin, 60
Sinner, 56
Siralvo, 163–164, 166
Sireno, 159, 161–162, 164
Slaves, 48
Smith, Paul Julian, 181
Smiths, 130
Social boundaries, theories of, 38
Socializing the pastoral, 164
Sodomy, 45
Solé-Leris, Amadeu, 168
Solitary women, 58
Soranzo, Francisco, 98
Sorceresses, 84
Sorcery, 46, 73
Soror ordinis, 12
Spain, 158–159, 181; help provided by, 114; military efforts against Portugal, 114; peripheral provinces of, 111; ruin of, 113
Spanish assistance to Archduke Ferdinand, 100; to Leopold, 114, 120; to Rudolf II, 100
Spanish Christian Kingdoms, 11, 15, 40, 43, 94, 99
Spanish court, 91; of Charles II, 113–122; French influence at, 119; of Philip III, 93, 98–100, 102
Spanish crown, succession of, 119, 121
Spanish currency, 83
Spanish decline, 92
Spanish empire, partition of, 121
Spanish foreign policy, 111–112, 116–117, 120

Spanish Golden Age, 60
Spanish government, 109, 113
Spanish grandees, 101, 113, 117
Spanish history, 110, 122
Spanish intellectuals, 180
Spanish literature, 58
Spanish military failures, 110, 113–114
Spanish monarchy, 118
Spanish overseas colonies, 110
Spanish physicians, 173
Spanish resources, 119
Spanish *romances*, 69
Spanish territories, invasion of, 114
Spanish theater, 141; degree of comic relief, 141; narrative outcome, 141; protagonists, 141
Spanish thinkers, 181
Spinners, 127; riot by, 133–134
Strategic subversions, 176
Studia humanitatis, 157
Styria, 98
Suevia, 143
Suevians, 143
Sufi mystics, 45
Sugar cane, 38
Superstitions, 46
Suprema, 57
Surgeons, 130
Sylvano, 159

Talavera, Hernando de, 39
Tapiner, 131
Tapins, 131
Taqiyya, 42
Tauriso, 161
Taxation, 79
Temple, order of, 4
Teresa of Avila, 55–56; describing nuns as melancholics, 176–177; hagiographer of, 56
Terrassa, María de, 13
Territorial difficulties, 110
Tertiary, 24
Teruel, 11–12
Thebaid, 55
Thirty Years' War, 110
Thomistic tradition, 30–31
Tilemakers, 39
Tirso de Molina, on melancholy, 180
Toledo, Antonio de, Don, 117
Toledo, Fernando de, 28

Toledo, 15; archbishop of, 115; bishop of, 79
Torcedors de ceda, 135
The Touchstone of Complexion, 173
Townspeople, 69
Tragedy/comedy, 141
Tragicomedias, 141
Trances, 27–28
Transatlantic trade, 110
Trastámara: authority, 79; campaign, 76; faction, 70, 77; family, 80, 84; regime, 71, 79, 82–83; succession, 70; wars, 83
Tratado de república, 97
Trent, 59
Tunis, 112
Turkish invasion, 116
Turks, 100, 114

Ubeda, 77
Uceda, María Eugenia de, Doña, 117
Uclés, 12; commandery of, 11
Umares, Luis Antonio de, 57
United Provinces, 116–117; invasion of, 118
Urban audience, 142
Urban patriciate, 14

Valbuena Prat, Angel, 150
Valencia, 39, 45, 94; kingdom of, 38
Valencia, Juan, 44
Valenzuela, Fernando de, 113, 116–117; "duende del palacio," 117; friendship with Nithard, 117; *valimiento* of, 117
Valido, 111, 113, 117
Valimiento, 113, 116–117
Valladolid, 15
Vanity, 26
Vendôme, Mathieu de, 158
Veil-makers, 134; masters' livelihood at risk, 134
Velásques, Andrés, 172
Venerated image, 58
Venitian ambassadors, 98, 101
Verisimilitude, 167–168
Versification, 142
Vicens de Jonqueres, Sant, monastery of, 13
Vice-Roy of Aragón, 133–134
Vidal de Palombar, widow of, 11
Vienna, 111, 113, 120

Vilar de Donas, 10; Master of, 12; prior of, 12
Villagarcía, Lord of, 12
Vinsauf, Geoffroi de, 158
Violence, 37
Virago, 71
Virginity, protection of, 8
Virgin Mary, prefiguration of, 150
Virgin/whore dichotomy, 70, 72, 85
Vita apostolica, 4
Vitalia, 11
Vitoria, Diego de, 25–29, 31
Vives, Juan Luis, 129
Voragine, Jacobo da, 56, 59
Vows, 4

War: for the faith, 9, 114; against France, 118, 120; against Muslims, 5; of religion, 143; by Spain in Europe, 110; against the Turks, 100, 114, 120
Weber, Alison, 176
Weeping, 28, 59
Western Christianity, history of, 23
Wetnurses, 47–48
Wheat, 38, 41
Widows, 8, 128; apprentices of, 132; childless, 132; solely responsible for the shop, 131
Wine, dietary prohibitions against, 41
Wisdom, 150, 153
Wisdom, character of an auto, 150–151
Witiza, 38; granddaughter of, 38
Women artisans, 127, 131–132; image of subordination and dependence, 130; independent, 129; unmarried, 131
Women authors, 172, 174
Women fishmongers, 129–130; against male fishmongers, 129–130
Women hagglers, 133
Women retailers, 129, 133
Women's accepted public domain, 101
Women's autobiographical literature, 24
Women's bodies, 60
Women's community, 3, 6–8
Women's desire, 178
Women's diplomatic role, 91–102
Women's discourse, 60
Women's hagiographical literature, 24

Women's historicity, as a circulating metaphor, 85; eradication of, 85
Women silkers, 134–135; illegal practice by, 135; selling hair nets, 135
Women's labor activities, 127–135; restriction in, 128
Women's labor force, 133–134; control by the city government, 134
Women's melancholy, 174; hierarchical discourse on, 174
Women spinners, 127–128; assault of Barcelona city hall by, 127
Women's political activities, 98, 121
Women's religiosity, 3–17
Women's religious life, 25
Women's sales practices, 129–130
Women's social status, 133; changes in, 133
Women's solitude, 58–59
Women's spirituality, 6, 8, 16
Women's voices, 92; poetic, 171
Women's work: multiplicity of images of, 128; political and economic issue, 134; recognition of, 129; traditional image of, 128; versatility and flexibility, 131, 133
Women thinkers, 172
Women weavers, 131; apprenticeship of, 131; informal examination of, 131
Women workers, 127; as liars and troublemakers, 129
Women writers, 171, 173, 176
Wool, 127; carding of, 128; combing of, 128; raw, 127; washing of, 128
Workshop, 128, 130–132
Writers: Catalan, 129; Spanish, 129

Xemeno, Dominga, commander, 13
Xérez, María, 43–44

Yo me estaba allá en Coimbra, 73
Yo por vos y vos por otro, 58
Yzquierda, Ynés, 46

Zamora, 78
Zaragoza, 46
Zayas y Sotomayor, María de, 145, 176–177
Zúñiga, Baltasar de, 100
Zúñiga, María de, 16

Contributors

JODI BILINKOFF is associate professor of history at the University of North Carolina at Greensboro. She is the author of *The Avila of Saint Teresa: Religious Reform in a Sixteenth-Century City* and a number of articles and essays exploring religion, gender, and authority in early modern Spain. Her current research focuses on the relationships between male confessors and female penitents and the construction of identities in Catholic Europe, 1450–1750.

JOELLEN M. CAMPBELL is a graduate student in the history department at the University of Minnesota. She holds a Masters of Arts degree in history from Tulane University and a Bachelor of Arts degree from the University of Nebraska-Lincoln. She is the author of a chapter in *La Tierra Mágica: Una Exploración Cultural de la América Latina*.

ANNE J. CRUZ is associate professor of Spanish at the University of Illinois at Chicago. She holds a Ph.D. in Spanish Golden Age literature from Stanford University. She is the author of *Imitación y Transformación: El Petrarquismo en la Poesía de Boscán y Garcilaso de la Vega*. She is co-editor of *Renaissance Rereadings: Intertext and Context*; *Cultural Encounters: The Impact of the Inquisition in Spain and the New World*; and *Culture and Control in Counter-Reformation Spain*. She is also the author of numerous articles in scholarly journals. She has been a visiting professor at Stanford University and has received several NEH stipends.

MARÍA ECHÁNIZ is a visiting scholar at Columbia University's Institute for Research on Women and Gender. She holds a doctoral degree from the University of Barcelona and is the author of several articles including "El Monasterio de Sancti Spiritus de Salamanca. Un Espacio Monástico de Mujeres de la Orden Militar de Santiago (Siglos XIII–XV)"; "María de Zúñiga. La Definición de un Modelo de Vida Espiritual Dirigida a una Comunidad de Mujeres"; and "Espiritualidad Femenina en la Orden Militar de Santiago, Siglos XII–XV."

MARY ELIZABETH PERRY is a research associate at the UCLA Center for Medieval and Renaissance Studies, and an adjunct professor of history at Occidental College. She is the author of *Gender and Disorder in Early Modern Seville*, which won the Sierra book award for best scholarly monograph for 1991. Her previous book, entitled *Crime and Society in Early Modern Seville* received the Sierra book award in 1982. With Anne J. Cruz, Mary Elizabeth Perry is the co-editor of *Cultural Encounters: The Impact of the Inquisition in Spain and the New World* and *Culture and Control in Counter-Reformation Spain*. She is the author of numerous articles and the recipient of many awards, including an American Council of Learned Societies Grant-in-Aid for 1990–1991.

ALAIN SAINT-SAËNS is assistant professor of history at Oklahoma State University. He received his doctorate from the University of Toulouse in France and his Agrégation d'histoire from the Sorbonne. He is the editor of *Religion, Body, and Gender in Early Modern Spain*, and is the author of *La Nostalgie du Desért. L'Idéal Eremétique en Castille au Siècle d'Or* and of *Art and Faith in Tridentine Spain, 1545–1690*. He is the editor of a forthcoming volume entitled *Between Pleasure and Violence. Sex and Love in Early Modern Spain*. Dr. Saint-Saëns is a past research fellow of the Casa de Velázquez in Madrid (1987–1990).

MAGDALENA S. SÁNCHEZ is assistant professor of history at Gettysburg College in Gettysburg, Pennsylvania. She earned her doctoral degree in early modern Spanish history from the Johns Hopkins University. She is a past recipient of a Quincentenary Postdoctoral Fellowship. Professor Sánchez is the author of several articles, including "Confession and Complicity: Margarita de Austria, Richard Haller, S.J., and the Court of Philip III," and Melancholy and Female Illness: Habsburg Women and Politics at the Court of Philip III." She is completing a book on Habsburg women in Spain during Philip III's reign.

TERESA S. SOUFAS is associate professor of Spanish at Tulane University. She has dedicated her research and teaching to Spanish Golden Age literature. In addition to article-length studies that have appeared in journals such as *Hispanic Review*, *MLN*, *Bulletin of Hispanic Studies*, and *Bulletin of the*

Comediantes among others, she has also published a book entitled *Melancholy and the Secular Mind in Spanish Golden Age Literature* (Columbia: University of Missouri Press, 1990). More recently, she has completed a book-length critical study of plays by seventeenth-century Spanish women dramatists and an anthology of their works, both forthcoming from University of Kentucky in 1996.

MARY LORENE THOMAS is professor of Spanish at Meredith College in North Carolina. She holds a doctoral degree from the University of Michigan. Professor Thomas is the author of *"Tu Prójimo como a ti": Volume I: Edition of the Two Versions* and of *"Tu Prójimo como a ti": Volume II: Paleographic Edition and Concordance*. She is currently preparing an edition of *La Hidalga del Valle*.

SYLVIA TRELLES is associate professor of Spanish at Guilford College in North Carolina. She holds a Ph.D. from the University of Michigan in Spanish literature. She has written an article entitled "Aspectos Retóricos de los Retratos Femeninos en *La Galatea*" in *Cervantes and the Pastoral* (edited by J. J. Labrador Herraiz and J. Fernández Jiménez).

MARTA V. VICENTE is a Ph.D. candidate in history at the Johns Hopkins University. Her dissertation is entitled "Artisan Families and Industrialization: The Case of the Sirés Cotton Factory, Barcelona 1770–1816." She is the author of "La Documentación Gremial: El Trabajo de las Mujeres en la Modernidad," in *Fuentes y Documentos para la Historia de la Mujer*; "El Treball de les Dones en els Gremis de la Barcelona Moderna," in *L'Avenç*; and "La dona en els Gremio en la Barcelona del Segle XVIII," in *Pedralbes*.